TO YOU

the reader, this book presents a Way of Living
. . . a Life which is inspired by the Ways of the
Old Ones who once lived in our Mountains,
swam in our Rivers, and hunted on our Plains.
These Old Ones have moved on—their Lands
have changed—their Ways have been neglected.

Now a new People are Seeking new Ways.
Experiences must Guide Them. Let this book
be, for You, an Experience. Let it help YOU
find a New Way.

Makwi Unoche
ADOLF HUNGRY WOLF

THE GOOD MEDICINE BOOK

Adolf Hungry Wolf

WARNER PAPERBACK LIBRARY

A Warner Communications Company

WARNER PAPERBACK LIBRARY EDITION
FIRST PRINTING: NOVEMBER: 1973

COVER ART: "INDIAN ENCAMPMENT IN THE ROCKIES," BY ALBERT
BIERSTADT. "WHITNEY GALLERY OF WESTERN ART,
CODY, WYOMING"

WARNER PAPERBACK LIBRARY IS A DIVISION OF WARNER BOOKS, INC.,
75 ROCKEFELLER PLAZA, NEW YORK, N.Y. 10019.

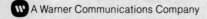 A Warner Communications Company

CONTENTS

Okohe! Okohe! Napi, Hiyo: Spumokit! Tamatautatsisama.
Spumokit! Nistoakok: Makwi Unoche.

This book is dedicated to my Spiritual Master. . . .
OnistaiPoka. . . .
His last years were my first—of a Life which is Meant.
He knew me but a short time during His 116-year stay
on Earth, but He knew He was to be my life-long Inspiration. His constant Presence is my Guide. To Him, I
dedicate my Life.

Makwi Unoche

INTRODUCTION TO THE GOOD MEDICINE BOOK

GREETINGS BROTHERS AND SISTERS!

Good Medicine is a Way to live in Harmony with Nature. A number of Us have been finding success and happiness by following the Path of the Sacred Circle, looking at the ancient footsteps and Ways in the Light of Today. We are following the Old Path in a New Way— we are combining the Spirits of the Past with the Light of Knowledge of Today, to make up our Good Medicine Life in Harmony with Nature.

During the four Winters that Good Medicine Books have been in existence many of the Spirits from the Past have come again to the People of today—to You, my Brothers and Sisters. We see and hear of this in many places, and it is Good—it is Good Medicine. The more of Us that there are, the stronger we will be, here on Earth.

The home of Good Medicine Books used to be on a farm in British Columbia. Sale of the Books helped us to build a small house with cold running water and kerosene lamps. We had a barn with Horses and Chickens and Goats. We snowshoed over frozen sloughs to get the mail in the Winter, and we followed Moose and Elk tracks to hunt our meat in the Fall. The Spirits of Good Medicine wanted to grow beyond the funky farm, so Good Medicine Books moved across the Rocky Mountains to a new home on the Northern Plains. Members of the Good Medicine Family ended up wandering in different directions— as their Spirits directed. The farm was sold and the proceeds helped the different members continue on in their Ways—most of it went to pay past printing debts and future costs of two new issues of the Good Medicine series —Tipi Life and Thoughts—that were being created at that same time. The Good Medicine Family was broke, scattered, and landless, but we had lots of Spirit and lots of books.

Out on the Northern Plains the Good Medicine Family became SikskiAki, Wolf Child, and myself. We moved to the Reserve where SikskiAki was born and where mine and Wolf Child's adopted People live. Because land on the Reserve can only be bought by those who were born here, we were able to obtain an old ranch house and a

4

small, fenced pasture around it, for the price of a few cartons of Good Medicine Books. The log house is the oldest inhabited one on the Reserve and nobody wanted it—nor did anybody want to settle on a place with enough grazing for just a few head of Horses. Most of the People here either have no livestock or else they have herds of them. Few of the first group would care to live out in the middle of nowhere—they prefer being closer to town— and none of the second group would be able to stuff a herd of Animals into the small pasture. The place was just right for Good Medicine.

After years of travelling short and long distances to visit my adopted People, beginning with my first Spiritual Master, who passed away a few years after we met, and after he gave me the Power to set out on the Path of Good Medicine, I finally joined them in the community and added the Good Medicine Spirit to the present efforts of continuing our Sacred Old Ways. The Good Medicine Path widened even more after another Sacred event which took place around that time. It happened like this:

A near-fatal accident to Wolf Child caused me to make a Holy Vow, in the Ways of our Old People, which led to the Good Medicine Family becoming the Keepers of a Sacred Medicine Bundle which has been among our People for longer than anyone today knows.

In brief, the Sacred Bundle contains an ancient, decorated Medicine Pipe Stem (one which is only rarely smoked during very Holy occasions), and the skins of Birds and Animals, along with some other ceremonial objects. Though the contents of the Bundle are very ancient and Sacred, they are not nearly so important as the Spirit which is with them—the combined Spirit of the many Holy Men and Women who have been past Keepers—the many Holy Families in whose households the same Sacred Bundle has given strength and Power and inspiration to live in a Holy Way according to our ancient Teachings. The Bundle is opened every Spring—after the first Sound of Thunder— as it always has been. The Opening Ceremony is a celebration for the end of the cold Season—when Nature is resting and the start of the warm Season, when life and

5

warmth return to our Mother Earth. Songs and dances are done according to tradition, each of the Bundle's contents having its place and symbolizing some major element of Nature—Land, Water, Air, Mountains, Trees, Birds, and Animals.

The keeping of our Sacred Bundle was a life-time Teaching of discipline and devotion, in the Old Days. Unfortunately, many of those Teachings have been lost in the years since our People were first forced to give up their Old Ways of Life in Harmony with Nature. Some of the Teachings lost their meaning when Life was changed. For instance, the place of the Buffalo within the Bundle and its ceremony no longer had direct meaning to our People after they lost the Buffalo. The songs and dances with many of the Bird and Animal skins became less meaningful as some of them were driven from our country and as the People stopped watching and listening to others. To some of our People the new changes made the ceremonies so meaningless that Sacred Bundle Keepers lost the desire to care for the Powerful Spirits until they might be needed again. Most of the Sacred Bundles were buried with their last devoted Keepers, or else were sold to museums to become parts of "collections of the past." In some cases certain greedy collectors took advantage of Bundle-Keeping families whenever misfortune struck. They rushed to the families and offered tempting amounts of cash for the Sacred things.

Among our People several Sacred Ceremonies have already come to a permanent end because of a lack of devoted participants and Sacred Bundles with which to carry them on. More ceremonies may soon come to an end because those who participate in them are all People over seventy years of age. The Good Medicine Family is now the youngest participating family in our Sacred Ceremonies, and hopes to learn enough of the songs and meanings from the remaining Old People so that a few of the ancient Ceremonies can be carried on far into the future. To help Us achieve this goal, the Good Medicine Family has some new Spiritual Teachers, about whom You will learn more in the years ahead. Let me briefly introduce them now:

6

Our "Grandfather," Wolf Old Man, is the last true Holy Man among our People. For most of his 92 years he has given the People spiritual counselling, has led their Sacred Ceremonies, has prayed for them, and has doctored them with Herbs and songs when they were ill. His Holy and Powerful character has served as an inspiration for many. He was the Keeper of our Sacred Bundle for ten years. He no longer doctors other People, because of his old age and "because the odd foods that People eat today causes strange illnesses." He devotes his time to praying and singing and to Teaching those Sacred Ways to his only students, our Family.

Our Uncle, Atsitsina, is one of our last People to know the old-time crafts and ways of everyday life—hunting, riding, camping, tanning, and so forth. After a rich life of rodeo riding, ranching, "running around," dancing and singing, pipe-making, and Bundle Keeping, he is now adjusting himself to live a life of Good Medicine and to teach what he can to his "grandchildren." At the age of 72 he has returned again to his Old Ways, wearing his grey hair in braids and his feet in moccasins. Our house is his second home.

As this is being written the green grass is again coming up from our Earth Mother, reaching out for the warmth of Sun and the moisture of Spring-time rains. We have heard the return of Thunder for the New Year—the Sacred Sound that has announced the coming of Summer to All the Spirits in our Prairie and Mountain Land. Ducks are beginning to nest along the River bottom, near our home, and Hawks and Eagles fly along the river in search of emerging Mice. Our Grandfather is preparing himself to lead the Ceremony of opening our Sacred Bundle, while we prepare ourselves to take some more of its Powerful Spirit of Nature and from the Past, as we sing its songs and see its Sacred Contents. Some of our Brothers and Sisters will be present at the Sacred Ceremony to celebrate along with Us and our Old People. The Good Medicine Family will use the Spiritual Power of that ceremony to guide Us as we make our move back to the Rocky Mountains this Summer. By the time we settle on our new Land, build our log cabins and barns, and prepare our Winter

7

supplies, it will be the end of Summer. The Good Medicine Family will have grown much larger, and the Good Medicine Spirit will have grown much stronger.

We invite you to come and visit with Us through the pages of this Good Medicine Book and the Books of the coming Seasons. Meanwhile, Brothers and Sisters of other places and Tribes, our prayers are with You.

GOOD MEDICINE

LIFE IN HARMONY WITH NATURE

ADOLF HUNGRY WOLF

To YOU, the reader, this book presents a Way of Living. . . . a Life which is thoroughly inspired by the Ways that were followed by the Old Ones who once lived in our Mountains, swam in our Rivers, and hunted on our Plains. These Old Ones have moved on—their Lands have changed—their Ways have been neglected.

NOW! A new People are Seeking new Ways. Experiences must Guide them. Let this book be, for You, an Experience. Let it help You Find A New Way.

1914   Stabs-by-Mistake and Family Glacier National Park

I have a song to sing,
To sing because We are All here;
We are All here as One,
The One makes us All.

We have the Power, My Woman and I,
We have the Power in Our Family;
We have the Power of Awareness,
Awareness that Others give Us spiritual Power.

Those others, We know Them through Our Old Man,
Our Old Man, He guides Us where We go;
We go where We can All be together,
We go where We can be just what We are.

With Our eyes far ahead, with Our steps big,
We can step over all obstructing logs;
Those logs, We just use them for Our fire,
Our fire that lights the way to where We Are.

If You are Seeking the True meanings of the many aspects of Life then Go into Nature. Go where You can enjoy evenings studying the Stars from the porch of your own home, on your own land. Go where You can see the trees that provide the lumber for your house. Go where You can see the crops that provide the food for your table. Go where You can follow the stream that provides your water. Go where You can wander for hours and think freely. Go where You can enjoy directly the fruits of your labor. Go and become what YOU think You are.

Are You clinging to the breast of ready-made living? Are You *afraid* to lose the "comforts" of such living by removing yourself to an unadulterated environment in Nature? Be honest with yourself—have you *really* even thought about changing your way of life? Not just day-dreamed and speculated, but really *thought* about it? It isn't hard to change and it's *never* too late. *All* You have to•do is set Your Mind on it! Review the factors in your present life. Review the factors of alternate lives. Let the facts make your decision, then let your Mind be your guide. Remember:

You Are What YOU Think You Are

Do you really think that You can be satisfied with your life if you spend the most important hours of the next *Forty Years* away from your family, your home, and your personal Self? Do You really believe that the benefits gained from selling your time to others are worth more to you than that time itself? Do you have to earn money so that you can pay others to do for you those things which you haven't the time to do yourself because you are busy earning money?

Decide Now that You want to have more time to Experience the many Natural aspects of True Life. Set your Mind to it. Save your money and buy a piece of land somewhere where the only thing between Earth and the Universe is You. Grow some crops. Raise some chickens and goats. Go to town occasionally for your supplies. Stop wondering about the ingredients of a bowl of soup—produce the ingredients yourself. Stop worrying about the taste of water—obtain that water yourself. Stop wondering what's inside the walls of your house—put those walls up yourself.

You owe it to your Life and the Life of your Family to consider the alternatives to acting as a cog in the world of mechanization. Don't let the intricacies of mechanical wonders amaze you into accepting them blindly as substitutes for processes of Life over which You should have direct knowledge and control.

WHAT IS GOOD MEDICINE

To understand the real meaning of the term GOOD MEDICINE, One must first realize the importance of the spiritualism that can be found in everything Natural. It is thus that People living in Nature can make a religion of their daily lives. GOOD MEDICINE means a Positive Spiritual Life. GOOD MEDICINE means realizing that there is more to Life than meets the eye. Belief in GOOD MEDICINE is one answer to the need that People in Nature find for expressing their humbleness to all that surrounds them.

Many people have asked, and others thought they answered: What do People believe when they live with Medicine—what do they pray to? They should learn that Medicine is not a subject for scholarly dissection, for it has no universal answers. For instance, tribal beliefs in North America varied widely. They depended mainly on the environment and daily pursuits of the People. Imagine the basic differences between the Arapahoe, who hunted Buffalo on the open plains, the Hopi, who still raise corn in the hot deserts, and the Seminole, who hunt and harvest in swamps and jungles. In addition to these tribal differences, caused by physical factors, were the personal differences, caused by mental factors. For the ultimate interpretation of spiritual life must be left to the wor-

14

shipping individual. It must depend on his spiritual awareness.

As all Truths must come from within the Mind, it is good to spend many times alone with the Mind. This is readily done in the Sanctuary of Nature. Thus, the follower of Medicine goes into the Great Outdoors with the same awe and respect that another would have upon entering an ancient cathedral.

The profound spiritual experience sought by those who follow the traditional belief in the Great Power of Nature is the Vision Experience. Visions, in this case, are those things experienced by the Mind when one is dreaming—when one allows the Mind to wander freely, without thoughts of social or physical restrictions. At such times many subconscious thoughts and abilities express themselves in the Mind.

The most sought-for Visions have been of visits with some spiritual element of Nature: a bird, an animal, a stone, or a star. Some have considered Visions of certain elements more powerful than others, but such decisions should only be made in the individual's own Mind. The Vision visit usually includes the ceremonial smoking of a pipe, the singing of songs, the performance of a ritual, and instructions to make or find certain objects and when to carry them. The ceremonies and material objects may later serve as physical reminders of one's spiritual ally, to provide comfort in a vast Universe where one may, at times, feel quite alone.

It has often been said that Medicine is a pagan belief that involves the use of witchcraft spells and weird physical doctoring. These claims have generally been made by un-Aware observers, who understood spiritual activity only as it was described in the rule-books of their own religions. One cannot write objectively about the spiritual beliefs of another's religion when he thinks that only *his* religion is "the right one."

First, witchcraft should not be confused with emotional spiritual experiences, which the followers of Medicine often seek. Furthermore, any power to perform physical doctoring had to come through very strong Dreams, and was often limited to the treatment of specific ailments. Relatively few Medicine Men were given such Power, and these were usually wise ones well versed in plant lore and human physiology. People living in a healthy, Natural environment have more need for spiritual guidance than medical help.

Young Stabs-by-Mistake—Pikuni

Visions might come at any time, during any kind of experience. Most properly, however, Visions are Sought during a Vision Quest. With preparation, one goes to a favorite and secluded place in Nature to meditate. Often a Vision Seeker goes forth with a specific element in Mind with which he would like to visit in Dream—the one he would most like to have as his spiritual ally. A powerful Vision experience requires intimate acquaintance with the physical aspects of the Seeker's environment. He should know the names and uses of plants and berries, the sounds and habits of birds and animals, and the signs of weather and

16

terrain. This way, he will be familiar with the elements encountered in the Vision, and know which aspects are to be most respected.

Most everyone who has spent any time out in Nature knows the feeling of an Unseen Presence. Such a feeling leads one to question what signs of the past may be visible and what unseen presence may still be there. It is good to question these things. It is good to realize that this kind of spiritual feeling is proof of a Power beyond that which is physical.

When you find a particularly moving spiritual place in Nature—one where you easily sense more than physical powers—then spend some time there. Stand before a large tree there, or sit on a big boulder—Realize YOUR place in the existence of all this. You should be humbled. Seek what others before you may have sought there also—look around for what might give spiritual guidance and motivation. Look Up at the Sky. Look Down at the Earth. Study the movements of Clouds. Study the details of Pebbles. See how beautiful this simple, Natural Life around you is. Ask yourself how You might permanently become a part of this beautiful Life.

Ask aloud how You might find a place in Nature. Ask aloud many times, and observe All that surrounds you. Become Aware of the Powers that you can see, and allow the unseen Powers to make You aware of their presence, too. Do this for an hour. Do this for a full day. When you have come to know Your place by daylight, stay there for a night. Do not fear Nature because you cannot see its details in the dark. Fear is only in your Mind. Give your Mind to Nature, as you become acquainted with Nature— *do not* try to control it with facts and figures learned in another environment. Do not discredit spiritual thoughts in your Mind with physical reasoning. Do not become distracted by thoughts of eating or sleeping—do them Naturally, if such becomes your desire. Spend your time singing, chanting, talking, and listening—all the while watching and thinking. Let the forces of Nature Guide your Awareness—*Respect That Guidance!*

If your eyes tend to distract your Mind from entering the spiritual realm, find some intriguing object to concentrate your Vision upon. Let that object filter the thoughts which enter and leave your Mind. Find a small stone, a seed, a piece of wood, or a bird's feather. Decorate it by polishing with your fingers or by attaching beads. Allow a ritual—short or long—to develop Naturally, whereby your Mind is cleared of all but spiritual thoughts. Use this as your key to the door of the spiritual world. YOU *can* do it, if Your desires are strong enough!

> *RELEASE YOUR MIND TO NATURE:*
> *Let Us Meet There. . . .*
> *Let Us Meet The Others There. . . .*
> *Let US ALL Be There Together. . .*

BRAVE BUFFALO'S DREAM

One's Medicine is a very sacred thing—not to be discussed lightly, or with just any person. Some people never reveal to anyone the details of their personal spiritual power. Here is the story of a Medicine Dream that was told by an old Sioux Medicine Man named Brave Buffalo (Tatan' ka ohi' tika) shortly before his death:

When I was 10 years of age I looked at the land and the rivers, the sky above, and the animals around me and could not fail to realize that they were made by some great power. I was so anxious to understand this power that I questioned the trees and the bushes. It seemed as though the flowers were staring at me, and I wanted to ask them "Who made you?" I looked at the moss-covered stones; some of them seemed to have the features of a man, but they could not answer me. Then I had a Dream, and in my Dream one of these small round stones appeared to me and told me that the maker of All was Wakan' Tanka (Great Spirit of the Sioux), and that in order to honor Him I must honor His works in Nature. The stone then said that by my search I had shown myself worthy of supernatural help, and that it would provide for me this help.

Brave Buffalo found a physical specimen similar to his Dream rock, which he covered with an Eagle down feather and wrapped in a piece of buckskin. Its presence reminded him of the strength promised in the Dream. Such objects may be attached to a buckskin thong and worn around the neck. Several Medicine objects may be included within one wrapping. When too many objects accumulate, or the size of an object becomes too large, a fringed buckskin bag or a cylindrical rawhide case may be used as a container. Wrapped with pieces of gaily colored cloth, silk neckerchiefs, or finely-tanned furs, the objects may become part of a Medicine Bundle. Such Bundles are never unwrapped without purpose, pipe smoking, incense burning, songs and prayers. They are generally hung, along with other Medicine objects, on a wooden tripod by the owner's bed. Incense is burned by them daily.

To the right is a Crow man, from Eastern Montana. He smokes his pipe next to the tripod that holds his sacred things. His dress reflects his spiritual creativeness. For each item he has intimate feeling.

PIPE SMOKING

A pipe is an essential object for important functions. In the old days, every man had at least one smoking pipe, often the kind referred to as a "peace pipe." Most of the "peace" made while smoking such a pipe was inside the smoker's head. Such pipes sometimes had bowls that measured six inches or more, and stems that were two feet in length. These were smoked whenever friends and visitors gathered. Both men and women had small pipes, with stems hardly longer than a man's finger, for personal smoking.

Imagine, for instance, the experience of pipe smoking during the Vision Quest: Seated on a large boulder, way up on the side of a mountain; your Mind drifts High up into vast Space with the quickly diffusing smoke of each puff.

Imagine pipe smoking while sitting in a circle on the floor with a gathering of friends: All sharing of the same natural mixture; the mouthpiece giving lips a common bond and bringing to all a spiritual unity that is allowing only for Truth.

Pipe bowls used to be fashioned from clay or short pieces of hardwood, with reeds or hollow sticks used as stems. Some were drilled pieces of hard stone or Deer antler. The popular peace pipes are carved from a red stone called Catlinite. Some of these are still being made by Native craftsmen near the quarry at Pipestone, Minnesota.

In the Rocky Mountain country pipes of various shapes have long been carved from different-colored soft stones. One popular kind is a gray-green calcareous shale that is found along many streambeds. This kind was favored by the Blackfoot people. A square piece of stone, of the right proportions, must first be drilled for bowl and stem. The desired shape is then worked around the holes, first with a file, then with a knife and a piece of sandstone (or paper). The Blackfoot often made bowls in the shape of a large acorn resting in a rectangular base. For a final effect the finished bowls are held in the smoke of a brush-fire until they turn black. A coating of grease is then worked into each one to produce a lustrous black finish.

Pipestem holes used to be made by splitting a branch lengthwise and scraping out the pithy center. The two sides were glued back together and wrapped with sinew (the muscle found along the backbone of large animals). Rosewood and Ash were preferred for stems. Holes can be made by using a straightened coat-hanger wire. Heat the wire in a fire and burn the hole straight through the stem. Partly dried Ash or Willow stems are best for this. Stems were carved, wrapped with beads, hung with bells and feathers, or just polished with fat to a natural finish.

A pipe used by the People of long ago can be easily made from the lower leg-bone of a Deer: The bone joints are sawed off. At the larger end is a cavity which may have to be scraped out—this will be the bowl. At the other end are two holes, which may have to be cleared out with a wire or nail—this will be the mouthpiece. Sand the rough spots away from the edge of the bowl, and smooth the mouth-piece down to feel comfortable. Rub the now-completed pipe with fat and polish it. It is ready to smoke.

What does one smoke in a pipe when one lives with Nature? Whatever one becomes guided to, and can locate, is what! A popular social smoke in the past consisted of dry Bearberry leaves mixed with a little Cedar bark. Many times plants were especially raised and harvested, some times to the accompaniment of ceremonies. The seeds for such sacred plants (and smoking was always considered sacred) were carefully saved in decorated pouches, and were kept with Medicine items. The first plant was usually given as an offering to the Powers that gave life to the crop.

The dried and crushed plants for smoking should be kept separate in decorated pouches. They are generally mixed just before smoking. Nature provides a great variety of blends.

Most men kept a complete smoking kit in a leather bag. This kit included pipe bowls and stems, carved sticks to use for tampers and bowl cleaners, pouches of smoking mixtures, matches, and a cutting board. Cutting boards are the smokers' catch-alls. On them the smoking mixtures are cut and blended with a sharp knife.

A fine cutting board can be made using a piece of hardwood, about one foot square. Sometimes a smaller piece is fastened to the bottom, to give a table effect. In the top center is a depression, where the loose tobacco is mixed. The board is divided into four sections by lines made with brass furniture tacks. Brass tacks were a favorite item for decorating wood items, like pipe stems and gun stocks.

For smoking, the pipe is first lit, then offered to the spiritual world as a symbol of respect and awareness. The mouthpiece may be held out to the Four Directions, or to Sun, and the Spirits that are Above us, on Earth with us, and Below us. Some people blow whiffs of smoke to the sacred places, instead.

Mr. & Mrs. Wades-in-the-Water—Pikuni—Inside their Tipi in Ceremonial Dress Glacier Studio

SWEAT BATHING

Sweat lodges were used by most native tribes. Many people today still take regular "sweats." The expulsion of dirt and germs through profuse sweating literally causes the removal of evil from the body. The plunge into cold water afterward serves to awaken both Mind and body. A "sweat" is a most profound spiritual experience—one that must be felt.

The sweat lodge is a small, round hut whose thick layer of coverings serves to keep the steam from heated rocks within. A typical sweat lodge is about eight feet deep and six feet wide.

To build a sweat lodge, clear a space big enough for the lodge. Locate the place for the door, which should face the rising Sun to the East. Dig a hole towards the rear of the lodge space for the rocks. This should be about two feet deep and two feet in diameter. Gather a quantity of flexible wood for the framework. Willow reeds, the thickness of a finger and ten to twenty feet long, are excellent. Working back from the doorway, plant the sticks firmly in the ground along both sides of the ground plan, perhaps a foot apart from each other. Tie together the ends of each pair of opposing sticks to form a series of arches. Allow enough head room for the number and size of intended bathers. Repeat this framework construction with the longer sticks arched from front to back. Remember to leave a door opening. Tie the arches together at intersections with buckskin thongs. Your framework should look like the neat beginnings for a gigantic basket, turned upside down.

Long ago, the Mountain People covered their sweat lodges with grass, or pine boughs, topped with firmly packed earth. The People of the plains used Buffalo hides over theirs. The desert-dwellers of the SouthWest used adobe. Later, canvas and blankets were often used for coverings in place of native materials. Today, popular covering materials include quilt, rugs, and layers of carpet padding. Some lodge covers are more than a foot thick.

Lay your lodge coverings over the framework so that an oval opening remains at the entrance. The coverings must reach the ground and drape outward. In bright Sunlight the interior of the lodge should be totally dark, and free from air passages. Use a folded blanket, or several small floor mats, for the door flap. This should be held in place at the top by a couple of heavy stones.

Properly prepared, the first sweat bath is an experience always to remember. Mine took place on a cool Summer evening in a grove of trees at the foot of the Rockies in Western Montana. I was "initiated" by two friends whose life in Nature includes sweats most every evening—Summer and Winter.

Jerome and I sat on a wooden bench between two trees and unbraided our hair. Pascal was already taking red-hot stones out of the fire with a shovel and placing them in the pit inside the sweat lodge. The stones hissed defiantly whenever they came in contact with the cool, damp earth in there. Pascal says he looks for dark, smooth rocks in places away from river beds. These "sweat rocks" are about the size of a fist, and are heated on a bed of good firewood. (Where fire is a problem, about six pounds

25

of briquets will heat rocks placed among them in a pit in two hours' time.)

We undressed and sat inside on a quilt-covered floor. When Pascal splashed water on the glowing rocks from a bucket, sounds like distant rifle fire filled our tiny chamber. Immediately we became enveloped by hot and heavy air. The steam was so thick, I thought I would suffocate. Jerome has been conditioned by more than fifty years of sweat bathing. He and Pascal, his nephew, took turns exclaiming the virtues of the "Good Sweat."

Three times we went outside for fresh air. The fourth time we went out singly to pour buckets-full of cold mountain water over our heads. I went out first, and passed out the second I stepped into the cold air. I fully dried and dressed myself before I again realized my physical location. I felt refreshed and hungry, as though I had just slept all night.

TIPI NOTES

A tipi is one of the most practical home styles ever made. Except for long poles, such a home can be compactly transported anywhere. Properly set up, it can house a dozen occupants comfortably—cool in Summer, warm in Winter. You will want one after the first time you sit in one around a blazing fire with friends on a cold night— or the first time you lie back on your bed, in one, and look up through the smoke-hole at a warm, star-filled Sky.

A 14-foot tipi is large enough to serve as a permanent home for a family of four. Drill, or unbleached muslin, makes good tipi covers. The material should be hemmed wherever it is cut, and reinforced with rope inside the hem around the smoke flaps and door opening. The best poles are made from straight pine saplings, scraped and dried. The number and type of poles, however, depend mainly on the individual.

Most tipis were between ten and twenty feet in size. A ten-foot camping tipi can be easily made in one piece from a large canvas painter's drop cloth.

Painted tipis were rare. The one on the left in the photo illustrated its owner's war and hunting exploits. Other tipis had colorful representations of mountains, stars, and animals. These were all Medicine tipis, representing power-ful Dreams. They should be respected as religious art, not copied or imitated for selfish reasons.

Tipi interiors are warmer and more colorful with the addition of dew cloths—six-foot-high linings of decorated canvas or colorful cloth tied to the inside of the poles all around the tipi. These serve to keep water from running down the poles, and to force upwards drafts from outside and smoke from within.

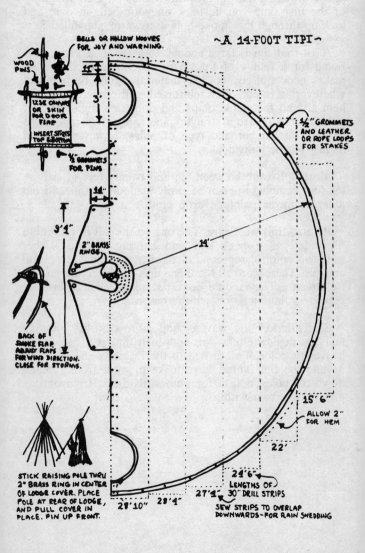

~A 14-FOOT TIPI~

BELLS OR HOLLOW HOOVES FOR JOY AND WARNING.

WOOD PINS

USE CANVAS OR SKIN FOR DOOR FLAP

INSERT STICKS TOP & BOTTOM

½ GROMMETS FOR PINS

11"

3'

½" GROMMETS AND LEATHER OR ROPE LOOPS FOR STAKES

11"

9'1"

2" BRASS RINGS

14'

BACK OF SMOKE FLAP. ADJUST FLAPS FOR WIND DIRECTION. CLOSE FOR STORMS.

15' 6"

ALLOW 2" FOR HEM

22'

24'6" LENGTHS OF 30" DRILL STRIPS

SEW STRIPS TO OVERLAP DOWNWARDS—FOR RAIN SHEDDING

27'1"

28'4"

28'10"

STICK RAISING POLE THRU 2" BRASS RING IN CENTER OF LODGE COVER. PLACE POLE AT REAR OF LODGE, AND PULL COVER IN PLACE. PIN UP FRONT.

OLD-TIME MOCCASINS

An old-time pair of moccasins is easy to make in one day. The effort is well worth the satisfaction of creating your own footwear. Soft buckskin is ideal for the tops. Untanned, or raw, hide wears well for soles. Thick Elk or Cow hide soles, however, are easier to sew. Split Cow hide can also be used for both tops and soles.

Begin by making a pattern as shown in figure 1, below. Trace your foot outline on a piece of paper. The pattern is cut slightly larger than the outline, as shown. This will allow the soles to mold upward around the feet. It will keep you from walking on the seam and wearing it out. Use the pattern to cut out your actual soles. Be sure to reverse for left and right. The grain side of the leather should be on the outside.

Use a large piece of paper to make the pattern for the uppers as shown in figure 2. Cut line A so that it measures 6 to 8 inches in length. Line B should be 2 to 3 inches wide to make the upper fit comfortably on your foot. Place the paper over your foot as in figure 3. Trace around the shape of your foot while pressing the paper to the floor. Add 1/8 inch around this tracing and cut out. Your upper pattern should look about like figure 4. Use this to cut your two uppers out of leather. Again, reverse for left and right.

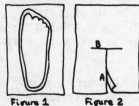

Figure 1   Figure 2

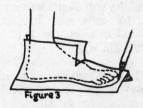

Figure 3

With an awl, make holes in the sole leather. Space the holes 1/8 inch apart, and make them at an angle as shown in figure 5. Place a sole and upper together and begin sewing the moccasin INSIDE OUT. The needle should not come out on that surface of the sole which will eventually touch the ground. As in figure 6, sew from the toe at C around one side to D, then from C around the other side to D. Use an over hand stitch and well waxed nylon or other unbreakable thread.

When both moccasins are sewn up, turn them right side out. Wetting the soles will make this easier. Sew up the moccasin backs as in figure 7. The flaps can be left standing, they can be folded and stitched down, or they can be extended with another piece of leather. Add a tongue, and cut thongs as shown in figure 8.

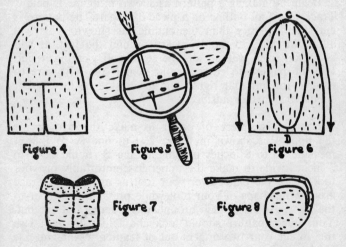

Figure 4   Figure 5   Figure 6

Figure 7   Figure 8

You now have a pair of Plains-style moccasins. This was the common footwear for people of the Plains, such as the Sioux and Cheyenne. It was well suited for their often-harsh country. It is today the most popular style of moccasin made.

For ceremonial wear moccasins were generally fully covered with beadwork. Everyday moccasins were left plain, or decorated with a beaded design on the toe. Winter moccasins were made of Buffalo hide with the fur left inside.

—Running Crane
Glacier Studio

—Black Plume
Glacier Studio

FUR CAPS

The caps worn by these two Blackfoot men are simple to make and comfortable to wear. Warmth and softness makes fur the most popular Winter headgear in cold climates.

On the right, old Black Plume is dressed for a Wintertime hunt, somewhere near his home by the Canadian Rockies. His cap is made of one piece of fur, sewn inside-out from the top of the front to the bottom of the back. The length of this piece is measured by holding it around the head the way it is to be worn. The height depends also on individual taste. The bottom of the cap is hemmed, and a cloth liner may be sewn to this hem.

The Pikuni leader Running Crane is seen dressed for battle. His Otter-fur cap is made in the two-piece style—a wide band sewn up the back, and a round piece sewn to the top. The main band can be hemmed at the bottom, or the fur may be doubled completely for extra warmth and strength.

Furs of all kinds, and even tanned birdskins, were used for caps. One's Medicine animal was often used for a cap, sometimes in a fashion that allowed the skin to be left intact. Dreams generally dictated any accessories that one might add to a completed cap.

Running Crane's style of shirt, incidentally, was worn on special occasions only, and represented dreams and accomplishments, in addition to skillful craftwork. When not being worn, these shirts were kept in rawhide containers, and treated as Medicine articles.

CABIN NOTES

"If you have built castles in the air, your work need not be lost. That is where they should be. Now put the foundations under them."

Henry David Thoreau

You can build a typical small frame cabin for about $250 if you live near a lumber mill. Such a cabin would have a solid door and a couple of windows, a wood floor, insulated walls and ceiling, and an attic for storage. There would be room inside for two beds, a wood-burning stove, a sink, some cupboards, and a small table. Additions could be made anytime later.

Log cabins can be built much cheaper than those made of milled lumber, if you have good trees on your property. The work is much harder, of course, and the logs take time to be seasoned. Log cabins are more difficult to heat and keep clean, and the chinking must be repaired regularly. The result of log cabin building is certainly an intimate home, as long as one has much more time than money. The house shown here is of a style which was popular among the Native People in the NorthWest country. Eight tree trunks were sunk in the ground to support the framework. Planks covered the outside, and an oval hole served as the doorway. The peak boards on the roof could be raised to draw out smoke and let in light.

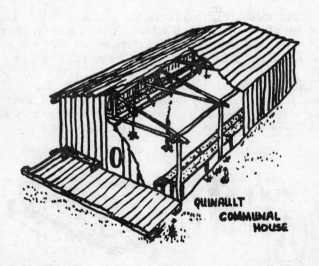

QUINAULT
COMMUNAL
HOUSE

Several families lived together in such houses, especially during the Winter. Sleeping platforms went around three walls inside. They were four feet wide and four feet from the ground. Sleeping is much warmer on this level than on the ground. Narrower platforms were built in front of the beds, two feet from the ground. These were used for seats and indoor work benches. In good weather the People preferred to work on the porch, outside.

❖❖BEADING❖❖

Beadwork decoration is a fine method for emphasizing pride in the design and workmanship of one's belongings. Beads vary in size from a pin-head to a pigeon egg, some rare types being even larger. After they became readily available from traders, the Native Americans used beads in countless different ways. With the tiny "seed" beads they developed a complex art form that was used to decorate clothing, tools, and even riding equipment. This art form was based on the ancient method of decorating by sewing down dyed and flattened porcupine quills.

Four methods of beadwork are commonly used. The easiest of these is done on a loom. A loom is easily made of wood, and should be about three inches wide and six inches longer than your planned beadwork. The tops of the upright pieces need grooves spaced 1/8 inch apart to hold the warp threads. Use heavy thread for the warp, and weave it back and forth across the loom and around the screws at each end, as shown in the drawing. Wax all thread with beeswax, to keep it from slipping.

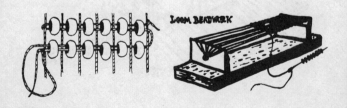

LOOM BEADWORK

Head bands, belts, and hat bands are generally made on a loom. Plan the design on paper, and leave two warp threads on each side, for strength. Beads are strung on the weave thread, spaced across the warp threads, and pushed down to be passed through again by the weave thread below the warp. Begin in the middle and work towards the ends. Weave back and forth a few times to

34

finish, and knot the warp threads together. Attach the completed bead strip to leather backing by sewing down the double-warp edges with strong thread.

More creative beadwork can be made with the "lazy-stitch" method. Finished pieces done this way are distinctive for their ridged rows of somewhat loose beads. This produced an appearance that was especially popular among the People of the Plains. It was done by sewing several beads at a time directly to leather, these being attached only at the ends of rows.

Lazy stitch beadwork is generally applied directly to the item to be decorated. A knot is tied at the end of a waxed thread, and hidden on the reverse side of the beadwork. From two to more than ten beads are strung at a time and sewn down in parallel rows. The needle does not go entirely through the material, but catches only the outer edge of it. Figure A is a top view of the beads before being pulled tight. Figure B is a side view.

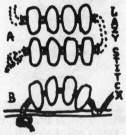

The third style of beadwork is known as the "appliqué stitch." Two threads are used, and every second or third bead is sewn down. This method produces the most perfect beadwork on leather. It is ideal for floral and pictoral designs. It was very popular among the People of the Rocky Mountain country, as well as the Woodlands People in the East.

The end of one thread is knotted and attached to the material. A number of beads are strung on it and laid in place. The second thread is then sewn across the first one, a stitch being taken at every second or third bead. Between stitches the second thread passes under the beads just below the surface, with leather. When beading on cloth the material must be backed for support, and the thread must be pulled all the way through. Beads may be sewn down in straight lines or in curves, as fits the design. Completed appliqué beadwork presents such a smooth, tight appearance that no threads are visible.

APPLIQUE STITCH

Circular pieces of beadwork are known as rosettes. They are often used where only a small amount of beadwork is desired—on leather vests, purses, and fur caps, for instance. They may range in size from a dime to a dinner plate.

Rosettes are generally made on backed felt or buckskin. Begin by drawing a circle on the material, and then draw in the design. Don't cut the circle out until you have done the beadwork. Knot the waxed thread, and sew down the center bead. Sew down the first row two beads at a time. Go back through the second bead again, each time. After the first row, sew down four beads at a time, and go back through the last two. At the end of each row, run the thread through all the beads again, if they need to be evened up.

For less than $5,000 you can have your own land and home and enough supplies to keep your family comfortable for several years. Money is *not* the barrier to Life in Nature—only Your lack of ambition is!

Some very fine small parcels of land can still be rented or leased from governments for just a few dollars. In Canada and the United States you can lease an acre or two of beautiful lake-front or national park land for less than $100 a year. Tax collectors' offices sometimes have lists of land that can be bought just by paying up the back taxes.

For real Peace of Mind it is best to own the land you live on—no matter how much the idea may contradict your belief in the Freedom of Nature.

Except in Alaska, homesteading is practically a thing of the past. Most of the good land was homesteaded long ago, and applications take years to be processed. Buying government land outright, unfortunately, is also time consuming. After choosing an area you wish to move to, however, you would do well to look into both methods of obtaining land. Then, you may wish to purchase your place privately.

37

Private land may either be bought from a realtor or directly from an owner. Realtors often charge high prices, while owners wishing to sell direct are more difficult to locate. Write to the chambers of commerce for lists of realtors in towns near any place you are interested in. Then, write to every one of the realtors and tell him what you are looking for and how much you can pay for it. Place the same information in the classified section of area newspapers. Finally, camp in the area and knock on doors during the day. Farmers and ranchers sometimes have separate grazing or woodcutting areas that are lying idle. Often such places are not considered for sale until you knock on the door and open your wallet.

The area you choose depends on you and the kind of life you intend to live. Let your skill and experience of living in Nature guide your land search. Don't risk your Life in Nature by withdrawing beyond the reaches of civilization. Consider the availability of medical help, supplies and building materials, experienced advice, and plain human companionship. A rural area that borders on wilderness is an ideal location for the inexperienced Nature seeker. Fortunately, such places are easy to find.

The price you will have to pay for land again depends on you. Don't ask a realtor "how much does land cost up there an acre?" Only tourists and businessmen try to apply regional acreage prices. You may locate a run-down 160-acre farm for $4,000, and find an 80-acre place with nice buildings down the road for more than twice that price. As a Nature-seeker you are not concerned with many of the things that the average land buyer is looking for— such as the land's money-production capabilities. For this reason you may find a bargain in a place that the commercial buyers have passed up.

Canada and Alaska offer the best deals in Nature for the land seeker. Millions of acres are available for homesteading in Alaska, where an island may be leased for as little as $100 a year. Most of Canada's relatively small population is concentrated within a short distance of the U.S. border, leaving the bulk of the country's land uninhabited, and often unexplored.

The province of British Columbia, for example, has a population of about two million people living in an area that is larger than the states of California, Oregon, and Washington combined. Of those people, seven in every ten are living within a short distance of the coastal city of Vancouver. Most of British Columbia consists of rugged and wild terrain which has kept the province from developing more than rural communities in most places. Farming is often done merely at a subsistence level, and most farms are huddled in small valleys between imposing stretches of wilderness.

The attitude of the Canadian government toward preserving the wilderness, as well as toward the welfare of its citizens is well worth looking into. The pioneer is still an active and important member of Canada's population, not a memory of the past. The future of Canada's vast undeveloped lands lies in the hands of today's pioneers.

"I'd rather sit on a pumpkin and have it all to myself, than be crowded on a velvet cushion."

Henry David Thoreau

RELEVANT ADDRESSES

LAND IN CANADA

For Government Land:
Director of Lands
Department of Lands,
Forests and Water Resources
Victoria, British Columbia

For Tax Sale Land:
Surveyor of Taxes
Department of Finance
Victoria, British Columbia

Alberta Government Land:
Director of Lands
Department of Land
   & Forests
Edmonton, Alberta

Saskatchewan Govt. Land:
Director of Lands
Dept. of Natural Resources
Prince Albert, Saskatchewan

LAND IN ALASKA

Land for Homesteading:
Bureau of Land Management
Box 1481
Juneau, Alaska

Division of Lands
344 6th Avenue
Anchorage, Alaska

LAND IN THE U.S.A.

National Forest Land
For Lease:
United States Forest Service
Department of Agriculture
Washington, D. C.

California Small Tract Lease:
Bureau of Land Management
2800 Cottage Way
Sacramento, California

TRADITIONAL CRAFTS MATERIALS

Send for Catalogs from these two leading suppliers by mail:

Del Trading Post
Mission, South Dakota

Western Trading Post
31 Broadway
Denver, Colorado

OUTDOOR MATERIALS

The Whole Earth Catalog
Portola Institute
558 Santa Cruz
Menlo Park, California:
"An evaluation and access device" for those interested in supplies and materials useful in outdoor life. No commercial interest in items reviewed. $8 per year.

Herter's Inc.
Waseca, Minnesota:
Long-time mail-order supply house for private and commercial outdoorsmen. You name it, they've got it. $1 for giant illustrated catalog.

NATURE'S FOODS

If you are going to spend your time in Nature you should know the plants, animals, and berries that can be of direct food value to you. The best way to learn such things, of course, is to speak with an experienced outdoor person in your area. All men once "lived off the Land." You should be inspired to learn some of the knowledge which they have passed on to us.

As an example of Nature's foods, here is a short list of common plants that can be beneficial to you:

CATTAIL—Grows in moist and swampy areas. Boil or bake the roots and eat them like potatoes. Powder the roots and use for thickening soups. Use the shoots for salads—similar to cucumber. Mix the yellow pollen half and half with regular flour to make golden pancakes.

CRABGRASS—Gather the seeds and cook them like rice for a good breakfast cereal.

DANDELION—Grows anywhere, and is commonly eaten in many countries. Use the roots for tea. The white area at the top of the roots makes a good boiled vegetable. Leaves are good for salad or boiled greens.

MILKWEED—Eat the flowers raw, cook the shoots like asparagus.

NETTLES—Leaves can be boiled and eaten like spinach.

PURSLANE—Grows anywhere. Gather whole plants and lay on sheet to dry in Sun. Then beat plants with stick to separate seeds, which make great pancake flour. Dried plants can be cooked in soups or stews. Fresh plants can be eaten as salad.

LAMB'S QUARTERS—Use young leaves for salads. Mix tiny black seeds in dough for nutrition.

GRANDMA

She lives alone in a little log house at the edge of a big field in Western Montana. Behind the house a path leads down to the creek and across a bridge made from a split log. On the other side of the creek the path leads to a small, tree-surrounded meadow. An old bathtub, with ornate legs, stands by the creek. Filled with mountain-fresh water in the morning, Sun makes the bathtub ready for service in the afternoon.

Next to the house stands an old woodshed, and the skeleton remains of a small wooden house that was once the home of Grandma's parents. Its old iron stove, with the stovepipe still connected, is used for cooking outdoors on warm Summer evenings. As much time as weather allows is spent outdoors. For this reason a small tipi is often set up and furnished near the house.

Grandma was born in a tipi in 1881. Her Salish-Flathead parents were members of a band of that tribe's people who stayed with their beloved Chief Charlot Bear Claw on their ancestral lands in a beautiful valley along the Bitterroot River. The rest of the tribe was earlier pressured to move to a government-appointed reservation in another valley. For ten years Grandma lived in the Bitterroot Valley, before Charlot was threatened into moving his people to the reservation. It seems that Charlot's people left too much of their Natural Wilderness undisturbed, for numerous settlers anxiously awaited Charlot's removal so that they could lay claim and "put the land to use."

Grandma was married most of her life to Louie. In old group photographs Louie stands out as a tall, thin man with a heart-warming jovial grin. His long hair was always neatly braided, and his dress style marked him as an individual who was proud of his appearance. He generally wore a colorful scarf around his neck, and he always had on a pair of moccasins that Grandma made from softly-tanned Deerhide. One of their kids was with them when the photo below was made, more than fifty years ago. They were dressed for a Sunday outing: He, with beaded vest, belt, cuffs, armbands, moccasins, and a blanket; She, with a velvet cape over calico blouse and skirt.

Louie has been gone for years, but Grandma's household still reflects his spiritual presence. She knows that she is really not alone when she goes down the old path to the creek to wash some clothes. Physical appearances may change, but no one can alter the spiritual feelings of a place once they have developed.

Several times a day Grandma's little form scurries out to the woodshed with a bucket and an axe. She returns to her kitchen with a fresh load of fuel for the old black stove with the shiny trim. Her daily dress is the same gay and colorful style of clothing she has always worn. Soft Deerskin, bright calico cloth, and little strings of beads are the materials. She loves her close, daily relationship with Nature, and is proud to do her part in making it more beautiful.

In the evenings smoke pours from the chimney of her little house. She sits by the front porch, appearing to be alone—knowing she is not. Over the years her eyes have weakened, but she still sees plainly the surrounding Mountains that are guarded in the twilight by the endless Sky. Her lips move silently in prayer, her eyes strive to see where only Her mind can go. Memories of other times and other people drift by like unseen clouds. She knows that soon she will be with them, and others will sit and feel her go by. The knowledge of her presence will give strength to their thoughts.

Grandma loves to reminisce about the days gone by. Days spent hiking through forests with Louie, or fishing in the creek with the kids. Warm days spent outdoors doing beadwork or tanning hides. Cold days spent inside by a fire, telling stories or singing songs.

Hunting for fresh meat, to supplement the vegetables from the garden, often meant a family camping trip up into the Mountains. Such trips were always made on horseback. Sometimes there was quite a caravan, if other families went along.

The families had favorite camping places where the tipis were set up. These spots were picked for their beauty, their abundance in wild game and plants, and the availability of water and feed for the horses. Some food was taken along, but the best of it was obtained in the vicinity of the camp.

The first successful hunter always shared his meat with everyone in camp. The choice parts were usually roasted and eaten immediately. A large roast was hung over the fire for a later meal. The rest of the meat was usually cut into thin slices and hung from poles or ropes near fire, there to dry into pieces that were easy to store.

The camp came to life early in the morning, when the men went out hunting. The women got their children up and ready, and then went out to fill the big pouches with wild berries, roots, and plants, which they gathered. The afternoons were spent swimming, hiking, or relaxing in the shade under a framework of poles covered with branches. In the evenings everyone gathered in one of the tipis, its owners acting as hosts for the evening. Pipes were smoked. Drums and rattles were brought out to accompany the singing. Stories were told. Cups of tea and bowls of berries were passed around. Weathered faces shone happily in the warm light of a wood fire.

THOUGHTS OF WISDOM

"That flowing water!
That flowing water!
   My Mind wanders across it.
That broad water!
That broad water!
   My Mind wanders across it.
That old age water!
That flowing water!
   My Mind wanders across it."

         Navajo Song of
         the Old Age River

The Ancient Ones had no written literature to shed a light from the past upon their days of thoughtful search. Each had his own Way of Seeking Truths. If You are seeking, You have the opportunity of choosing from their many Ways. For NOW there is literature that tells us of Their Ways. Wise Men of many lands, many cultures, and many generations have left Us their Ways. They meant for us to use them. Their Words they meant for us to hear.

"Grandfather:
   A Voice I am going to send!
Hear me,
All over the Universe:
   A Voice I am going to send!
Hear me,
Grandfather:
   I will Live!
I have said it."

         Sioux Opening
         Prayer of the
         Sun Dance

Learn about the Ways of the Ancient Ones. Study

literature and listen to Wise Men. Let the Old Ways help You to decide where you are going. Let the Old Ways help You to get there.

> *"Many Paths lead through the Forest,*
> *But They All come out on the other Side."*
>
> *OnistaiPoka*

Think NOW of your Direction. Think NOW about your Path. Make your Trail meaningful—make every Step count. Don't stop to weep for those who would rather sleep. Stay Awake and Seek: from All that you meet.

> *"Often in my travels I come to the land of Spirits.*
> *As day approaches I travel and*
> * come to the land of Spirits.*
> *Often in my travels I come to the land of Spirits.*
> *As Sun drops, I travel and come to the land of Spirits.*
> *Often in my travels I come to the land of Spirits.*
> *In my Dreams I travel and come to the land of Spirits.*
> *Often in my travels I come to the land of Spirits.*
> *As a Spirit I travel and come to the land of Spirits."*
>
> *Osage Spirit Song*

If you become lost, do not hesitate to take a new Path. Do not make a soft bed under a Bush, and there await your End. You may never know if the right Path is nearby. Do not let fear of the Unknown keep you from discovering the Unknown. Do not let discomforts keep you from finding more than comfort.

> *"The Old Men Say—The Earth only Endures.*
> *You Spoke Truly—You are Right."*
>
> *Sioux Song to overcome fear*

Choose Surroundings of which you will want to speak well. Praise them often, in words and in songs. Find Good in All, and see that you replace it. Give, without expecting to take. But always Give, if You take. Goodness is Giving. Happiness is Giving. Giving is Goodness and Happiness.

> *"Footprints I make! I go to the field with eager haste.*
> *Footprints I make! Amid rustling leaves I stand.*

47

Footprints I make! Amid yellow blossoms I stand.
Footprints I make! I stand with exultant pride.
Footprints I make! I hasten homeward with a burden
of Gladness.
Footprints I make! There is joy and gladness in
my home.
Footprints I make! I stand amidst a day of contentment.
Osage Corn-Gatherers Song

It is the song of a content Mother who has brought home to her joyful family some of the fruits of her own labor. Her burden is a load of gladness.

Four Principal Directions are there in Nature. Four Principal Seasons Change the Scenes. No wonder that the Ancient Ones thought of Four as the Sacred Number. It added to All more sense of unity.

Looking Westward:
"Over there are the mountains.
May you gaze upon them as long as you live.
From them you will get your Sweet-Pine as incense."
Looking Northward:
"Over there is The-Star-that-never-moves (Pole Star).
From the North will come your strength.
May you see the Star for many years."
Looking Eastward:
"Over there is Old Age.

From that Direction comes the light of Sun."
Looking Southward:
"May warm Winds from the South bring you plenty of
food."

Pikuni Good-Luck Song for Medicine
Pipe Man

The Ancient Ones knew that there is a Place for Everything, in Nature. With Faith in Nature, One is sure to Find His Place.

An Old Sioux named Shooter once said: "Wakan Tanka teaches the birds to make nests, yet the nests of all birds are not alike. . . . The seeds of the plants are blown about by the Wind until they reach the Place where they will grow best—where the action of Sun and the presence of moisture are most favorable to them, and There they take root and grow."

. . . . . AND ONLY TIME WILL TELL IF EACH GENERATION IS ABLE TO IMPROVE ITS LIFE WITH THE WISDOMS OF THE GENERATIONS BEFORE . . . . .

Silver Skies reflect Our Way,
Sun Guides Us,
Moon Guides Us:
Nature is Our Way!
Sleep. . . . Vision. . . . Dream. . . .
All Can Be Heaven!
First, You Must Release:
Don't hold back, to Wander.

No feet to walk
The Trail of All,
No eyes to see
No footsteps;
Above Ones—Below Ones:
We on Earth Seek Guidance;
Awake Us. . . . Awake Us. . . .
And let Us find All.

COME TOGETHER

Where one man can survive, two will fare well;
Three and their Families will form a tribe.
A thousand like-Minds form their own Nation,
With Nature as the ruler of their Lives.

Brothers: Find Your Brothers!
Like Minds: Share Your Thoughts.
Let Customs and Traditions develop,
Let Respect be the Medium of Exchange.

Find Your Own piece of land to envelope,
Let Brotherhood of Your Minds grow along;
Love Your Brothers the way you love your own self;
Give Your children Paths to choose from that can't go
*   wrong.*

Come Together, Oh Brothers! Come Together,
Your Life on Earth is just so long;
Dig the Earth—know what comes of Your Digging,
Learn the simple Life of Nature—relax, let It Guide You
*   along.*

If Dreams of a Life of culture accompany Your desires
for a home in Nature, then look for Companions. Seek
others whose Dreams are like Yours. Get Together—give
each other motivation. Get Together—Your ideas and resources. The results of Respectful coalitions will be seen
in the strength of Your success.

Native People seldom traveled alone. They knew that Strength comes from Unity of Numbers. Families and friends camped together, hunted together, and defended together. The success of One meant success for All; none were left to suffer alone. Allegiance to the Group came before allegiance to self, thus the self was supported by the Group. With neighbors like Brothers, and Brothers for neighbors, no thoughts were kept hidden, no property hoarded. Generosity made a good man a leader; greed was the sign of discontent.

In the old days large groups of People, known as Tribes, seldom lived together in one body. The effect of such a mass on the Natural environment would have been unbearable to them. Water would have become polluted, forage would have been overgrazed, and game overhunted. Instead, smaller groups, known as Bands, were formed. These were People who were related (physically or spiritually—the Old People saw no difference), or who wished to follow the leadership of a successful man. New bands were formed regularly, and change of membership was not uncommon. And always: The bands could call on the rest of the Tribe in any case of need.

Leaders remained so only as long as they had followers. Band members remained so only as long as they put Group success before personal gain.

Bands of the same Tribe were often camped far apart from each other most of the year. Sometimes they only

51

assembled once a year, for the great Summer Spiritual Gatherings which have been generally referred to as Sun Dances.

Sun is the ever-present symbol of the Great Power of All. When making a vow, in time of danger or need, Sun was often respectfully addressed as the Center of the Universe—the Great Power. Such vows were then often fulfilled during the sacred Sun Dances. Friends and relatives who lived with separate bands met and celebrated their continued Life on Earth together. Band leaders met and exchanged hunting and travelling information. Tribal leaders emerged as those whose actions and counselling were most sought after and admired by the People. The Sun Dance was the last opportunity for a great gathering of the tribe's bands before they set out in small groups to make preparations for the Winter.

What better time to gather in honor of Sun than in Summer, when Sun is nearest to the People who live all year beneath Its presence. At that time the trees are in full leaf, the berries are ripe, and the flowers are blooming—all with their faces to Sun in search of life and growth. At that time the weather is most pleasant, and the food is plenty.

And what great gatherings there were! Steady processions of People and Dogs arrived for days before the Sun Dance ceremony itself was to begin. Some groups traveled great distances to reach the Sacred Grounds. Many hundreds of tipis made up the tribal camp circles, each band having a space reserved for it by tradition. In the center of the circle was built the Sacred Lodge—the central point of the spiritual gathering. Nearby were the meeting-tipis of the various men's and women's societies, which furnished the policemen and attendants. A particularly large lodge in the center of camp served as the meeting place for the People's leaders.

Sun Dance ceremonies Naturally differed among the numerous tribes who performed them. The reasons for attending the ceremonies even varied among People of the same tribe. Some came to fulfill religious vows made

52

during the year. Some came to exchange spiritual knowledge and Medicine articles. Some came to show their abilities as spiritual leaders. Many came simply for the Spiritual Strengthening that resulted from the joyous gathering of so many like-Minds. Colorful clothing, tearful reunions, exchanges of presents, and happy singing were some of the common features of these gatherings.

To get an idea of the typical aspects of most Sun Dances let Us go back and visit a Dance of the Past. Let Us be with the Northern Cheyenne People, at their town of Lame Deer, Montana, around the turn of the century:

Multitudes of tipis and tents dot the Plain in a huge circle. Horses are seen grazing everywhere—singly and in herds. Buggies, buckboards, and covered wagons are parked by their owner's lodges, and show how households are easily transported. Outside a few lodges can still be seen travois poles, leaning against tipi sides like upside-down V's. The small cross-braces, to which loads are tied when the poles are being dragged by a horse, serve as steps for a handy camp ladder.

Hundreds of People are seen doing many things: visiting with each other; going to the river for Water, or a swim; hanging Meat over pole frames to dry; or beading a new pair of moccasins in the shade of a pine-branch Sun shelter. Others continue to arrive throughout the day, coming in various-sized groups and often from remote Villages on the Reservation. The arrival of such groups is often announced by their own young men, who charge into the huge camp circle on their horses, singing songs, yelling, and firing rifles into the Air. Some men ride into camps like this with their fraternal group, whose members all share some mark of identification, and who generally perform a few on-the-spot group songs and dances for the camp. All the new arrivals are dressed in their finest decorated clothes, and in just a short while their homes are set up and the fire is going.

As evening settles on the prairie the hundreds of fires light up the darkness. The air is filled with the smells of Cottonwood burning and meat cooking. The sounds of People talking and laughing are mixed with the sounds of drumming, as some sing their Spiritual songs and others meet in groups to practice lively tunes used for dances. It is a time for lighting pipes—for no good host would fail to offer his guests a smoke.

By the time the camp is completely set up the Leaders of the Sun Dance itself have already undergone some time of preparation: singing songs, sweat bathing and purifying, and preparing of the Sacred Articles to be used. A number of days might be spent before everyone is ready to concentrate on the Spiritual Experience of the Ceremony.

The first of the Four Important Days begins with the gathering of poles and branches for the Medicine Lodge. This is done by men who are respected for their wisdom and courage, while the members of the Tribe look on. Old, respected men are then sent out to cut down a sturdy Cottonwood Tree, which will serve as the important Center Pole in the Medicine Lodge.

During construction of the Lodge, the Leaders of the Ceremony emerge from the preparation lodge and seat themselves on the ground near the new poles. There are three People who vowed during the past year to make this Summer's Sun Dance—they are called Pledgers. The wives of these Pledgers led the procession from the preparation lodge. Their bodies are painted according to custom, and they are wearing Buffalo robes wrapped around them. Bunches of fresh-smelling Sage are tied to their wrists and the sides of their heads.

The Pledgers are taken over to the partly-constructed Lodge to see the progress and to achieve Spiritual Communion by rubbing the poles with Sacred Red Earth Paint. Meanwhile, the women of the camp are given an opportunity to achieve Spiritual Communion with the Ceremony by bringing their children to the Sacred Women, who take each individual in their lap and say a prayer of Spiritual Strength for them. Presents are left before the Sacred Women by these callers in thanks for the hardships of fasting and self-sacrifice which these three Women are undergoing to aid the People with the Ceremony of Spiritual Strengthening. The Sacred Men, meanwhile, are looking on while sitting in a semi-circle to the right of the Women. Each of these Men was once a Pledger of the Sun Dance for his People.

Much shouting, shooting, and singing around the Center Pole, by all the People, is the signal of cheer that the Lodge is completed. The Sun Dance is now begun, and the People have given their approval. The Leaders of the Ceremony now enter to remain within the Lodge during the four days and nights of Ceremony.

That night, after dinner, comes the first assembly of the People to see the entrance of the Sun Dancers— mostly young men who have vowed to fast and dance for four days and nights in Spiritual recognition of some Powerful event which brought them Good during the year.

Older men, who have themselves once undergone the Sun Dance, accompany the Dancers and serve as Guides: giving the Dancers instructions, and painting their bodies. Drumming and singing accompanies the dancing for the whole time. At intervals all activity halts, the Dancers wrap themselves in blankets, and there is a period of rest.

Most of the time, however, the Dancers face the Center Pole, look up toward Sun, and rise up and down on the balls of their feet in time to the drumming.

The Dancers are painted several times daily, and the designs are changed regularly during the days of the Ceremony. Clays, Earths, and Charcoal furnish most of the paint, which is then mixed with animal tallow for application. Breechclouts and waist wraps are the only clothing worn. In addition, each Dancer has wreaths of Sacred Sage on his head and wrists, and strung as a bandolier across one of his shoulders. Whistles of Eagle wingbones hang suspended from each Dancer's neck. Fine Eagle plumes on their ends seem to float in air as the Dancers blow in unison to the drum-beats.

During one of the earlier rest periods in the dancing the Spiritual Leaders ceremonially construct the Altar of Life. This serves as a central place where those seeking Spiritual communication may go to pray and get strength. The center of the Altar is a Buffalo skull, with symbols of Nature painted on it. Around it are piles of dark Earth. Before it is a small pit for sweet-smelling incense, and an arch made of twigs to represent a Rainbow in the Sky. These are things from the People's daily Lives.

A public feast follows completion of the Altar. Wagonloads of food are piled up in the Medicine Lodge, while the Spiritual Leaders make prayers of thanks for It All, and ask that the Good Spirit continue with the People.

All too soon the Great Summer Celebration is over. Homes are taken down and packed up. Groups of People head back out on the Prairie in All Directions. The events of the few days and nights will become topics of conversations during coming Fall and Winter campfires. The new Spiritual Strength will help Guide the next year's daily Life.

around the household

Housework in the days of tipi camps was a full-time job that often did not even allow for mistakes. The woman, in those days, usually owned the tipi and all the household

57

goods, and was responsible for them. The husband was the provider and protector, but he often only watched when the tipi was being set up by the women, or when a new tipi was being made. The woman did all the cooking, tanning, sewing, and child-raising, as well as the firewood and berry gathering. Older children helped a great deal with this work, and many men had more than one wife to take care of all the housework. A wife's younger sisters, for instance, were often absorbed into the same household and generally made good companions this way.

The basic food item for most tipi-dwelling People was meat. On the plains, of course, this was primarily the meat of the Buffalo. In the mountains the meat was largely that of Deer, Elk, and Moose, supplemented by occasional Buffalo hunts out on the plains. Tipi-dwellers who lived by lakes and rivers learned to rely on Fish and Ducks, while some of the tribes on the prairies to the East even raised corn and other vegetables.

The best parts of an animal were often cooked over a fire and eaten as soon as possible. The Summer's heat and the constant travelling required preparation of the bulk of the meat so that it would not be subject to spoiling. Thus, most meat was dried by being cut into large, thin slices and hung out in Sun's light or over a constant fire. Drying racks were made like the one pictured above, or with a four pole foundation (like a topless table). The four pole type can be covered with chicken wire for practical use. Slice the meat into thin strips and slabs and lay them across the wire or hang them from the poles. Some pieces can be sliced in half again after they have dried and toughened a bit. A smoky, almost-flameless, fire underneath will dry an immense quantity of meat, without burning, in a day or two. At night the meat should be covered or taken inside to keep it from getting moist.

The dried hunks of meat can be broken up and stored in large bags. It may be kept this way indefinitely, and eaten just as it is. It may also be toasted over a fire, fried in a skillet, or cooked with soups and stews. The same methods, incidentally, also apply to Fish.

Pemmican—the energy snack of the Outdoors—is made by pounding dried meat until it is fine and then mixing it with fat and berries. Hold the dry pieces briefly over the fire to make them soft and oily, then pound them with a heavy stone. Then heat some animal fat, bone marrow was particularly preferred, and mix it with the meat and crushed berries. A few leaves of wild peppermint were often added for flavoring. Five pounds of fresh meat will make one pound of Pemmican that can be divided and wrapped in small pouches to take on Winter hikes or hunting trips.

Here is how to make 10 pounds of Pemmican by the modern method: Take 5 pounds of dried meat and grind it until it has a meal-like consistency. Mix the ground-up meat with 1 pound of raisins (in place of berries) and ½ pound of brown sugar and then stir into 4 pounds of melted fat. Pemmican cakes were generally kept in rawhide bags, but canvas pouches will do. It may be eaten raw or fried.

Berry gathering was an important pursuit at Summer's end, in the old days. Bushes were often lightly beaten with sticks so that the berries would fall on robes spread out underneath. The robes were then taken back to camp and spread out again, so that the berries could dry in the Sunshine. Sometimes berries were spread out where the ground sloped, and a fire was built at the base to speed up the drying. Dried berries were stored whole and pulverized. Sometimes the fresh berries were mashed and pressed into cakes and then Sun dried. Several species were often mixed together for these berry cakes, which provided a nutritious change in fare during the long Winters.

SACRED TOBACCO

CEREMONIES

Most Native People made a ceremony of the gathering of their smoking mixtures. They used the occasion to make known their wishes for success and happiness which they hoped would accompany their smoking times during the next Season. They prayed that Spiritual Awareness of the existing Powers should accompany their times of pipe smoking: while at home before the evening fire; while passing the pipe around a circle of friends gathered in the sweat lodge; or while blowing out whiffs of smoke to the

Universe while seated on a rock outcropping far above the valley floor.

Certainly the time of harvest is a time to smoke in quiet contemplation of the Good Times Yet to Come! It is a wonderful occasion for singing songs and chants of the Montana region. For instance, tobacco planters among the Crow People used words like these in their songs:

> *"Tobacco is plenty, it is said,*
> *on the Mountain where I stay."*
> *and:*
> *"Some plants good—put on your heads."*

In the past an individual sometimes went out into the tobacco garden after the planting and spent the night there to seek a Vision. An old-time Crow man named Gray Bull, in 1911, described an experience of this sort that he had had:

"I once lay at the garden for three days and nights. I slept. In the morning I got into water up to my breasts, faced upstream and downstream, and stayed all day until Sunset (Summer days in Crow country can be extremely hot). My body felt as though pricked. All my body was wrinkled up when I got out. I got out quickly and lay down in the shade. All my body felt as if pricked with needles. I lay down again by the garden and saw a man singing this song:

> *"I am Tobacco. My body all over is Tobacco."*

At the first sentence he moved his clenched hand forward. At the second sentence he touched his body with it. The People asked me whether I had seen anything and I told them of my Vision. Then all said: 'Thanks! We shall surely have a good crop.'"

The Crow People developed a complex ritual for their Sacred Tobacco planting ceremony. The participants were members of the Crow Tobacco Society, whose ceremonial activities in the tribal life of the Crow were second in importance only to the Sun Dance. Members of the Society were trained for the respect and ceremony which was considered essential for the successful planting of the Sacred Tobacco.

Ceremonial meeting of Crow tobacco society on a summer day

Members of the Tobacco Society "adopted" new members and taught them the pertinent songs and ceremonies. These new members thought of their adopters as Mother or Father in Spirit, and the adopters called them Children, in turn. Such Spiritual Relationships were generally lifelong, and were no less important than physical relations. Children sought advice from their adopted Parents, and provided for them whenever the need arose. Presents were exchanged between the two whenever the situation seemed appropriate. A complex ceremony of adoption often took place inside an "adoption lodge." Songs were sung, gifts of appreciation were given by the new member, and Society Medicine objects were transferred to him by older members. The new member was shown ways to paint and dress at ceremonies.

The Blackfoot People raised their Smoking Plants in Sacred Gardens in which each family had its own plot. A band of the People would locate their Garden site and prepare it for planting in early Spring. The women and children helped to prepare the site. They removed debris, spread brush over the ground and burned it, and then swept the area clean with brush brooms. The soil was then broken up and raked fine by everyone present.

Tobacco Seeds were prepared by the Blackfoot for planting by being mixed with Elk, Deer, and Mountain Sheep droppings which had been pounded up. Sacred Serviceberries were then added to the mixture. Spiritual thoughts, songs, and prayers accompanied all phases of the planting ceremony.

The planters and their wives all met at the Garden on the actual day of planting. The planters stood before their own plots and then went across the field in a line, one step at a time. At each step they made holes in the ground before them with short, pointed sticks. Then the women followed behind and dropped some seed into the hole, and the Medicine Men sang one of the Tobacco Songs. This ceremony was repeated until the planting was done, at which time the Tobacco Dance was held. Then the People left the area of the Sacred Garden and went on their Summer hunts.

While the People were absent from the Sacred Garden they performed ceremonies at which prayers for the success of the crop were made. Some asked for protection of the crop from grasshoppers and other insects. While praying and singing they sometimes kept time with a stick, which they tapped on the ground as though they were killing these insects.

At harvest time the People all gathered and camped by the Garden again. The day before the Sacred Plants were gathered the wisest of the Medicine Men went to the Garden and brought back one plant. He then directed a young boy to take the plant to the center of camp. There he showed the boy how to fasten it ceremonially to a stick and leave it in the ground as an offering of appreciation to the Great Power which had caused the crop to grow successfully and to be ready now to Unite with the People.

On the day of the harvest a ceremony was held in the center of camp. A feast was served, prayers were offered, and songs were sung. . . .

"Sun goes with Us,"

were the words of one of the songs. The group of People

63

then proceeded to the Garden and gathered their own plants. Fine pouches had been made and decorated prior to this, and these were now filled with the Sacred Plants to be smoked. Little decorated sacks were also on hand—these to preserve the precious seeds until the next Season's planting. The old-time Blackfoot People believed that these seeds were the ancestors of the first seeds given their forefathers of the long ago by a Medicine Beaver. The ceremonies of raising the Sacred Tobacco have, today, all but been forgotten.

THE GHOST DANCE:
SONGS & VISIONS

Father, I come;
Mother, I come;
Brother, I come;
Father, give us back our arrows.

. . . . so went the continuous chant of the Sioux People as they gathered for the Ghost Dance—a spiritual revival ceremony in which the object was to lose consciousness of the physical state (which was at that time one which most People would not want to be conscious of)—a state of confined life on reservation land which seemed barren and desolate without the Buffalo herds and tipi camps that were everywhere a generation before. While under the spell of the Dance's excitement those who were fortunate fell to the ground in a trance and went on Spiritual Visits to places of beauty—visiting the camps and People of another day.

The history and anthropology of the Ghost Dance has been well described in several books. Let us see here about some of the Dance's spiritual methods. Ghost Dance leaders among different tribes patterned details of the ceremony to compliment traditions that already existed within their own tribes. Styles of dress and types of songs, for instance, were common tribal variations in Ghost Dance Ceremonies.

. . . . As We join an Arapaho Ghost Dance camp of the past We find ourselves in the midst of almost 100 tipis. The People have located the Camp in a grove of tall Cottonwood trees next to a little river. It is late in the afternoon, and the People are putting on beaded clothing and combing their hair in preparation for the Dance. Some wear only aprons—they are painting elaborate designs all over their bodies with red, yellow, green, and blue mixtures of sacred paints. Red and yellow paint lines the parting in their hair. Dots like hailstones are seen on some faces. Sun, stars, crescents, crosses, and birds are seen on bodies. Others have these designs painted on white clothing.

The Dance leaders of the camp are the first to assemble around a tree which marks the very center of the dance area. They hold hands and quietly begin singing this song:

> *Eyehe'! na'nisa'na,*
> *Eyehe'! na'nisa'na,*
> *Hi'na cha'sa' aticha' ni'na He'eye'!*
> *Hi'na cha'sa' aticha' ni'na He'eye'!*
> *Na'hani na'nitha'tuhu'na He'eye'!*
> *Na'hani na'nitha'tuhu'na He'eye'!*
> *Bi'taa'wu' da'naa'bana'wa He'eye'!*
> *Bi'taa'wu' da'naa'bana'wa He'eye'!*

In English the song says:

> *O, my Children! O, my Children!*
> *Here is another of your pipes—He'eye'!*
> *Here is another of your pipes—He'eye'!*
> *Look! thus I shouted—He'eye'!*
> *Look! thus I shouted—He'eye'!*
> *When I moved the Earth—He'eye'!*
> *When I moved the Earth—He'eye'!*

The song is sung a number of times and it grows in strength, as voices become louder and others join in. The dancing starts slowly to the left, in rhythm with the singing —right feet shuffling after left. The People of the camp join in with the handholding, shuffling, and singing until All become a part of a sacred, revolving Circle of men, women, children, and Old People. The Mass becomes a gigantic Vibration.

No one notices that evening is slowly coming on. Some of the dancers have unclasped their hands and are sitting on the ground smoking and talking. Others are beginning to shake noticeably from the intensity of the spiritual feeling.

From within the ring advances one of the spiritual leaders, dancing in unison with the group, but facing a Young Man who is shaking. The leader is wearing a cotton apron and a white flannel shirt with many birds and insects drawn upon it. His hair hangs loosely over his shoulders and he holds a black and white Eagle feather in his left hand, a red scarf in his right. He twirls first the feather, then the scarf in front of the Young Man's face, all the while muttering a low Hu! Hu! Hu! Hu! The words of the song that fills the now-night air are: "Na' nanu' naatani'na Hu'hu!" Soon the Young Man loses his place in the dance circle as he looks at the handkerchief and Eagle feather—or looks through them to the beginnings of his Vision beyond. Having the Young Man's full attention the Older keeps him spellbound by waving the feather swiftly, then slowly, then twirling it, then fanning his hands in the air, then in front of the Young Man's face, then, finally, drawing his hands from in front of the Young Man's eyes, slowly up into the Star-filled Sky, until the Young Man stops shaking, becomes rigid, and falls to the Earth to go to his Vision. The Experience of the Older has brought the Youth from his state of physical hopelessness to a state of Spiritual Ecstasy whose moments of delight and happiness are worth the hours of daily toil + + + +

The other dancers continue, and the leader moves on to another person. Everyone is careful not to disturb those who are having Visions—carefully dancing around them where they lie on the Earth. These Dreamers often stay gone for several hours.

It is supposed that the popular Ghost Shirts originated in a Dancer's Vision some time ago. On the white background the owners of these shirts paint sacred symbols representing Nature, and illustrating some aspect of a Vision they have had. While Dancing, the Shirt is worn as an outside garment by many men, women, and children. Many, in the Past, wore it underneath their daily garments at all times. They believed that the Shirts gave them exceptional Power.

Ghost Shirts are made of white buckskin, whenever this is obtainable. Most of the Shirts are made of white muslin,

67

and are sewn with sinew instead of thread. The sleeves, shoulders, and necks of the Shirts generally have extra strips of cloth sewn between the seams, and this is cut into fringe. Eagle feathers are often attached to the shoul-

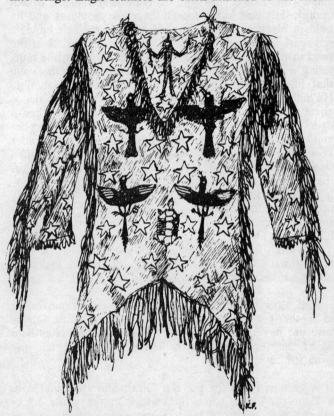

ders and sleeves. The designs are generally applied with colored painted, but some of the fine buckskin shirts and dresses of the Past were completely decorated with bead-work. Some Shirts have only a few designs on them, while others are completely covered with Sun, Moon, Stars, and other Natural symbols.

Most Ghost Dancers of the Past were antagonized into believing that going beyond physical reality to seek spiri-

tual experiences was evil. Yet the doctrine of Wovoka—
the Ghost Dance messiah of the Past—is still believed by
some to describe one of the Paths that lead to Happiness:

"You must not fight. Do no harm to anyone.
Do Right always."

MORE GHOST DANCE SONGS

Verily, I have given you my strength,
Says the Father, Says the Father.
The shirt will cause you to live,
Says the Father, Says the Father.

Sioux Ghost Shirt Song

My Children - E' e' Ye'!
My Children - E' e' Ye'!
Here it is, I hand it to You.
The Earth - E' e' Ye'!
The Earth - E' e' Ye'!

Arapaho

I love my children - Ye' ye'!
I love my children - Ye' ye'!
You shall grow to be a nation - Ye' ye'!
You shall grow to be a nation - Ye' ye'!
Says the Father, says the Father.
Ha ye' ye' Eya' yo'! Haye' ye' Eya' yo' yo'!

Sioux

I Fly around yellow,
I Fly around yellow,
I Fly with the wild rose on my head,
I Fly with the wild rose on my head,
On high - He' e' e'!
On high - He' e' e'!

Arapaho

ON NAMING PERSONS

Names of many Native American Persons are well
known for their color and beauty. The stories behind such
names are often even more colorful and beautiful, for

many such names originated in Visions or were given as a permanent reminder of some notable event.

Methods of name-giving varied among the many tribes. Most individuals, however, had more than one name, and some changed their names a number of times during their life-time. A given name at Birth, and an earned name for adulthood was the most common system by which Persons were named.

The parents of a newborn child generally called some respected old person to their lodge to give the baby a name. This person would ask if a particular name was preferred—one Dreamed of by the parents, or, perhaps, one that was asked to be passed on by some relative. If not, the old person might give the child the name of some animal or other Natural Being whose presence was noted at the time of the Birth. Or, the old person might previously have Dreamed of a name to be given to the next child that needed one. Or, the person might pick out a name or event from his or her own past with which to honor the child. It was quite common for an old warrior to name a baby girl for some battle exploit of his. Names such as Two Strike Woman and Night Horse were carried by women of the past.

An event during childhood often brought a new name to an individual. Sometimes this became the life-long name, at other times it represented an embarrassing aspect in the person's life. Such names as Lazy Boy, Round Head, and Sits Like A Woman were life-long names of the past. If the individual showed dislike for the commonly-given nickname he might find the name turned into "Not Want to be Called Lazy Boy."

Upon reaching adulthood an individual could take on a new name by several means, such as through Dreams. Sometimes a person who was in the midst of accomplishing some brave deed would choose a new name and shout it aloud for all to hear. Or, again, an outstanding event might be condensed into a name by which the person became popularly known.

Names given to the People of the past were of a much

greater variety than the common "White Eagle" and "Morning Star" of cinema fame. Two word names were often abbreviations of names that made complete statements. Thus, a man known as Eagle Walker might actually be named "Walks as quietly as an Eagle flies." Inventory Clerks for last century's Leaders of Manifest Destiny were often the first ones to "officially" record the names of Native tribe members—names that were then applied permanently to the offsprings of these members. Generally these names were given in their short forms by the obliging People, and were then translated into suitable words for ledgers.

Among many tribes it was considered respectful not to ask a person his name, or the origin of it, lest he be forced to draw unwanted attention upon himself or his Spiritual beliefs. Some old-time People, in fact, never spoke their own name for that reason. Other individuals, however, were publicly proud of their names and had pictographic signatures by which they were known. Below here, for instance, are the "signatures" of a few of the followers of the old Sioux chief Red Cloud. When the government agent "chose" a new chief for the tribe, Red Cloud's People showed their opposition through a petition of several paper sheets of these signatures. These were sent to Washington, D.C., where they were, no doubt, respectfully received.

SMOKING BEAR   SCRATCH-THE-BELLY   GOOD BIRD

LEAVES   LITTLE BEAR   OLD HORSE   EAGLE HORSE

WOLF-ON-A-HILL   CHARGE AFTER   HIGH BEAR

"Peaceful People" means Hopi—far and wide reaches the Earth around them: Why quarrel with another about the distance of the far-ness, or the method to cross the width? Let each one wear the moccasins he makes for himself—let him choose the Paths to wear them.

Far and wide is the Earth around the Hopi: with no signs of trees—no signs of Water. OMNIPRESENT is the Desert to the Hopi: to them, the Earth. Spiritual Strength is in everything known to the Hopi: how else could anything survive in their World? Why little hidden places of Water—there in the trackless sands? Why little groves of trees—there between the barren ridgetops? Why little crumbling catacombs—built by the Ancients there on the Sunburnt mesas? Why All these things: if no Great Spirit were to draw them together?

For more than 800 years have the Hopi centered their lives around several little villages built separately on distant desert-hilltops. For all those centuries have the People of that tribe lived their totally-Spiritual lives: leaving little offerings at their few gathering places of water, to demonstate their thankfulness for even that amount; having cere-

72

monies to pay their respect to Sun, and give thanks for the *good* done by Sun for them; singing songs of praise to the hardy little plants of corn and squash that thrive in the sands of the Desert to give the People most of their food.

Sometimes feeling miserable even with shade and Water, the stranger in the Land of the Hopi questions the availability of anything but sand and heat. Yet, the Hopi have learned that everything in the Nature of the Great Spirit was intended to harmonize together. So it is that the Hopi cherish all the Natural elements that let them go on living: the cultivated Maize, Beans, Squash, Watermelons, Peaches, and Sunflowers; the Salt, brought ceremoniously from waters far away; the Clays, dug from remote hillsides and packed home for the making of utensils; and the hunted Coyotes, Rabbits, Prairie Dogs, Rats, Hawks, Owls, and Foxes, taken home for their sparse meat and their furs, feathers, and bones.

Farming has always been a struggle with the elements of Nature for the Hopi: hot Sunshine and no Rain; or Rainstorms to wash away seeds and destroy tender, young plants; or Hailstorms to smash mature plants before harvest; or Windstorms to tear up plants and smother gardens in knee-deep sand; or weeds to drain the precious moisture and strangle growing crops; and, of course, a variety of small animals and insects who, like the Hopi, have to make use of everything they can find in order to subsist in the Desert.

Hopi couple going to their cornfield near Mashongnavi

Can You fail to succeed finding Spiritual Happiness, no matter what your conditions, with the knowledge that the Hopi people have been succeeding for centuries? Is it not ample proof of the strength of a Natural Spiritual Life?

The Hopi have usually started their first crops in April. Sweet Corn is at that time planted in holes dug four inches deep, the seeds being covered by two inches of soil. Mice, rats, and worms have never lost any time in searching for the seeds, and often the whole crop has had to be replanted. Windbreaks are made around the holes with small twigs and pieces of brush. Tin cans, opened at both ends, have been used in later days, for they also cut down on animal damage.

Other crops are planted according to the condition of the Weather. Melons, Squash, and Beans are usually in by the end of April. Muskmelons, Watermelons, and Lima Beans are planted in May. The Melons are planted in sandy soil, and the hills are placed five steps apart. By the middle of June most planting is completed with a final crop of Corn—the main staple of the Hopi People.

Corn planting has often been done co-operatively by several men. Holes are dug 6 to 9 inches deep, and several feet apart, with Greasewood planting sticks. 12 to 15 grains of Corn are dropped into each hole. The resulting clumps of Corn plants are easier to keep moist than long rows. The plants are fertilized—a common old-time mixture was composed of dried roots, dung, and pulverized parts of animals, which was mixed with water and sprayed on the plants.

Stakes are used to mark the location of crops, as sandstorms regularly cover all signs of planting. Dirt is packed tightly around the plants, once they come up, to help keep worms away from the roots. And to avoid offending the Corn Maiden Spirits, who spiritually protect the crops, Hopi farmers have been careful not to have intercourse with a woman in the cornfields.

Harvested Corn is brought home, shucked, and left to dry on the roofs of the houses. It is then stored indoors in bins—the People being always careful to keep enough on hand to take care of a whole Season's crop failure. The dried Corn is ground to make the popular, crispy-thin Piki bread. It is also ground into corn flour, corn mush, corn bread, and hominy. The husks are used to make a Hopi tamale. And the stalks are ground and fed to the livestock.

The many spiritual dances and ceremonies held by the Hopi throughout the Seasons are all tributes to Earth fertility and life-giving Rain, and to the Spirits who share these Benefits. Out on the Desert, across the centers of the Villages, and down in the underground Kivas are sung the songs and said the prayers that give to the Hopi a spiritual meaning for everything in Life.

BROTHERS: FIND YOUR BROTHERS. . . .

. . . . LET COMPANIONSHIP MAKE
LIGHT THE BURDENS IN LIFE. . . . .

GOOD MEDICINE

IN

G L A C I E R

NATIONAL
PARK

ADOLF HUNGRY WOLF

INSPIRATIONAL PHOTOS AND STORIES
FROM THE DAYS OF THE BLACKFOOT PEOPLE

A drive through Glacier National Park, in NorthWest Montana, today, gives many people a wonderful opportunity to see vast areas of unspoiled wilderness land from the comfort of their automobile seats. Few of these people are aware of the tremendous spiritual value that this region has held for those who have ventured out to seek it.

For untold centuries the wonders of the Glacier National Park country were held in awe by various Native tribes such as the Blackfoot, Kutenai, Stoney and Cree. The Blackfoot People were jealously guarding this region from all intruders when they were first visited in the area by white men during the early 1800's. These People, who were well acquainted with the vast NorthWest country, considered the many peaks within the park as "The Backbone of the World." A wealth of myths, tales, and stories of the Blackfoot days in the Glacier Park region were recorded by historians, both Native and white. This booklet presents a selection of these accounts. The photographs that accompany them were taken at a time when tipis were still a common sight within the park boundary, and when campfires still illuminated the wrinkled faces of the old men and women who related many of these stories as firsthand experiences.

Today, the outward signs of Native life are all gone from Glacier National Park. Gone are the tipis, and gone are the old, wrinkled faces. Yet, the Spiritual Powers that attracted the People of the Past are as strong today as they were then. Read these stories. Study these pictures. Then, visit one of the places that sounds most appealing to YOU. Walk to a secluded spot and sit down. Study closely all that surrounds you. It really hasn't changed at all! The spiritual powers that enchanted the people of the past who sought them are just as available to the people of today who will seek them.

How inviting look the waters of Punak'iksi Ituktai—the Cut Bank River—on a Summer's afternoon. How refreshing looks the green field that winds along as a narrow valley next to the river. Nearby is a forest of towering pines, whose countless numbers lie like an endless Buffalo robe at the foot of the majestic, snow-covered mountains.

Along the river's bank is a small camp of half a dozen tipis. Colorful religious designs on the covers of some of the tipis tell that they belong to the Blackfoot Tribe. Divided into three divisions, the powerful Blackfoot for years ruled the plains and Eastern mountain passes in

Montana and Alberta. The mountains that bring forth the waters of Cut Bank River were well-known for their spiritual powers and were jealously guarded by the Blackfoot as their own sacred domain.

The tipi camp by the river amply illustrates the close relationship between its occupants and the surrounding Nature. Tipi doors all open to the East, out of respect to the direction of Sun's first rays each morning. Sun is representative of the Great Spirit, which includes all the Universe. It is Sun's energy which stimulates all Life.

Sun's afternoon rays help create a relaxing atmosphere among the tipis of the small camp. Near the river sit the men, each one smoking leisurely. Whenever necessary, the pipe is refilled with tobacco from a fringed bag of softly-tanned Deerhide. The tobacco is a mixture of native plants, herbs, and bark; sweet of taste and aromatic of odor.

STABS-BY-MISTAKE, SUN WOMAN, AND LITTLE OTTER
IN CUTBANK CANYON

Not far from the men are gathered their women and children. The younger children are playing with buckskin dolls and miniature bows and arrows. Some of the older children are putting up a play-tipi, while others are watching the women's skillful hands as they make and decorate clothes for their families. Using sinew thread, made from strips of animal muscle, they are sewing together soft buckskin hides and decorating them with dyed porcupine quills and tiny glass beads that were imported from Europe.

Many of the stories being told by the men are about their own experiences on war trails or with hunting parties. Every social and religious gathering is an opportunity for those with brave deeds or adventuresome tales to stand before an enthused audience and relate them. Many stories were so popular that they were proudly told again and again. Often they were passed from generation to generation. Sometimes they gained so much romance by retelling that they were better called myths than stories. Let us hear about one that was told often when camp was made along the Cut Bank River.

THE MEDICINE BEAR OF CUT BANK RIVER

This happened not long after the time the first white men visited the Blackfoot. A small band of People was camped down by the Cut Bank River one Summer. It was early in the evening, and the men were gathered in one of the tipis to talk. Outside, children were still playing, while the women gathered firewood and brought in water. One of these women carried her pouch of water right into the tipi in which the men were gathered, thereby interrupting the conversation. While down at the river, she told the surprised men, a stranger had watched her from a clump of bushes. She had hurried back without arousing any suspicion.

Quickly, the men gathered their weapons from their tipis. Silently, they made their way down to the water's edge. On the opposite shore they saw the members of a small enemy war party preparing to cross the river towards the camp. They watched silently as the would-be attackers removed their clothes, wrapped their weapons with them, and held them over their heads while crossing the river.

Only the flowing water could be heard in the night air until—suddenly—came loudly the war-cries of the watchers as they attacked the war party of startled men. Left and right the enemy fell, until only their chief got to shore alive.

Some of the warriors watched the thicket in which the chief had managed to hide, while the rest took the trophies of battle to which they were entitled. From within the thicket came a torrent of insults, accompanied by loud grunting sounds and challenges to those outside to come in and fight. Remembering the chief's ferocity in the open, no one dared to enter the dense brush to accept the challenge.

It was not until the following morning that the men were able to charge the thicket and slay their opponent. Around his neck they found a string of huge Grizzly Bear claws. Recalling the sounds he had made while fighting, the men knew that this was a Grizzly Bear Medicine Man. They feared his power, even as he lay dead. Camp was immediately packed up and moved.

The tipis had not even been set up at the new campsite when a great commotion took place. A very powerful Grizzly Bear had come into camp and knocked down one of the lodges and killed its occupants. The rest of the People tried to escape, but several more were killed before the huge Bear disappeared.

For many years after that battle camps that were made near the site were troubled by a large Grizzly Bear. The People felt that this was the enemy chief. They named the Bear Akoch'kitope—the Medicine Grizzly—and they feared his supernatural power.

Camps made along the Cut Bank River were strategically located. An ancient trail follows the river for many miles. Some parts of it can still be seen today. Other parts were widened to become automobile roads. The trail has been best preserved amid some of the tall stands of timber that border the river.

Hunters once used the Cut Bank Trail to reach the Buffalo herds which grazed on the plains to the East. Warriors used the same trail to cross the Rocky Mountains and raid the Indian tribes on the West side. These West-side Tribes, as they were called by the Blackfoot, included the Flathead, Kutenai, and Pend d'Oreille. They often hunted for Elk and Sheep on the Western slopes of the mountains of Glacier Park. They also used the Cut Bank Trail to cross the mountains for occasional Buffalo hunts on the plains. Such hunting parties often consisted of members from several Westside tribes, making up a sizeable group. Small parties constantly faced the danger of attack by the more numerous and aggressive Blackfoot. The Blackfoot considered the Westsiders thieves for "stealing" their Buffalo, and fierce battles were fought whenever the two sides met. Such a battle once took place in the thick woods near the head of the canyon that lies East of the summit of Cut Bank Pass.

BATTLE AT CUT BANK PASS

This battle was the result of a chance meeting between two war parties on the Trail. Headed downhill were the mounted members of a group led by the famous Blackfoot Chief Siyeh—the respected and fearless Mad Wolf. They were returning from successful horse raids against the Westside People. Hearing the sounds of horses coming uphill, Mad Wolf had his men take cover to see who it might be. The other group turned out to be a war party of Kutenai, heading home after a successful raid on the Blackfoot.

Mad Wolf opened the battle by shooting the Kutenai chief from his horse. Although caught by surprise, the Kutenai outnumbered their enemies and held their ground. Mad Wolf pursued the wounded Kutenai chief through the dense brush and finally killed him. As he reached down to take his enemy's scalp a familiar sight shocked him. Tied to the Kutenai chief's belt were the scalps of Mad Wolf's own two brothers. They had started out with Mad Wolf, on this war expedition, but turned back home before crossing the mountains. They had met their fate along the Cut Bank Trail, just like this Kutenai chief met his fate.

Mad Wolf told his retreating warriors of the discovery, and then led them on a violent attack for revenge that ended in death for all but one of the Kutenai, that one being an old woman. They gave her food and extra clothing and sent her on her way home, praying that someday they would be helped when in need, just as they had helped this old woman and shown mercy. Mad Wolf died of old age, in his home near the Cut Bank River, in 1903. North of Upper St. Mary's Lake is Mount Siyeh and Siyeh Pass, both named in honor of the respected chieftain.

TWO MEDICINE LODGES

From Cut Bank Pass to the South and East another trail winds its way from the rugged crags North of Mount Rising Wolf down to the lush and mystic meadows and forests of the three lakes in the Two Medicine Lodge area. The campground that is known today as Two Medicine Lake is located in a most spiritual area. Campers and trailers stand today where tipis and Medicine Lodges stood in the past. This was a favorite camping place for the

Blackfoot People, and many religious ceremonies were conducted there. To the Blackfoot the place was known as Ma'toki Okas Omu'ksikimi—the Lake of the Two Medicine Lodges.

The very name—Two Medicine Lodges—recalls a time of deep spiritual need in the history of the Blackfoot Tribe. It was here, at the foot of majestic Mount Rising Wolf and the outlet of middle Two Medicine Lake, that the Blackfoot People gathered in a long-ago time of drought and famine. The Buffalo had left the neighboring plains, streams had gone dry, and only in the vicinity of these lakes could the women find enough berries to calm the hunger of their families. Because of the desperate need, and the many People who were gathered, it was decided to build two Lodges for the great Medicine Lodge Ceremony—the grand annual religious festival of the Blackfoot Tribe.

The spiritual leaders of the People who had gathered— the Medicine Men and Holy Women—fasted and prayed, asking the Spirits of the Universe for aid. Through dreams and visions these People were told to send seven of their wisest patriarchs North to Chief Mountain. Here was thought to dwell the spirit of the Winds, for these often blow fiercely along the walls of the 9,000 foot high mountain.

The old men were chosen, and soon found themselves at the foot of the noble mountain. A strong wind had been blowing across the plains, growing stronger as they approached. The summit of Chief Mountain was barely visible to the old men, as they struggled through the dust and debris that filled the air. None of the party had the strength or courage to climb the desolate reaches of the wind-swept mountainside. They went back to the camp by the Lake and told the People of their failure.

Another group of men was chosen to pray on Chief Mountain. This time the selection was made from among the daring and brave young warriors. Fourteen were chosen to go. Their arrival at the Mountain was also marked by terrific winds and almost unbearable dust. Wrapping their robes tightly about them and leaving behind their travelling packs, the group of warriors climbed up towards the forbidding peak. As they neared the summit they were almost overcome by heavy clouds that cut off all visibility to their wind-swollen eyes. Here, they sat down in a tight circle and began the prayers and songs that make one's mind leave the body in search of spiritual contact.

Rain drops fell steadily on the party of men as they climbed back down the mountain's side. Clouds covered the top of Chief Mountain like an immense turban, and reached out for the plains—North and South—like long, white wings. The much-needed rain that fell from these clouds brought back life to the Earth that it entered. Great was the rejoicing among the People, and many were the offerings of thanks that were hung in trees and on boulders as signs of appreciation to the unseen Spirits who had helped them.

Scene of the past at Two Medicine Campground

Many a young man had his favorite sacred place there around Two Medicine Lake, where he went to be alone with the wonders of Nature and the Spirits of the Universe. Visions were sought during sleep or in deep meditation at such lonely, spiritual places. The vision might tell the seeker of something to do, or to avoid doing. More often, the vision showed the seeker certain items, ceremonies, and songs which could be used at a later time to again summon the spiritual feeling that was present at the time of the vision. Taking only a robe for warmth, and a pipe for meditation, the vision seeker often spent several days and nights trying to establish communication and understanding with the many elements of Nature.

STABS-BY-MISTAKE

CAMP IN TWO MEDICINE VALLEY

Besides being a most spiritual place to camp, the area of the Two Medicine Lodges was once a wonderful hunting ground. In those days game conservation in the Park region was not required. Hunters were few, and animals were so very many. What the hunters did shoot, however, they made all possible use of. The meat of a fine buck, for instance, was roasted and eaten, or dried and stored for later meals. The hide was tanned and sewn into shirts, dresses, leggings, moccasins, pouches, and quivers. Thin strips were cut from the left-over pieces of hide for use as strings and straps. The hooves were cleaned and boiled, then carved or strung plain with bead spacers on leather straps to make jingling bandoleers and necklaces. The horns made nice handles for knives and awls. With holes drilled through them they were used as arrow-shaft straighteners. The teeth were often hung on necklaces. Leg bones made good brushes for applying native powder paint to large surfaces. Properly cut, these bones make wonderful pipes for smoking. Intestines make good paint powder pouches, as well as containers for the Porcupine quills used in decorating. Tendon fibers make the sinew for sewing and beading. Even the hair on the Deer's tail has a use in making the dance roaches which are worn in the hair. The true hunter would not consider killing an animal merely to take a small portion for glory.

Back in the days when there were tipi camps at Two Medicine the hunter had a wide choice of game animals and birds that lived in the surrounding valley and woods. Fortunately, these animals can all still be seen here. The lakes abound with fish (although some People in the old days never ate them for religious reasons), and waterfowl visitors are still frequent. Higher up the hunters used to seek the Mountain Goat and the Bighorn Sheep. The Naturalist-Writer George Bird Grinnell wrote that Rising Wolf told him: "The Gray Sheep used to be very plenty. . . . in old times when the Piegans were camped. . . . he has gone up on top (of mountains) with a lot of young fellows and driven the Sheep down to the plain below where the People were waiting on horseback. There they would kill hundreds of them. . . . their skins were used for making war shirts and women's dresses."

Grinnell loved to camp and explore the Glacier Park region. He was called Fisher Cap by his many Blackfoot friends, some of whom took him for his first visit to the Park area in 1885. He was so inspired that he used his persuasion in national articles and important friendships to make the area a national park. He would have preferred that it remain a sacred domain for the Blackfoot People, but he realized that the greed of the advancing new "civilization" would find some way to swindle the tribe out of this choice land and then destroy its primitive beauty.

The hunters are gone now, but not so the game. Look up to the higher reaches of Mount Rising Wolf from your campsite at its feet, the Two Medicine Campground. Early in the morning or late in the afternoon you may catch the movement of tiny white specks. With field glasses you can watch the Goat or Sheep as they wind their way along treacherous trails in a world that belongs almost exclusively to them. It required great skill and patience for a hunter to come within shooting distance of these wary animals. It required just as much in strength and daring for the hunter to carry the carcass of his kill back down the precipitous trails.

RISING WOLF

And who was the Rising Wolf whom this noble mountain is named for? He was the trader and trapper Hugh

Monroe who, at the age of seventeen, was the first white man known to have visited this part of the Rockies. He was an employee of the great Hudson's Bay Company and roamed the Blackfoot country as an adopted member of that tribe. He married a young Blackfoot woman, joined Blackfoot hunting and war parties, and was given the name Makwi Powaksin—Rising Wolf. He loved to camp and hunt in the area around the mountain that bears his name. When he died, in 1896, he was buried along the Two Medicine River, not far from the mountain.

When not in need of the fine pelts of the Goat or Sheep up on the high ridges, the native hunters preferred to seek game in the valleys and forests down by the lakes. Deer, Elk, and Moose have always been plentiful in the area. Bears, too, are quite common in the region. Many a hunter was foiled in his tracking by suddenly meeting a Grizzly Bear in his path. The Blackfoot name for the Grizzly is "the Real-Bear," and the People most always gave the animal wide berth. Few warriors cared to prove their bravery the way one well-remembered Blackfoot hunter did. Weasel Tail was armed only with his good hunting knife when he engaged a huge Grizzly in a hand-to-hand encounter. The Battle was short, brave Weasel Tail

THE OLD WAY OF TRAVELLING THROUGH THE PARK. OLD THREE BEARS, THERE, WAS A GREAT ORATOR AMONG THE BLACKFOOT PEOPLE.

emerging as the victor. Forever after he proudly wore the Grizzly's big claws on a necklace.

On the road to Two Medicine Camp, not far below the main lake, is a most spectacular waterfall. A short and interesting trail leads the visitor from the paved road back to an enchanting trout pool, at the head of which is the waterfall. It is known today as Trick Falls. It was a favorite bathing place of the legendary Pitamakan, after whom the Blackfoot named it. Pitamakan was a warrior's name which means Running Eagle, but it was earned, in this case, by a brave Blackfoot woman.

THE STORY OF PITAMAKAN

Pitamakan was a young girl known as Weasel Woman when both of her parents were killed. With her brothers and sisters she worked hard to keep their orphaned family together in one tipi. By necessity she learned to do many of the chores usually done by men. So it was that she joined one day a war party bound for the Westside tribes. She did so without telling anyone, and against the wishes of some of the men in the party. The party was successful, and the young girl returned with several fine horses which she had captured. The People were amazed by her bravery, and an old Medicine Man gave her the name of an honored Blackfoot chief of the past—Pitamakan.

There followed, for Pitamakan, a career of horse raiding. She even led some of her own war parties against enemy tribes, for no man was ashamed to join with her. Whenever leaving for a raid Pitamakan would exchange her woman dress for warrior's clothing. Her takings of horses were many, and she counted coup on three men whom she herself killed. Her end came when she was discovered one night leading horses from the midst of an enemy camp. Her Blackfoot People kept alive the memories of her with stories about her exploits, and by naming these falls for her.

ST. MARY'S LAKES

The area around the St. Mary's Lakes was popular in the old days because of the large camping space in the valley by the lower lake, and the abundance of game that was found there. Rising Wolf took one of the early Jesuit missionaries (Father DeSmet) to the lakes in 1846. There he helped plant a wooden cross at the foot of the lower lake, while the priest said a prayer and christened the lake St. Mary. The Blackfoot People know Saint Mary by the name Patoaki—the Good-Spirit-Woman. The lakes, however, were known to them by the name Puhtomuksi Kimiks—the Lakes-Inside.

Rising Wolf first visited these lakes in 1816, when his adopted Blackfoot People camped down by the lower one of the two. That same location later became his favorite hunting and trapping place. With his Blackfoot wife and four children he spent many seasons there, collecting furs and enjoying the freedom of nature. Sometimes he was forced to fight off war parties from enemy tribes like the Crows, Assiniboin, and Yankton Sioux. His lodge was always protected by a stockade, or a trench dug around its perimeter. He kept every member of the family armed and trained to help in defense. His take of furs included Beaver and Otter. For hides and meat of larger game he could take Moose along the lake, Deer and Elk in the valley, or Sheep and Goats high in the mountains. Even Buffalo herds came to this, the Western boundary of their home on the great plains.

STABS-BY-MISTAKE WITH HIS SACRED MEDICINE, AT THE LOWER END OF UPPER ST. MARY'S LAKE. SURROUNDED BY MOUNTAINS ARE THESE "LAKES-INSIDE." LIKE NATURE'S BOWL OF TREASURES IS THIS COUNTRY: LAKES AND STREAMS FULL OF FISH, VALLEYS AND WOODS FULL OF GAME, TREES AND SKIES FULL OF BIRDS.

In the long ago members of the Crow tribe made their home in parts of Glacier Park. A popular story around Blackfoot campfires tells how the Crow were driven from the Glacier area down to their present homeland in South-East Montana by the Blackfoot. At that time most of the Blackfoot bands were living North of the United States border, in Alberta and Saskatchewan. A Blackfoot man named One Horn came down to the St. Mary's Lakes area to camp with the Crows and discuss with them his desire for a permanent peace between the two tribes.

ONE HORN'S PEACE MISSION

One Horn stayed with the Crows for some time in their camp by the St. Mary's Lakes. His women kept up their household there, amid the Crow tipis. They had many guests and, in turn, were often invited to the lodges of others. The Crow chief and One Horn became good friends, and often went hunting together.

So it was until a Crow braggard, one night, told his fantastic story of bravery against the Blackfoot. The tipi was filled with guests that night. The Crow claimed that he had been wounded and his partner killed, while they were attacked by a whole village of the Blackfoot. Despite a bad arrow wound, the Crow stated, he made an heroic escape through all the People. To prove his tale, he produced the Blackfoot arrow and showed everyone there his wound.

One Horn laughed when he saw the arrow. "That arrow is my own," he told the listeners. "I surprised two horse thieves in our camp one morning, and killed one. The other one dropped his weapons and ran. I wounded him with an arrow from my quiver." At that he reached into his quiver and pulled out an identical arrow and laid it before the murmuring crowd. The braggard hurriedly left the lodge, while the guests jeered him.

One night, soon after, one of the Crow chief's wives stole into One Horn's lodge and brought him a warning. She had overheard her man agree to help the braggard kill One Horn for the price of five horses. The next morning One Horn dressed in his finest clothes, took his weapons, and rode his horse into the middle of the camp circle. From there he shouted to the Crow chief, for all to hear: "My friend, your plan to help that braggard in killing me has been found out. I have the spiritual guidance of my Grizzly Bear Medicine, and I challenge you both to fight me here, now." The Crow chief made no reply, and remained in his tipi. The braggard, whose lodge was at the other end of the camp, grabbed his horse and hurriedly rode into the woods.

One Horn packed up his belongings and returned North to his People. After telling them of his adventures he called on the men to help him in driving the Crow people far away from the Blackfoot country. War parties were formed among all three Blackfoot divisions, and the Crows were soon put to flight. They never again moved back to the Glacier Park country.

GOING-TO-THE-SUN

By the head of Upper St. Mary's Lake looms a mountain whose contemplative face looks like it might belong to an ageless old man who is always looking towards Sun. This is the imposing Going-to-the-Sun Mountain. The Blackfoot name for it is Matapi Ostuksis, meaning Person's Face. Unfortunately, no legend for either name has been recorded. Apikuni (writer James Willard Schultz) says that he named the mountain after one of his old Blackfoot friends told him that, were he still physically able to, he would like to "go up on that mountain to fast and pray and visit the Sun." Certainly the mountain was a popular place for the spiritual vision quests that men used to take. Since vision seeking often involved complete surrender of one's spirit to Sun, the mountain was very sacred to those who used it for "going to the Sun."

Apikuni named many of the Park's geographic points during his life in that region. His fabulous books tell of some of his adventures there. His "Blackfeet Tales of Glacier National Park" and "Signposts of Adventure" are both devoted to the Park. He was also the companion and guide of George Bird Grinnell when that Naturalist and writer made his first visit to the Park region in the Fall of 1885. They encountered horse thieves along the Cut Bank River, trespassing gold miners near the St. Mary's Lakes, and hunting parties from tribes who still considered themselves enemies of the Blackfoot People.

On September 7, 1885, for instance, Grinnell recorded in his diary: "A Kootenay came to camp just at Sunset. He is one of a party of 8 lodges camped on Swift Current, a mile or two above its mouth. They are hunting with good success. Have been out 50 days and have killed plenty of Sheep, two Bears (1 bl., 1 grizzly), a Moose, a few Elk and a lot of Beaver."

SINGLE SHOT MOUNTAIN

A few days later, on September 10, he gives an account of the story which led to the naming of Single Shot Mountain. He says: "Today about 10:00 the Kootenay who speaks Piegan, and who says his name is Hi-clough, and another (cap bound with Goat skin) came to camp and proposed to go for Sheep. . . . I explained to the Indian that I was a poor climber and that they would have to go slowly to have me keep up. . . . when I got to the point of the Mt. they were nowhere in sight. . . . soon it began to snow and blow and was very cold, and I performed my customary operation of sitting on a rock and shivering. . . . After going a mile or more I stopped to look and listen as I was standing there. I saw the head of a Sheep appear over a ridge coming toward me. It was walking but discovered me at the same time I saw it and stopped. . . . after pausing a moment (it) started to run by me on the upper side. . . .twice it stopped. . . . I tried to shoot, but the snow blew so thickly that I could not see the sights on my rifle. A third time it stopped. This time at about 150 yards and behind a pile of rocks so that I could see only its head and neck. . . . so I fired. . . . springing from rock to rock I hurried to a point where it had passed along. Some spots of blood on a little patch of snow told the story, which the wide spread hoofmarks in the loose shale confirmed. I followed it at a half run down the mountainside. . . . then down over a ledge 12 or 15 feet high I saw the game stretched on its side. It was quite dead."

Grinnell's fine shot was matched by his next feat of carrying almost 100 pounds of Sheep, plus his rifle, some three miles over treacherous terrain. This included a climb of "Perhaps 1500 feet, a long journey along the rough face of the mountain and then a descent of about 2,000 feet to the horses." Somehow he made it back to camp, and he says: "When I detailed to Schultz the circumstances of my shot he proposed to call the mountain where it had been made Single Shot Mountain."

LAKE OF THE JEALOUS WOMEN

Nestled amid towering mountain peaks, melting glaciers, dark canyons, and green, wooded valleys is the awe-inspiring Lake McDermott. The Lake's blue waters are Nature's mirrors. They are able to describe the surrounding scenery like no man's words. To the Native People of long ago, such a scene was an experience that no modern form of entertainment could rival.

Lake McDermott was sometimes known as Beaver Woman's Lake, but is best remembered in old stories as Jealous Women's Lake. It was given this name by the Kutenai People, from the Westside, who told this story of its origin:

There once lived a young Kutenai warrior named Big

HUNTERS OF THE PAST: STABS-BY-MISTAKE, LITTLE PLUME, BLACK BULL & EAGLE CHILD (AT LEFT), BLACK WEASEL & IRON BREAST (WITH BONNETS), AND SHORT FACE (ON RIGHT).

Knife whose two wives were twin sisters. The family got along well, except that one sister worked quicker than the other. This sister, whose name was Weasel, also talked a lot. She sometimes complained that the other sister, whose name was Beaver, was not doing her share of work and was often trying to become Big Knife's favorite. Beaver thought Weasel to be foolish for having such bad thoughts.

Big Knife was out riding his horse one day when he came upon two Otters at the bank of the Kamoak-skasee Naya-tahtah—the Swift Current River. "What nice presents those two Otter skins would make for my women," said Big Knife to himself. He quickly strung his bow, fitted an arrow, and shot one of the Otters. Before he could shoot again, however, the other Otter disappeared. He took the one skin home and gave it to Beaver, telling them both that he would go back the next day to get the other skin for Weasel.

Big Knife searched all the next day for the same Otter, but could not find it. For several days he searched in other areas near camp, but nowhere did he see another Otter.

Weasel, meanwhile, was getting more cross at home. She told Beaver that the Otter skin was sure proof of her favored position with their man. Beaver could not convince Weasel that their man was very distressed about not finding another Otter.

Finally, one day, Weasel told her twin sister that the two could no longer live together in the same lodge. "I will challenge you in any way to determine which of us shall remain in this lodge with Big Knife," she told her sister.

The two then decided that they would swim the lake by which they were camped, up and back until only one was left swimming.

So it came that Beaver found herself crawling up on the lake's shore. She looked all around the quiet lake top, but could not detect any sign of her sister. She went home weeping, and Big Knife wept too, when he heard what had taken place. Together they wept, and for a long time they were sad. It is so easy to disturb the beauty of Nature.

CAMPED BY THE LAKE OF THE JEALOUS WOMEN

LIFTING HIS STONE-BOWLED PIPE, OLD MAN
TAIL-FEATHERS-COMING-OVER-THE-HILL
MUTTERS A PRAYER FOR US:

*Hi-Yo Spirits With Us. . . . Guide Us As We Follow The
Many Paths That Lead Us Through Life. . . . Show Us
In Dreams The Ways To Live Right. . . . Give Us The
Strength To Learn From Our Failures. . . . SUN Give
Us Warmth With Your Eternal Light.*

As The Winds That Blow, Here, Let My Mind Wander. . . . As The Tree That Stands Here, Give Me Strength And Old Age. Let Me Bend, And Mold, To Stronger Forces. . . . Let Solid Ground, Forever, Hold My Feet.

I Am Three Bears—An Old Pikuni—Here In The Mountains. . . . I Came To Think—To Look Ahead—To Hope And Pray:

. . . . May My Ancestors—In All The World—Still Have The Wisdom, To Live With Nature. . . . To Come and Pray, To ALL, Our Spirits There. . . .

WITH TEARS PLEADS OUR MOTHER EARTH:

Remain Close To Me, My Children.
Pray To Your Father—Sun
Live In Harmony With Nature
Respect The Will Of EVERY One!

And So Was Crossed The "Backbone Of The Earth" In The Days When Time Was Counted By Moons And Snows. . . . Two-Guns-White-Calf And Friends Leaving Two Medicine.

Horses! Fleet On Foot—Flowing In Mane—Gentle In Character—And Ever Aware.

Together: Man And Horse. The Strength To Travel . . . . The Ability To Know. Trusting Each Other To Trust In Nature. . . . Trusting All Others To Trust The Same.

Along The Rivers. . . . Through The Forests. . . . Up The Canyons. . . . Into Mountains On Paths Lined With The World. . . . Every Path An Experience To Learn From: Up And Down, Left And Right. And (Like Life) Forever Luring On.

SOME OLD TIME NAMES OF PLACES IN THE PARK

Almost a Dog Mountain—Named by Apikuni for one of the few survivors of Baker's Massacre in 1870. When Baker's soldiers opened fire on the innocent camp of Chief Heavy Runner, on the Marias, the People were still sleeping. Almost A Dog's father and mother were killed almost instantly, his wife next, and his little daughter died in his arms as he tried to find a safe place for them to hide. He was crippled from his wounds, and died in 1894. He was buried under the Buffalo cliffs of Two Medicine River.

Apikuny Mountain—One spelling of the name given to James Willard Schultz by his adopted Blackfoot People. Its translation means something like "Far-Off White Robe." His many experiences in the Park region were the basis of several fine volumes for interested readers.

Chief Mountain—Has always been considered the Chief of the Mountains.

Cut Bank River—Named for the cliff-like banks which are found along the lower course of the river.

Mount Jackson—Named by Grinnell in 1891 for his guide, and Apikuni's companion, William Jackson. He was a scout for Custer, and the grandson of Rising Wolf. His other name was Siksika-kwan, or Blackfoot Man.

UPPER CUTBANK CANYON

Little Chief Mountain—Little Chief, or Kinuks-Inah, was a famous Blackfoot warrior who was killed in 1865 when his horse fell while he was hunting in the midst of a Buffalo herd.

Little Dog Mountain—Little Dog is a name that has been held by several respected Blackfoot leaders of the past. The last of these was a war chief at the end of the Buffalo days.

Logan Pass—Was known in the old days as Misum Oksokwi, or the Ancient Road. It was used by numerous tribes of the past as a favorite pass.

Lake McDonald—Was known in the past as the Sacred Dancing Lake. It used to be the gathering place for the area's tribes during their annual Summer religious celebrations.

Norris Mountain—Also known as Tall Man Mountain, which was the Blackfoot name of Henry Norris. He was married to a Blackfoot woman and lived and hunted in this area until his death in 1918.

Red Crow Mountain—Named in honor of the head chief of the Blood division of the Blackfoot People.

Red Eagle Mountain—Known in Blackfoot as Mekotsipitan Kokwito, in honor of the noted Medicine Man and leader, Red Eagle. He died in 1897 and was buried near the Buffalo cliffs of Two Medicine River.

Rising Wolf Mountain—An old Blackfoot name that was given to trapper Hugh Monroe because of his habit of sleeping lightly.

Mount Siyeh—Named for the respected and fearless Chief Mad Wolf, in 1888 by Grinnell.

Sherburne Lakes—Was known as Kyoioiks Otsitaitska Omuksikimiks, or Fighting Bears' Lakes. Rising Wolf and a Blackfoot hunting party once witnessed a fight to the death between two large Grizzly Bears between these lakes.

Triple Divide Mountain—Was called Three Rivers Mountain. Waters from it flow North to the Saskatchewan, South to the Missouri, and West to the Pacific Ocean.

Waterton Lake—Was called Kutenai Lake, as it was a favorite camping place for the people of that tribe.

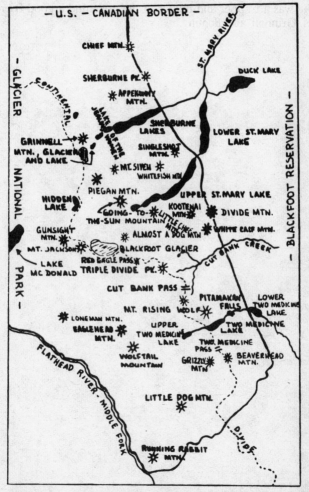

GOOD MEDICINE MAP OF GLACIER NATIONAL PARK

White Calf Mountain—Named in honor of Piegan head chief OnistaiPoka, who lies on a bluff overlooking the Cut Bank River.

Yellow Fish Mountain—Was named for the half-breed Charles Rose, whose Blackfoot name was Yellow Fish. He was a trapper and hunter of the area, and a good friend of Grinnell and Schultz.

LEGENDS

TOLD BY THE OLD PEOPLE

A GOOD MEDICINE BOOK

In the Old Days the often-long Season of Winter was a time spent mostly indoors, around the central fireplace, whether the home was a tipi, an Earth lodge, a Brush lodge, or an igloo. The men were often gone hunting, raiding, or taking care of the Horses. The women were kept busy cooking, sewing, and hauling wood and water. So, it was often left for the Old People in the home—grandfather, or an old aunt, to watch the children and entertain them. They played games, learned songs, and practiced skills that the parents were busy doing. But, as with children everywhere, the favorite pastime was listening to the Old Ones' stories—real or imaginary.

The following stories are a random selection of the countless numbers that have been recorded from some of those Old People. Miles of paper could be filled with more—the ones that follow are just some Good Medicine favorites. So, put another chunk of wood in your stove, turn up your lamps so you can see good, and gather Your Family around You. Read these stories aloud. You may become inspired to make up some stories of Your own. And have a pleasant evening!

LEGENDS
From the Old People

CONTENTS

THE STONE BOY

A Sioux Story of the Creation of Man and Woman

The Four Brothers lived together without any woman, so they did the woman's work. One time, as the eldest was gathering wood after nightfall, something ran into his big toe. This pained him but little and he soon forgot it, but his toe began to swell and was soon as big as his head. Then he cut it open and found something in it. He did not know what it was, but his brothers washed it and found that it was a baby girl.

The Four Brothers kept the baby and gave it good food and fine clothes so that it grew to be a beautiful young woman. She could do a woman's work well and quickly and never allowed anyone to leave their tipi cold or hungry. She could dress skins so that they were white and soft and from them make good clothing, upon which she put beautiful ornaments, and each ornament meant something.

Many young men tried to induce her to live with them, but she would not leave the Four Brothers. They told her that they would always keep her as their sister, and they did everything to please her. The eldest Brother said, "I will go and hunt Deer so that our sister may have the skins to make clothing for herself." He went away and did not return. Then the next eldest Brother said, "I will go and hunt Buffalo so that our sister may have the skins to make robes for herself." He went away and did not return. Then the next youngest Brother said, "I will go and hunt Elk so that our sister may have meat for herself." He too went away and did not return. Then the youngest brother said, "Sister, our Brothers have gone away and have not returned. I will go and find them." So he went away and did not return.

When the youngest Brother had been gone one Moon, the young woman went to the top of a high hill to mourn, and to seek a vision. While she was mourning she saw a pebble which she looked at for a long time, for it was very smooth and white, and then she put it in her mouth to keep from being thirsty. She fell asleep with the pebble in her mouth and swallowed it. While she slept the vision came to her in the form of a great beast, which told her that the Four Brothers were kept by a stone and that a stone would find them and bring them back to her.

She told this vision to Shaman and asked him to tell her what it meant. The Shaman told her to marry and name her son the Stone. But she would not live with any man, for she remembered how good and kind the Four Brothers were, and she wished to live with them only.

Soon, she grew big with child and gave birth to a boy baby. The flesh of this baby was as hard as stone, and she knew that it was mysterious (Wakan) and came from the pebble she had swallowed. She went far away and lived alone with her son. She taught him all the games and songs and all about Roots and Plants and Animals and Birds, so that he was cunning and wise. She gave him fine clothes and good food so that he grew up strong and brave though his flesh was as hard as stone. She would not allow him to hunt or join a war party, for she was afraid he would go away and never return like the Four Brothers.

Each Moon she went to the top of a hill to mourn. When her son had grown to be a man he asked her why she went to mourn each Moon, and she said to him, "My son, you are now a man, and I will tell you why I mourn." So she told him the story of the Four Brothers, of her coming to them, of how they went away and did not return, of his own birth and the vision of the great beast.

Then she sang this song to him:—

> I am a mysterious woman.
> I am like no other woman.
> You are a mysterious man.
> Your flesh is like stone.
> You are the Stone Boy.
> You are the stone the great beast told of.

Then he sang to her.—

> I am the Stone Boy.
> I am the stone that will aid you.
> I will bring back your brothers.
> My mother, I will make you happy.

He then said to her, "Mother, I will go to find your brothers. I will bring them to you." She said, "I am afraid you too will go away and never come back." He said to her, "What did the great beast tell you? I am the stone." She said, "Go my son, but first you must be prepared with magic."

She made a great feast and invited a wise Shaman, a wise old woman, a great brave, a great hunter, and four maidens as the chief guests, and all the People as common guests. She placed the People as they belonged according to the bands with her son among the chief guests. When all were satisfied with eating she stood before the People and told the story of the four brothers; of her coming to them, of their going, of her vision, and the birth and life of her son. She then told them to examine her son that they might know that he was mysterious (Wakan). The People all examined the young man, and when they found that his flesh was hard like stone they said he was indeed mysterious and that he was the Stone Boy. She then told them that her son was to go in quest of the Four Brothers and she had invited the chief guests so that they would help her to prepare her son with magic for his quest.

The chief guests agreed to do what she should ask of them. The Shaman gave the Stone Boy a charm (Pajuta-wakan-rea) that would keep all harm from him. The old woman gave him a robe on which she had painted a dream which made the robe magical and made anyone who wore it invisible. The warrior gave him a magical spear that would pierce anything, a magical club that would ward off anything, and a magical club that would break anything. The hunter showed him how to find anything he wanted. His mother made clothes of good Deerskin and the young women put ornaments on them. While ornamenting his clothing, they sang love songs and the

Shaman conjured the ornaments (Ca Kina wakan kaga) so that they were magical. On the sides of his moccasins they put mountains so that he could step from hill to hill without touching the valleys; on the tops they put dragonflies so that he could escape all danger; on his leggings they put wolf tracks so that he would never grow weary; on his shirt they put the tipi circle so that he would find shelter anywhere.

He stood before the People, clothed in his magical garments, his shield on his back and his spear and club in his hands. His face was towards the rising Sun. Before him was his mother, on one side the Shaman, warrior, and hunter, and on the other, the old woman and the four young maidens. He said to his mother, "I will bring the Four Brothers to you." To the young women, "When I return I will take you four as my women." To the men, "What you have taught me I will use to release the Four Brothers." Then turning his face towards the setting Sun he said to the old woman, "I go."

Then the old woman threw the robe about him and he was seen no more, but there was a Wind as if the Thunderbird flew towards the setting Sun. His mother fell on her face as one dead, but the People heard a voice high in the air, clear and loud like the voices of the cranes when they fly towards the region of the Pines, and this is what it said: "A stone shall free the Four Brothers."

When the Stone Boy went from the People, he stepped from hill to hill more swiftly than the Stars (meteors) fall at night. From each hill he looked carefully into the valleys so that he saw all there was in every valley, but he saw nothing of the Four Brothers until he came to the high hills far toward the setting Sun.

In the valley there was much game of every kind and in one of them he found a stone knife that he knew belonged to the eldest brother. In another valley he found a stone arrowhead that he knew belonged to the next eldest brother. In a third, he found a stone axe that he knew belonged to the next to the youngest Brother, and in a fourth he found a stone bone breaker that he knew belonged to the youngest Brother. Then he knew he was on the right road to find the Brothers and looked carefully into each valley.

Near the mountains he saw a valley that was barren, with nothing in it but a stone, a tree, and a little brown hill from which he saw smoke rising. He took off his robe and sat down to watch this. Soon a huge Coyote, larger than a Buffalo, came out of the hill and began to jump up very high and yelp very loud. Then the stone began to roll and bump about and the tree began to move from place to place. The stone went to a pool of water and took a drink.

The Stone Boy continued to watch, and soon a growl like Thunder came from the hills beyond. The Coyote, when he heard this growl, jumped very high and fast and yelped and yelled; the stone again moved about and bumped on the ground, the tree moved from place to place, and a little old woman came out of the hill and looked towards the growling. Soon a huge Bear as large as a Cloud came over the hills. He walked upright like a man and held some People in his forepaws, and his growl sounded like Thunder. He came into the valley and held the People up to the tree. The Stone Boy saw that each branch of the tree was a Snake. These snakes bit the People as the Bear held them up so that they were paralyzed. When they were still as if they were dead, the bear threw them down on the hard smooth ground and the stone rolled over them and flattened them so that they were like dried Buffalo skins.

Thus the little old woman laid them on the little brown hill and the Stone Boy saw that the hill was made of flattened People piled one on top of another. When the People had all been placed on the hill, the Coyote sniffed towards the hill where the Stone Boy stood and jumped and yelped. Then he sniffed and jumped up again; he sniffed very hard, jumped very high, and yelped very loud and the little old woman pointed to that hill and the Bear growled and came to it. But the Stone Boy put on his robe and stepped to another hill. The Bear looked foolish and said, "That must have been a Thunderbird (Wakinyan), a Winged God."

116

Then the Bear came towards the hill he was on, running very fast, and growling like Thunder. Then the Stone Boy quickly put on his robe, and when the Bear was almost near him, he stepped to another hill. The Bear stopped and looked very foolish. and said, "That must have been a Thunderbird that passed by me." Then the Coyote sniffed towards him again and jumped up and down, and the Bear ran towards the hill he was on, but when he got there the Stone Boy stepped to another hill and the Bear looked very foolish and said, "I think that is a Thunderbird going by."

Thus the Coyote sniffed towards the hill where the Stone Boy stood and again jumped up and down and the tree walked that way and the Stone came also. The Bear growled like very heavy Thunder and came creeping towards the hill, watching everything very closely, but when he got near, the Stone Boy stepped to another hill. Then the Bear was afraid, and ran back to the little hill, whining and whimpering, for he thought it was a Thunderbird. Then the little old woman came out of the hill, and the Coyote yelped and jumped up and down and ran around and around, and the branches of the tree squirmed and licked their tongues and hissed like a great Wind. The stone jumped up and down, and every time it came down, it shook the Earth.

Then the Stone Boy stood up and took off his robe and jeered at them and mocked them. They saw him. The old woman screamed and the Coyote yelped louder than ever and jumped up and down, and the tree walked towards him, every snake hissing louder. The stone rolled and tumbled towards him and the Bear came very fast towards him growling like a Thunder Cloud. When the Bear was very close, he raised his paw to strike, but the Stone Boy shot one of the arrows through heart and he fell dead.

Then the Coyote came jumping up and down. Every time he jumped up, he went higher and higher, and when he was near enough he jumped up so as to come down on the Stone Boy, but the Stone Boy set his spear on the ground, and when the coyote came down the spear ran

117

through his heart and killed him. Then the stone came rolling and tumbling and smashing everything in its path. When it was about to roll over the Stone Boy and smash him, he raised his war club and struck it a mighty blow and broke it to pieces.

The tree could not walk up the hill, so the Stone Boy went down into the valley, and when he came near the tree the branches began to strike him. But he held up the shield the warrior had given him, and when one of the snake branches would strike it, its teeth would break off and its head would be smashed. So the Stone Boy danced about the tree and sang and shouted until every branch had smashed itself to death against his shield.

The little old woman then went into the little hill, and the Stone Boy came near it and cried, "Ho, old woman, come out." But the old woman said, "My friend, I am a weak old woman. Have pity on me and come into my tipi."

The Stone Boy saw that the hill was a strange kind of tipi. He found the door, went in, and the old woman said, "My friend, I am a weak old woman, but you are welcome to my tipi. I will get you something to eat and drink." The Stone Boy noticed that her tongue was forked, so he was very wary and watched her closely.

She said, "My Friend, you must be tired. Lie down and rest while I get food for you." The Stone Boy lay down and the old woman passed close, saying to him, "The meat is behind you." As she leaned over him she stabbed him over the heart, but her stone knife broke off when it struck him.

She said, "My Friend, I stumbled and fell on you." The Stone Boy said, "I will sit up so that you will not stumble over me." So she said, "My Friend, sit near the center of the tipi, so I can go about you without stumbling over you."

So the Stone Boy sat near the center of the lodge, and the old woman moved about him. As she passed him she struck him on the head with a warclub, but it only bounced off without hurting him, so she said, "My Friend, that was a stone that fell from the top of the tipi." The Stone Boy said, "I will sit out by the door of the tipi so that stones will not fall on me." He sat outside by the door of the tipi. The old woman said, "My Friend, you must be hungry. I will make soup for you." She made soup with bad medicine in it and gave it to the Stone Boy, who drank it.

The old woman said, "Ho, you are the one I hate. I am Iya, the evil spirit. I hate all People. I destroy all People. I have given you that which will destroy you. You have swallowed poison. It will kill you. I am Iya the evil one. I know whom you seek. You were hunting for your mother's brothers. They are there in that tipi. They are like tanned skins. You will soon die and I will make a tanned skin of you. I must have a living stone to flatten you out, but there is only one other living stone and I must find it. The living stone was my master. He is the only one I feared. He is the only one who could hurt me. No one else can do me any harm. His only relative is a living stone. He is now my master and none other. But you will die from the poison I have given you and I will sing your death song."

She sang:—

A young man would be wise.
A young man would be brave.

He left the places he knew.
He came to strange places.

He came to death valley.
He came to Iya's tipi.

He slew Iya's son, the Coyote,
He slew Iya's daughter, the Snake Tree.

He broke the living stone.
He broke Iya's master.

Iya will be revenged on him.
Iya will see him die.

He slew my friend the Bear.
Iya will laugh and see him die.

Then the Stone Boy said, "May I also sing a song?"
Iya said, "Ho, sing what you will. It is your death song
and it is music that will make my heart glad."

The living stone was Iya's master.
The living stone had but one relation.

He had a son that was little.
A pebble that was white as snow.

Iya feared this pebble and stole it.
Feared it because it was white.

Iya carried it into a far away country.
Iya threw it from him on a hilltop.

Where it would not be nourished.
Where it would not be life warmed.

He thought no one would find it.
He thought it would be there forever.

A woman born mysterious.
Found this pebble mysterious.

She gave to it the warmth of life.
The son of the living stone.

The wisest Shaman taught him wisdom.
The bravest warrior taught him bravery.

The oldest woman taught him cunning.
The best of women taught him kindness.

The People taught him justice.
To strive for the right against evil.

He was charmed from harm by the shaman.
He was armed against evil by the warrior.

On his robe was the dream of the old woman.
On his feet was the magic of the young woman.

Thus he came to death's valley.
Thus he came to Iya's tipi.

He slew Iya's friend, the Bear.
Because he enticed the People away.

He slew Iya's son, the Coyote,
Because he did evil only.

He slew Iya's daughter, the Snake Tree,
because her faults were many.

Iya's knife would not harm him.
Iya's club would not kill him.

Iya's broth would not kill him.
It only makes him warm and strong.

I am the pebble you threw away.
I am the Stone Boy, your master.

Then Iya said, "How shall I know you to be my master?"
The Stone Boy said, "Do my bidding or I will punish you."
Then Iya said, "I am a weak old woman. Have pity on me
and do not punish me." The Stone Boy said, "Your tongue
is forked, and you do not tell the truth. You are not a
woman. You are an evil old man. You have pity on no one,
but do evil to everyone. Tell me, where are my mother's
brothers?" Iya said, "I do not know. I was only boasting
when I said I knew where they were. Have pity on me. Do
not make it hard for me." Then the Stone Boy said, "I will
have no pity on you. Tell me where my mother's brothers
are." Iya said, "I do not know."

Then the Stone Boy seized him by the foot and placed
it on the ground and trod on it, and Iya's foot was flattened
like a piece of dried skin and he howled with pain. But the
Stone Boy demanded he tell where his mother's brothers
were, and Iya declared that he did not know. Then the
Stone Boy flattened his other foot in the same way, and

Iya sobbed and cried with pain and said he would tell all to the Stone Boy if he would not punish him any further, for Iya recognized that the Stone Boy was truly his master. Iya said:—

"In ancient times, I found game plentiful in the valleys below here, and good hunters and brave men came here to hunt it. These good men could not be made to do evil at their homes, so I could not do them mischief. So I made a bargain with your father, the living stone, and with the great Bear and brought my sons and daughters with me and we all lived here in this valley. [Iya was a giant; he fought with the living stone. The stone conquered him and became his master. He kept Iya with nothing to eat until he grew smaller and became a little old person.]

"The bargain was that the Bear would go out among the game, and when a good man came to hunt, the Bear would show himself and, being so big, the hunters would chase him until they came where they could see my son, who would jump up and down and scare them so that they would fall down with no strength. Then the Bear would take them in his arms and bring them to my daughter, who would sting them so that they would be paralyzed. Then the living stone would roll on them and flatten them out like skins and I would heap them on my tipi poles. As they were alive, this would always be a torment to them. In this way I could do mischief to good men.

"We often heard of the four men who lived alone and did women's work and who never did evil to anyone, so that I could not torment them. But they would not hunt or go on the warpath, and we thought they would never come within our power. So I determined to get a woman into their tipi that they might do some evil, but I could not get an ordinary woman among them. Then I tried to break off a branch from my daughter, the Snake Tree, and put it into their tipi, but the branches would not break and the only way I could get a part of my daughter was by digging out a part of the heart of the tree. This I did and placed it near the tipi of the four brothers so that when one of them went to get wood he would step on it and stick it into his toe. These men were so good that when they cared for this child it grew up a good woman—as they were good men—but I waited patiently, for when she grew to be a woman I knew they would not live as they had before. When she was a woman they came to hunt game for her, and the Bear enticed them and they were caught and flattened and are now tormented on my tipi poles.

"When I threw the white pebble away, I knew that no ordinary woman could nourish it into life and growth, and when your mother grew up to be a woman, I did not think of her being a mysterious woman who could give life and growth to the pebble. So my own evil has brought the punishment on me, for I know that you are my master and that you will not let me do evil anymore. But those who now lie on my tipi poles will still be tormented."

Then the Stone Boy said, "Tell me: how can these people that are on your tipi poles be restored to their natural condition?" Iya said, "I will not." The Stone Boy said, "I am your master. Tell me or I will punish you." Then Iya said, "Remember, I am your grandfather, and do not punish me." The Stone Boy said, "I broke my own father in pieces because he was evil. Do You think I would spare you because you are my grandfather?" Iya said, "I will not tell you."

Then the Stone Boy said, "Give me your hand." He took Iya's hand and trod on it and it was flattened like a dried skin and Iya howled with pain. Then the Stone Boy said, "Tell me or I will flatten your other hand," and Iya said, "I will tell you."

"You must skin the Bear and the Coyote and stretch their skins over poles so as to make a tight tipi. Then you must gather all the pieces of the broken living stone. You must make a fire of the wood from the Snake Tree and heat the stones over this fire, and place them in the tipi. Then get one of the flattened People off the poles of my tipi and place it in the tipi you have built. Then place the hot stones in the tipi and pour water over the stones. When the steam rises onto the flattened Person, he will be as he was before the Bear enticed him."

123

Then the Stone Boy did as he was told, but the skins of the Bear and the Coyote would not make a full-sized tipi, so he made it low and round on top. When he made fire of the Snake Tree, the branches were so fat that one would heat all the stones red hot. He had plenty of fuel to heat the stones as often as he wished. So he placed the flattened People in the sweathouse and steamed them and they became men as they were before they were enticed by the Bear.

He did not know who his mother's brothers were, so he took the arrow he had found and called to all and asked them whose arrow it was. One man said it was his. He told him to stand to one side. He took the stone knife he had found and asked whose it was. A man said it was his and he told him to stand to one side. He then took the plum seed dice he had found and asked whose they were. One man said it was his, and he told him to stand to one side. Then he told the men he had asked to stand aside to look at each other. They did so, and when they had looked at each other they embraced each other, and the Stone Boy knew they were brothers.

Then the Stone Boy told them the story of the four men, of the birth of his mother and how the four men went away and never came back. Then the men said, "We are those four men." The Stone Boy knew that they were his mother's brothers, so he told them the story of his own birth, and they said, "We believe you, because we know the birth of your mother." Then he told them of his preparation to come for them, of his coming and his fight with the Bear, the Coyote, the Stone, and the Snake Tree, and how he was master of Iya. They said, "We believe you, because the Bear did entice us and the Coyote did jump up and down and the Snake bit us and the Stone did roll over us and make us flat like skins and the old woman did spread us on her tipi and we were tormented."

Then the Stone Boy counselled with them as to what he should do to Iya. They advised him to make him flat like a skin, but the Stone Boy said, "There is no Snake Tree to bite him." He came back to Iya and said, "You have been very evil, but now I am your master and I shall punish you for all the evil you have done so that you will always be in torment as you have kept all these People." Iya was a great coward and he begged the Stone Boy to spare him and not punish him. But the Stone Boy said, "I shall flatten you like skin and spread you on a pole."

Then Iya said, "I am Iya, the giant, and I will grow so big that you cannot flatten me." He began to grow and grew larger and larger so that he was a great giant. But the Stone Boy began to trample on him. Beginning at his feet, which he had already flattened, he trampled on his legs, so that Iya fell to his knees; he trampled on his thighs so that Iya fell to his buttocks; he trampled on his hips so that great floods of water ran from him. This water was bitter and salty and it soaked into the Earth, and where it comes out in springs or lakes it makes the water very bad and bitter.

Then he trampled his belly, and Iya vomited great quantities of cherry stones, and the Stone Boy said to him, "What are these Cherry stones?" and Iya said, "They are the People that I have sucked in with my breath when I went about the Earth as a giant." The Stone Boy said, "How can I make these People as they were when you sucked them in with your breath?" Iya said, "Make a fire without smoke." So the Stone Boy got very dry Cotton Wood and made a fire and when it was burned to coals Iya said, "Get some of the hair from the great Bear's skin." He got hair from the great Bear, and Iya said, "Put the hair on the fire," and he put it on the fire. Then there arose a great white smoke, and it was like the smoke from wild Sage branches and leaves. Then Iya said, "Blow this smoke on the Cherry stones." The Stone Boy did so, and Iya said, "This drives away all my power to do these People any harm." Iya said, "Get the hair of many women." The Stone Boy did so and there was a thick blue smoke like the smoke of Sweetgrass and Iya said, "This gives you power to do what you wish to these People."

The Stone Boy said to the People, "Be as you were before Iya sucked you in with his breath." Every Cherry stone arose. They were transformed into more women and children, so that there were a great many People there.

These People were all very hungry, so the Stone Boy said to Iya, "What shall I give these People to eat?" Iya replied, "Give them the flesh of the great Bear." So he cut off a piece of the flesh of the great Bear and gave it to a woman. It grew to be a large piece, and this woman cut it in two and gave half of it to another woman. Immediately each of these pieces grew large. Each one of these women cut their pieces in two and each of those pieces grew large. Each time a piece was given away it grew large. Then the women built fires and cooked the meat and all feasted and were happy and sang songs.

The People spoke many different languages and could not understand one another, but the Stone Boy could speak to each one in his own language. He addressed some in their own tongue, "Where was your place?" They replied, "Over the Mountains." He said to them, "Go to your People." As he said this to everyone, he gave to the oldest woman of each people a piece of the flesh from the great Bear, so that they had plenty to eat while they traveled. Then the Stone Boy said to his mother's brothers, "Now we will go back to your sister, to my mother, but before we go I will destroy Iya so that he may do no more mischief or hurt the People."

He trod on Iya's chest and his breath rushed out of his mouth and nostrils like a mighty Wind and it whirled and twisted, breaking down trees, tearing up grass, throwing the Water from the Lake, and even piling the Rocks and Earth over the carcasses of the Coyote and the Snake Tree, so that the Thunderbird came rushing through the Air to find out what all this tumult was about. With his Cloud shield he rushed into this great Whirlwind, and while the Lightning spit and flashed from his eyes, he fought the Whirlwind and carried it away into the Sky.

Then the Stone Boy said to Iya, "I will now tread your head and your arms out flat like a dried skin and you shall remain forever here in this evil valley where there is no Tree, nor Grass, nor Water, and where no living thing will ever come near you. The Sun shall burn you and the Cold shall freeze you and you shall feel and think and be hungry and thirsty, but no one shall come near you.

Iya grew so large that he almost lay across the valley. His hands were upon the hill where the Stone Boy first showed himself. When the Stone Boy told him his fate, his hands grasped for something, and he felt the Stone Boy's robe. This he quickly threw over himself and immediately he became invisible. But the Stone Boy saw what he was doing and jumped quickly to trample the breath out of Iya, his mouth gaped wide open. He got the robe over his head before Stone Boy could get his feet on him. When the Stone Boy did trample Iya, he stepped into his mouth, so Iya closed his jaws like a trap and caught both of the Stone Boy's feet between his teeth.

Iya could not hurt the Stone Boy, but he held the feet very tightly between his teeth, and when the Stone Boy drew out one foot, he closed still closer on the other so that when that one was dragged out, the Moccasin was left in Iya's mouth and was invisible and could not be found.

FIRST CREATOR AND LONE MAN

A Mandan Origin Story

It is our custom to tell an old-time story when the Corn is ripe. We have a man called Only Man. As he was walking along he came to himself. He stood and thought. A pipe was lying in front of him, over his head flew a Raven. And he sang a song which said, "Where did I come from?" He thought, "Where did I come from? How did I happen to come here?" The Earth about him was Sandy and he could plainly see his own tracks, so he followed them back to see where he came from. He came to a wet spot, then farther on to a great Water, beside which was a Plant with spotted leaves. A Buffalo Bug was jumping about in the Sand. The Plant said, "I am your mother, it was I that bore you; that is your father," and the Weed-mother told Only Man that he was born to arrange matters on the Earth. "Go back to the wet spot and there you will find a tall Weed. That is your pipe. I am just a Weed, this is all I am for. If anyone has a sore eye or stomach trouble, let him take me and boil me up for medicine. Go ahead and create things in the World." When he

127

came to himself he had a Wolf blanket and a cane with feathers tied to the end. He came to the wet spot, and there grew a tall Tobacco Weed and around it buzzed a Tobacco Fly—buzz, buzz. The Bug said, "I am blowing your Tobacco Plant—use it to smoke." Again he sang the same song—"Where did I come from?" and he pulled up the Tobacco Plant.

As he was trotting along at a gentle pace, another man came up suddenly. The two argued as to which was the older. They agreed: "You lie here and I there and the first one that gets up will be the younger." Only Man said he would leave his cane standing as the other turned about and lay down, and Only Man sang the same song—"Where did I come from?" He went on his way, and traveled over the whole World from one end to the other. Then he thought of his cane, and returning to the spot where it stood, he found it tottering and ready to fall. Grass grew where the other lay. He said, "This fellow can never get up again!" He took his cane and it became like new and he sang his song and was about to trot away again when the other man got up from the heap of dust where his body had been and said, "I told you that I was older than you!"

The two traveled to create the World. They looked for Mud, but there was Sand alone. They came to a great Lake where there were two Mudhens, a male and a female. They called them over and made them their servants, and the Mudhens dived and brought Mud, and the Men made all creatures. They would throw the Mud in the Air and at once it became a Bird. One Bird had no place to go, so it flew over to the stoney places and became a nighthawk. Another stuck its head into the red paint, saying it was hungry, and when it pulled its head out, the head was red, so they said it should have a hard time to get a living out of rotten trees. This was the Woodpecker.

They made many kinds of different Birds and Animals and at last a grandmother Frog came and said, "You are making too many Animals; we must make death so that the first ones may pass away and new ones come." The two said, "You have nothing to say about our business!" and they picked up a stone and hit Grandmother Frog on the back. That is why her legs spread out so. That is how death started, and the child of Grandmother Frog was the first to die. Grandmother Frog came to the Men and said, "I am sorry! Let us take it back and have no deaths!" But the men said, "No, it is impossible; it must be so."

The two said, "Let us improve the Earth—it is all Sand!" So they took the Mud that was left and Only Man took his lump and smoothed it over the Earth and the Earth was flat. First Creator took a little bit and put it here and there and formed hills and bluffs. Only Man used his cane and leveled the North side of the Earth and made Lakes. First Creator's idea was that when the Snow flies there should be rough Land and Trees and Springs to protect Men and Animals from the cold. First Creator made nothing but Buffalo to roam over the land and in every herd he made a White Buffalo and he said that this White One should be precious. From the East this way Only Man created and First Creator created the South side of the Earth. Thus it has been told from generation to generation.

After the creation Only Man was never seen again. First Creator turned him into a Coyote and from him came the Coyote today. He never knew where he came from.

CROW NECKLACE AND
HIS MEDICINE CEREMONY

A Hidatsa Story

There was a party of Gros Ventre Indians who went out for a hunt from Knife River where the old camp was, and while they were hunting, the Assiniboins came and attacked the hunters. Some got away and were saved. A young man among them looked for his sister and could not find her. So he trailed them to their camp. This man was an Assiniboin who had been as a little boy captured by the Gros Ventre and made a slave. The girl called him brother, but was not really related to him. When all was quiet at night he went through the camp to look for his sister. He came to a big tipi and heard talking. Looking through a hole, he saw two men wounded whom he recognized as his own brothers. Now he had shot two Assiniboin in the conflict (and he recognized these two as the ones he shot.) Drawing his robe over his head, he entered and sat down beside their father, who was his father too. The wounded men told their father to fill his pipe and smoke with the stranger. The boy had not forgotten his own language, so he spoke to the old man and said, "Father, it is I." When he told what had happened to him, the father put his hands about his neck and fainted; the mother did the same. When he told them it was he who had shot the two brothers, they all laughed over it. He told them that he was looking for his sister, and the wounded men advised the father to call in the chiefs and tell them about her. So the chiefs arranged not to move camp for four days, but to have a feast and call together all the slaves taken from the Gros Ventres and let them eat. Then they had a dance called the scalp-dance, but the sister was not there. According to the old custom, slaves are supposed to belong to the tribe by which they are captured, so the slaves too got up and danced with them. All the slaves knew the young man. They called him "Crow Necklace."

Before the four days were passed he said to the slaves, "Go steal some moccasins and dry meat and one of these nights we will run away." On the last of the four nights they were all prepared. They stole sinew and cut pieces of Buffalo hide from the tents for moccasins. It was storming when they left—young women, old, and children, the young women carrying the children on their backs—and they ran North instead of East in the direction from which they came. Coming to a dry Lake, they lay down in the deep Grass and the Snow covered them. Meanwhile, the Assiniboin discovered their absence and tracked after them, but could not find them. They came to the Lake but, seeing nothing of them, went home except one who stood looking. Him Crow Necklace crept up and killed and took his scalp.

That night they went until daylight, traveling North-East, until they came to another dry Lake thick with Grass. There they stayed all day. Four days they traveled in the night and hid all day. By this time they were up at the head waters. From there they came around toward the Missouri River and came out at a place we call "Timber Coulee." At that time it was full of timber. Crow Necklace was about to push down an old Tree which had an Owl's nest on top. An old Owl said, "Don't push down that tree or my young ones will get cold. We are the ones who have helped you get around to your home again. It will be best for you to go back to your own tribe; there you will find a chief's daughter waiting to marry you." So when they wanted him to marry some of the women he refused and said, "No! the young ones are my sisters and the old ones are my mothers." The Owl directed him, "After leaving this place, go directly to the Short Missouri to camp, then on to Wood-trap (right across the river west of here). Here all the Spirits will set traps to catch all kinds of wild Animals for you to eat. When you get there, build a tipi out in the bush. Go inside and do not go out, and they will bring you meat themselves." So they did this—fixed up nice and went in. Outside they could hear the noise of butchering going on around them. When the noise ceased they went out and found meat cut up or wrapped in hides and laid up on scaffolds. The Owl told Crow Necklace that they were now not far from the tribe —at the next move they would reach home. The next day they moved until they came to a high hill. Crow Necklace fixed up a skull and painted their faces black. As they approached, they saw a woman crying on top of a hill and someone pointed her out to Crow Necklace; it was his sister. He called to her, and when she saw him she fainted. Then the whole camp came out to meet them and everybody made much of Crow Necklace. He told the story of their adventures and brought the food for them to eat.

All the hides he had asked to have tanned in order to make Medicine after he got back home. Among them was a White Buffalo hide. So after he had married a chief's daughter as had been foretold, he made Medicine in order to understand all the mysterious beings and leave out none of them. And that cost him everything he had prepared— a hundred moccasins, a hundred robes, a hundred blankets —everything in hundreds.

THE STORY OF HUNGRY WOLF

An Assiniboine Story

A Young man and his wife were up hunting in the breaks North of Little Missouri, back by Kildeer Mountains. The man camped there with his wife. He was successful as a hunter, and his wife cured the hides and fried strips of jerked meat. One night he told her to pack up everything, as the next day they would be leaving. The next morning early he went out to get some fresh meat for the journey and returned with parts of a Rocky Mountain Sheep and its hide, which the People regard as very valuable. He found the packages on the scaffold just as he had left them, but his wife and Dog were gone.

Circling about the tent he found no trace, but the fourth day he found a few tracks of men. With the tracks of men were the tracks of his wife and dog heading South. He went back to camp and pounded the meat and roasted the fattest meat and stored it away in bags to eat on the way, then he followed the trail. The fugitives hid their trail by spreading out and then coming together again, so that the tracks were hard to follow. Thus he followed a party which he judged to consist of twelve persons. When he came to Looks-Like-a-Chicken-Tail butte, he turned South-West and saw smoke rising from a camp. He waited until Sunset, then walked into the camp. There he stood a while, considering. He covered his head with his robe, carrying bow and arrows under his robe in case of attack. He could see young men walking about engaged in courting. As he went from tent to tent listening for signs of his wife, their Dog ran out from a tent and jumped about its master. He gave it meat. The Dog returned inside the tent, whined, wagged its tail and ran out again to its master. He went and stood in the doorway. Within he could see his wife sitting. An old woman came in, and to his surprise his wife spoke to her in Gros Ventres. She was an old woman who had also been taken prisoner and had lived among the enemy until she was old.

He surveyed the situation of the camp. On the outskirts was a ravine where a spring had made a small pond. A trail led down to this pond, made by the women going after water. Beside the pond grew Beaver Grass, long and fine, right down to the water's edge. There he hid, hoping that when his wife came down to get water, they might plan an escape. His plan was to start in the night, go westward toward the mountains, and come back home. In the morning a stream of women came down after water. At noon fewer came. In the early afternoon he saw the Dog coming down the bank wagging his tail. His wife came to the edge of the spring and, standing on a stone, leaned over to dip water. He said, "Stay just where you are, my own heart, I heard you talking last night with the old woman. My plan is for you to come out here when everyone is asleep. The People will expect us to go back to our old camp, so we will go toward the mountains and live on game on the way home. Afterwards we will go back and get our packages at the camp.

He lay behind the grass. In the evening after the women had left who came down after water, the men came down and encircled the pond. They overpowered him, took away his bow and arrows and carried him away to a tent and gave him food. His wife came and looked into the tent. He said, "I believe that it is you who have betrayed me."

They dug two holes in a circle, set in two posts, lanced his muscles next to the bone at wrists and ankles, stretched his arms and legs to the posts; then they scalped him, and, tying the scalp to a long pole, they sent out drummers and all came out and danced the victory dance and carried his scalp about on the pole. They brought firewood and made a pile of it before and behind him, intending to burn him; but just then an old man came out who seemed to have authority, and stopped the dancing and made signs towards Sun, but his words were unintelligible. The old Gros Ventre woman came to him and said, "My dear, it is all your wife's fault. You communicated with her when she went down to get water. When she returned she told the camp that there was a Corn Man down in the water-hole. I was taken away when young by these people and have been here ever since. I married and have children and grandchildren and hence have been contented to live among them. When they brought this Gros Ventre woman

133

here, as she was one of our tribe, I went over to her tent to comfort her. It was your wife who advised that you be captured and tortured to death. You cannot expect a woman to keep a secret. The men who spoke to the People told them that when we fight and kill an enemy we kill him quickly. He said, "The great God in the Heavens is looking down upon us. If you burn this man, that great Spirit will some day avenge this deed. He will punish us. Let us wait and see what will happen.' "

The next day when the People broke camp, some came over and pierced his eyes; then they left him and went away. For four days he remained hanging. On the fourth day toward dusk he heard an Owl hooting. He came nearer and hooted again. He could hear the grass rustling as from a man walking close to him. The steps stopped in front of him and a man said, "My son, the hooting of the Owl was myself. I have come to see what I can do to restore your sight." He heard him spitting on his hands and rubbing the palms together. The man told him to look up, and he rubbed the palms of his hands over his eyes, and his eyesight was restored. The man told him, "Fear not, the torture from which you are suffering has been caused by your wife. But you shall live and see your home again. You must stand and listen at daybreak when Sun comes over the hills, and you will hear the Earth trembling and the sound of something falling to Earth. That which you hear falling and whose vibrations you feel is white clay, which is being made for you in the Sky and dropped from the Sky to Earth. You will find it near Red Grass butte beside Knife River. When you get home, when you give a dance, let the Grandma society clean a lodge site and pile the grass in the center as a symbol of your standing here. Strip a cane in four places as a symbol of the four days you have stood here without food and water. It will be a token of long life and prosperity. Give another such cane to a brother or some relative. The two canes are symbols of the two torture posts. There shall be a circle for the Wolf society and the old scouts shall circle around you. Take one Winter to prepare all the articles for the dance. Ask all your friends and relatives to help you. They shall make arrows and give them as payment to the scouts who sing and tell of their exploits and they shall give them to their sons and young relatives to use against those who tortured you. Next year you will find these same People camping here, and you shall kill a hundred of them. You shall capture this old Gros Ventre woman and your wife. Save their lives, but do not make the woman your wife again. You shall marry the daughters of your chief. Teach your warriors to use in the battle shields made of buffalo hide hardened by burning with hot stones."

The Owl Man told him that in the morning he would see Wolf-of-the-Sunset dancing with his warriors. He must watch their dress and learn their songs and make this dance a part of his Mystery. In the morning the Wolf-of-the-Sunset came with his warriors, who were a pack of Wolves. They freed him and took him into their company by the name of Hungry Wolf. The scouts come in the rear. The Raven as he flies over the country seeing all that is going on is like the scout. It was the Raven who had told the Owl how the man was being tortured and had reported it to Wolf-of-the-Sunset. That is why the two men who led in the Wolf Dance and impersonate Wolf-of-the-Sunset and Hungry Wolf wear Raven feathers. Just as the Wolves do for the fasters in the dance, so the Wolves came that day, removed the rawhides that bound him and gave him the feast of fat of the Buffalo to eat. They said, "This will drive away the pain of the torture. When your People kill a Buffalo, after skinning the breastbone, they must take a mouthful of the fat, and whatever their sickness this will cure it. They took fat and anointed his wounds in his arms and feet and on the forehead. They daubed him with white clay all over and then, as a sign of healing, they made scratches with their fingernails in the clay on his calves, his forearm, and on his forehead, thus leaving the clay in streaks. This white clay is used at the Wolf ceremony. The heap in the center of the clearing is the symbol of his torture. When they dance about, they must go over to the right side (and dance from the right to the left) in order to insure long life and prosperity; if they start from the left, it is a sign of misery. So when People smoke, the pipe is handed to the extreme right of the circle and then handed around.

The Wolves told him to follow them. When he got over the divide, he found a Buffalo butchered and blood and kidney, liver, guts, laid aside for him to eat raw. The Wolf placed on his head a piece of hide from the Buffalo's head, sang a song, and his torn scalp was healed and the hair turned the color of his own hair. Thus he reached home. Then he climbed up on his old lodge, face to the West, and said "Hee-hay!" (which signifies "Listen!"). He spoke to the Wolves of the West and said, "This Winter I shall have bedding [Buffalo hides] scraped for you and shall bring the Wolves into my lodge [meaning warriors] in order to conquer my enemies." Taking hunters and Dogs, he returned to his old camp and brought back his bundles. He placed food in those lodges where the societies met and in return they gave arrows and other things for the ceremony. He sent one of his sisters to the chief's lodge and asked for the hand of the chief's two daughters in marriage.

During the Winter he instructed the Wolves in the scout songs he had learned from the Wolves. In the Summer he sent for the white clay and had the dance performed. After this he called for the young men through the announcer and for the old men who had endurance and speed and provided them with moccasins and provisions for the war path. On the outskirts of the village the warriors assembled. When they reached the butte, he was told that this was the place to mine the bright red ochre which is to be found there in pockets. Since he had too many scouts, he selected from the forty-five the fourteen who were the fastest runners. They had to run one by one between two goals while the rest in the center tried to catch them. This is called "running by." If anyone was caught before he reached the opposite goal, he was put out. They went on and sent out scouts ahead. They reported a hundred and fifty tents. There were 2500 persons in the village. They got close to camp, whooped, and attacked at daybreak. After a hundred warriors had been killed, he gave the signal to stop by waving his robe in the air. No women or children were killed, or any old people. The old Gros Ventre woman and the young man's wife were taken. The old woman was allowed to go back to the tribe; the wife was brought back to the village. No one would marry her, and it was she who introduced harlotry.

In the village they danced the greatest victory dance ever known. Hungry Wolf lived to old age and had children and grandchildren. The mystery he conferred upon his son, and so it was handed down from generation to generation.

ORIGIN OF THE SWEAT LODGE

A Nez Perce Story

Long ago, in the days of the Animal People, Sweat Lodge was a man. He foresaw the coming of Human Beings, the real inhabitants of the Earth. So one day he called all the Animal People together to give each one a name and to tell him his duties.

In the council, Sweat Lodge stood up and made a speech: "We have lived on Earth for a long while, but we shall not be in our present condition much longer. A different People are coming to live here. We must part from each other and go to different places. Each of you must decide whether you wish to belong to the Animal beings that walk, fly or creep or those that swim. You may now make your choice."

Then Sweat Lodge turned to Elk. "You will first come this way, Elk. What do you wish to be?"

"I wish to be what I am—an Elk."
"Let us see you run or gallop," said Sweat Lodge.
So Elk galloped off in a graceful manner, and then returned.
"You are all right," decided Sweat Lodge, "You are an Elk."
Elk galloped off, and the rest saw no more of him.
Sweat Lodge called Eagle to him and asked, "What do you wish to be, Eagle?"
"I wish to be just what I am—an Eagle."
"Let us see you fly," replied Sweat Lodge.

Eagle flew, rising higher and higher and with hardly a ripple on his outstretched wings.

Sweat Lodge called him back and said to him, "You are an Eagle. You will be king over all the Birds of the Air. You will soar in the Sky. You will live on the crags and peaks of the highest Mountains. The Human Beings will admire you."

Happy with that decision, Eagle flew away. Everybody watched him until he disappeared in the Sky.

"I wish to be like Eagle," Bluejay told Sweat Lodge.

Wanting to give everyone a chance, Sweat Lodge said again, "Let us see you fly."

Bluejay flew into the air, trying to imitate the easy, graceful flight of Eagle. But he failed to keep himself balanced and was soon flapping his wings.

Noticing his awkwardness, Sweat Lodge called Bluejay back to him and said, "A Jay is a Jay. You will have to be contented as you are."

When Bear came forward, Sweat Lodge said to him, "You will be known among Human Beings as a very fierce Animal. You will kill and eat People, and they will fear you."

Bear went off into the woods and has since been known as a fierce animal.

Then to all walking creatures, except Coyote, and all the flying creatures, to all the Animals and Birds, all the Snakes and Frogs and Turtles and Fish, Sweat Lodge gave names, and the creatures scattered.

After they had gone, Sweat Lodge called Coyote to him and said, "You have been wise and cunning. A man to be feared you have been. This Earth shall become like the air, empty and void, yet your name shall last forever. The new Human Beings who are to come will hear your name and will say, 'Yes, Coyote was great in his time.' Now, what do you wish to be?"

"I have long lived as a Coyote," he replied. "I want to be noble like Eagle or Elk or Cougar."

Sweat Lodge let him show what he could do. First, Coyote tried his best to fly like Eagle, but he could only jump around, this way and that way. He could not fly, the poor fellow. Then he tried to imitate the Elk in his graceful gallop. For a short distance he succeeded, but soon he returned to his own gait. He ran a little way, stopped short, and looked around.

"You look exactly like yourself, Coyote," laughed Sweat Lodge. "You will be a Coyote."

Poor Coyote ran off, howling, to some unknown place. Before he got out of sight, he stopped, turned his head, and stood—just like a coyote.

Sweat Lodge, left alone, spoke to himself: "All now are gone, and the new People will be coming soon. When they arrive, they should find something that will give them strength and power.

"I will place myself on the ground, for the use of the Human Beings who are to come. Whoever will visit me now and then, to him I will give power. He will become great in war and great in peace. He will have success in Fishing and in hunting. To all who come to me for protection I will give strength and power."

Sweat Lodge spoke with earnestness. Then he lay down on his hands and knees and waited for the first People. He has lain that way ever since and has given power to all who have sought it from him.

WHY THERE ARE NO SNAKES ON TAKHOMA

A Story from the Cowlitz People

A long, long time ago, TyheeSahale became angry with the People. Sahale ordered a Medicine Man to take his bow and arrow and shoot into the Cloud which hung low over Takhoma. The Medicine Man shot the arrow, and it stuck fast in the cloud. Then he shot another into the lower end of the second. He shot arrows until he had made a chain which reached from the Cloud to the Earth. The Medicine Man told his klootchman and his children to climb up the arrow trail. Then he told the good Animals to climb up the arrow trail. Then the Medicine Man climbed up himself. Just as he was climbing into the Cloud, he looked back. A long line of bad Animals and Snakes were also climbing up the arrow trail. Therefore, the Medicine Man broke the chain of arrows. Thus the Snakes and bad Animals fell down on the Mountainside.

Then at once it began to Rain. It Rained until all the Land was flooded. Water reached even into the Snowline of Takhoma. When all the bad Animals and Snakes were drowned, it stopped Raining. After a while the water sank again. Then the Medicine Man, and the klootchman, and the children climbed out of the Cloud and came down the Mountainside. The good Animals also climbed out of the Cloud. Thus there are now no Snakes or bad Animals on Takhoma.

DOG GOES FOR FIRE

From the Coeur d'Alene

People had a fire. Wolf had no fire. Wolf and Dog were friends. Wolf said to Dig, "Go steal a spark from the People."

Dog went to the People. They fed him and he forgot to steal the spark. That's all.

ESKIMO MYTH OF THE ORIGIN OF SUN, MOON AND STARS

At a time when darkness covered the Earth, a girl was nightly visited by someone whose identity she could not discover. She determined to find out who it could be. She mixed some soot with oil and painted her breast with it. The next time she discovered, to her horror, that her brother had a black circle of soot around his mouth. She upbraided him and he denied it. The father and mother were very angry and scolded the pair so severely that the son fled from their presence. The daughter seized a brand from the fire and pursued him. He ran to the Sky to avoid her, but she flew after him. The man changed into the Moon and the girl who bore the torch became the Sun. The sparks that flew from the brand became the Stars. The Sun is constantly pursuing the Moon, which keeps in the darkness to avoid being discovered. When an eclipse occurs, they are supposed to meet.

ESKIMO STORY OF THE NORTHERN LIGHTS

Auroras—or Northern Lights—are believed to be the torches held in the hands of Spirits seeking the souls of those who have just died, to lead them over the abyss terminating the edge of the World. A narrow pathway leads across it to the land of brightness and plenty, where disease and pain are no more, and where food of all kinds is always ready in abundance. To this place none but the dead and the Raven can go. When the Spirits wish to communicate with the People of the Earth, they make a whistling noise, and the Earth People answer only in a whispering tone. The Eskimo say that they are able to call the Aurora and converse with it. They send messages to the dead through these spirits.

SIOUX STORY OF THE QUARREL OF THE SUN AND MOON

In the days of the first grandfather, the Moon and the Sun lived upon the Earth. Then they quarreled.

Said the Moon: "I am out of patience with you. I gather the People, but you scatter them. You cause them to be lost."

Said the Sun: "I wish for many People to grow, so I scatter them. You put them in darkness; thus you kill many with hunger." Then Sun called to the People, "Ho! Ye who are People. Many of you shall grow strong. I will look down on you from above. I will rule all your work."

Said Moon: "And I, too, will dwell above you. I will gather you when it is dark. Assembling in full numbers, you shall sleep. I myself will rule all your work. We will walk in the trail, one after the other. I will walk behind you."

SIA LEGEND OF THE COYOTE AND RATTLESNAKE

The Coyote's house was near the house of the Rattlesnake. The Coyote said to the Snake, "Let us walk together," and while walking he said to the Snake, "Tomorrow come to my house." In the morning the Snake went to the house of the Coyote and moved along slowly on the floor, shaking his rattle. The Coyote sat to one side, much afraid; he became frightened after watching the movements of the Snake and hearing the noise of the rattle. The Coyote had a pot of Rabbit meat cooking on the fire, which he placed in front of the snake, inviting him to eat, saying, "Companion, eat." "No, companion, I will not eat your meat; I do not understand your food," said the Snake. "What food do you eat?" asked the Coyote. "I eat yellow Flowers of the Corn," was the reply, and the Coyote immediately began to look around for some, and when he found the pollen, the Snake said, "Put some on the top of my head that I may eat it," and the Coyote, standing as far off as possible, dropped a little on the Snake's head. The Snake said, "Come nearer and put enough on my head that I may find it." He was very much afraid, but after a while the Coyote came close to the Snake and put the pollen on his head; and after eating the pollen the Snake thanked the Coyote, saying, "I will go now and pass about," but before leaving he invited the Coyote to his house: "Companion, tomorrow you come to my house." "Very well," said the Coyote, "tomorrow I will go to your house." The Coyote thought much about what the Snake would do on the morrow. He made a small rattle (by placing tiny pebbles in a gourd) and attached it to the end of his tail, and, testing it, he was well satisfied and said: "This is well"; he then proceeded to the house of the Snake. When he was near the house, he shook his tail and said to himself, "This is good; I guess when I go into the house the Snake will be much afraid of me." He did not walk into the house, but moved like a Snake. The Coyote could not shake the rattle as the Snake did his; he had to hold his tail in his paw. When he shook his rattle, the Snake appeared afraid and said, "Companion, I am much afraid of you." The Snake had a stew of Rats on the fire, which he placed before the

142

Coyote and invited him to eat, saying, "Companion, eat some of my food," and the Coyote replied, "I do not understand your food; I cannot eat it, because I do not understand it." The Snake insisted upon his eating, but the Coyote continued to refuse, saying, "If you will put some of the Flower of the Corn on my head I will eat; I understand that food." The Snake quickly procured some Corn pollen, but he pretended to be afraid to go too near the Coyote, and stood off at a distance. The Coyote told him to come nearer and put it well on the top of his head; but the Snake replied, "I am afraid of you." The Coyote said, "Come nearer to me; I am not bad," and the Snake came closer and put the pollen on the Coyote's head and the Coyote tried to eat pollen; but he had not the tongue of the Snake, so could not take it from his head. He made many attempts to reach the top of his head, putting his tongue first on one side of his nose and then on the other, but he could only reach either side of his nose. His repeated failures made the Snake laugh heartily. The Snake put his hand over his mouth, so that the Coyote should not see him laugh; he really hid his head in his body. The Coyote was not aware that the Snake discovered that he could not obtain the food. As he left the Snake's house he held his tail in his paw and shook the .rattle; and the Snake cried, "Oh companion! I am so afraid of you!" but in reality the Snake shook with laughter. The Coyote, returning to his house, said to himself, "I was such a fool; the Snake had much food to eat and I would not take it. Now I am very hungry," and he went out in search of food.

ESKIMO STORY OF OWL AND RAVEN

Owl and Raven were close friends. One day Raven made a new dress, dappled black and white, for Owl. Owl, in return, made for Raven a pair of Whalebone boots and then began to make for her a white dress. When Owl wanted to fit the dress, Raven hopped about and would not sit still. Owl became very angry and said, "If I fly over you with a blubber lamp, don't jump." Raven continued to hop about. At last Owl became very angry and emptied the blubber lamp over the new white dress. Raven cried, "Qaq! Qaq!" Ever since that day Raven has been black all over.

PIT RIVER STORY OF THE
CREATION OF MANKIND

Silver-Fox and Coyote lived together. Silver-Fox gathered some Service Berry sticks and whittled them down, working all night. The shavings were to be made into common People. The finished sticks were to be warriors and chiefs. About Sunset the next day he was ready to make them alive. They turned into People. Then Silver-Fox sent them away, some in one direction and some in another. Then he and Coyote had a big feast.

But Coyote also wanted to make People, so he did everything he had seen Silver-Fox do. He gathered some Service Berry sticks and whittled them down, working all night. About Sunset the next day he was ready to make them alive. They turned into People. But right away Coyote ran after some of the women, and after a long chase caught them. But as soon as he touched them, they turned back into shavings.

SHASTA MYTH OF HOW OLD MAN
ABOVE CREATED THE WORLD

Long, long ago, when the World was so new that even the Stars were dark, it was very, very flat. Chareya, Old Man Above, could not see through the dark to the new, flat Earth. Neither could he step down to it because it was so far below him. With a large stone he bored a hole in the Sky. Then through the hole he pushed down masses of Ice and Snow, until a great pyramid rose from the plain. Old Man Above climbed down through the hole he had made in the Sky, stepping from Cloud to Cloud, until he could put his foot on top of the mass of Ice and Snow.

The Sun shone through the hole in the Sky and began to melt the Ice and Snow. It made holes in the Ice and Snow. When it was soft, Chareya bored with his finger into the Earth, here and there, and planted the first Trees. Streams from the melting Snow watered the Trees and made them grow. Then he gathered the leaves which fell from the Trees and blew upon them. They became birds. He took a stick and broke it into pieces. Out of the small end he made Fishes and the Animals except the Grizzly Bear. From the big end of the stick came the Grizzly Bear, who was made master of all. Grizzly was large and strong and cunning. When the Earth was new he walked upon two feet and carried a large club. So strong was Grizzly that Old Man Above feared the creature he had made. Therefore, so that he might be safe, Chareya hollowed out the pyramid of Ice and Snow as a tipi. There he lived for thousands of snows. The Old People knew he lived there because they could see the smoke curling from the smoke hole of his tipi. When the foreigners came to our country, Old Man Above went away. There is no longer any smoke from the smoke hole. The foreigners call the tipi Mount Shasta.

NEZ PERCE STORY OF CHIPMUNK AND SNAKE

Chipmunk and Snake lived together. Their fire was one long burning log. Each of them had a stick with which to poke the fire. Chipmunk poked the fire: "U ya had ya ha." Snake poked it. "Winter" was the noise he made. When the log was burned through the middle, it would be Spring. Chipmunk was hurrying it to make Spring come quicker. Snake was trying to delay it because he wanted Winter. The only time they ceased arguing was when they slept. At dawn, as soon as they woke up they took up the stick. Suddenly, the Chipmunk said, "I'll go outside and see."

She went out the door. Already the ground was clear of Snow. Small blades of Grass showed through. She nibbled them. She went in again and took up her stick to poke the fire. Snake said, "Is it clear yet?" "No, there is still Snow on the ground." Then Snake repeated, "Winter." Suddenly she said, "You smell of green grass." "No, it's that mat you smell. I just turned it over."

Outside all was green. "Tsatapi," spoke Snake. "Ya, ya," said Chipmunk. Patsatsa, Chipmunk ran out. Snake said, "My! She does smell of green grass!"

Then he went out. The ground was clear. Sun was shining. Snake ate Grass and curled himself up on the ground.

The end of my road.

KIOWA LEGEND OF WOLF BOY

There was a camp of Kiowa. There were a young man, his wife, and his brother. They set out by themselves to look for game. This young man would leave his younger brother and his wife in camp and go out to look for game. Every time his brother would leave, the boy would go to a high hill nearby and sit there all day until his brother returned. One time before the boy went as usual to the hill, his sister-in-law said, "Why are you so lonesome? Let us be sweethearts." The boy answered, "No, I love my brother and I would not want to do that." She said, "Your brother would not know. Only you and I would know. He would not find out." "No, I think a great deal of my brother. I would not want to do that."

One night as they all went to sleep the young woman went to where the boy used to sit on the hill. She began to dig. She dug a hole deep enough so that no one would ever hear him. She covered it by placing a hide over the hole, and she made it look natural so nobody would notice it. She went back to the camp and lay down. Next day the older brother went hunting and the younger brother went to where he used to sit. The young woman watched him and saw him drop out of sight. She went up the hill and looked into the pit and said, "I guess you will want to make love now. If you are willing to be my sweetheart I will let you out. If not, you will have to stay in there until you die." The boy said, "I will not." After the young man returned home, he asked his wife where was his little brother. She said, "I have not seen him since you left, but he went up on the hill." That night as they went to bed the young man said to his wife that he thought he heard a voice somewhere. She said, "It is only the Wolves that you hear." The young man did not sleep all night. He said to his wife, "You must have scolded him to make him go; he may have gone back home." "I did not say anything to him. Every day when you go hunting he goes to that hill." Next day they broke camp and went back to the main camp to see if he was there. He was not there. They concluded that he had died. His father and mother cried over him.

The boy staying in the pit was crying; he was starving. He looked up and saw something. A Wolf was pulling off the old hide. The Wolf said, "Why are you down there?" The boy told him what had happened, that the woman had caused him to be in there. The Wolf said, "I will get you out. If I get you out, you will be my son." He heard the Wolf howling. When he looked up again, there was a pack of Wolves. They started to dig in the side of the pit until they reached him and he could crawl out. It was very cold. As night came on, the Wolves lay all around him and on top of him to keep him warm. Next morning the Wolves asked what he ate. He said he ate meat. So the Wolves went out and found Buffalo and killed a calf and brought it to him. The boy had nothing to butcher it with, so the Wolf tore the calf to pieces for the boy to get out what he wanted. The boy ate till he was full. The Wolf who got him out asked the others if they knew where there was a flint knife. One said that he had seen one somewhere. He told him to go and get it. After that, when the Wolves killed for him he would butcher for himself. Some time after that, a man from the camp was out hunting, and he observed a pack of Wolves and among them a man. He rode up to see if he could recognize this man. He got near enough only to see that it was a man. He returned to camp and told the People he had seen a man with some Wolves. They considered that it might be the young man who had been lost some time before. The camp had killed off all the Buffalo. Some young men after butchering had left to kill Wolves (as they did after killing Buffalo). They noticed a young man with the pack of Wolves. The Wolves saw the men, and they ran off. The young man ran off with them. Next day the whole camp went out to see who the young man was. They saw the Wolves and the young man with them. They pursued the young man. They overtook him and caught him. He bit at them like a Wolf. After they caught him, they heard the Wolves howling in the distance. The young man told his father and brother to free him so he could go to hear what the Wolves were saying. They said if they loosed him, he would not come back. However, they loosed him and he went out and met the Wolves. Then he returned to camp. "How came you to be among them?" asked the

147

father and brother. He told how his sister-in-law had dug the hole, and he fell in, and the Wolves had gotten him out, and he had lived with them ever since. The Wolf had said to him that someone must come in his place, that they were to wind Buffalo gut around the young woman and send her. The young woman's father and mother found out what she had done to the boy. They said to her husband that she had done wrong and for him to do as the Wolf had directed and take her to him and let him eat her up. So the husband of the young woman took her and wound the guts around her and led her to where the Wolf had directed. The whole camp went out to see, and the Wolf Boy said, "Let me take her to my father wolf." Then he took her and stopped at a distance and howled like a Wolf, and they saw Wolves coming from everywhere. He said to his Wolf father, "Here is the one you were to have in my place." The Wolves came and tore her up.

ORIGIN OF THE SACRED ARROW

A Story from the Gros Ventres

Charred Body had his origin in the Skies. There was a big village up there and this man was a great hunter. He used to go out and bring in Buffalo, Elk, Antelope until the Buffalo became scarce—they scattered out far from the village. So one day he told his close relatives, "The Buffalo seem to have gone far away from here, and I am tired of hunting them so long. Some day they may multiply again, but now I am going to build a mound to sit on and look over the country. He made a practice of going up to this mound at intervals of three or four days to survey the land and listen to its sounds. One day toward nightfall he heard Buffalo bellowing. He was excited. He could not tell from what direction the sound came. He was in the habit of changing himself into an arrow shot from a bow and thus making in one day a journey such as a man would ordinarily make in ten days. The next day he went out to the mound, changed himself into an arrow, and went in every direction, but found no buffalo. Back on the mound he again heard the Buffalo, and they seemed so close that he thought it strange he could not place them. The next day when he went out to the mound he took an arrow and stuck it into the ground, and as the ground opened up a crack, he worked the hole a little larger and, to his surprise, could look down through the hole. There below he saw Buffalo as if the Chokecherries are half ripe, and the bulls were fighting and bellowing. This was the sound he had heard.

He went back to his lodge and told his relatives that he had seen the Buffalo, thousands upon thousands, but since, if he went down below, it would be difficult to pack the meat back, he decided to go down ahead and build a dwelling and his brothers and sisters-in-law should follow afterwards. They could themselves see by looking down the hole that there would be Buffalo enough for all.

The chief of the village was named Long Arm. He was regarded as a holy man. He usually knew what was going on from day to day. Charred Body told him of the land he had found, so beautiful and plentiful in game. Charred Body said, "I want to leave this place and go down there, but it will not be possible to pack the meat back up here or to drive the Buffalo up here from the Earth. So I shall go down there to live and take with me all those near relatives of mine who are bound to me like the thread of the Spiderweb, and we will make our home there." Long Arm said neither yes nor no; he uttered no word. The hunter went back to the hole, transformed himself into an arrow and flew through the air to Earth.

He came down so swiftly that as he landed on the ground the arrow point struck the Earth, and it seemed as if he were stuck there for good. The place where he landed was near Washburn by a creek. Some People call it Turtle, but we call it Charred Body Creek. There was an evil spirit in the creek whose moccasin tops were like a flame of fire so that when he went through the forest the Cottonwood Trees would burn down. He would undo the flap of the moccasin when he went to Windward and wave it back and forth over the ground; when he tied it up again the flame ceased. This man feared the man from Heaven lest he establish villages or take away his land or even kill him, so he caused a Windstorm and set the Prairie on fire and the flames charred the arrow here and there. Hence the name "Charred Body" is derived. Since the arrow could not pull himself out, he decided to make a spring; thus he loosened himself. So he decreed that the spring would flow as long as the World should last; you can see even today where the spring is.

Charred Body established thirteen lodges. First, he looked about and found a good site and established one lodge, then another, until he had thirteen built. Then he went back into the Heavens and told what had happened and how the old man with flame about the foot had tried to kill him, how he had found the spring and how good the game was. He made it sound very attractive. He said that he went by the arrow and hence could take down only as many families as there were parts to the arrow. He would take his nearest relatives only, with their children. The groove at the end of the arrow to put the string into was one lodge. The three feathers were regarded as lodges; that made four. The two sinews bound about it were two others, making six. The three points of the arrowhead were three other lodges, making nine. The three grooves circling around the arrow in a spiral made twelve. The arrow itself was the thirteenth: there were thirteen lodges all told. The spiral is considered as Lightning; hence the arrow's power. If it does not come in contact with a bone, it will penetrate the Buffalo right through.

He called his nearest relatives and embraced them, and in embracing them he gave them the power of the arrow and encouraged them to follow him. First, he went down, then all came after and he assigned them lodges. When they first came down, the Mysterious bodies down there knew that he was also Mysterious and tried to kill him, but when he pulled himself out (of the hole made by the arrowpoint) they knew that they had no power against him. Before coming down, the People had made preparations and they brought seeds of Corn, Beans and so forth and began to plant Corn on the ground by the river and to build scaffolds for drying the Corn and the meat. So they lived happily for a long time. You can see today the remains of their thirteen villages, but obscured by high water and the ploughing farmers. I have heard that People have found arrowheads in the thirteen villages.

After a number of years, First Creator happened to come to the village. He asked some boys playing outside who was the chief. They showed him the way to the large lodge in the center of which was Charred Body's lodge. He asked Charred Body how he came there and Charred Body told him. He said it was well and that he wished to make friends with Charred Body; when there were two they could talk matters over and act more effectively (than one), three were even better, but two were strong. They must therefore love one another. So they became friends, ate and talked together, and First Creator stayed in the lodge several nights before he went on again.

When he came back, he reported that there was a big village East of them whose chief had a beautiful daughter. It was the custom in that village after noon for the maidens to go along a wide path to the river for water and for the men to line up along the path and do their courting. The married women would go along the path outside the row. When a young girl came opposite a man who liked her, he would clear his throat and if the girl looked at him, it was a good sign. The next day he would ask a drink, and if she gave him a drink it was a still better sign. So People took notice, and if a girl gave a man a drink it became a matter of gossip, the parents came together to find out whether the two were industrious and able to run a household, and if everything was favorable, they were married. Now the chief's daughter had a strong will and never looked at the young men. When they tried to catch her eye she paid them no attention. "Now, my friend," said First Creator, "You are handsome, not too slender, too tall or too short. Your hair is long and beautiful. No one could find a blemish upon you. You would certainly make a hit with the girl, so let us go over and try our luck. If you can get her and be son-in-law to a great chief, you will be a renowned man."

So it was agreed, and when they came to the edge of the village to a place where the moles had dug up a mound of Earth, they began to dress themselves up. Charred Body mixed the dirt with water and daubed mud across his chin from ear to ear and upon his cheeks, brought his hair together in a big pompadour in front and stuck a plume in at the place where he tied it up. This feather the wind waved to and fro. His robe he wore open with his bow and arrows inside. Today we say of a person who combs his hair to the side in a pompadour that "he wears his hair like Charred Body."

They went to a certain lodge in the village and were kindly received. When First Creator told them who Charred Body was they said, "We have heard about him and how he had a beautiful land in the Skies and liked the country down here." When he said that they had come courting the People said, "It is well." They went down to the path by the river and stood opposite each other and Coyote which is another name for First Creator, said he would give a signal when the chief's daughter came so that his friend would pay no attention to the others. She came dressed in tanned white Deerskin with a robe of Elkskin from which the hair had been scraped, light and pliable as a plume. Charred Body stepped in front of her and she swerved. He turned also and she swerved again. When he was almost in front of her he said, "I wish to drink out of your cup." She said, "What you have done is not according to our custom; you should not have moved from the line but just cleared your throat, and I shall give you no drink!" Do you make those streaks across your face in imitation of the charring?" He was angry, took out his bow and arrows and, as she turned to flee, shot her twice in the back and killed her. A tumult arose and the two visitors fled back to their own village.

Coyote warned Charred Body that he had done an evil deed and that this would not be the end of it. The chief was not likely to sit still and do nothing. He had owned the land before Charred Body came there, and Charred Body must therefore build barricades and protect himself. Charred Body paid little attention to him. "I go by the arrow and it can pierce through them," he said. "Even then," said Coyote, "You are often out hunting, and while you are away they may send out scouts and kill all in the village. More than one village may combine against you. You may think that you can fight them single-handed, but you have done a bad deed and this will cause your mind to stray, and while it is occupied with other things, they will overcome you. So whatever you do, don't let anything distract your attention or you may be destroyed."

Day after day, Charred Body would go and sit on the top of a hill where he had a mound and look over in the direction of the village where he had committed the crime. He told the young men to cut up sticks for arrows and sort them out into bundles and put them under his bed. When they came back, the sticks would be already made into arrows. Soon all the young men were supplied. But he was always in deep thought, first because of the crime he had committed and second lest the village come against him. One day Coyote offered to go over to the village and find out what they were planning. He said that he would take Cornballs and Pemmican and spread them on the outskirts of the village, and if anyone was wounded he would give him the food and tell him it was Good Medicine for wounds. He would pretend that he had left Charred Body because of his crime. He met them on the way in such numbers as completely to surround the village. All who had children remained. When he had passed them, on the other side of the hill, he saw Meadowlark and sent him on an errand to fly to Charred Body on his mound and tell him to prepare four barricades as a great force was coming against him to avenge his crime. Meadowlark carried the message, but as soon as Charred Body got back to the village to prepare the barricades, he forgot all about it. The enemy employed a Holy Man to make him forgetful; the Holy Man raised his hand against him and Charred Body forgot what was to happen. Three times Coyote sent Meadowlark with the message, and three times Charred Body forgot it as soon as he reached the village. The fourth time Meadowlark told him to make some sign on his body to attract attention. Charred Body stuck a bunch of Grass in his hair and went back to the village. Again he forgot the message. He went into his lodge, but his head itched; he told his wife to scratch his head, and she found the Grass and said, "This is the cause of your itching!" He gave a groan and sent word to the People that the next day the enemy would come against them; they must prepare a barricade, get arrows ready and be brave even to death. He went out and cut Bog Brush, put it under his bed, and commanded it to turn to June Bushes.

153

When he took it out, it had become June Bush, and he peeled the bark and made more arrows.

Coyote (in the enemy's camp) said, "You have been sending out scouts but their reports are not clear. I will go myself to see what is going on." He started on a run, fell with his foot out of joint, and claimed it was too painful to put in again and that he was now too disabled to fight with them in the attack against the village. He said, "Way down on the river they are performing rites for Medicine, so I will go there and bring back Corn-balls and Pemmican." He caused an announcement to be sounded at a distance (He must have been a ventriloquist) which said—

"All you who have Medicine Bags and Mysteries, come and join in this ceremony to be performed."

He told them that he had an adopted son in the enemy's camp who was Mysterious in battle. He could not be shot by an arrow and they must keep away from him. "You will find him dressed with a bladder covering his head daubed with white clay. His body will have streaks length-wise and crosswise. His quiver is a Coyote's hide. He will wound many of you, but I will bring a hide for the wounded to lie on and feed them with Cornballs and Pemmican." As soon as he was out of sight, he threw away his crutch, set his foot again, turned into a Coyote and ran around another way into the village and became a man again. He asked after Charred Body and learned that he was making arrows. But a weasel had just been in to see Charred Body, and it had scattered and trampled arrows. Charred Body had been angry and struck four times at the Weasel, the fourth time it ran out and Charred Body after it. "I told him whatever happened, not to allow anything to distract him!" said Coyote. "But never mind, I am here. Don't turn into women!" Charred Body's sister was at this time with child, and Coyote told her to go inside a cellar-hole, and he would cover her over so that she would not be burned.

When the battle took place, there were four among the enemy's band who had supernatural power. One had no head, but only a big mouth from shoulder to shoulder into which he sucked his enemies; another was an old woman with a basket which, wherever she turned, sucked in People or Birds of the air; a third was the man with flaming moccasins; a fourth was a Beaver (called Tail-With-a-Knife) whose tail was sharp on both sides. These four helped the enemy. Tail-With-a-knife chopped down the barricade, Flame-Around-His-Ankle encircled the village and set it on fire. Coyote was in the thick of the battle dressed as he had described. When he saw that all was lost, he disappeared in a cloud of smoke.

Meanwhile, Charred Body was still chasing Yellow Weasel. It seems that there was a transformation of the Earth so that Charred Body found himself far to the North. Yellow Weasel said, "Look back and see your own village!" He looked and saw the smoke. He wanted to get back as quickly as possible. His eyesight would be too slow, for he would have to stop at the end of each sight, so he used his thinking power, transformed himself into thought, and wished himself back at his village. There he found the place in flames.

Now after the battle, the enemy had withdrawn and were relating their exploits. It seemed to them as if Coyote had fought in the Battle, and Coyote heard their word as he came limping back with the hide, Cornballs, and Pemmican. An old Bear was appointed to discover whether Coyote had been in the battle. The way he did this was to lift up his paw and put it upon a Person, then put his paw to his nose and smell it. When Coyote entered, the paw was raised to test him, but Coyote put a cornball into the paw, saying, "You greedy fellow, you want this all for yourself!" then he had the wounded brought in and laid upon the robe, and gave them Cornball and Pemmican. He said, "However wounded you may be yourselves, you have destroyed the village and enticed Charred Body away." And he said, "These People were just like relatives to me, and I want to go back there and walk through the place where young men and maidens formerly walked, and think about their sports and laughter and mourn there for them." So they consented and he went on his way.

Close to the village he saw Charred Body walking among the dead. As was the custom in those days, Coyote walked up to him, put his arm about his neck, and wept over him. Then he told him where he had hidden the sister, and they went to the cellar to see if she were alive. When they lifted up the hide she came out, but when she saw the desolation of the village she wept and the men with her. Coyote proposed that they have a lodge, to live in together. He faced the North, raised both eyes, and he said, "I wish for a lodge facing South furnished with bedding and all things necessary and with a scaffold in front." When they opened their eyes, there it stood just as Coyote had said. There was no food, so Coyote said, "There is all kinds of food on the hoof; let us go out and see what we can take." They followed up the creek and killed a Buffalo, cut it up, left the backbone, head and shoulders and took the best pieces. The kidney, backgut and liver they washed to be eaten raw. These raw parts are considered a tonic today to keep one from sickness. The woman at the lodge cooked for them. She began to slice the meat and roast the ribs close to the fire and they felt themselves at home once more.

After they had lived thus from day to day, bringing in game until there was plenty, Coyote went away to the enemy's camp to see what the People were doing, promising to return again. It is an old custom with both Mandans and Gros Ventres that when a sister is alone in a house, a brother must not enter out of respect to his sister. Only if someone else is with her is it right for him to enter. Hence Charred Body did not think it right to stay alone with his sister, so he went off hunting by day to bring in choice bits of food for her and told his sister on no account to let anyone into the house if anyone should come around asking for the door. "No one can come in if you do not take out the crossbar," he said. One day when he came back from hunting, he saw his sister standing outside looking as if she were laughing, and he took the meat and waited for her, but she did not come in. This is what had happened. While he was away on the hunt she had heard a voice crying, "Tuk, tuk, tuk! my daughter, where can the door be?" She forgot what her brother had told her and undid the door for the stranger. There entered a headless monster. He said, "Place me on the West side between the pillows." She said, "Grandfather, what will you have to eat?" He said, "The best is the fat of the stomach. When I eat this fat I must have a pregnant woman lie on her back and then I place the hot fat upon her and eat in this way." The woman was frightened and only half cooked it. He held it himself to the fire, and the flames wrapped his hands but he did not seem to feel it. He made her lie down on the floor and placed the hot fat upon her. The woman screamed and twins were born as the woman died. The monster took one by the leg and threw it into the center of the lodge and said, "Lodge center, make this boy your slave!" The other he threw into the spring and said, "Spring, take this child for yours!" Then he took the doorposts which were forked and set them outside and placed the woman against them and held out her lips with two sticks as if she were laughing. Then he gathered up all the food and was gone.

When Charred Body knew that his sister was dead, he made a burial scaffold for her and by means of a rude lattice he placed her body upon it and cried bitterly. In the evening he came home and was preparing an evening meal when he heard a wee voice from the center of the lodge say, "Brother, give me something to eat." Twice this happened; then he investigated. He cut a splinter and wrapped fat into it and, using this as a torch, he looked into the dark spot from which the voice came and found a baby boy. He brought the child to his knee. This was the child who had called him "brother" (among these People a mother's brother is called "brother," a father's brother is an "uncle").

When Coyote drifted back, he found to his amazement that their sister had been killed, and he mourned her loss. One day he said, "Can't we do something for our brother here? Let us take this baby up and wish that he grow to a certain height." This is the song that Charred Body sang: First he took Sweet Grass and smoked him; then he raised him up and sang, "I want my child to grow this high!" Coyote did the same. Charred Body raised him again and sang and he became like a boy of twelve. Coyote got up and raised him and sang, "I want my brother to be the height of a man," and he became like a boy of eighteen. And at the same time, since the boys were twins, the Spring-boy attained the same height also.

Since the boy was now grown, he was left to look after the lodge when the two went hunting, and every time this happened, Spring-boy came out and played with him. The name of Lodge-boy was A-tu-tish, which means, "Near-the-edge-of-the-lodge," and the Spring-boy was Ma-hash from Ma-ha, meaning "spring." He was dark and his brother was light and a little taller than Spring-boy. The two men kept Buffalo tongues strung up and wondered why they disappeared so rapidly. "Are there two of you?" they asked, but the boy denied it. They had him bite the tongue, and compared the mark left by Spring-boy's teeth, and they were different. At last, Lodge-boy confessed that he had known all the time what happened when his mother was killed by the stranger and he was taken by the leg and given to the edge of the wall as a slave, and his brother had been thrown into the spring. The brother did not recall this. Spring-boy seems to have been a kind of maverick— he did not belong to anyone. He had a long tusk and lived on water creatures and was influenced by his wild life in the Spring. If anyone tried to catch him, he would tear him to pieces with his tusk. They arranged a plan to catch him. The boys used to play with gambling sticks and a round stone with a hole bored through. The men fixed up two Buffalo hides as a kind of armor with a lace down the back to hold it tight. In the game there was to be a dispute, and when the boy got down on his knees to look and see if the ring lay on the stick, Lodge-boy was to jump on his back, tangle up his hair and thrust in a stick to which a bladder was fastened. If he ran for the spring, they could catch him by the bladder. They then prepared a sweat lodge with hot stones and water ready, and transformed themselves into arrowheads. Spring-boy came trotting up, quick and agile, and encircled the lodge to see if there was anyone about. He complained of smelling his brother, but Lodge-boy told him that was because they had been there before going out hunting. He came into the lodge and was surprised to see the bladder; Lodge-boy told him it was used to separate the marrow from the bones. He asked about the sweatbath and was told it was for the men when they came home from hunting. They began to play, and when Spring-boy knelt down to see how the ring had fallen, Lodge-boy jumped upon him, wound his legs about his body, and the two boys rolled on the ground, and Spring-boy's tusk could be heard snapping at his brother. The two men dashed in, dragged him to the sweatbath and began to switch him, crying, "What kind of a person are you? You are a human being and should behave like one." Spring-boy cried out, "I am coming to myself!" They drew him out and examined his mouth, but the tusk still showed. Three times they returned him to the bath and poured water and switched his flesh; the fourth time the tusk had disappeared and he lay exhausted. So they fastened up his hair and thrust a stick through it, to which the bladder was attached. The moment he was released he ran to the spring and jumped in, but was unable to go under because of the bladder. After the fourth time of trying to get under water, he surrendered. They gave him water to drink, inserted two fingers into his mouth, and he vomited up all the water creatures which he had eaten and was restored to the ways of men.

Now there were four occupants of the lodge. Several days passed before Spring-boy came entirely to his senses. The men he was accustomed to call "Your brothers," and one day he said, "I wish you would tell your brothers to make a bow and arrows, two painted red and two black for me and the same for you." Lodge-boy said, "You always speak indirectly to our brothers, but we are twins. We are from the Sky. There is a big village where we came from. The chief is Long-Arm and he knows everything that is going on and is called a Holy Man. When our brother Charred Body wanted to come down here to this Earth, he asked for permission, and although Long-Arm said neither yes nor no, he took it upon himself to come down here, and this had led to the destruction of all our relatives. But the Holy Man knows what is going on below there. Our brother and Coyote went courting and our brother killed the chief's daughter. So there was a fight, but our other brother Coyote stowed our mother

159

away in a cellar, and I knew all these things that were going on. One of the formidable men who took part in the fight was a monster with no head but a big mouth from shoulder to shoulder who lives around the bend of the creek. He killed our mother, and I knew all about it and thought that you did too." Spring-boy said that, through living in the spring, he had forgotten all these things. The arrows he had asked for the men made for the boys. Then they went through a ceremonial and Spring-boy said that these arrows, one painted black and one red for each boy, were to be kept sacred and used in emergency, and they were to have other arrows for daily use.

One day as they walked near their mother's grave, Spring-boy proposed that they use the sacred Arrows to bring their mother to life. The two boys had watched the arrow rite. When the two hunters had gone out before Sunrise, they took down the arrows from the quiver, burned Sweet Grass and sang the arrow song. They did the same for the bow, resting one end of the bow on Buffalo-bull manure while they strung it. Then they went where their mother lay. Spring-boy placed one arrow in position, sang the arrow song and let it fly. They could see it go up into the Sky like a streak of flame. As it fell the boys cried, "Mother! Mother! Look out! The arrow is going to hit you!" The figure began to move. Spring-boy sent the third arrow, and this time the mother sat up. Lodge-boy shot the fourth arrow and the mother yawned and stretched her arms. She said, "I must have slept a long time; I feel tired." The boy set up a ladder to the scaffold and the mother came down to embrace them and said, "My spirit has remained here and was about to return to my People when you sent the arrow. You are motherless and it is a joy that you have done this for me and my Spirit has returned to my body." When they returned to the lodge, she noticed at once how the meat was cut in strings, not in the nice flat pieces that a woman is accustomed to cut. So she ate a hearty meal. In time came Charred Body and Coyote home from hunting, and as Charred Body threw down his pack he recognized his sister and they all cried for joy, and she told him how her Spirit had pitied the children and had lingered about until it had been restored to her body by means of the Sacred Arrows.

Charred Body warned the boys that although they had more supernatural power than he had, they must never lie down to take a nap without setting four arrows in the ground, one at each of the Four Directions, and lying within the arrows with the head resting to the North or to the West (for even an ordinary person should never rest his head to the South or to the East) and they must place their moccasins to point toward the West, not toward the East, because all the Spirits go to the East. Among both Mandan and Gros Ventre a dead person is always placed with head to the East.

One day the boys went out to survey the country and came to an old man whom they knew to be Flame-Around-the-Ankle. They stood side-by-side and asked him to give them a demonstration of his power. He loosened the strings of his moccasin, let the flap fall, and they saw flames leaping. They asked him to run about a Cottonwood Tree; he trotted about a tree; he trotted about it in a circle and ran about a Cottonwood Tree; he trotted about it in a circle and the tree fell over in flame. Spring-boy asked to try the moccasin. "Surely you may!" He ran about a tree, then back to his brother, and then all at once he circled the old man and burned him to ashes. Then the boys ran shouting and laughing home to their mother pretending that Flame was chasing them.

Again the boys wandered out, and as they followed up the creek, Lodge-boy said, "Brother, right in that dense timber on the side of the hill lives the monster without a head who carried his mouth on his shoulders. Let us go over and have a look at him!" They approached cautiously; then, turning into Chickadees, they flew over the monster's den and, perching on a tree, began to call. They filled a water bag made out of a Buffalo paunch and had heated a stone red-hot and caused it to shrink so that they could carry it in the curve of a stick. They first got a big stone, then went into their Mysteries and rubbed it until it became small. To this day, when we heat a stone red-hot for the sweatbath we call it "The Chickadees' stone." When the monster came out and opened his mouth to swallow them, they dropped the hot stone. As it went down his gullet, he thought, "It must be their claws that scratch so!"

161

"Enlarge, enlarge!" called the boys to the stone. He snatched the water-bag to drink and they said, "Enlarge yourself and hold more water!" The water began to boil in his stomach and the monster burst. The boys burned up his lodge, skinned him and placed the skin on Spring-boy and ran back to the lodge as if the monster were after them. Its body was black; it had two tails and claws like a wild-cat's. The mother was so delighted with the victory that she danced for joy, so from that time they dance when one wins a victory, generally the women but sometimes both women and men.

There was another mysterious spot where an old woman sucked People into a basket hung upon a post. They asked her to demonstrate her power. The woman was afraid of them, knowing that they had supernatural power. A flock of Birds was passing; she waved her basket to and fro and then to the side, and brought down the Birds into the basket. Spring-boy asked her to let him try. He took the basket, waved it as the old woman had done, and drew the woman into the basket. Thus he killed her. Great was the joy of their mother when he brought her home dead in the basket.

All those Mysterious beings lived in the vicinity of Turtle Creek, which the People called Charred Body Creek, just about a couple miles East of Washburn.

Some time later the boys heard about the Beaver-with-Tail-Like-a-Knife, who could tear open the Earth with a blow. Even today you can see where his tail struck the Earth; it looks something like a shellhole. The Beaver had sharp ears, but the boys lay in wait for him and Lodge-boy shot an arrow through his head as if it were a big Pumpkin. When the Beaver was dead they cut off the tail and brought it home.

These were the beings who lived about Washburn and had allied themselves with the enemy. There might be others living at a distance, but those who lived near were all destroyed. So their mothers' brothers urged them to attempt no more such exploits, and the boys agreed that their mother's safety was now assured. They wished, however, to wander further into the country, so they told their mother not to worry if they did not return, and took their leave.

While all this was going on down below, the People in the Sky became uneasy lest the boys who had killed so many Mysterious beings below come up to the Sky and kill them. So they held a council and asked Long Arm to bring Spring-boy, who was dark and reckless, up into the Sky and put him to death. Long Arm told them he saw nothing wrong with the boys and did not wish their death. They belonged to their own People. The father and mother had had hard treatment and they had avenged themselves justly. But the People cried out all the more against Spring-boy, and Long-Arm accordingly used his magic power to throw the boys into a sleep in the Moon. That is the origin of daytime napping. The boys grew sleepy and, remembering their brother's instruction, they set up the arrows and placed their moccasins Westward with the bow and arrow beside them and went to sleep. Sun cast His direct rays upon them, making them drowsy. Then Long-Arm reached down to Earth to where Spring-boy lay and picked him up and carried him up into the air.

The People arranged for Spring-boy's death. They dug a hole and the chief bade them set up a tree there with forked branches, but all feared to cut the tree lest Spring-boy come out alive and destroy the one who cut it down. They tried to persuade the women to cut it, but they said, "If you are afraid, how much more should we weak women fear!" Then the chief decreed that a hermaphrodite should cut the tree on which Spring-boy was to be hung. As soon as Long-Arm brought Spring-boy up, the people rushed upon him and beat him until he was nearly dead. They had already prepared the form of death he was to die. A rawhide was stretched across the arms of the crotch and wound around the tree while it was wet; when dry it was much tighter. The boy's arms were lanced next to the bone and his feet through the cords, and rawhide strips were run through and brought right around the tree so that he hung by wrists and feet. After he was securely tied, they raised the tree and set it into the hole. They had put an Antelope hide, tanned soft, about his waist so that it hung below the knee, this on account of the number of women present. Over the tree they erected a kind of bower, the cross-pieces of which were inserted into the rawhide at the top of the tree. The whole was covered with leaves. All this time the boy said nothing, but now he spoke: "I have been delivered into your hands and I do not think evil of you, for my mother was one of you and I do not wish to destroy you. If this were done by an enemy it would not be strange, but as you are my own People, it does not seem right for you to cause me this agony. But you need not fear me." The People did not answer; they could accuse him of nothing. (Today they do not put up a man, but they kill a Buffalo and cut a strip along the back leaving the tail and raise it as if the Buffalo were angry and on the other end they put the Buffalo skull without the horns and hang this up to represent the Buffalo. They set up a bower about it and gather up the Earth into a ridge on the North side and stick Bog Bush into it, beginning at each end and leaving a place vacant between. They used to leave this space so that when the boy died his body could be laid down. Today they lay there the sacred Weasels or other Animals used in the ceremony. To the ridge of the West side sits the Holy Man in a robe worn hair side out.)

For three days Spring-boy hung on the tree, then he began to get weary. Now when Lodge-boy awoke from sleep and could not see his twin brother, he was alarmed and, taking the shape of a flaming arrow, he flew over the Earth even to both sides of the Ocean, calling the name of Spring-boy and, finding nothing, he returned to the place from which his brother had vanished. There he lay looking up into the Sky, when he saw a streak of light at the point where Spring-boy had been taken through. Flying through the air he entered at the same place and saw that the land was empty where all the multitude had flocked after Spring-boy. So he changed himself into a little boy with shaggy, uncombed hair and a big belly, who was nevertheless old enough to talk, and followed the People to the field where they were massed about the bower. At the edge of the field was a lodge in which an old woman was sitting. He asked for food and the old woman adopted him as a grandson; he waited upon her and she was glad. All this time they could hear singing going on in the bower. He said, "Grandmother, what is going on there?" So she related the whole story of Charred Body's descent to Earth and his crime and how the People feared the boys and especially Spring-boy because he was dark and reckless and how they had cut the tree and what Spring-boy had said about his own People destroying him. "This is the third day and night and tomorrow at noon they will place his body on the ridge in the bower," she said, and she told how they danced in the morning, at noon and in the evening and sang ten songs in rotation, and how they could not stop dancing until the ten songs were sung or extend the dance beyond them. For a drum they used a long rawhide without hair which they beat with sticks, and the dancers whistled to the rhythm of the song. The best singers beat with sticks on four small round drums of wood covered with skin on one side like a tambourine, which were to indicate the four nights of the dance. It was difficult to remember the order of the songs correctly. These four led the singing and the whole society must sing with the leader.

So the little boy asked the woman to take him to the bower. At the door she picked him up so that he could see and asked the People to make way for her and her grandchild. They were singing a song and dancing with whistles in their mouths and shouting to the man on the tree, "be a man for one day more." As Spring-boy looked about and saw his brother, a light shone about his head and he began to move and stretch as if he had been strengthened. Lodge-boy, fearing he would be recognized, begged the old woman to take him outside. That evening they heard again the sound of songs and dancing. An announcer came through the village warning the young men and maidens not to sleep that night, but to keep watch lest Lodge-boy come to his brother's rescue, for the Holy Man thought when he saw the light that Spring-boy's brother must have come there to strengthen him. "My grandchild, did you hear what he was saying? He says that Lodge-boy is here!" said the grandmother. There she was, speaking to Lodgeboy in person!

Rows of People slept at the bower to watch the place. When the old woman was snoring, the boy got up, took some Buffalo fat and went over to the place. Some slept, others were talking and moving about. It seemed impossible to reach his brother. He changed himself into a great Spider and crawled up to the post where his brother was. With the fat he greased the wounds, then he cut the thongs and they came down to the ground. There he found a stone hatchet with eyes, the very one used to cut the pole, and the Holy Man knew all about it but could do nothing because the two together were too powerful for him. Long-Arm went and placed his hand over the hole by which they passed through so as to catch them. Spring-boy made a motion with the hatchet as if to cut it off at the wrist and said, "This is the second time your hand has committed a crime, and it shall be a sign to the People on Earth." So it is today that we see the hand in the Heavens. Some People call it Orion. The belt is where they cut across the wrist; the thumb and fingers also show; they are hanging down like a hand. "The Hand Star" it is called.

The boys went back to the place where they had left the arrows sticking in the ground, pulled out the arrows, and went home to their mother. She told them that the People in the Sky were like Birds; they could fly about as they pleased. Since the opening was made in the Heavens, they may come down to Earth. If a person lives well on Earth, his Spirit takes flight to the Skies and is able to come back again and be reborn, but if he does evil, he will wander about the Earth and never leave it for the Skies. A baby born with a slit in the ear at the place where ear-rings are hung is such a reborn child from the People in the Skies.

While the People sang and danced about Spring-boy in the bower, he had the ten songs learned, and he instituted the ceremony on Earth in order to get power from the Skies. In place of a man's body he told them to use a Buffalo skin. They should hang themselves at the wrist and tie cords to their bodies and suspend the cords to the nose of the Buffalo skull and hang there just as he had been suspended. He said, "The person who performs the cere-mony in memory of me may have the picture of the Sun on his chest and the half Moon on his back. The Sun causes things to grow and the Moon causes the moisture. Since I have named the Buffalo hide as my own body, the Buffalo shall range where People are. In regard to the tree, the maidens of the village must be examined, and one who is a virgin shall cut down the tree and a young man, brave and unblemished, shall help her haul the tree to the dance place. In course of time they shall marry and their seed multiply so that the People may live and not go out of existence."

The Gros Ventre (Hidatsa) People have believed in those rites. You can see where I have been lanced across the chest in those ceremonies. They took hold of the flesh, lanced it through with a sharp knife and thrust a Juneberry stick cut about four inches long and wet with saliva through the lance-thrust and tied it with buckskin so that it would not slip off, then pushed back the chest. It hurt at first but not later. As I ran around (after being suspended to the tree) my feet would leave the Earth and I was suspended in Air. Above my head I heard sounds like those made by Spirits and I believed them to be the Spirits of my helpers.

The chief celebrant at these ceremonies has usually killed an enemy. He cuts off the hand, brings it home, skins it, removes the bones, and fills it with sand. After it dries he empties out the sand and wears it at the back of the neck, where it flaps up and down as he dances. It represents Long Arm's hand. He wears a hand at the back and a white Antelope hide about his loins just as Spring-boy wore it. Every night he uses the ridge of Earth as a pillow. Since Spring-boy hung on the tree three days, and it took a fourth to escape back to the lodge, the ceremony lasts four days. The men lanced have to fast. The man who sleeps with his head on the ridge is naked and sage is strewn. The ceremony is called the Sundance in some tribes, but among the Hidatsa it is the "Hide-beating."

The Boys were worried for their mother's safety and the mother for that of the boys, so they sent the two older men and the mother to join the People in the Sky and take back the hatchet and give it to the owner. The boys promised their mother to stay below and help the People on Earth in Spirit as long as the World lasted and at the end of the World she would see them again. The greasing of Spring-boy's wounds by Lodge-boy was the origin of the use of grease and tallow to heal wounds.

UNKNOWN ONE, SON OF TWO MEN

The twins now went by the name of Two Men. Their former lodge was abandoned and they roamed at will all over the country and made a permanent camp on the West side of the Missouri by Knife River. There you can see the ruins of the old village. The Two Men would come back to the village for ceremonial rites, then they would be off again. When a young man of the village performed such a ceremony, if he had a young wife he would call together all the men of the clan and deliver her to them in turn. Meanwhile they sang the Holy songs and prayed for blessings upon their daughter-in-law. Thus these Two Men were given their son's wife and they took her out and sang songs and, without having any intercourse with her, she bore them a son. As he grew, Two Men visited him in spirit as often as they could until he attained manhood. They drove the Buffalo within hunting distance of the village and caused Rain to bring good Corn crops. Thus one day his father was killed in an Indian war and his mother died through miscarriage. Before dying she called in a man whom she had adopted as a brother because, though not a blood relative, he belonged to the same clan, and entrusted her son to him as a brother and her mother to him as a mother. The man accepted the charge and the woman died. She was her mother's only child. From this time on the man looked after the boy and loved him dearly. His lodge was placed close to the grandmother's, and if they went on a Winter's hunt, their camps were always beside each other. The two never quarreled; hence it is a rule that when two camps are beside each other, there is to be no quarreling or backbiting between them.

From time to time they went hunting, as the custom was, or made gardens. Sometimes before the Winter hunt the women and old men would recount the deeds of the hunters and compare their ability to find a helping Spirit or to endure bravely the torture of hanging themselves over a cliff. Then, pipe in hand, they would proceed to the lodge of some warrior who had shown himself brave and give him the charge of the Winter camp for that year.

One year the leader decided to place the Winter camp

near the mouth of the Yellowstone. The people harvested their Corn and stored into cellars what Corn and Squash they could not carry. In those days, nine varieties of Corn were known, differing in color or in hardness of grain, but some of these varieties have today disappeared. Almost up to today it was the custom for heralds to go through the village four days before the start and announce the departure. In those days they depended upon Dogs for transportation and the Dogs were well fed and cared for. They were harnessed with a strap of soft fur cut from the Buffalo where the fur is thickest and fastened to poles on each side. Almost over the back was a round withe bent in a circle to which were fastened rods as in basketwork, and to this luggage was fastened. This year they made camp at Beaver Creek (on the South side of the river). Below this creek is a creek called Bear-dancing creek where there is a big meadow, like a river flat, and here they made their fourth camp.

Unknown One was now grown to be a young man and was a good hunter for his age. As they came up the river, he was successful in killing Deer, Elk and other game so that his brother was well provided. One night he came in with only a small portion of the game he had killed and said to his grandmother, "On our way up I went in advance of the camp and saw a few herds to be sure, but the bulls looked scabby. I think it is going to be poor hunting and propose that you and I go home and I will provide for you through the Winter. But let us not tell my brother anything." So the next day he delayed starting until the camp had gone over the hill and then the two packed up and returned to the village. At a certain place where a man eloping with a girl had tried to shoot a rabbit and always missed it, hence called "The place where the man missed the Jack Rabbit," they could look over the whole village and from one hut they saw smoke rising. The boy said, "Grandmother, there must be someone remaining in the village." That must be the man who broke up the gambling-stick. I have heard that although he is only a middle-aged man he has been poisoned and cannot use his legs." It was in fact this man; he had remained with his wife and daughter, a girl of marriageable age. She ran out joyfully to meet them and the young man shared his game—the ham of the

Deer, a rib, and such pieces also as are eaten raw. They insisted that the two must share their lodge, the cornmeal was already cooked, and bullhide was placed for the old lady to sit upon.

Early next morning at dawn Unknown One rose and went hunting. About daybreak he came to a river where the antelope crossed, killed four and carried back the parts eaten raw and as many ribs as he could carry. In those days they had a big log of wood burning all night covered with ashes and the ashes were brushed away to kindle a fire in the morning. The old man was overjoyed—"I had thought that we would make snares and catch Snowbirds, but now we are to be provided for the whole Winter," he said. Toward Spring the old man proposed to his wife that as they liked the young man, he should become their son-in-law. The wife consented. They proposed the match to the old woman, promising to look after her until the day of her death. She told her grandson of the proposal, but he refused to consent—"I should be the laughing-stock of the People if I should marry before performing any warrior's deed!" The old woman begged him to consider her loneliness, but he refused to yield. Three times the proposal was made, three times he rejected it. The fourth time was the last chance. The old lady sat by the fire mending. She told him how old she was and how she could not live much longer, how his own mother would wish the match, and even threatened suicide unless he would marry the girl; so rather than this happen he promised to marry. The old people rejoiced at the news. All was prepared and there was a marriage. The young girl loved the man dearly, as he was a handsome fellow, and she herself was a beauty. Her father gave to his daughter for his son-in-law his Eagle-tail ornament made of twelve feathers, and the young man was well pleased with it and hung it up in its case.

One day as he was out hunting, he shot a Deer and was skinning it when he saw two men whom he recognized as his fathers. The men told him that in order to honor their daughter-in-law, they were driving down a herd of Buffalo from the North and among them a White Buffalo out of which to prepare a robe for their daughter-in-law to hang on the scalp-pole in front of the lodge. They bade him cover the fire so that there should be no flame, muzzle the dogs so that they would not bark. He must burn incense, the wife prepared a dish of Corn cooked with fat, the father-in-law's tobacco for smoking (by greasing leaves and drying them on the fire). At night as the Stars appeared one by one in the Heavens they would come to visit the lodge. So all was done as directed and at the appointed time Two Men lifted the bullhide at the door and entered the lodge. The coals burned without flame and the lodge was dim. Unknown One took the pipe from a square of buffalo hide and passed it to Spring-boy who lit it at the coals and smoked by inhaling the Sweet Smoke; it was then cleaned out, refilled and passed to Lodge-boy. Unknown One then divided the Eagle-feathers, giving six to each, which they stuck in their hair. It is for this reason that feathers are valued today by the People. Unknown One dished out the sweet Corn and in no time they had cleaned out the pot, neglecting the meat which was there in abundance. After smoking again, the visitors advised them to bring in ice and drinking water in preparation for a heavy fog which would last four days while the Buffalo were being brought in; then they left the lodge.

Two Men had observed that the father-in-law was lame, and Spring-boy now agreed to doctor the man. They came to the Lodge a second time. Spring-boy had the fire re-kindled with split wood and water brought in. He dipped up some of the water into his mouth and gargled four times. Then he took more water into his mouth, chewed up some black medicine and, going over to the man, took hold of the leg by the ankle, lifted it up and blew the finely chewed medicine four times from the man's leg up to his hips. Something was seen twitching in the man's leg. Spring-boy reached into the instep and drew out a male bull Snake and placed it in the ashes. Lodge-boy did the same and drew out a female bull Snake from the left leg, which he laid on the ashes beside the other. He told the husband and wife to tie cords to the Snakes, spit black medicine over their legs and draw the Snakes out on the snow and leave them with their heads pointing to the West, then cleanse their hands with Sagebrush and lay Sagebrush

171

at the rear, pointing to the West. The man was now perfectly well. All that night they kept a light in the house lest the Snakes escape, and the next morning they took them far outside the village and left them on the Snow as directed. Four times the young man would have stopped to leave them, and four times the wife insisted that they should be carried farther from the village.

When the two returned they hauled the ice as directed and placed it on blocks of wood close to the door. Four days the fog lasted when they must muzzle the Dogs and keep inside. Voices were to be heard like those of Women, which were Spirit voices. After four days they could see through the smokehole that the Sky was clear. Outside they found all the scaffolds throughout the village loaded with meat, the scaffold outside their own door as well, and on the scalp-pole hung the white Buffalo hide. This the mother took down immediately to tan. Buffalo were to be seen roaming about everywhere. The old man was delighted. Day by day he went through the village to drive the Ravens and Magpies from the meat. Their own store of meat the family put away, the old grandmother helping as she could. The bones were then crushed with a stone hammer over a flat stone, the grease melted out and stored in Buffalo bladders. When Spring came, the man erected shelters over the scaffolds to protect the dried meat. One day the Two Men came to the boy and told him that the People were returning and would camp that night by the Little Missouri. They would send four runners to the village and these must be well fed and given bundles of meat to carry back, for the People were famishing. So they got a good rib roasting slowly by the fire to feed the runners and give them bundles of jerked meat to carry back to the others. Just about where the ferry is today, that is where the camp began, and it was stretched West to the upper crossing. The next day there was a string of young men and women all the way from the camp into the village, some hurrying to preserve the meat and others to take food back to the others. Old People hobbled along on their canes eager to see what had happened. Soon the whole village was lively with People.

Unknown One was hunting and his two fathers came

to him. They told him that they could not come to his lodge now, for his father-in-law was the kind of man in whose lodge men congregate. They warned him that although he had Mysterious power, he was nevertheless human and the evil spirits would not fear him as they did his two fathers. Whatever happened therefore, he must never allow himself to feel fear or they would get the better of him.

He was more cautious after this and formed the habit of going up on the lodge and looking off in a Southwesterly direction over the village. One day he saw a big Buffalo on a ridge headed toward the river and, thinking to get a shot at it as it came to the river, he took his bow and arrows, explained to his wife where he was going and hid himself in a ravine in the Buffalo's path. As it came along he was surprised to see that at times its body appeared to contract. He shot, but the animal contracted its body so that all the ribs showed, and the arrow fell off harmlessly. The Buffalo ran; he pursued. Four times he shot, but the arrow had no effect. He followed it up a coulee, came to a lodge, and was amazed to see the Buffalo change into a human being and walk into the lodge. "I told you to bring him along; did you bring him?" said a voice inside. "Yes, he's standing outside," said another voice. "I had all the points arranged where he was to shoot, but the four shots were the limit of my power. With every shot I drew the distance toward me and succeeded in getting him here." "Son, enter in!" said the first voice.

Inside was a great serpent with a concave Snake face, a big mouth, four legs with claws and a tail coiled in a heap. As the boy entered there came a hissing sound and flames shot forth. This so frightened him that he went around the fireplace, and because of this fear he lost his memory and could not recall his own Mysterious power. A man reproved the Snake and said, "Only if he brings home no game or tries to escape are you to kill and eat him!" and to the youth he explained how the Buffalo had drawn in the country at every shot with its paw so that he was now in the North country in a land of springs and running water where it was useless for him to try to escape. His task was

173

to hunt Deer and bring home the whole body without skinning it. He must then skin it and boil the guts and head for the serpent and feed him without tasting a bit himself. Then he must fill the pouch with water and raise it to the Snake's lips, throw out the remainder and taste no drop himself. This man had been in the fight with Charred Body and had formed an alliance with the chief whose daughter he had killed. He knew that Unknown One was his enemy's grandchild and had sent the Buffalo to draw him to his lodge.

The boy went out, shot and killed a Deer, cut down the skin over the shinbone and took out the bone, leaving the hoof, which he brought crosswise through a slit cut in the skin so that he could hang the deer over his shoulder. The Snake hissed loudly as he came in, and even when the man quieted it, still it humped its back and grumbled. The boy saw no way of escape. He skinned the Deer in the customary manner by cutting the throat and drawing out the insides. These he threw to the Snake and watched him swallow them down without chewing just like feeding grain to a threshing machine. He roasted ribs, brought pieces of board and placed them in front of the man and laid cooked meat before him. When the man had eaten, he threw every bone into the fire so that the boy should not get a taste. After this the boy took the water-bag made of Buffalo pouch laced into a kind of kettle, carried it to the river and, wading out to the middle where the water ran clear and cool, he brought it back filled to the brim and, lifting it with great difficulty to the man's mouth, gave him what he could drink and poured out the rest outside without tasting a drop. Then he took string and a stone axe and went after firewood. He was commanded to bring no rotten sticks but dry wood fit for firewood and to drink no water on the way—"Should you disobey me in the slightest in one of these commands," said the man, "you will die. This Earth with us is like a small dish out of which you cannot escape." So during his captivity the boy had little liberty except when out hunting; it was just as if he were shut up in a penitentiary. During the night the fear of the serpent kept him awake. The man slept on the left of the door, the boy on the right, the bull near the center.

Under him there was not even straw and he had neither pillow nor robe.

For three days the same thing happened. On the fourth day he had become so weak that when he got the Deer on his back he was unable to lift it. As he lay on his back crying he saw a bright light pass across the Sky and heard a voice crying, "Where are you?" The Two Men had become alarmed and were out looking for him. With their backs against each other they were traveling all over the Sky. They had searched the mountains in the West, the Ocean, but had not thought of the North. The boy suddenly realized that he also had Mysterious powers but had allowed his Mind to become distracted. He got up, took up his arrow that slid the farthest and wet it across his mouth to indicate that it was the voice that the arrow was to carry, with a call for help. Had he not wet it, the arrow would have gone through the air with a flash of light but carried no sound with it. He strung his bow, tested the string, strung the arrow and called out twice to Spring-boy and Lodge-boy, "Heh-h-h! Heh-h-h!" Then he let go the arrow and it shot through the air like a flame with a sound tearing and came down again beside the boy. The Two Men followed it and he was overjoyed. Lodge-boy looked at him sadly, thinking how he must have suffered, but Spring-boy laughed and asked how he could possibly have become so emaciated—"Whoever it is, the enemy shall not escape my hand today," he promised.

The boy related his story and as he laid his ear against the Deer he heard a ringing sound in his right ear. This is the sign of glad news; a ringing sound in the left ear is a sign of bad luck. The men told him that the serpent had caused him to lose his wits and this ringing sound was the return of his consciousness of power. The men shot a fat old Buffalo for the boy to eat. They cut out the leg bone and used it to strike the backbone loose so that they could cut up the ribs. They told the boy to drink four times of the blood from the ribs and gave him a piece of the raw liver to eat. Then they accompanied him to the lodge and told him to go in as usual, but when the man had finished drinking to throw the rest of the water upon him and they would enter and take care of the situation.

All was done as they had said. They bound the serpent from its head to its tail and threw it into the fire. They shot the man and burned him with the serpent. But the Buffalo they spared. This was the leader of the Buffalo who had brought in the herd for the boy's marriage feast, but he had been taken into captivity by the man. He promised to do them no harm; only when they made sacrifices and did not perform the ritual correctly would he allow them or their ponies to be gored. Then the two set the boy between them, Spring-boy to the right and Lodge-boy to the left, and made a leap and landed beside the river near the village. All the family who had been mourning for him rejoiced. The young man became a great chief.

THE BIRD THAT TURNED THE MEAT BITTER

A Mandan Story

Looking about the lodges in the village, Coyote saw strings of jerked meat, but the People were lean. He asked why this was. The People said, "When we go hunting, only the fastest butchers can get their meat home in good condition. There is a Raven which flies over calling 'Get bitter! Get bitter!' (gi-ba in Mandan) and the meat turns bitter." Coyote asked for a sample. He chewed but he could not swallow the meat, it was so bitter. He said, "I must have this thing righted." He sent the young girl after firewood and had it piled ready to light, first laying down manure because it keeps the flame a long time. Then he had the men get timber rope and make a snare. He filled up his pipe and asked help of his fellow creatures. The big Spider came to his aid, and he lighted the pipe for the Spider to smoke. Now the Raven lived in a hollow tree out of which it flew when the men were butchering. Big Spider said, "It is easy to snare that Bird. Be ready to snare him into the fire and let him burn. Some of his feathers will fly into the air and turn into Birds. When you see a White Raven fly out and cry, 'At the end of the World there shall be seen a White Raven as a sign that the World is coming to an end,' that will be the last of it."

They sent out young men into the hills scouting. These reported Buffalo. They made ready for the hunt. The fastest runners went ahead to encircle the herd. Buffalo always run toward the Wind, but the runners drove them toward the other hunters. These formed a corral where they slaughtered the whole herd. The men with large families packed meat home; others followed behind. Meanwhile, some watched by the hollow tree. When the Bird came out, before it could cry, Coyote caught it by the neck and pulled it to the ground. It had the head of a man and the body of a Bird. The face was human but it had no hair. The body had wings and a long neck. It was a frightful thing to see. Coyote clubbed the Bird and threw it into the flames. Feathers flew up and turned into Birds and flew away. The unburned bones Coyote crushed with his club. Finally out flew a White Raven and said, "When the World is about to end I will come to you again!" So Coyote told the People that was to be a sign to them.

SENDEH CHEATS THE SOLDIER

A Kiowa Story

Sendeh was going along. He met someone who he had never seen before. They both stopped, and Sendeh greeted him. He said, "I do not know you, but I think I have heard about you. You are the man who cheats everybody." Sendeh answered, "Yes, I am he who cheats, but I have left my Medicine at home, about four hills away. So I cannot cheat you." The man said, "That makes no difference. If you are the one who cheats, you can cheat me without your Medicine." "I cannot cheat you without my Medicine. I wish I had it, I would cheat you." Sendeh said to the soldier, "If you want me to cheat you, loan me your Horse and I will go and get my Medicine and come back and cheat you." So the soldier said, "All right, I will loan you my Horse, but you must come right back with your Medicine." So Sendeh got on the Horse. As he rode off he secretly punched him so he balked. Sendeh said, "This Horse won't go. Maybe he is afraid of me. Loan me your hat." The soldier gave him the hat. Sendeh punched him again, the Horse balked. "This Horse is afraid of me. Lend me your coat." Sendeh got on the Horse. He punched him secretly again and turned back and told the soldier he might as well let him have his blanket. "I think it would be well to give me your quirt."—"All right, here is the quirt, too. Make haste, get your Medicine and come back and show me you can cheat me." The Horse went forward. Sendeh looked back and said, "Soldier, I have already cheated you. I have all your things. I have no Medicine. Now you go your way, and I will go mine.

JAY'S SKINNY LEGS

A Flathead Story

The chief had a daughter who was old enough to marry. He informed the young men that one with the strongest legs could have her. Coyote showed how long and fast he could run and claimed the girl. Bear flexed his leg muscles to show how big and strong they were, and he claimed the girl. Jay sneaked off into the woods where he gathered some black Moss that hangs from trees. He wrapped the Moss around his legs to make them look large. The chief was fooled by his trick and proclaimed him the winner. Jay had to carry his new wife across a stream in order to reach his teepee, and the water softened the moss so it fell from his legs. When he climbed the bank on the opposite side of the stream, everyone saw his little skinny legs, and they all laughed.

THE FINDING OF THE TSOMASS

A Legend of Vancouver Island

Near thirty miles from where Alberni pours her crystal stream out of the mighty fjord that cleaves Vancouver's Island nigh in twain, a tribe of Natives lived. Their village nestled at the foot of wooded hills, which everywhere on this indented coastline rise straight up from out the North Pacific. They were a powerful tribe, E-coulth-aht by name; seven hundred strong, with many fighting men, and many children who played upon that shore. I think even now I hear the echo of their voices round the bay, and how marvelously clear an echo may be, among the inlets of that rockbound coast! I have heard my call flung back from side to side alternately, till it was lost among the rocky heights and ceased to be.

Across the bay from where the Natives lived ran a stream, called Po-po-moh-ah. Here every Autumn, when the Salmon came, they stayed and caught the Fish for Winter use. Yet strange to say these ancient E-coulth-ahts seemed unaware that at their very doors, a Nature-hewn canal had its entrance. One fine September morning Ha-houlth-thuk-amik and Han-ah-kut-tish, the Sons of Wick-in-in-ish, or, as some say, Ka-kay-un, accompanied by their father's slave See-na-ulth, were paddling slowly to Po-po-moh-ah, when half across the near to Tsa-atoos they saw dead Salmon floating on the tide.

The Salmon had spawned, and is it not strange to think that this, the king of Fish, should struggle up the rapid tumbling streams for many miles, against strong currents, over falls where the water breaks the least, perchance to fall within the wicker purse of People's traps placed there so cunningly to catch them if they should fall back? And even if they escape the traps and find the gravel bar where they four years before began their life, and having spent themselves in giving life, sicken and die, their bodies even in death give sustenance to Gulls and Eagles circling round those haunts.

"These Fish have come from where fresh water flows, so let us follow up from whence they came. Let Quawteaht direct our course, and we shall find new streams where Salmon are in plenty and win great glory in our tribe." Thus spake the sons of Wick-in-in-ish, and they turned the bow of their canoe upstream and followed where the trail of Salmon led, to the broad entrance of that splendid fjord.

Soon they paddled by the harbour U-chuck-le-sit, long famed for its safe anchorage and quiet retreat, when Winter storms lash the waters of the sound. Leaving this quiet harbour on the left, they followed where the wider channel led to Klu-quilth-soh, that dark and stormy gap, where People say the dreaded Chehahs dwell among the rocky heights—"The Gates to Hell," and when men seek to pass those gates, the Chehahs blow upon them Winds of evil fates from North and South and East and West. The water boils in that great witches pot, People seek a sheltered beach in vain—no beach is there; no shelter from the storm. The mighty cliffs frown down relentlessly; the Whale She-she-took-amuck opens his great jaws and swallows voyagers, at which the Chehahs laugh, and their wild laughter, Klu-quilth-soh's heights re-echo far away.

In this eventful day, the evil Chehahs were absent from their home and the Yukstees Wind blew not too strong to cause the waves to dash along in wild commotion, and after paddling uneventfully through Klu-quilth-soh, the three E-coulth-ahts stopped beside Toosh-ko. Looking back they could see Nob Point, which hid their home from view—it was as if the mountains which formed those stormy gates had closed and barred them in.

"What chehah," they cried, "has lured us within this inland sea and shut those gates? A-ha-A-ha!" they called with anxious cry, and prayed Kah-oots to save them from all dangers. To the Saghalie Tyee, the chief above, they also prayed to potlatch kloshe to guide them, and guard them from the evil chehahs hovering around. After the relief of prayer, their Spirits rose, and once again the splashing of their paddles marked their onward progress.

Soon they glided by Hy-wach-es Creek and, rounding Wak-ah-nit, they came in view of the great valley where Tso-mass flows. At once they ceased from paddling to gaze with pleasure on that favoured land, and so they looked they heard the sound of song up the river valley.

The evening fell, the pleasant Yukstees Wind blew more faintly, and as it passed away, over those calm inland waters swelled again the sound of many voices chanting songs.

"There are People dwelling there," they said. "It would be well if we delayed until morning." Agreeing to this plan, they crossed the channel and camped at Klu-quilth-coose.

Next morning while the grass was damp with dew, and long before the U-ah-tee Winds had ceased, the sons of

Wick-in-in-ish, hearing again the quaint alluring song, took their canoe and paddled on, to where between two grassy slopes, the Tsomass ends. When they approached the river mouth, they saw extending from the bank a Salmon trap, and even today the People will show at Lup-se-kup-se some old rotten sticks, which they affirm formed part of that same trap. The land was green, the wild Duck's quack was heard among the reed which edged the river bank while flocks of Geese were feeding on the grass which grows thickly upon the tidal flats, the flats the People call Kwi-chuc-a-nit.

Upon the Eastern bank the young men saw a wondrous house, which far surpassed their father's lodge at home beyond the hills in Rainy Bay, in size of beams and boards. The sons of Wick-in-in-ish were afraid and would have turned the bow of their canoe home-bound, but from the house they heard a woman call. "Oh come and stay with us, go not away. Our land is full of all the riches Nature gives; our woods are bright with o-il-lie most luscious to the taste; on yonder hill the nimble au-tooch feed; in every stream the silver Salmon swim, so come within our lodge with us and stay awhile." Ha-houlth-thuk-amik was mesmerized by the sweet welcoming and entered in, whereat the klootsmah said to him, "We welcome thee strange one unto our lodge, for we have never seen a man before."

Now Han-ah-kut-ish was alarmed and much afraid that if his brother listened to the klootsmah and was attentive to her blandishments, he would forget the mission in which they were engaged; therefore he called to him to come, and after much persuasion the elder brother left the lodge and joined the younger and the slave See-na-ulth, and together they paddled up the stream to Ok-sock-tis opposite the present village of O-pit-ches-aht. Across the river there were houses in which more klootsmah lived, but at this time they were employed in gathering Kwanis in the land behind, and when the young men sought them out, they were afraid, and all but one took flight, escaping to the woods. This one had no fear, but coming near to Ha-houlth-thuk-amik, besought him with favour to look on her, but Han-ah-kut-ish again reminded him that they had not as yet attained the object of their quest.

Still further up the stream they went, until they came to where they found the Ty-see Salmon spawning on the gravel bars. Believing they had found the object of their search, they camped the night at Sah-ah-hie. All through the darkness they listened to the rushing of the Fish, when the gaunt and savage males with flattened heads and upper jaws curved like a hook about the lower, and armed with Dog-like teeth, fought for the females of their choice. With great satisfaction they heard the wallowing of the Fish, as with their heads and tails they formed the elongated cavities in the gravel in which to lay their eggs. Then Ha-houlth-thuk-amik declared that this, the Tsomass River, was the source from which the dead Fish came which they had seen when paddling to Po-po-moh-ah.

To Lup-see-kup-se they returned next day, and there they saw, among the women in the lodge, the girl who spoke to them when they had landed on the river bank opposite Ok-sock-tis. Then Ha-houlth-thuk-amik, desiring to convey her home with him, took her aside and said, "If thou wilt come with me, say not a word, but unbeknown make haste and leave the house, and run across the point which forms the Eastern bank where this the Tsomass River joins the inland sea, then hide thyself until we take thee in, as we are paddling home."

The klootsmah did as she was told, and as the young men passed she jumped within the canoe and was away with them. That night they stayed at Chis-toh-nit not far from Coleman Creek, so named because in later days a man of that name took up some land and dwelt there some little while.

Next morning the Klootsmah said to Ha-houlth-thuk-amik, "I am Kla-kla-as-suks and I am now thy rightful wife, and therefore I desire to make of thee a famous hunter of Whale, so come with me and climb the mountain called Kuk-a-ma-com-ulth where high above the timber line the green grass grows, and I will get for thee an Ow-yie Medicine."

They climbed the mountains and she secured for him

the Medicine so desired by all who hunt the Whale, and early next morning blown by a strong U-ah-tee Wind, they started from Po-mo-moh-soh, and when they came to Klu-kwilth-soh, they found the gates wide open and passed safely through between the frowning cliffs, arriving home before the break of day.

Then Ha-houlth-thuk-amik aroused his father who was still asleep and bade him light a fire, and when the fire was lit told him how they ventured up the unknown way, between high cliffs, where they had lost all sight and sound of Rainy Bay. He told of the Tsomass land, and the Salmon stream which far eclipsed their own Po-po-moh-ah, and then described the great and wondrous house, where the Klootsmah dwelt, and how they sang to him "Yah-hin-in-ay." He told him also of Kla-kla-as-suks, the Klootsmah who had left her home to be his rightful wife.

Then Wick-in-in-ish sent for all the tribe, and when they were assembled in his lodge, he told to them the story of the Tsomass land. Among the braves was much talking, and after speeches from the lesser chiefs, it was decided that the next day before Sun had cast His shadow North and South, with Yuk-stees Wind, they would set sail for Tsomass land.

That day in every house, in varied occupation, each family busied. The Cedar boards which form the sides and roof of all their houses were piled upon canoes. Atop of these were set their household goods, the mats of Cedar bark, the wooden tubs in which they boiled their Fish, the spears of flint, their hooks of bone, their fishing lines of Kelp, and mattresses of Water Reed. Large quantities of Clams and Mussels, also Salmon cured by smoke they took with them, for Wick-in-in-ish planned to give a great potlatch to the strange tribe of girls, from which his eldest son had chosen one to be his wife.

Next morning long before Sun had reached the Zenith they had set sail for Tsomass land. It truly must have been a sight to see, that fleet of dark canoes piled high with all the wealth of that great tribe, as with the sails of Cedar bark filled with the Yuk-stees Wind, they glided by the green and rocky shores which led them inland to the pleasant Tsomass land. Before the shadows of the night had spread among the gloomy conifers, the dark canoes had rounded Wak-a-nit when, taking down their sails of Cedar bark, they paddled silently close to the shore.

When near Tin-nim-ah, where the People say they find good stone for sharpening arrow points, they rested on their paddles, and first heard the women singing in their Cedar lodge. Then Wick-in-in-ish addressed his tribe. "My children we have sailed for many miles, and our little ones are hungry and weary. Let us sojourn near this old Spruce."

Thus they encamped near the conifer and called the place Toha-a-muk-is after the Spruce they were afraid to touch. Water they carried from near Kak-mak-kook, named from the Alders growing round the streams. All through the night they heard the Salmon splash to free themselves, so many People say, from Sea Lice clinging to their silver sides, and their hearts were happy with that refrain, which spoke to them of great supplies of food.

Early next day, before the forest trees were gilded by the glorious rising Sun, the People heard the call of many Birds, and looking Northward where the Tsomass flows forth from the mist, which in the early morning hangs like a veil of gauze among the trees, they saw a flock of Sand hill Cranes appear. They flew far above their heads and, gradually ascending to the Sky, vanished from their sight. These were the maidens, so the People say, who left behind them all this lovely land for regions unexplored, taking with them both Clams and Mussels. This is the reason People give for the lack of these Shell-Fish now, upon the shores of the great inland sea. The maidens also took the Kwa-nis bulbs, but as they flew they dropped a few upon the ground; hence the Kwa-nis bulb is still found in Tsomass land.

Wick-in-in-ish, with his sons, now made haste to paddle to the river mouth but lo, the house was gone, no sign of it was left, and with it all the klootsmah tribe had fled. Then he turned to Ha-houlth-thuk-amick and said, "This is thy land, and this thy future home shall be; thou and thy chosen one Kla-kla-as-suks shall dwell therein, and may thy children be many."

GOOD MEDICINE
TRADITIONAL DRESS ISSUE

KNOWLEDGE AND METHODS OF OLD-TIME CLOTHINGS
✝···ADOLF HUNGRY WOLF···✝

Jack Red Cloud—Son of Oglala Sioux Head Chief, Red Cloud:
*"I want you to look me in the face, and I hope the Great
Heavenly Father, who will look down upon Us, will give All the
Tribes His blessing, that we may go forth in peace, and live in
peace all our days, and that He will look down upon Our Children
and finally lift Us far above this Earth, and that Our Heavenly
Father will look upon Our children as His children, and that All
the Tribes may be His children. . . . We have assembled here
today as chiefs from all over the Land, we eat the bread and
meat together, we Smoke the Pipe of Peace, and we shake the
Hand of Peace. And now we go out as one Chief, and I hope we
shall be as Brothers and Friends for all our lives and separate
with kind hearts."*

So spoke young Red Cloud at a council of many chiefs, in Montana in 1909. He was photographed there by the council's origina-
tor—Rodman Wannamaker.

The Native American People, back in the Old Days, dressed according to tribal tradition *and* personal desire. Like everything else in their lives, appearance was dictated foremost by Visions and Dreams. Sometimes a totally new article or method came about this way—often with spiritual meaning that was respected, and not copied by others. More often, however, the Visions of personal appearance were based on pleasing articles and methods that the individual had seen previously on another tribe member, on a member of another tribe, or even, on a person from other culture. For instance, it is believed that many of the intricate geometric beadwork designs were inspired by similar designs on Oriental rugs that were brought into the frontier country by white settlers. Again, the famed *"war bonnet"* was used originally by the Sioux tribe, and a few neighbors, to distinguish warriors who had accomplished enough brave deeds that their representative Eagle feathers could be made up into a headdress. The style and meaning of the bonnet was adopted by numerous tribes during the latter part of the 19th Century. By the beginning of the present century no Native dress was considered complete without a war bonnet. So, virtually every tribe adopted the style, and the traditional bonnet all but lost its meaning.

The Native People in the Old Days certainly placed as much pride in their personal appearance as any group of People ever have. Their dress consisted of handmade clothing, necklaces of natural materials or wonderful, prized beads, little bunches of feathers and furs worn here and there, hats made of skins—each thing with a story behind it that was sure to recall some prior happy moments at any discouraging times.

The following presentation is meant to inspire Your thoughts about personal appearance. It does not give step-by-step instructions for week-end diversion. Rather, it gathers together some old styles and some old methods, with the hope that You will be tempted to gather the materials at Your disposal and make some of the items to suit Your own personal thoughts and way of Life.

THE OLD WAYS OF DRESSING

"It has always been observed that all the various tribes have a close resemblance in their dress; that of the North Americans in their original state, consists entirely of furs and hides; one piece is fastened round the waist, which reaches the middle of the thigh, and another larger piece is thrown over the shoulders. Their stockings are of skins, fitted to the shape of the leg; the seams are ornamented with Porcupines' quills; their shoes are of the skin of the Deer, Elk, or Buffalo, dressed for the most part with the hair on; they are made to fasten about the ankles, where they have ornaments of brass or tin, about an inch long, hung by thongs. The women are all covered from the knees upwards. Their shifts cover their body, but not the arms. Their petticoats reach from the waist to the knees; and both are of leather. Their shoes and stockings are not different from those of the men. Those men who wish to appear gay, pluck the hair from their heads, except a round spot of about two inches diameter on the crown of the head; on this are fastened plumes of feathers with quills of ivory or silver. The peculiar ornaments of this part are the distinguishing marks of the different nations. They sometimes paint their faces black, but more often red; they bore their noses and slit their ears, and in both they wear various ornaments. The higher ranks of women dress thair hair sometimes with silver in a peculiar manner; they sometimes paint it. They have generally a large spot of paint near the ear, on each side of the head, and not unfrequently a small spot on the brow. These People, it is true, have made several improvements in their dresses, since they commenced to receive European commodities."

So wrote John McIntosh in the 1840's in his book, *"The Origin of the North American Indians."* The manner of dressing had already been quite affected among some of the Eastern tribes by their contact with the new cultures, when McIntosh wrote. The spectacular dress of the People on the Plains, and many of their neighbors, was then beginning to go through a period of changes that reached their artistic climax during the following fifty years. In that period, the People took advantage of the many new materials available from traders to make and design articles that were inspired by their spiritual past and their still-Natural lives.

YOU are like the People of that period. You can take advantage of the multitudes of materials and tools that are available today to make and design articles inspired by Your spiritual knowledge of the Past and Your opportunity to seek a Natural life in the present. Be proud of Your Person—take pride in the appearance of Your Body and the manner of Your dress. Seek Beauty in everyone, and let everyone appreciate the beauty in You. Would You not rather behold a meadow of wild flowers than a field of weeds and grasses? And would You not find much more satisfaction with the colorful birds of the forest than with the sparrows of the city?

Most anything is easy to sew by hand, as long as You use common sense. Patience is the most difficult requirement. Anyone can produce fine work who has the patience to take short, even, and tight stitches.

TOOLS

In the old days the only tools for sewing were: a knife for cutting, an awl of pointed bone for making holes, and stripes of sinew to sew the materials together with. For inspiration, as well as for appearance of certain items (such as Medicine bags) nothing is better than the old-time process. You separate the piece of sinew into strips of the thickness required for the project. Soak one of the strips in your mouth until it becomes soft and workable. Then draw it across your lap with your left hand, from right to left, at the same time rolling your other hand over the strip with a downward motion. Thus twisted, the strip is poked through the awl-holes and pulled tight. Leave the end used for poking dry and untwisted, so that it will be stiff and hard, like the rest of the strip when it dries. Sinew sewing is tedious, and beginning attempts are often clumsy. For making practical clothing You would do well to keep in Mind the efforts of the past, while proceeding with the methods that follow.

191

The basic sewing tools of today are the needle and thread. Scissors, wax, and thimble are almost as important. A few dollars will buy a life-time supply of all of these materials in any department store that carries notions.

A dime-store package of assorted needles will take care of most sewing needs. Large needles are easier to handle, and will take rougher treatment without bending or breaking. Smaller needles are easier to push through the material. Three-cornered needles are particularly good for leather sewing. When sewing leather try to use the smallest practical needle—one with an eye just big enough to take your thread—or you will be struggling to push each stitch through. An awl is a handy tool to use when tough leather is being sewn. Perforate a number of holes with it and then follow with the needle and thread. A sharpened ice pick works well as an awl.

Thread should always be at least as tough as the material you are sewing. A good standard type is made of nylon. This comes in tiny rolls as well as mile-long spools, and is virtually unbreakable. Use it doubled for extra strength and rigidity.

Scissor types are many, the most important factor to consider about them is sharpness. You will wear out patience and hands with dull scissors, and your work is likely to look ragged, besides. Get a good pair of scissors that will keep a sharp edge, and have them sharpened once in awhile. Scissors will cut cloth and most leather. For tough leather it is better to use a ruler and razor blade. For fur, use a razor blade and cut on the skin side, to avoid damaging the hair.

If you've ever perforated your fingertip with the fat end of a needle that you were attempting to push through thick material, then you appreciate the value of a thimble. Learn to handle the needle with your thumb and middle finger, so that your index (or thimble) finger will always be free to give that helpful boost once your needle point has found its mark. Buy a good-fitting thimble—too loose or too tight will distract your efforts at smooth sewing.

Pulling your length of thread back and forth over a small piece of Beeswax will greatly improve the appearance and effort of your sewing. It will eliminate the slippery feeling of your thread, and allow your stitches to remain snug after you pull them tight.

SEWING METHODS

Hand-sewn items are generally stitched-up inside out. When the completed item is turned right side out, the stitches should be barely visible between the even seam. These stitches can be hidden altogether if a thin strip of material is sewn between the two main layers, and the stitches are kept quite firm. Sometimes a strip of contrasting material is used this way, with very pleasing results. Red wool cloth, for instance, makes a beautiful *"welt"* between a leather seam. Fur strips look very well when used as welts between heavy wool material.

After you have made a wrapping-paper-pattern of your proposed work, and then cut out your actual material (allowing ¼ inch for the seams), line up and pin the whole piece along the seams with stick pins. This will help keep your work properly lined up and will counter the stretching that your material may do while you are sewing. Two-piece items that are to be sewn most, or all, of the way around (such as pouches and two-piece moccasins) should be begun in the center and sewn first down one side, then the other—again to outwit the material's tendency to stretch and end up lopsided.

Fasten your thread to the material either by knotting the end, or by leaving a tail and taking several close stitches and then tying a double knot with the tail and the main thread. Knotted ends alone sometimes tend to pull out during use. The basic stitch for sewing material inside out is the simple overhand (or loop) stitch. Again, keep the stitches even and tight, and sew close enough to the edge of the material to avoid unsightly and large stitches from showing when right side out (but not so close that pressure from use will rip the stitches through the material). At the end of a seam, or when running out of thread, either of the methods for tying thread may again be used. Waxing the end of the thread and taking a half dozen close, tight stitches is often sufficient for the end of sewing.

LOOP STITCH & STARTING KNOT

WELT

A few comments may be worthwhile here: If you buy your material, get the best you can afford. Endless hours of careful sewing will be wasted if your material shrinks, tears, or pulls out of shape. The best deals on cloth can generally be found in thrift stores and in the remnant selections of quality clothing manufacturers. Taxidermists often sell unclaimed, tanned hides for a fair market price. They may also have a wide selection of furs available, while thrift stores will sell used fur pieces much cheaper.

Buckskin (the common name given to tanned Deer hides) is the best all-around leather for clothing. It is extremely tough and durable, yet soft, and easy to cut and sew. The money you save by buying cheap, commercial "*splits*," and so forth is as nothing when compared to the stiff, uncomfortable piece you may end up with. The feel of new leather does not change much for the better with age, so buy accordingly.

Rawhide for clothing: don't embarrass yourself by asking for it. A rawhide is just what the name implies—an untanned hide. You would do as well to make your clothing from plywood sheets.

If money is no object, then buy Deer, Elk, or Moose hides that have been tanned by Reservation People. Sold as "*Indian-tanned*" hides, this kind of leather is expensive and hard to find, but feels smooth and soft like velvet. If you buy it "*smoked*" it will have a nice brown color, an aroma you will never forget, and will dry fairly soft after wetting (smoked and unsmoked "*Indian-tan*" can be softened by kneading). The "*Indian-tan*" process is not patented, so make your own, if you have the hides, space, and ambition. Look for instructions in the GOOD MEDICINE series.

THE EVERY-DAY CLOTHES WORN BY THESE ARAPAHO PEOPLE ARE EASY TO MAKE BY HAND WITH SIMPLE MATERIALS. THEY INCLUDE: LEATHER MOCCASINS, COTTON DRESSES AND SHIRTS, WOOL LEGGINGS WITH BEADED STRIPES AND SCARVES TO WEAR AROUND THE NECK.

On the following pages are outlined several styles of moccasins—though many more existed, of course. Most tribes used certain traditional characteristics by which their moccasins could be told from those of similar styles used by other tribes. The two-piece moccasin style of the Plains, for instance, was worn by the People of many tribes. Some wore theirs without much decoration, while others liked to cover them partly or fully with lazy-stitch beadwork, and still others decorated theirs with applique beadwork. Everyday moccasins were often plain.

The beaded designs, of course, differed among the tribes. The Cheyenne and Sioux preferred white backgrounds for their beadwork, and often used complex geometric designs. The Blackfoot People preferred blue backgrounds and geometric designs made up of little squares and rectangles. On partially decorated moccasins they often sewed down a piece of colored cloth of a basic design and edged it with beads. Along with the Flatheads and other Western neighbors, the Blackfoot also decorated their moccasins with beautiful flowers in applique beadwork.

The two-piece moccasion style practically replaced the old one-piece style among the Blackfoot in more recent years. Their neighbors to the West, however, still use the one-piece style today. They invariably sew on ankle flaps to give their moccasins high tops for warmth, security, and protection against brush and snow.

Southern Plains moccasins were often cut quite low, but the People liked to add long fringes to the seams and cuffs. Women's moccasins, in this area, often had a top piece added on that reached almost to the knee. These top pieces were either buttoned up the sides or held up by a thong around the top. The tops were sometimes cut into fringes, which hung back down to the feet, or above.

Moccasins worn by the desert People in the SouthWest generally had separate soles made from thick hide and curved upwards around the edges. Sharp rocks and hot sands lined their trails, and influenced their moccasion designs.

Tough, pliable leather is necessary for moccasins that are to be worn daily over trails. For soft-soled and one-piece styles thick Moosehide is best. For the bottoms of hard-soled styles Buffalo or steer rawhide is thickest and best. For Winter wear use Buffalo hide with the fur turned in. The one-piece style is best for this—well greased or covered with water repellent. Sinew is excellent for sewing up your moccasins—it is very tough, and adds to the appearance. People in the old days always carried an awl and some sinew in a small pouch for moccasin and clothing repairs. When travelling away from home one or more extra pairs of moccasins were carried in the pack or hung from the belt. It was common to find discarded moccasins next to the campfire remains of a passing hunting or war party. Others were thus often able to tell what tribe the campers belonged to.

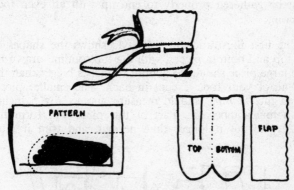

ONE-PIECE ROCKY MOUNTAIN STYLE

This is really a simple style of moccasin to make—even for one who has never sewn anything before. It is also one of the most handsome and comfortable styles to wear.

Make a paper pattern first, as shown, allowing the extra widths to make up for foot height. Use the pattern to make your leather pieces—be sure to reverse for left and right. Sew the pieces inside out and begin on the short sewing side. When nearing the end of the long side, slip the piece on your foot, bring the two sides together up the heel, and mark the line of your heel on each side. Cut the ends slightly larger than marked, then sew from top down to the cut-out rounded piece. Turn the moccasin right side out and stitch down the rounded piece to look neat. Trim the tongue and sew on an ankle flap to reach to your desired height. Cut laces long enough to wrap around the ankle flap several times, and your new moccasins should fit securely.

NORTH WOODS STYLE

This style of moccasin is still common today among the

People of the widespread Cree and Chippewa tribes, many of whom continue to live by hunting and trapping in the remote Northern Woods. The making of this moccasin style requires patience and skill. The puckered toe section must be gathered properly to end up with an even foot covering.

The first illustration of this style shows the shapes of the top and bottom pieces, with the foot outline drawn in. The large piece should be about two inches bigger than the outline of your foot, except in back. The smaller piece, called the *"vamp,"* should measure about 3 by 5 inches for a man's moccasin. Part of this piece will form the tongue, so cut it longer than needed, and trim it after sewing.

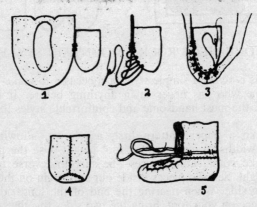

Begin by stitching the two pieces together at the point where the curve begins, as in Figure 1. Figure 2 shows how the gathering is done—by taking stitches twice as large on the big piece as on the vamp. After the vamp is sewn on, insert a piece of wood or stone under the gathered ridges, inside of the moccasin, and pound the ridges down flat on the outside with a hammer. Slip the moccasin over your foot (either one—this style has no left or right) and hold the sides up so that you can mark the heel line. Trim the surplus off the heel from the top down to the cut-out rounded piece. Stitch it on neatly to look like Figure 4. Add laces long enough to wrap around your ankles several times, and your moccasin should look like Figure 5. The vamps are often fully-beaded with the floral patterns used by the North Woods People. This should be done before sewing.

SOUTHERN SWAMP STYLE

Variations of this moccasin style are worn by People in the forests and swamps of the deep South—tribes such as the Seminole, Cherokee, and Muskogee.

Begin by cutting two rectangular pieces of leather like in Figure 1—each measuring about 12 to 20 inches. Cut the lacing strip round and round out of the corners that you trim off the pattern, as shown.

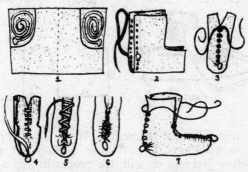

Punch holes along the longest straight section and run one lace in and out of the holes about one inch up on either side from bottom, as in Figure 2. Pulling this lace tight should give you the puckered heel seen in Figure 3. Lace up the rest of the back of the moccasin, round and round, as shown, and tie a knot at the end. Put a long thong through the top pair of holes to serve as ankle tie strings. Figure 4 shows the open front of the moccasin, with the laced-up heel showing in back. Insert a lace through the leather at the bottom front of the moccasin, and lace it up as in Figure 5. Pulling the laces tight will pucker-up the toe and bring together the top of the moccasin as in Figure 6. Figure 7 shows the completed moccasin. The ankle flaps can be cut so that they are taller, or so that they can be wrapped around the ankles, by changing the pattern.

TOP-SEAM STYLE

This style of moccasin has the main seam running up the front center of the moccasin, beginning at the toes. The Kutenai variation is cut so that the two sides will fit perfectly together up to the vamp, which also serves as a tongue. The back and flaps are completed in the usual way. Of the other variations here illustrated, the one from the Shasta tribe (of Northern California) is cut at an angle so that there will be a left and right to each pair.

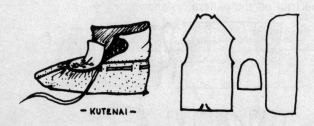

— KUTENAI —

This requires careful gathering. With these top-seam styles you may have to tear your stitches out several times before you end up with the proper fit and appearance. The other top-seam style was used in the East by the Ojibwa, Iroquois, and Shawnee.

— SHASTA —

- EASTERN -

PUEBLO WRAP-AROUND

This style of moccasin is commonly worn by the Zuni People, but is popular in other Pueblos as well. The point marked A1 on the upper is sewn to the sole at the point marked A. When the upper has been sewn all the way around the point marked A2 is sewn down and cut off to slightly overlap A1. The piece B is then attached as a flap, with a buttonhole cut into it. The toe and heel of the sole is puckered, and a silver button holds the flap shut.

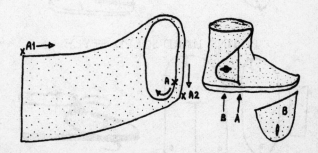

SOUTHWEST HIGH TOP

This style of moccasin is used by the People who live in the Pueblos of the SouthWest. It has rawhide (or thick hide) soles and white Deerskin uppers. The high top is sewn on first, and the toe piece is joined to it. The stitches are made on the outside and the sole leather is gathered at the toes and heels.

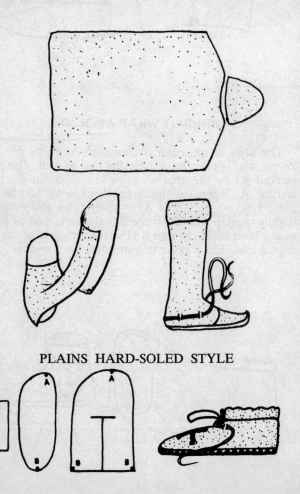

PLAINS HARD-SOLED STYLE

This has always been one of the most popular moccasin styles. It is today's basic pow-wow style, and was worn on the Plains, in the past, by the Sioux and their many neighbors. Sew inside out, beginning at A, first one way to B, then the other. Sew up the back, add tongues and laces, then turn right side out.

A YOUNG SIOUX COUPLE AT THE TURN-OF-THE-CENTURY. SHE WEARS A TRADE CLOTH (WOOL) DRESS, WITH RIBBONS, CROSSES OF BRASS SEQUINS, ROSETTES OF TUBE BEADS, A FEW ELK TEETH NEAR THE BOTTOM AND A CAPE-COVERING OF MANY DENTALIUM SHELLS. HER BREASTPLATE IS OF LONG HAIRPIPES. THE MAN WEARS TRADE CLOTH BREECHCLOTH AND LEGGINGS (WITH WHITE "SELVEDGE EDGE") THE LEGGINGS HAVE BEADED STRIPS, MIRRORS AND SHOE BUTTONS SEWN ON. HIS CLOTH SHIRT IS COVERED BY A SCARF, A LONG BREASTPLATE OF HAIRPIPES AND A LEATHER VEST WITH QUILLED EMBROIDERY. THE BONNET NO DOUBT BELONGED TO AN OLDER RELATIVE AND WAS BORROWED. THIS COUPLE IS WEARING THE ULTIMATE IN TRADITIONAL PLAINS FINERY, NOT THEIR EVERYDAY CLOTHES.

FUR ROBES AND WOOL BLANKETS

The fur robe was, in the Old Days, the most important item of dress—one of the most important single material items used by the Native People. With their robes, the People felt as secure as snails with their shells—they could curl up under any bush and go to sleep in a warm bed. Or, they could travel in any kind of weather and cover or uncover themselves as needed. If you have ever sat around an outdoor campfire wrapped up in a fine blanket then You have some idea of the pleasure of robe-wearing.

The best fur robe in the old days was, of course, from the Buffalo. Ideally, it was from a two-year old cow. Many tribes who lived far from Buffalo country sent good hunters on long journeys to bring back hides—or else traded eagerly for them with tribes who had an extra supply. For years, any material thing among these People could be given a Buffalo robe value—for, along with the horse, this was the standard item of exchange.

Buffalo robes can still be bought, and are well worth their cost. Native tanners and reservation pawn shops sometimes sell tanned robes for as little as $50. Taxidermists and fur suppliers will ask closer to $200 for a new robe. Salted, untanned Buffalo hides can at times be bought cheaply from private and government Buffalo ranches and reserves, and from a few trading posts.

When worn, Buffalo robes were generally wrapped the long way around the wearer's body. Among some tribes it was the custom to wear the head of the robe on the outside and facing to the left—among others it was a matter of preference. Robes with the fur left on (which were most common) were worn hair in or out, depending on the weather. Summer robes of Buffalo and Elk were worn without the hair. Some People cut the head and tail pieces off their robes for convenience, while others used only a part of a hide for their robes. Among some tribes it was the custom to skin the hide of a Buffalo in two long halves, tan it, and then sew the halves back together.

Robes were often decorated. The simpler styles involved painting the robe a solid color, or covering it with red or black lines, Medicine designs, or pictographs of personal exploits. A more time-consuming method of decoration involved making a long, belt-like strip of quill or bead-work—as much as a foot wide and eight feet long—which was sewn down the center of the robe, the long way. Usually four immense rosettes were spaced through this long strip, and quillwork or buckskin thongs dangled from the center of these. Perhaps the most spectacular robe decorations were those which usually identified the chiefs and leading men—the skin sides of their robes were often nearly covered by yellow, orange, and red geometric designs, done in quillwork, which combined to form gigantic Sunbursts. Powerful, indeed, was the sight of a man with flowing feather headdress and long hair, mounted on his war horse, and wrapped in a robe with the quilled image of Sun blazing brightly from it!

Rabbit skin blankets were popular among People who could not easily obtain Buffalo robes. The whole skins sewn together do not make a very strong or neat blanket. Rather, the People cut the raw pelts into long strips about two inches wide, which they sewed end to end and rolled into a ball. After a period of days or months, when the ball appeared to be large enough, a wood frame loom was made—slightly larger than the desired blanket. The ball was unrolled and part of the long strip was wound upon the frame to form the warp. The remainder of the strip became the woof and was woven in and out of the warp, as in the sketch. A light, fluffy, coarsely woven blanket was the result. Sometimes the fur strips were twisted as they were being rolled up, and dried this way for the blanket.

Other light robes were made by the People from such furs as Bear, which required two hides, Wolf, which required four hides, and Coyote, which sometimes required eight. These were trimmed to match, and sewed with the fur sides together, using an overhand stitch. Worn fur out, the seams appeared as even ridges that contrasted the different skins.

Red Squirrel skin robes were sometimes popular, according to one Sioux craftsman, who said: *"Old women also tanned the hides, and when they got enough together, they made little robes on which to sit to smoke their pipes."*

Blankets became very popular, after their introduction by traders, because they are lighter and less bulky than robes. Blue wool blankets with white, undyed edges were most common among the central and Southern tribes. In the North the Point blankets from the Hudson's Bay Company were and are a favorite with all outdoor People. In the NorthWest and Plateau areas the many-colored Pendleton-made blankets and shawls have long been favorites, and are today very commonly seen at pow-wows from Oregon to Oklahoma.

Robes and blankets were worn in a variety of ways, both for comfort and for particular style. For instance, young men generally wore theirs wrapped around the body so that the arms remained free, or else over their heads so that only their faces were showing (a common style when courting). Women generally wore theirs over both shoulders, or over their heads in colder weather. They often fastened a belt around the robe at the waist, so that the blanket could be dropped to free the hands for working. Old men often left their right arms free and held the ends of their robes with their left hands from underneath.

For sleeping, the robe or blanket is spread open on the ground. The sleeper then lies on one end, folds the blanket over him, and tucks the other end beneath himself. The bottom of this bed roll is then folded up underneath the legs.

OLD-TIME OVERCOATS

A handmade overcoat is one of the easiest and most

functional old-time dress items, that You might like. Two basic styles exist—the Blanket Capote and the Northern Parka. Both have sleeves, hoods, and are very practical for Life in the Outdoors. Capotes are generally made from warm blankets, while Parkas are generally made from furs. However, any material which You may have on hand or wish to obtain, can be used. The main consideration is Your intended use of the coat.

NORTHERN PARKA

The Parka is the simpler to make of the two overcoats. Make a paper pattern as illustrated—allow yourself a loose fit for heavy clothing underneath—then cut your material accordingly.

Begin by sewing the front and back together at the shoulders (A). Next sew up the sides, beginning at the bottom and up to the sleeve holes (B). Attach the sleeve pieces, beginning at A, and then sew these from where they are attached up to the cuffs. Stitch the hood together from the front (C) on up, and the Parka will be completed.

Parkas are often made in contrast—soft, warm material worn inside; tough, waterproof material covering the outside.

BLANKET CAPOTE

French trappers in the Canadian woods gave this fine coat its name, and all those who have worn one understand its Winter fame. Easy to make and enjoyable to wear —all You need is a blanket and a little time.

More Capotes have been made with the striped Hudson's Bay Point blankets than any other. The white ones with colored stripes were especially popular, although the red ones with black stripes were also often used. Any large wool blanket will make a nice warm Capote, however.

Cut up your blanket according to the drawing. To avoid

much unravelling, tear your material whenever the line for cutting falls along the "*straight*." Notice that the body of the Capote (back and fronts) is all one piece—all you need to sew is the shoulders. The extra lengths that are shown folded back on the sleeves, neck, and front of hood are for fringes, and may be left out. Next, sew up the back of the hood, and attach it to the body at the neck and lapels. Hoods generally had tassels hanging from them, one sewn to each of the three sides at the tip. Your

NORTHERN PARKA

HOOD

C   C

A

BACK

B

A

HALF FRONT

SLEEVE

A

B

BLANKET-CAPOTE

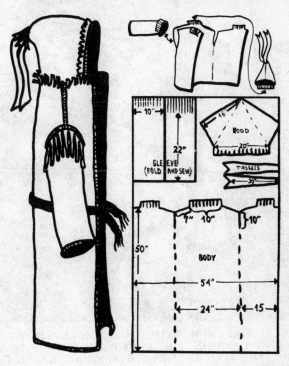

Capote is now ready to wear. Tie strings may be sewn on, or a belt or sash used to hold the Capote closed.

For pleasing appearance bind all exposed edges with colored cloth or ribbon, as shown on the drawing. Use the same material to cover the shoulder and sleeve seams. These last two bindings were sometimes fully or partially covered with beadwork. Large rosettes were sometimes added to the front of the hood, while beads and sequins were often tacked on top of, or parallel with the bindings. Capotes can also be made of Moosehide or Buffalo fur.

SOME STONEY MEN WITH THEIR CHILDREN, AT A HUNTING CAMP IN THE ROCKY MOUNTAINS NEAR BANFF. THE MAN IN THE FOREGROUND HAS A CAPOTE AND LEGGINGS MADE FROM A HUDSON'S BAY BLANKET. THE BOY WEARS A SCARF AND BLANKET LEGGINGS. THE MAN AT LEFT WEARS HIS BLANKET OVER ONE SHOULDER AND HOLDS IT FROM INSIDE.

Photo from Archives of the Canadian Rockies

MITTENS AND SOCKS

Footwear in the Winter time and during cold rains was no easy matter in the Old Days. One old Comanche woman once told an anthropologist who wondered about the Native secret for Winter warmth: *"Some folks were just awfully cold all Winter.*" The Old People would have gladly traded their most prized possession, in the Winter, for a pair of modern, insulated boots.

For basic foot warmth tall Winter moccasins were made of Buffalo hide with the fur turned in. Extra Buffalo fur, or other warm skins, were wrapped around the feet for more protection, and pieces of dried and shaped rawhide were tied over the outside to keep out moisture. Bear or other animal fat was often melted and used to coat moccasins to keep out water. Unfortunately, moisture always got in, leather slipped on snow and ice, and a pause in cold weather sometimes meant frozen lumps at the ends of the legs.

Socks were often cut and sewn in the form of foot-sized pouches. These were folded around the ankles and held up by the wrapped tops of the moccasins.

Gloves were apparently not made in the old days, but mittens were generally worn over the hands in cold weather. Mittens keep the hands warmer than gloves by allowing the fingers more movement. Mittens are also easy to remove in a hurry—they were generally attached to each other by a thong worn over the shoulder, so that they could be allowed to fall from the hands. Two basic styles were made, one with the thumb and hand cut as one piece, the other with a separate thumb piece sewn over an opening for the thumb. Both kinds were made from single pieces folded over and sewn up, or two pieces sewn all the way around.

BLANKET SOCK

Belts

Belts were very important articles to People who lived outdoors and whose clothing had no pockets. From belts hung their knives, awls, and handy pouches. Men used belts to hold up their leggings and breechcloths—women used them to keep their dresses in place.

Belts were commonly made out of heavy leather or rawhide. Commercial harness leather has long been a favorite belt material, and was used exclusively whenever it was available. Men's belts were generally no more than three inches wide, but women's belts of five and six inches were not unusual. The simple method of fastening a belt was to have a buckskin thong attached through two holes in one end, and then slipped through two matching holes in the other end and tied in front. Harness buckles and uniform buckles were sometimes sewn on instead.

Beads, brass tacks, and metal conchos were the main items used to decorate belts. Small brass tacks (similar to those used on upholstery) were often pushed through the leather and the protruding points broken off. These were the popular "*tack belts*" of the Northern Plains. Tack belts were either solidly covered by even rows of tacks, or designs were made by using tacks or leaving certain areas untacked.

"*Panel belts*" were another popular type on the Northern Plains. These were decorated by sections, or panels, of lazy-stitch beadwork (often with rows so long between stitches that they hung loosely over each other), which alternated with undecorated sections or with sections of brass tacks.

Fully-beaded belts were used most everywhere. Lazy-stitch and applique beadwork was done on the belt itself, which was usually made of stiff leather or soft leather with heavy backing. Beaded belts made on a loom were generally sewn to a stiff backing.

Belts covered by trade metal, or silver, conchos (from

less than one to several inches in diameter) were most popular on the Central and Southern Plains. The conchos were usually attached by a long thong running behind the belt. Women's concho belts often had a matching piece hanging down one side, and sometimes ending with an ornate silver tip.

In the SouthWest and NorthEast very fine hand-woven sashes were often used instead of belts. The sashes of the Hopi (which are woven by the men) have become standard items for the ceremonial wear of many SouthWest tribes. Sashes are often quite wide, and so long that they have to be wrapped several times about the waist. Long fringe often hangs from the ends. In the North a popular belt was the "*Hudson's Bay Assumption Sash*," which is basically red, with many colors interwoven. It was worn by Natives and trappers alike.

Arm bands and anklets were, and are, usually worn with dance outfits, but were not as often worn with everyday dress. Arm bands were decorated with quill or beadwork, or made from strips of fur (often the foot sections, with claws or hooves were attached). Metal bands were cut from brass sheets and tin cans. Strips of Angora or Buffalo fur were worn over the feet, tied beneath sleigh bells that were fastened to leather straps.

BEADING

Beadwork decoration is a fine method for emphasizing pride in the design and workmanship of one's belongings. Beads vary in size from a pin-head to a pigeon egg, some rare types being even larger. After they became readily available from traders, the Native Americans used beads in countless different ways. With the tiny "seed" beads they developed a complex art form that was used to decorate clothing, tools, and even riding equipment. This art form was based on the ancient method of decorating by sewing down dyed and flattened porcupine quills.

Four methods of beadwork are commonly used. The easiest of these is done on a loom. A loom is easily made of wood, and should be about three inches wide and six inches longer than your planned beadwork. The tops of the upright pieces need grooves spaced ⅛ inch apart to hold the warp threads. Use heavy thread for the warp, and weave it back and forth across the loom and around the screws at each end, as shown in the drawing. Wax all thread with beeswax, to keep it from slipping.

Head bands, belts, and hat bands are generally made on a loom. Plan the design on paper, and leave two warp threads on each side, for strength. Beads are strung on the weave thread, spaced across the warp threads, and pushed down to be passed through again by the weave thread below the warp. Begin in the middle and work towards the ends. Weave back and forth a few times to finish, and knot the warp threads together. Attach the completed bead strip to leather backing by sewing down the double-warp edges with strong thread.

More creative beadwork can be made with the "lazy stitch" method. Finished pieces done this way are distinctive for their ridged rows of somewhat loose beads. This produced an appearance that was especially popular among the People of the Plains. It was done by sewing several beads at a time directly to leather, these being attached only at the ends of rows.

Lazy stitch beadwork is generally applied directly to the item to be decorated. A knot is tied at the end of a waxed thread, and hidden on the reverse side of the beadwork. From two to more than ten beads are strung at a time and sewn down in parallel rows. The needle does not go entirely through the material, but catches only the outer edge of it. Figure A is a top view of the beads before being pulled tight. Figure B is a side view.

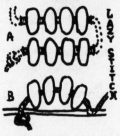

The third style of beadwork is known as the "applique stitch." Two threads are used, and every second or third bead is sewn down. This method produces the most perfect beadwork on leather. It is ideal for floral and pictoral designs. It was very popular among the People of the Rocky Mountain country, as well as the Woodlands People in the East.

The end of one thread is knotted and attached to the material. A number of beads are strung on it and laid in place. The second thread is then sewn across the first one, a stitch being taken at every second or third bead. Between stitches the second thread passes under the beads just below the surface, with leather. When beading on cloth the material must be backed for support, and the thread must be pulled all the way through. Beads may be sewn down in straight lines or in curves, as fits the design. Completed applique beadwork presents such a smooth, tight appearance that no threads are visible.

APPLIQUE STITCH

Circular pieces of beadwork are known as rosettes. They are often used where only a small amount of beadwork is desired—on leather vests, purses, and fur caps, for instance. They may range in size from a dime to a dinner plate.

Rosettes are generally made on backed felt or buckskin. Begin by drawing a circle on the material, and then draw in the design. Don't cut the circle out until you have done the beadwork. Knot the waxed thread, and sew down the center bead. Sew down the first row two beads at a time. Go back through the second bead again, each time. After the first row, sew down four beads at a time, and go back through the last two. At the end of each row, run the thread through all the beads again, if they need to be evened up.

WOMEN'S CLOTHING

The simplest style of dressing, among Native women, was that seen among tribes in warm weather regions in the old days—they brushed their hair neatly and enjoyed the warm Sunshine on their bodies.

Skirts of tule, woven grass, and shredded bark were worn by women of many tribes—along both sea coasts. Aprons and skirts of animal furs were also common. Blankets and robes of various styles were worn by such women when the weather got cold, or at nighttime.

The simple styles mentioned above can be assembled using your own imagination. We will limit this discussion to the more complex dress items—leather and cloth dresses and leggings—as they were made and worn from the deserts of the SouthWest to the woods of the North-East.

216

The most common style of leather dress in the long ago was made like a slip, with shoulder straps and separate sleeves tied around the neck and sometimes under the arms, as illustrated. It was seen among numerous tribes.

Another old style of dress, though apparently more recent than the one just described, was made from two Deer skins. The three drawings show the steps in making this dress: The skins are laid together, the dotted line marking the eventual shoulder line. The bottom of the dress is trimmed to suit the wearer's taste (or the tribal style) and also the size. Commonly, the bottom of the dress was arranged so that all or part of the legs on the skins were left hanging at each side, and sometimes the tail was left to hang down in the front and back centers. The two pieces are sewn together with sinew or thread, or laced with leather strips, with an in-and-out stitch along the dotted line. The sides are sewn down with an overhand stitch. The tops of the hides are folded down, front and back, to form the yoke, as shown. A neck opening is cut and hemmed. The sleeves may be sewn shut, laced together, or just left hanging open. Sometimes the hides were sewn so that their hinds formed the yoke, and the Deer tails were left to hang down the front. Sometimes they were tailored so that fringes could be cut right into the dress itself; at other times strips of leather were sewn on separately and fringed, often up along the side seam.

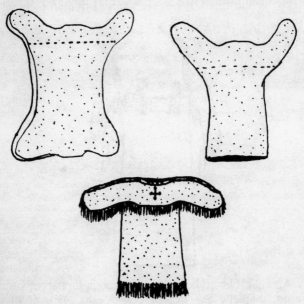

James A. Teit, who was married to a woman of the Salish People, described their styles of dresses thusly:

"Women's dresses were made of two whole Deerskins or small Elk skins sewed face to face, heads down. The sides were sewed up to near the armpits. At the upper ends of skins the edges were folded over and sewed down to the body of the garment. There were no sleeves, the extensions of the shoulders consisting of the hind legs of the skins falling over the arms almost to the wrists. The side seams and all the outer edges were fringed. Generally the tail-pieces were cut off and the bottom of the dress was trimmed so that it was longer at the sides. Usually one or two rows of inserted thongs depended from the dress near the bottom. In later days some cloth dresses, generally red and blue, were used instead of skin. They were cut and ornamented in much the same way as the skin dresses."

DRESS DECORATIONS

Tribal styles of dress decorations were generally similar to the decorations on men's shirts and leggings. Tribes of the SouthWest and Southern Plains liked to paint their leather clothing solid colors, sometimes with contrasting lines along the edges. They had a strong liking for long, thin fringes hanging in profusion. Items of silver, especially buttons and conchos, were common on their dresses, leggings, and moccasins. Heavy beadwork on yokes was rare, but narrow lines of beadwork were often used to decorate seams and edges.

Yokes fully covered with bead and quillwork were most common among the Sioux People and their neighbors. These women certainly looked striking with their long braids falling over an immense section of beadwork, that was covered with geometric designs, and sometimes reached the waist. Some women who could afford the vast quantities of dentalium shells covered their yokes with row upon row of these fine items. Elk teeth, however, were the most prized of all dress decorations—among many tribes in addition to the Sioux. Those who could not afford solid rows of the teeth (and few could) were often content to space the rows far apart, or to add some teeth to the bottom of a row of beadwork. Cowrie shells gave a similar effect for much less expense, and were particularly popular on the heavy wool replacements of skin dresses. By that time the restricted hunting had made teeth even more valuable. The Sioux even carved Elk teeth replicas from bone.

Old-time Blackfoot dresses were commonly decorated with a band of beadwork across the front that curved downwards toward the center. Another beaded band often covered the shoulders, and small beaded symbols were applied on other parts of the dresses. A downward-pointing triangle was generally beaded on the lower front of the dress—presumably as some traditional symbol of womanhood. A narrow beaded band usually edged the bottom of the dress, while thongs and fringes often hung in profusion. Blackfoot women preferred larger-than-seed beads for their dresses. They used both pony beads and

CHEYENNE MOTHER & DAUGHTER WITH COWRIE SHELL-COVERED TRADE CLOTH DRESSES.

glass tube beads on the capes. Time saved made up for beauty lost. Large beads were also strung on the long thongs, while thimbles and drilled coins were attached to their ends, and Deer hooves and cowrie shells were tied into the fringes.

Cloth dresses were decorated in a variety of ways, in addition to, or instead of beadwork. Cowrie shells were popular, and ribbon edging was almost always applied around the bottom. The heavy wool dresses were usually edged with one or more rows of narrow ribbons, and sometimes with wide ribbons at the bottom. Brass sequins, shoe buttons, and similar items were often sewn down next to the narrow ribbon edging. Designs, such as crosses and circles, were also made with them. Dresses made of light cloth usually had one or two wide ribbons sewn on at the bottom. Chippewa women commonly attached many rows of tin cone jingles to their cloth dresses. Women of Prairie tribes, such as the Osage and Sac & Fox, developed elaborate cloth skirts and dresses by using ribbon decoration. Ribbons (and ribbon-like strips of cloth) were sewn down in vertical and horizontal rows of varying widths.

220

Contrasting ribbon was then folded in half and cut, like children's paper cut-outs, in floral and geometric designs. Either the cut-out pieces, or the ribbon with the pieces cut out were then sewn over a row of ribbon already in place. Often a third ribbon was sewn between the basic ribbon and the one with the cut-outs in such a way that it could be seen beneath the cut-out openings down one side of the piece, while the basic ribbon could be seen down the other side. Much careful sewing and hemming is required to give this style the beauty that its design highlights. At some present-day pow-wows all the women's dresses are of this style.

Other common articles of women's clothing included belts, moccasins, headgear, and necklaces, which are all described elsewhere. Little pouches for toilet and sewing articles, as well as a slender case for an awl, were often carried from a belt or tied elswhere on the dress. Bracelets of small beads and metal as well as rings of metal and silver were much desired. Fringed shawls have been very popular shoulder coverings since they have been available.

Native women of today, in general, have taken much greater care to maintain at least a semi-traditional appearance (braids, calico dresses, and moccasins) than have the men (crew cuts, cowboy hats, and cowboy boots). It is easier to be one's self at home than among spirit-less critics.

JICARILLA APACHE DEERSKIN DRESS

Of the two basic styles used in the making of most buckskin dresses, Teit describes one, and this Apache dress illustrates the other. It is, basically, a dress made of two hides, sewn up the sides and across the top, except for a neck opening and the openings of the short sleeves.

221

when travelling on hot days, or when cooking in crowded lodges, or when gathering wood, water, berries, and stray children from near and far.

For warmth and style, heavy, wool "*trade cloth*" was the most popular for dresses. These were generally made like the old skin dresses. Often, in fact, buckskin fringes were sewn on at the bottoms, and buckskin thongs were suspended in rows across the dresses, sometimes anchored to small pieces of colored cloth. Two methods of attaching these thongs are illustrated. Many times the beaded or quilled yokes from worn-out skin dresses were repaired and worn over plain cloth dresses.

The large, and sometimes annoying, sleeves of many old skin dresses were often modified on cloth dresses. Sometimes the cloth sleeves were just made slimmer, other times they had cuffs that buttoned. With the latter a loose blouse was often worn which had big, open-end and elbow-length sleeves. At other times the dress had these flaring sleeves, and a blouse with cuffs was worn underneath. The combination of blouse and dress gave more warmth and the appearance was pleasing—especially when contrasting calico materials were used. Aprons were sometimes worn in the form of a second skirt—made of yet another contrasting pattern of calico material. This style became the every-day dress for numerous women after the start of the reservation period, and variations of it may still be commonly seen today.

Instead of folding over the top of the dress, however, a separate yoke is added. In this case, the yoke falls down a short distance, front and back, and is generally sparsely decorated. Yokes that were basically similar were made by Sioux women. Theirs came down much lower, were usually cut straight across at the bottom and were often fully covered with beadwork of much weight.

The dimensions given for this dress are for proportions only. The fringes were cut from separate pieces of leather that were sewn along the inside edges and between the side hems. Pieces of leather were sometimes added between the side seams to make the skirts fuller.

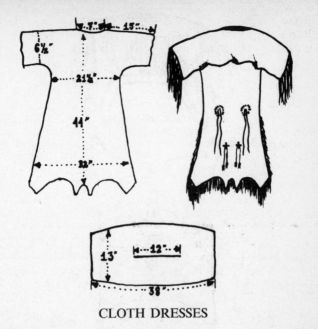

CLOTH DRESSES

Women, more than men, must have been greatly pleased with the coming of cloth. The majority of full-dress wearing tribes adopted a physical modesty that must have made the heavy skin dresses of the women a sheer burden

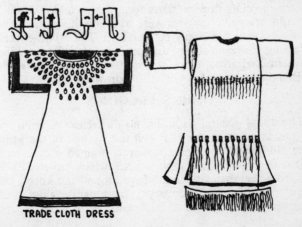

TRADE CLOTH DRESS

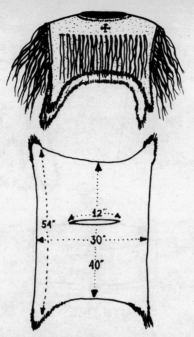

APACHE SKIN PONCHO

Leather ponchos were commonly worn by women of many tribes over bare skin in the long ago, and over leather and cloth dresses, more recently, for added warmth and appearance. The styles were basically the same, while the decorations can easily be imagined. The Apache liked very long fringe on theirs, and often painted them a solid color. In cold areas, these ponchos were sometimes made of Buffalo or other fur with the hair worn inside.

WOMEN'S LEGGINGS

There was generally little or no difference between the moccasins worn by the men and the women of the same tribe. In the Plains area, however, women wore snug-fitting leggings beneath their dresses which covered their legs from the ankles to somewhere around the knees, the height depending on tribal style. Everyday leggings were often simply two pieces of buckskin, cut to wrap around the lower leg—wider at the top than bottom. Several thongs were used to tie the leggings together along the outsides of the legs. Long thongs were used to hold the tops up. When worn with high-top moccasins the leggings were usually wrapped around the outside of the ankle flaps.

One style of legging was made to be worn inside the ankle flaps of high-top moccasins. In the drawings this style is shown with shoe buttons along the side. These were sometimes used instead of tie strings, whenever they could be obtained. A strip of colored cloth was sometimes sewn down one side, over the buttonholes, for decoration.

The most common decoration on leggings consisted of a panel of beadwork that usually covered the bottoms of the leggings. Women on the Southern Plains often made and decorated their leggings to match their moccasins. In the North the decoration generally contrasted with the moccasins, and usually consisted of designs done within narrow bands of beadwork. Sometimes the beadwork was solid, often times it merely highlighted a background of colored cloth, such as dark green velvet.

EVA SUN-GOES-SLOW, A GIRL OF THE CROW TRIBE,
WITH SKIN DRESS AND PANEL BELT.

A MOTHER AND SON OF THE SOUTHERN UTE PEOPLE
FROM THE SOUTHERN ROCKY MOUNTAIN COUNTRY.
SHE WEARS A COTTON BLOUSE BENEATH A VELVET
DRESS WITH CAPE-LIKE SLEEVES. A SPLIT OTTER SKIN
COVERS THE BOY'S SHOULDERS AND BEADED ORNA-
MENTS HANG FROM HIS HAIR.

A CANADIAN OF THE YEAR 1900

A SYMBOL OF PRIDE AND BEAUTY IN PERSONAL AP-
PEARANCE. THIS YOUNG DENE MAN IS DRESSED IN
TYPICAL NORTHERN PLAINS FASHION OF THE PERIOD:
BEADED MOCCASINS, WOOL LEGGINGS, TRADE-CLOTH
BREECHCLOUT WITH RIBBONS, BEAD AND FRINGE-
DECORATED SHIRT, BRASS ARMBANDS, AND LOOP
NECKLACE; PLUS BELLS AND PORCUPINE-HAIR ROACH
FOR DANCING. HIS HAIR IS IN THREE BRAIDS AND
HAS A POMPADOUR.

MEN'S SHIRTS

Buckskin shirts were not as common in the Old Days
as has often been assumed. In fact, shirts were not made
or worn by the men of many tribes until fairly late in the
period of the old life. Those shirts that were worn long
ago were generally in the style of ponchos, with loose
sleeves attached. They were often left open along the sides
and only fastened by a couple of thongs underneath the
sleeves. The neck opening was usually a large slit that was
tied shut with thongs at the shoulders.

227

A simple style of shirt was worn by men in the North-West forests—and probably in other areas, as well. It consisted of a large Deer hide that was folded in half and had a slit cut along the fold for a head opening. It was stitched or laced up the sides and arms (which were simply left as part of the hide when the sides were trimmed), or tied with thongs that also served as fringe.

Another simple shirt was made of two Deerskins that were sewed together heads up. The heads and necks were trimmed off and the resulting gap allowed the wearer's head to pass through. The forelegs were fastened together in .pairs to form the sleeves. The shirt was sometimes trimmed straight across the bottom, often fringed, and other times left complete, with the legs hanging far down on each side of the wearer.

Warm shirts for Winter wear were made in a number of ways—generally from hides with the hair left on. A small Buffalo robe, for instance, was commonly folded in half, an opening cut for the head, and the sides fastened together. Two coyote skins were sometimes worn over the front and back, with tails hanging down. Pieces of other skins were used to attach these two together at the shoulders and sides.

SHIRT DECORATIONS

Two basic methods of ornamenting shirts were used by most all shirt-wearing tribes, and were found to some degree on most all leather shirts. One of these, of course, was fringe. Some Hopi shirts had only a few short fringes cut from the excess material that protrudes from their style of seams. Some Kutenai shirts had amazingly long fringes sewn into the seams at the sides, shoulders, and across the shirt bottoms. These, no doubt, produced some memorable experiences when their wearers chased after game, or tried to escape from enemies in the dense brush of their country. The People of the Southern Plains, too, liked long fringe on their shirts and garments. They often cut their fringes very thin and numerous. Each fringe was moistened and then rolled with the palm of the hand across the lap, which left the fringes with a very pleasing spiralled appearance.

Along with fringe, the other basic shirt ornament was the triangular flap which hung down from the front and back of the neck. This flap helped to cover the often large neck opening, besides adding a pleasing dimension to the front of the shirt. The flaps were commonly fringed on the edges, and covered with paint or painted designs, as well as quill and beadwork.

Buckskin shirts are often called war shirts, though among many tribes the shirts that were used in war were of a particular, and sacred, character, and seldom worn.

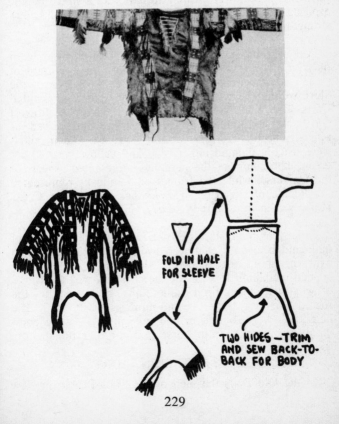

FOLD IN HALF
FOR SLEEVE

TWO HIDES—TRIM
AND SEW BACK-TO-
BACK FOR BODY

Many shirts were, however, painted and decorated for war purposes, even if used at other times. The specific decorations were, of course, first seen in Dreams. They included these methods: Shirts painted a solid color; shirts painted several colors, such as yellow top and sleeves and red bottom; shirts covered with painted designs, such as large stripes all around, crosses, dots, and other Medicine figures; and shirts perforated all over with circles or other designs.

Other war shirts were recognizable by certain tribal styles, and by the knowledge that the wearer was a successful warrior. Sometimes the wearers of these shirts belonged to societies, and often they were offered large payments if they were willing to part with a shirt to some aspiring young man who felt that he would gain extra strength through its wearing.

Among the Sioux People, decorated shirts were worn only by leaders in the Old Days. The most important of these leaders belonged to a group called the Wicasas—the Shirt Wearers. They were the only ones to wear painted shirts. The Wicasas were chosen from among the bravest and most honorable men of the tribe, and served as official executives—men above reproach. Their shirts were usually painted either blue and yellow, or red and green. The colors of the paintings represented aspects of the Universe, while the fringes of hair locks represented the People of the tribe. The famous Sioux chief Crazy Horse was such a Shirt Wearer.

Other common shirt decorations were the stripes of quill and beadwork that were worn down the arms and over the shoulders. Blackfoot shirts often had a large beaded medallion in front of the chest, as well as fringes of white-with-black-tip Ermine skins. In later years the sacred hair-lock shirts became more generally used. The hair locks were sometimes enemy scalps, but more commonly were made from horse hair, or hair donated by friends and relatives.

TAOS ELK SKIN SHIRT

In the Old Days the men of the Taos Pueblo in New

Mexico often travelled North to the Plains country in order to hunt Buffalo. Though they were members of the SouthWest Pueblo culture—the Life of farming and permanent villages—they saw many appealing aspects of the Buffalo-hunting tribes on the Plains, some of which they brought home and adopted themselves. This shirt is a typical example of a Taos-Plains article.

The shirt requires two Deer hides, or one large Elk hide. The main section is one piece that is cut like a poncho, as seen in the drawing. The measurements given are only for proportion—yours will depend on your own size and desires.

Begin by cutting a 10 or 12 inch slit for the head opening in the piece which you have cut to shape. Then lay the body and sleeve pieces on the floor, attaching them as shown, and sewing them together. A long, rectangular piece of buckskin is sewn between each sleeve and the body. This is later fringed. These fringe pieces should hang lower than the bottoms of the sleeves. The sleeves and shirt sides may either be sewn shut (for warmth) or tied shut with several short thongs (for better air circulation). The short fringes at the bottom of the sleeves and body may be cut into the material itself, but are usually separate pieces (as shown for the sleeve) that are sewn on after completion. Triangular flaps hang down both front and back. They are sewn across the top only. Generally, these were painted with red or yellow pigment, and edged with beadwork, cloth, or strips of fur, along with leather pieces for fringe, as on the sleeves. Sometimes lines of contrasting colors were carefully painted next to the beaded edgings on the sleeves and flaps.

SHOULDER COVERINGS

Vests and capes can be worn in Summer over the bare skin, and in colder times over a cloth shirt when a jacket would be too cumbersome. . . Both kinds of coverings were commonly worn with old-time dance outfits, and capes are still a basic dress item for many dancers today. Pow-wow outfits in the Northern Plains area, for instance, often center on a decorated cape and matching aprons.

231

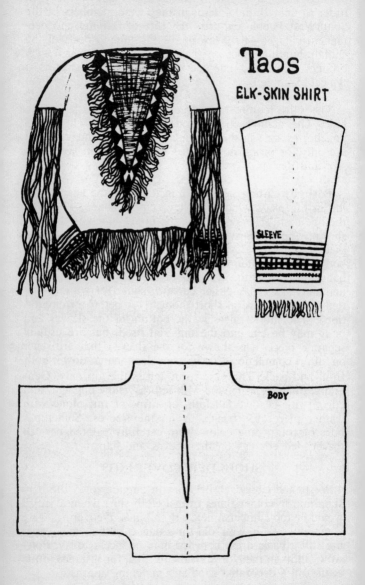

Taos

ELK-SKIN SHIRT

SLEEVE

BODY

HAIRLESS, A COMANCHE CHIEF, AS HE APPEARED
BEFORE RODMAN WANNAMAKER AT THE MONTANA
COUNCIL IN 1909. HIS CLOTHING IS OF THE SOUTHERN
PLAINS STYLE, WITH MUCH TWISTED FRINGE. HIS
RATTLE AND TIE SLIDE ARE AMONG THE MANY SYM-
BOLS HE WEARS TO ACCLAIM HIMSELF AN OLD-TIME
PEYOTE MAN. HIS SACRAMENT IS BEADED ON THE
BOTTOMS OF HIS HAIR DROPS.

VESTS

Native vests were originally copied from the vests of the invading culture. In fact, manufactured cloth vests (gambler's vests) were quite popular with men when "*dressing for town*" during the latter part of the nineteenth and early twentieth century. Older conservative men on many reserves today still wear dark cloth vests and black scarves for their daily dress.

Cloth vests can be bought cheaply at thrift stores. They can be decorated with beadwork or with ribbons sewn along the edges. Elk teeth and cowrie shells were commonly drilled and hung in rows to partially or fully cover cloth vests.

Leather vests can be made of buckskin, or of heavier hide such as Moose. They should be backed with colorful calico cloth—for beauty, extra warmth, and comfort, and to keep thinner leather from stretching out of shape. If the lining is cut slightly larger than the vest it can be folded over the outside to make a nice edging. It is best to cut the lining to shape as it is being sewn down, rather than beforehand, for the leather vest may stretch while you are sewing. Vests should be cut to fit loose. For a pattern use a cloth vest that fits you, or make one out of paper. Begin sewing the three pieces together at the shoulders, and end up by sewing the sides down to the bottom. Add tie strings in front to complete the basic vest.

Beadwork makes beautiful decoration on vests. Some of the finest examples of traditional art in beadwork were seen on many of the old-time, fully-beaded vests, like those worn by the Flathead men in the photo. The Eastern tribes, who lived in the Woods, preferred profuse designs of connecting flowers and leaves for their vests (as well as most other beadwork). The People who lived on the wide-open Plains used intricate geometric designs with straight lines, done in lazy-stitch style, to decorate their vests. The People of the Northern Plains and Mountains also used geometric designs, in applique style, but preferred simple designs of colorful flowers and leaves. In the final years of their popularity, some fully-beaded vests displayed such un-ethnic designs as crossed flags and hatted cowboys on rearing horses.

CAPES

Capes of fringed leather were a basic part of the long-ago clothing worn in the Eastern Woodlands. For dancing and special occasions these People made capes of dark velvet—heavily beaded with floral designs—which were a part of elaborate, matching outfits.

Skins of animals such as Otter, Bobcat, and Coyote were often slit down the middle so that they could be worn over the shoulders for warmth and appearance, as well as for spiritual power. The skins were left intact, often lined, and worn with the head on the chest and the tail down the back. Sometimes mirrors or other decorations were sewn to the skins, other times Medicine items were attached.

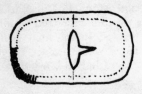 

LEGGINGS

When the People were given government rations and presents in the old days they generally went home and reworked many of the useful things to suit their own needs. Metal utensils were often cut up and made into knives, arrowheads, or arm bands. Shoes and boots had their tops cut off and used for wristguards and such— while the buttons were sewn onto other things for decoration. Trousers were turned into leggings by having the crotch cut-out of them—a practice which some old-timers continued well into the present century.

The use of crotchless pants appears to be quite ancient. It is believed that many of the Northern tribes used leggings long before adopting breechcloths and shirts. Even in Winter they wore only moccasins, leggings, and a Buffalo robe. The leggings provided warmth, as well as protection from brush and brambles.

In the long ago, Deerskin and Elkskin leggings were worn in the Summertime, while Buffalo or other skins with the fur turned inward, were used for Winter leggings. The skin leggings were made like hollow tubes that covered the legs from the ankles to the thighs, where they were tied to the belt with thongs. They generally had fringes or wide flaps along the seams, down the outsides. Often they were also fringed around the bottoms, and sometimes the fringes, or side-flaps, trailed for a foot or two on the ground behind. Decoration consisted mainly of painting—either stripes, spiritual designs, war deeds, or solid colors covering the whole leggings—and long, narrow strips of quillwork in front of, and parallel with, the seams.

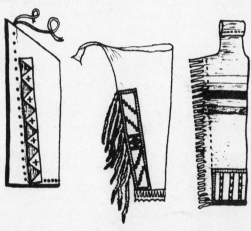

With the coming of blankets and beads, leggings were often made of wool, and the decorations consisted mainly of beadwork. These wool leggings had flaps of varying widths, which stood out and away from the legs. Beaded strips were done on separate material and then sewn to the main part of the legging, just ahead of the seam. Another style of decoration that was used widely—especially by the tribes of the Northern Plains area—was the beaded panel. Panels consisted of rectangular pieces of thin wool or velvet, usually four to six inches high, and long enough to go either all the way or half way around the bottom of the tube part of the legging. These cloth panels were backed with stiff material, covered with beadwork (fully or partially—often the color of the cloth served as a background) and sewn to the bottom of the legging.

237

To make a pair of leggings you will need two average hides or one blanket. The front and back of each legging is cut out as one piece, then sewn, laced, or tied together along a straight line drawn at an angle from the large part of the leg, at the top, to the narrow part at the ankle. The flaps will be narrow at the top and wide at the bottom. They are left open, not sewn together. If you wish more warmth, or don't like wool next to your skin, cut some calico material about one-half inch wider all around than your legging pieces, and sew this on before closing up your leggings. Fold the extra material around to the front and stitch it down neatly, and you will have a nice trim all around. Also, the inside of your flaps can be quite flashy this way. Sew cloth loops or leather thongs to the front side of each legging, so that the leggings hang properly when fastened on to your belt. A SouthWest style of legging is knee-high and made from thick hide. It is tied on at the calf with sashes. It was worn out on the deserts as a protection from cactus, brush, and snake bites.

After breechcloths gave way to full pants many men still wore leggings in the Winter time. Slipped over regular pants, your leggings will really keep those cool Canadian winds from biting through!

UTE SKIN LEGGINGS

The leggings in the large drawing are the old style worn by men of the Ute tribe of Colorado. They are typical of leggings worn by other tribes on the Southern Plains and in the SouthWest. Each legging is made from one Deer hide. These are cut as shown in the lower drawing, folded in half along the center line, and sewn up as far as the outside dotted lines. The separate piece in the drawing, with the ragged edges, was commonly sewn to the inside bottom of the leg tubes, so that it would protrude beyond the bottom fringe. In wearing, this piece covered the moccasins, the fringe trailed on the ground, and the legging was tied to a belt by the two pieces extending from the top. Beaded strips were applied as shown. Bells, Deer hooves, pieces of hair and fur, and other small things were attached to the strips, fringes, and wherever else the wearer wished to have them.

BREECHCLOTHS

In the warm Summertime a breechcloth held up by a soft leather thong is often all the clothing necessary for physical pleasure with minimum security. This has long been the favorite style of Native dress in warm areas and warm times. Warriors preferred it when going into battle, for it allowed their bodies free movement. Young boys of most tribes seldom wore anything else while playing in warm weather. Even girls wore breechcloths before they reached the age of puberty, among a number of tribes.

A breechcloth is a piece of skin, or cloth, that is seldom more than a foot wide, and is passed between the legs, up over the belt, and left to hang down in front and behind. The softest tanning was required for those made of skin, to help avoid chafing. Blue wool tradecloth was favored, for warmth and comfort, by many men after it became available. Breechcloths were generally worn plain—those of skin were often fringed. Cloth breechcloths for dress were decorated with colored ribbons and metal sequins, which were generally sewn on in many parallel lines, or combinations of lines and V's. Circles and crosses were made with sequins, and sometimes beadwork was added.

Breechcloth lengths varied—from barely-covering, to tails that hung down to the ground.

Tribes in the East, and in some other areas, wore aprons instead of breechcloths. These were just leather or cloth flaps that hung down from a belt in front and behind. Sometimes they were just tied together at the sides, and worn without a belt. Some of them were beautifully decorated with floral designs done in applique beadwork.

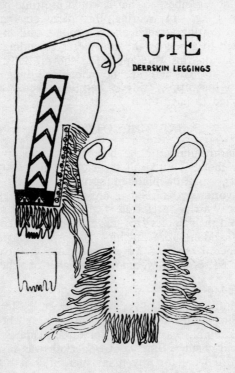

UTE

DEERSKIN LEGGINGS

BLACK-TAILED DEER, A UTE, AS HE APPEARED DUR-
ING AN OFFICIAL VISIT TO WASHINGTON, D. C. IN
1868. THE SILVER SPOT OVER THE FOREHEAD WAS AN
OLD LIFE SYMBOL FOR WARRIORS—HIS WAR EXPLOITS
ARE DRAWN ON THE FLAPS OF HIS "WAR LEGGINGS."
A HANDY MIRROR IS PARTLY COVERED BY HIS LITTLE
POUCH OF PAINTS AND SUNDRIES.

NECKLACES AND EARRINGS

Like an artist with an empty canvas, the old-time individual loved to decorate any exposed areas of his body. These were places to present calling cards—necklaces with mystifying little pouches, breastplates of fine, polished bones, beadwork to exclaim artistic talent, or strings of animal claws to testify for the wearer's prowess.

BREASTPLATES

Though an occasional arrow must have been deflected by the hard, little, bone "*hairpipes*," worn on breastplates, during old-time battles, these served basically as items of beauty, not as pieces of armor. The hairpipes are made from Deer leg-bones (in factories, not by hand—they have long been an important part of traders' stocks), and strung up in various ways to hang over the chest. Some long breastplates reached from the neck down past the waist, while others were barely six inches long, hanging like white chevrons from their thongs around the neck.

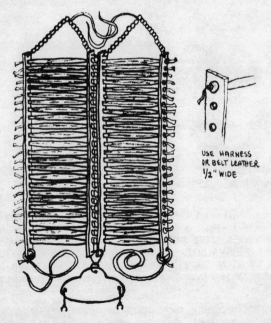

USE HARNESS
OR BELT LEATHER
1/2" WIDE

Hairpipes have always been costly. Many dancers today
buy imitation bone pipes, or make their own from bird
and animal bones or corncob pipe stems. Long hairpipes
(3 inches or more) are generally worn in two parallel
rows, while shorter pipes are often mounted in three, or
even four rows—the length depending on desire and
money.

Lay your hairpipes out in the way you wish to mount
them. The drawing shows a *"typical"* example. Use soft
thongs to string the pipes between tough, but pliable
leather straps. Old harness leather, found in a corner of
your barn, works well for such purposes. One strap goes
on each side of the breastplate, and two go down the
middle, with large necklace, or *"Crow"* style beads strung
in the center. With really long hairpipes only one strap,
and no beads, may be used down the center. At the top of
the completed plate is a pair of thongs that tie around
the waist.

Some item was often attached to the bottom center of a
breastplate. Little bunches of Ermine tails, a large coin,
or a small pouch of Medicine paint or herb were common
items. The drawing shows a *"pectoral"* worn there. These
items were taken from or copied after early Spanish horse
gear. They were often made on the Plains from trade
metal, such as German *"silver."* Large, Christian-style
crosses were made and used the same way. Scenes and
designs were often scratch-engraved on pectorals and
crosses—pictographs of battle exploits and designs with
spiritual meaning were most common. Sometimes these

metal items were worn on a thong like a necklace, but more often they were fastened to the bottoms of breast-plates. Chains and little metal crescents and designs were attached to holes drilled into the pectorals.

The drawing shows the basic style for the loop necklaces that were more popular in the Northern Plains area than breastplates. Some tribes, like the Crow and the Flathead, preferred small "*disc*" beads (looking like bone-washers) strung on loops of buckskin, while others, such as the Blackfoot and Sarsi, wrapped tiny seed beads round and round on the buckskin loops with thread. Still others strung large necklace beads or short hairpipes on the loops.

The most difficult part of making the loop necklace is obtaining enough beads to string up. After you have done this, cut the number of buckskin thongs you wish to use—usually eight to twelve. These get progressively longer as they go down. They are strung to harness leather straps on each side and knotted on the ends. Buckskin tie strings are used to tie around the neck and waist.

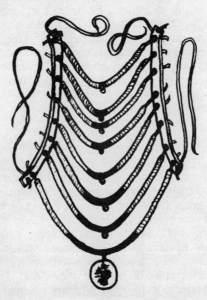

EARRINGS

Most Native People had their ears pierced at an early age. Among some tribes this was done in a ceremonial manner, among others it was done simply by the mother at home. Long ago, a greased Porcupine's quill, a cactus spine, or a sharpened twig was thrust through the earlobe and broken off close to the surface. In later times, a piece of sinew or buckskin thong was pulled through with a needle, or an open ring was pressed against the lobe and left to wear out an opening by constant pressure.

Each lobe generally had one hole. However, some People, like the Comanche and Wichita, thought it fashionable to have a number of holes up along the outside of the ears, and to wear a small earring in each.

Silver wires were preferred for earrings. Some tribes, like the Utes, often wore only large, heavy hoops made from wires. Round pieces of shell were popularly worn from small or large hoops. Sometimes whole shells, or pieces of shell carved into shapes were hung from wire hoops. In the same way, silver and glass beads were worn on hoops. The Sioux prized earrings made of dentalium shells, strung in rows like the chokers, and tied to the wire hoops. Ball and cone earrings were made by hanging a metal bead and a tin cone from the wire hoop. Members of the Native American Church often wear symbols of their religion on earrings today.

The silversmiths and jewelry workers of the SouthWest tribes produce earrings and necklaces of a very artistic type. This craft was influenced by Mexicans and Spaniards, and the products have long been eagerly sought by members of other tribes. Their manufacture, however, requires more knowledge and material than the general reader of these words will easily find.

SOUTHERN UTE PEOPLE IN "MODERNIZED", EVERYDAY CLOTHING. NOTICE THE DIFFERENT STYLES OF EARRINGS. THE CLOTHES OF THE MEN WERE STORE-BOUGHT, THOSE OF THE WOMEN WERE SEWN BY HAND. IN LATER TIPI-DAYS, TREADLE SEWING MACHINES WERE SOMETIMES SEEN INSIDE OF LODGES.

OTHER NECKLACES AND CHOKERS

Most any material that suits your fancy can, of course, be strung up and worn as a necklace. Claws were usually attached to a heavy thong, which was run through holes drilled at the base of the claws. Smaller holes were then drilled at the half-way point of the claws, so that a strip of sinew could be run through to give the necklace more rigidity. Pieces of fur can be folded over the two thongs and sewn together for added appearance.

Long necklaces were sometimes worn as bandoliers— hung over one shoulder and under the other arm. They were strung with seeds, beads, Deer hooves, gun shells, and other fancy or noisy items. Necklaces, like everything else, were worn for appearance as well as for personal spiritual reasons.

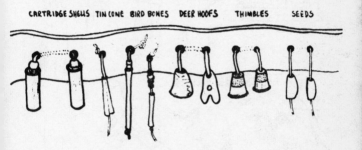

CARTRIDGE SHELLS   TIN CONE   BIRD BONES   DEER HOOFS   THIMBLES   SEEDS

Chokers worn around the throat were also of many kinds—some that could be worn all the time, others that were impressive, but so fragile or awkward that they were worn for special occasions only. The tribes of the Plains area seem to have used chokers much more than others. The Sioux People preferred the tusk-like dentalium shells for theirs, strung in rows on buckskin thongs, with leather strips and brass beads for spacers. They also liked to string up short hairpipes this way. Glass tube beads were similarly strung up and worn as chokers among many tribes. Everyday chokers were commonly made up of one or two strands of necklace beads. The Blackfoot People often strung Elk teeth or cowrie shells between the beads. Strips of beadwork were sometimes worn as chokers. Some later-day dance outfits were complete with a choker that was patterned after the common high-collar and tie, but was made of buckskin and fully beaded. Shells, metal items, and strips of fur were sometimes tied to chokers so that they would hang down in front. Chokers are most always tied behind the neck.

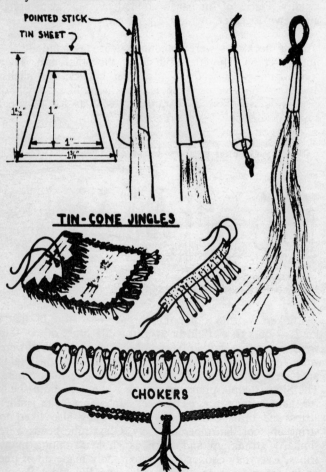

POINTED STICK

TIN SHEET

1½"

1"

1"

1¾"

TIN-CONE JINGLES

CHOKERS

BEAR'S GHOST–CHIEF OF THE YANKTON SIOUX. WHEN PHOTOGRAPHED BY RODMAN WANNAMAKER HE SAID: *"I REJOICE THAT A RECORD IS TO BE MADE OF THIS COUNCIL THAT IT MAY LIVE FOR FUTURE GENERATIONS."* HIS SHIRT IS DECORATED WITH PORCUPINE QUILL WORK AND HE WEARS HIS WAR MEDICINE IN HIS HAIR.

HAIR

The manners of wearing the hair were many and varied —but most People in the Old Days allowed their hair to grow Naturally long. Pride and personal satisfaction come with hair which flows about the shoulders and ripples gently in the Wind. The desire for individual expression, too, can be fulfilled in a number of ways in and about the hair. And finally, present-day hair specialists claim that hair cropped close to the scalp falls out at a rate of more than ten times that of waist-length hair.

HAIR STYLES

The following list describes some of the ways that various Native American People wore their hair. Some individuals always wore their hair in the same way, others changed styles often. Members of some tribes copied and adopted hair styles generally considered to be specifically from some other tribe. Personal dreams and tastes, as well as tribal traditions, determined the style of hair worn.

1. Hair worn loose and long—This is certainly the basic style of wearing long hair. It was the common style for Apache men, who often wore wide cloth bands around their heads to keep the hair back. It was a common style for men of the Mojave tribe, who just wore it straight down. It was also a common style for men and women of the Pacific NorthWest, who kept the hair out of their eyes, when working, with a headband of fur or skin. Individuals who normally wore their hair in one of the more dressed styles often wore their hair loose for ceremonial occasions, such as Vision Seeking and Sun Dancing—to obtain a more complete feeling of freedom and flowing with All. The hair was generally parted in the center or on the side when it was worn this way. This was also one of two styles used most commonly by Native women.

2. Hair worn loose and cropped—Among some tribes the men commonly wore their hair shoulder-length and kept it always cropped that way. The Messiah of the Ghost Dance, the Paiute named Wovoka, wore his hair

this way. Kiowa and Sac-and-Fox men liked this style. Widows and mourners of many tribes generally hacked their hair off to shoulder length to show their grief.

3. Hair worn long with bangs—This style was commonly used on children to keep the hair out of the face. The Pueblo tribes of the SouthWest have been particularly fond of bangs. Long ago, men on the Plains sometimes cut a small lock short and let it hang over their foreheads and noses.

4. Hair worn back—
a. For practical reasons many individuals used buckskin thongs to simply tie their hair behind their heads.
b. Some wore their hair in one braid down the back. Married Iroquois women wore one braid doubled up and tied with buckskin.
c. Another style consisted of a number of braids made after the hair was combed back. The braids were then tied together into one bunch.
d. The People in the SouthWest still comb their long hair back and roll it up in a queue, then wrap it with cloth. The Navajo wear it this way; Navajo men usually wear a wide band of cloth around the head, also. Hopi men wear the back of their hair in this fashion. They crop the sides shoulder length, and often cut bangs above the eyes. For ceremonies they wear all their hair loose.

5. Hair worn in two braids at the sides—
a. With a part down the center, one braid on each

side covering the ears. This is the other basic style for the majority of Native women, many of whom still wear their hair this way. They often tie the braids together and throw them behind while working. This is also the most common old-time style among the People of the Plains and many neighboring areas. Sioux and Cheyenne men favored it, Chippewa men to the East used it, and many Buffalo-Plains oriented men and women living in SouthWestern Pueblo villages also wore their hair in the handsome two-braid, center-part style.

b. A similar style differed in leaving the ears uncovered. This was done by some for comfort, by others because they lacked enough hair to cover the ears properly. Men more often did this than women.

c. Another similar style differed in having the part off to one side. This was the common men's style on and near the Northern Plains.

d. Parted on one side, with a lock cut shorter in front—the lock was combed and trained to lie to one side and cover the hair that went into the braids, though it often ended up hanging into the face. This was a man's style among tribes like the Utes of Colorado and the Blackfoot of Montana.

e. A similar style was used by some men—the lock was left long enough to be gathered from the forehead back into a bunch and then tied to the rest of the hair at the crown with a buckskin thong. This lock covered the part, and was usually gathered loose enough to form a slight pompadour over the forehead. It was a favorite style among Flathead men.

f. In a similar style the lock was cut from two to six inches long, coated with Bear grease or Buffalo dung, and trained to stand straight up over the forehead. It was an identifying style of Crow men, though it was also worn by a few men of neighboring tribes—notably Chief Joseph of the Nez Perce and Weasel Tail of the Blackfoot tribe.

g. Another variation worn by men with two braids at the sides left a third section of hair hanging loose down the back.

6. Hair worn in three braids—

a. The favorite style among Blackfoot men was to divide the hair into three even parts for braiding—one braid was made high at each side, in front of the ears, and another hung down the back. Less often the braids at the sides covered the ears. Sometimes the side part was used with this style, more often it was worn with the long lock tied back.

b. Another three-braid style seen among many tribes really consisted of two main braids and a thin "*scalplock*" down the back. This was a warrior's hair style from the Old Days, worn to tempt the enemy. If the wearer was knocked down or slain in battle, the first enemy to reach him usually grabbed the braided scalplock, put one of his feet on the victim's head, and gave a swift, curving slash with his knife, neatly severing the braid and skin to which it was attached. Wounded men often survived this "*scalp-lift*." The victor scraped the skin clean, then laced his little symbol tightly to a small willow hoop and took it back to camp to represent the slain warrior. During the Victory Dance war widows often danced with the scalps, then flung them into the fire to signify that the past was now over.

7. Hair worn in several braids—Two braids at each side, and sometimes one more in back, was another style sometimes used in the old days, particularly among Northern tribes like the Crees. Rarely, a man might have a number of braids all around his head, generally in fulfillment of a Dream.

8. Hair worn straight up—an old-time warrior's style used for its grotesque effect. The Chippewa, when going to war, tied the thin scalplock with stiff material at its base, so that it stood straight up for several inches, while the rest of the hair fell back down loosely, like a water fountain. Others did this with all their hair. Still others mixed grease or Buffalo dung into their hair and made it stand up in a huge point or curve back like a horn. Often this projection was smeared with paint. Kutenai warriors used a bunch of tule reeds as a base to tie their hair up to.

9. Hair worn in a knot on the head—this was a religious hairstyle, used primarily by the sacred Medicine Pipe Men of the Blackfoot tribe. The knot was usually worn over the forehead, with braids at the sides and back. Individuals who were totally devoted to their spiritual leadership often put all their hair into one braid, which was then coiled and fastened to protrude above the forehead. Sacred paint generally covered the hair.

10. Hair worn long down the center of the head—the well-known "*Mohawk*" style. This was a common style for men among many East Coast tribes, as well as some tribes in other areas, such as the Pawnee of the Eastern Plains. The hair on the sides of the head was generally plucked (yes, plucked!) out, and only a narrow srtip down the center was allowed to grow long. This was sometimes worn in a braid down the back.

HAIR CARE

The Bishop of Meaux long ago observed of the Native People:

"They are certainly fond of their hair, and they would consider themselves disgraced if any part of it was cut off. To preserve their hair they grease it often and powder it with the dust of spruce bark, and sometimes with vermillion; then they wrap it up in the skin of an Eel or serpent. . . ."

The trader Alexander Henry said this about the Blackfoot men whom he saw:

"The young men allow theirs (hair) to flow loose and lank about their necks, taking great care to keep it smooth about the face. . . . the elder men allow their hair to grow, and twist it. . . . they wear it on the forehead, projecting seven or eight inches in a huge knob, smeared with red Earth."

The anthropologist Clark Wissler found, even after the turn of the century, that they still *"spend a great deal of their time brushing and caring for their hair. They admire long hair and use charms to increase its length."* Buffalo hair and hair collected from mourners was often attached to the end of the hair with spruce gum, for added length.

Though Native People had body and face hair, most of them kept all exposed hair plucked, save that on the head. Many men kept hand-made metal tweezers fastened to a necklace or pouch, and spent much time seeking stray hair and plucking it out. Facial hair grew thicker among some tribes than others, so that mustaches and even beards were commonly seen in some areas. The men along the Pacific Coast, for instance, regularly wore full mustaches and sometimes long goatees. Buckskin Charlie, a Ute Chief from Colorado, was known for his mustache, which curled down around his mouth. A number of Flathead men trained mustaches and even waxed the ends. Names like Hairy Face and Bearded One were heard occasionally among tribes on the Plains.

Combs were not known in the Old Days, but the hair was often brushed. A primitive brush consisted of a handful of flexible twigs, bound together with buckskin. The most common brush on the Plains was made by inserting a stick of wood into a Porcupine's tail. Again, a handful of horse hair was sometimes bound and doubled over to make a soft hair brush.

Hair tonics and washes were prepared by the Native People from various plants which grew in their areas. Cactus suds were commonly used by the Hopi, and others in the SouthWest. SweetGrass, which was widely used as a sacred incense, was also boiled in water and used as a hair tonic. Sometimes it was mixed with cedar leaves, or other plants, for aroma and medicinal effect. The common Bear Grass was often boiled and used to control falling hair.

HEAD WEAR

Numerous things were worn over, in, and around the hair. Headbands of buckskin or strips of fur were worn, especially during the Winter, by both men and women (though not as commonly as one might think). Winter hats of fur, whole animal skins, and even bird skins were popular everywhere. Woven hats (made like baskets) were worn by women of many basket-weaving tribes. Eye-shades were made from rectangular pieces of rawhide with head-holes cut out of them.

Men often wore head coverings that identified their tribal roles or spiritual powers. Feather bonnets and single feathers, worn in back, top, or front of the head, generally represented war deeds. Headdresses with horns, worn with caps of Buffalo fur, Ermine skins, or feather bonnets, often signified membership in a men's society or power as a Medicine Man.

Personal Medicine items were quite often attached to the hair—especially during hunting or war expeditions. Animal claws, bird feathers and parts, and sacred little pouches were common.

Silver conchos were tied into the hair—often to the small scalplock in back. Some men tied leather straps to their hair that were covered with conchos (like belts), often reached the ground, and weighed many pounds.

Thongs with beads were often tied into the hair above each temple, and allowed to dangle in front of the eyes. Beaded headbands were uncommon, in most areas, and "*princess headbands*" were invented by non-Natives along with the term that gives them their name.

Fancy young men among the Sioux commonly wore a feather ornament in back of their heads that consisted of one or more upright Eagle feathers, a strip of bead or quillwork, and the tail of a bull, hanging down behind. Their Blackfoot counterparts often wore an item down their backs that was made from a number of long strands of human hair, joined by pieces of gum, and otherwise decorated.

Scarves and hats of every kind were worn by both men and women, after their introduction. Hats were commonly worn as they came from the factory—with flat brims and rounded crowns. Feathers and scarves were two of the most common hat decorations.

Scarves are very functional items that were eagerly acquired in the Old Days. Mainly, of course, they were tied around the neck, the ends hanging down the front or back. Some People just tied a double knot and let the ends hang loose, while others used tie slides made of silver, buckskin, or animal vertebrae, and tied the ends into knots, too. In warm weather thin scarves of cotton or ones made from calico material were used. In cold weather heavier material was used, and more than one scarf was often worn. One might be tied around the neck, another one around the neck was tied behind so that it could be pulled up in front to cover the mouth and nose in icy cold, and still another one might be worn over the head, peasant style, to protect the ears and sides of the face. Men often wore scarves on their heads beneath fur hats, in this way. The most common style of headband, especially in the SouthWest country, was made by rolling up a scarf and tying it behind. Women usually wore scarves in the manner of caps—covering the head and tied behind.

PAINTING AND TATTOOING

Prince Maximilian, during his travels on the continent in the last century, made this observation:

"They paint their faces red with vermillion; this colour, which they procure by barter from the traders, is rubbed in with fat, which gives them a shining appearance. Others

257

colour only the edge of their eyelids, and some stripes in the face, with red, others use a certain yellow clay for the face and red round the eyes; others, again, paint the face red, and forehead, a stripe down the nose, and the chin, blue, with the shining Earth from the Mountains. . . ."

Little leather pouches filled with paint powders were often attached to articles of clothing or in the hair, in the Old Days. Most People back then kept their paint applied as carefully as they kept their hair combed. And, though men going to war often used grotesque designs and patterns in an attempt to frighten the enemy with their power, most painting was not considered *"war paint."* Many People made a daily practice of painting the part in their hair, or the upper part of the cheek, to add a highlight to their personal appearance. White clay was often used to coat the face skin if a day in the bright light of Sun was planned —for many preferred light skin to that tanned dark by Sunshine. People in Mourning kept their faces, and sometimes their bodies and clothing, covered with black paint. And, for religious occasions, there were many reasons and methods of painting. Dreams, in fact, dictated most individual styles, while ceremonies, and their functionaries, always required traditional manners of painting. In such cases the pigment was called *"sacred paint,"* or *"sacred Earth,"* and represented the spiritual presence and oneness with the Mother Earth.

Complete *"toilet kits"* were kept in small decorated pouches and bags, which were often worn on belts or at the end of necklaces. Inside were little bags of the paints that the owner used, some wrapped-up tallow or fat, some shells or tiny stone bowls for mixing, and pointed sticks (often the carved and sharpened ends of antlers) used for applying some of the finer designs. Mirrors, of course, were added when they became available. When painting, the tallow was generally rubbed into the palm of one hand and some paint mixed with it. This mixture was then applied with the thumb and forefinger of the other hand, or with a stick. In the case of sacred paints, any excess was rubbed on Medicine bundles and articles, and also on pipe stems, robes and clothing, or into the hair. Devout

Medicine Men in the Old Days often had sacred paint caked on virtually everything they owned, and the fragrance of ceremonial incense always informed others of their presence.

Sacred paints were often gathered at special locations. Other paints were found or produced in the user's area. RED paints came from earths, clays, and rocks that were powdered. WHITE came from chalk-like earths and from clays. BLACK was made from charcoal. BLUE came from a dark blue mud; BLUE and GREEN were both made by boiling certain kinds of rotten woods. GREEN was also made from an algae. YELLOW came from an earth, and from Buffalo gall stones. Some People travelled great distances to procure material for certain kinds of paint, which they then traded to others in their tribe, or even to People of other tribes.

A YOUNG MAN OF THE DENE TRIBE FROM THE CANADIAN PLAINS. HE IS WEARING A BLANKET CAPOTE AND A METAL CHOKER, AND IS PAINTED FOR ADVENTURE. THE DENE ARE ACTUALLY COMPOSED OF A NUMBER OF LITTLE-KNOWN TRIBES IN THE CANADIAN INTERIOR. INTERESTINGLY, THE NAME IS ALSO USED BY THE NAVAJO TO DENOTE THEMSELVES. IT MEANS "THE PEOPLE."

Tattooing was done to some degree by all tribes in the long ago. Most tribes gave up the practice sometime before the reservation period. Tattooing was sometimes done for beauty, but mostly it was dictated in Dreams and had personal spiritual meaning. Many times it was merely a permanent style of face and body painting. Married couples sometimes tattooed similar designs on each other as part of spiritual vows. Individuals often tattooed some representation of their personal Medicine on themselves—often where it could not be seen by others.

The Bishop of Meaux made these comments about tattooing among Eastern tribes:

"Many men make various figures all over their bodies, by pricking themselves, others only in some parts. . . This operation is not painful itself. . . they begin by tracing on the skin, drawn very tight, the figure they intend to make, then they prick little holes close together with the fins of a fish, or with needles, all over these traces, so as to draw blood. Then they rub them with charcoal dust, and other colours, well ground and powdered. These powders sink into the skin, and the colours are never effaced; but soon after the skin swells, and forms a kind of a scab, accompanied with inflammation."

The People of the Thompson tribe, in British Columbia, applied their tattooes with needles of bone, (or) cactus spines or other thorns, often tied in small bunches with their points close together. In later years they preferred a steel sewing needle and thread. They blackened the thread with powdered charcoal and drew it underneath the skin, where the design had been drawn. A few of their tattooing and painting styles are illustrated on the next page.

FOR BETTER OR WORSE

Some Sources for Dress Knowledge and Materials:

AMERICAN INDIAN CRAFTS AND CULTURE—Magazine. $4.50 for 10 issues. Tulsa, Oklahoma.

AMERICAN INDIAN TRADITION—A series of magazines describing various cultural crafts and aspects in thorough

detail. No longer issued—existing copies now collector's items.

AMERICAN MUSEUM OF NATURAL HISTORY: ANTHROPOLOGICAL PAPERS. Several volumes from early 1900's covering material and spiritual culture of several specific tribes.

BUREAU OF AMERICAN ETHNOLOGY: ANNUAL REPORTS. Various cultural studies beginning in late 1800's.

CANADIAN WHOLE EARTH ALMANAC—Quarterly. $9 for four issues. Handicrafts Issue gives knowledge and sources relative to Canadians. 341 Bloor Street West, Box 6, Toronto 181, Ontario.

Ewers, John C., BLACKFEET CRAFTS. Bureau of Indian Affairs, Haskell Institute, Lawrence, Kansas, 1955.

Hunt, W. Ben, THE GOLDEN BOOK OF INDIAN CRAFTS AND LORE, New York. Golden Press, 1954.

Lyford, Carrie A., IROQUOIS CRAFTS. US Dept. of the Interior, Education Division of the Office of Indian Affairs, 1945.

Lyford, Carrie A., OJIBWA CRAFTS. US Dept. of the Interior, Education Division of the Office of Indian Affairs, 1943.

Lyford, Carrie A., QUILL AND BEADWORK OF THE WESTERN SIOUX. Indian Handicraft Series, US Indian Service, Haskell Institute, Lawrence, Kansas, 1940.

Mason, Bernard S., THE BOOK OF INDIAN-CRAFTS AND COSTUMES. A.S. Barnes & Company, 1946.

MATERIAL CULTURE NOTES: $3.80 for set of 22. The Denver Art Museum, 1300 Logan Street, Denver, Colorado.

*Murdock, George Peter, ETHNOGRAPHIC BIBLIOGRAPHY OF NORTH AMERICA, Human Relations Area Files, New Haven, Connecticut, 1960. Large volume which lists countless books and articles according to Native tribe and area.

DEL TRADING POST
Mission, South Dakota

ORLEY INDIAN CRAFTS & SUPPLIES
3437 South Broadway
Inglewood, Colorado

WESTERN TRADING POST
31 Broadway
Denver, Colorado

GREY OWL INDIAN CRAFTS
Box 86
Jamaica, New York

PLUME TRADING & SALES CO.
Box 585
Monroe, New York

ROBERTS INDIAN CRAFTS
Anadarko, Oklahoma

Write for catalogs—include money for postage

GOOD MEDICINE

THOUGHTS

BY ADOLF HUNGRY WOLF

Dramatic changes in one's daily Life tend to bring about new Thoughts about the meaning of that Life. Such changes can only *add* to Life's fullness, if we learn from them the new lessons which they bring Us, and accept their results as we would a patch of Flowers, a grove of Trees, a winding brook, or an uphill climb in the continuous Path of Life. The following Thoughts were inspired by some of the new changes along the Path of Good Medicine Life. May our Spirits continue to Travel together!

On the Prairie the Wind often blows. It is a constant reminder of the Great Power of the Universe. These words are now being written while at home on the Prairie . . . while the Wind blows outside, and Winter Sun shines brightly. . . .

. . . To the cabin on the valley floor came the call of the Spirit of the Prairie: "Not enough just to visit here in Summer—camping with the Old People—the Spirit is here all year, all time—we must keep Your Spirit over here with Us, now—better you bring your body, to live right. The devotion You gave to building your valley home will give inspiration to the good People who will come behind You—perhaps they will find their happiness with our spiritual ancestors there, in that valley—below the towering and overpowering rocky peaks, whose tops are always the last sign of Winter in Spring, and the first sign of same in Autumn. There, by the peaceful, tree and brush-lined river which flows past many spiritual lives and places before its wide mouth sings its Forever-Water Song on the shores of the mighty Ocean. There, by the coulee behind the cabin which was your home—back through the trees and bushes along the little creek—back to the rock-faced waterfall from where we, here on the Prairies, could barely hear your prayers for advice and guidance to us. It is better you stay with Us, over here, for the songs you sang while hunting your Moose in the meadow were the songs of our Old Prairie People. They were as sacred as those of the River People, who used to live there, but not sung with their Spirit. You must go on forward, young man— though the cost may be high—You must not sorrow for what you leave behind—for the Spirit of that which is meant to be Yours will never leave You—though its body might. When the brief Experience of physical Life is over, Your Spirit will be again fully in the presence of All those Spirits whom you seek—from the Past and the Present. Forget your body and let The Spirit be your Guide—if others feel their physical needs are more important, give them no less than a smile—no more than whatever You can to add to their happiness. If anything you have seems more important to them—let them have it. Work hard to put yourself in a position where you will not have to fear the trust of others—become fully spiritual and you will be able to give full trust through the Spirit—nothing will be able to take away your Spirit for It Is! It Exists—and will for All Time, which is no time, for it just Is . . ."

Now my Spirit is on the Prairie. I miss some of the People and Places that were a part of my daily Life and Love. I miss them physically—but they are always with me in Spirit. The strongest of these are before my eyes at any time, happy, smiling, their Spirit doing me only good. If I start to become lonely I remind myself that I am not alone, for with me are all those Spirits who are with mine in the Great Spirit of the Universe. And with me are new Spirits, who are uniting with the Spirits I bring with me from the Past. And more Spirits will unite with Us in the future as others find the Great Spirit in the same way.

I am going forward into the Great Spirit and I welcome All those who wish to come along.

Do Your physical desires distract You from a spiritual life? You say No? Can you pray at any time that The

Spirit makes you want to? Can you pray out loud—and feel free to put into words the thoughts that Your Mind carries? If You want to—if Your desire to Seek is strong enough—I pray that You can put Your physical self where it will be the least distraction to Your spiritual self, for that is the never-ending You.

It is true that physical life here, on this Earth, lasts only an Earth time. Perhaps those who are only concerned with that physical life are not following the wrong path, either. Exploring the endless physical experiences can certainly be a lifetime endeavor—leaving no time (Earth time) for abstract journeys into the unseeable. But, the physical life ends in a physical death—not a very pleasant physical experience. The body wears out long before the physical hunger can be satisfied, and long after it has become addicted to those things that will help wear it out.

Why not, instead, come with All of Us who are on the quest of a Spiritual Life. Come travel with Us that Path which leads to complete Heaven of the Mind, for that is where Heaven is. Be ready to sacrifice physical pleasures for spiritual ones—dream with Us of the day when We can leave our bodies sitting in lotus positions Up on Our favorite hilltops—when We can All be at the gathering of the Minds—as The Great Spirit of the Universe—and we can all turn to our bodies whenever—if ever—we feel that we should. Give Us All that You have, and We will give You All that We have. Let Us follow the Holy Order that is given to those who are looking for It—let Us climb together the unseen steps of ultimate Universal Brotherhood and Love. Let Us inspire each other—many others—to come along.

"Do not disturb he who knows not, and knows not (or cares not) that he knows not, for you may make him unhappy. Look, rather, for he who knows not, and knows that he knows not, for he is searching and you may help to make him happy."

Come along, my friends, wherever (or whoever) You are. Let Us not expect *anything* of each other. Let us only give All that we have to each other—to All our Brothers and Sisters who wish to come along. We must learn to love and share for happiness, not by bargaining. We must love and share simply for happiness.

Are You one of the People who can—who *will*—give up *anything* for the Great Spirit? If the Spirit comes into Your Mind and says, "Go, Now!", will You go? Or will you ignore The Spirit—will you reply: "I can't," or "not yet," and suffer, instead, the ultimate physical experience of *death* as a reward for your life of physical desires? The Great Spirit of the Mind knows no death. It knows no sickness. It knows no wars—no hate—no money. It does not exist on a level of communication with the "physical devils" that lure bodies away—it is beyond those tests of strength and courage that must be pleased to achieve complete control over it while living on this Earth.

I have seen this Great Spirit of the Mind in my Dreams and visions. I know It is everywhere. But, like You, I have been tempted by the "physical devils" to walk on the thin layer of their Garden of Eden—where any wrong step could mean a fall into Hell. Often have they invited me into their brightly-lit houses of wealth and fame, where a wrong word could mean a collapsed house. At every corner on the Path of Life they beckon to me to cross, with the traffic of life's physical dangers between us. But at every corner there are fewer beckoning—the traffic becomes continually less. Ahead, I can see the Path opening out into a never-ending meadow to which there seems to be no other sides.

Minds at Peace are left outdoors while the meals of greed and opportunism are devoured on a man-made table. But, while the diners loosen their belts and clean the unused surplus away from their sight, the Peaceful Minds continue with the Feast of Everlasting Life.

A Dream to be like a Tree—never complaining—always growing in strength with each Experience brought forth by Nature. . . .

A Dream to be like a Berry Bush—emerging from each trial of difficulty with a colorful tune of Life—being thank-

268

ful after each experience of good time by giving to others the fruit each bears best. . . .

A Dream to be like an Insect—remaining in the physical state only long enough to perform that which needs performing. . . .

A Dream to be like a Bird—always flying high and singing a song—being thankful for each twig in the Forest, each raindrop in the Sky, and each seed in the Ground. . . .

"WHERE THERE IS A WILL THERE IS A WAY"–IF YOU PRAY

If we will assume that the words "Will" and "Mind" can be interchanged, then we find ourselves saying, in effect, that "the Mind is everything." If You can clear your Mind of all but good things, then your desires will all be good; your ways to those desires will be good—Your life will be Good! But how to clear the Mind of all but good things?

Decide that goodness in Life is all you want—and You can clear Your Mind of all but goodness. I say this not from a righteous throne—I confess to having other-than-good thoughts much too often (for my Mind's desires). I am only too well aware that the Way may come much later than the Will. The paycheck often comes much later than the work—for those who are on that path. The Harvest, after all, is not expected to be on the same day as the Planting. Plant in your Mind the desire for good thoughts —water that desire with inspiration, regularly—weed it objectively—and convince Yourself (as countless others have, now and then—as I have) that the Harvest time will come, and you will reap a lifetime supply of good thoughts. Your desires should be able to preserve them quite well—even through stormy weather.

How do you plant, in Your Mind, the desire for good thoughts? Well, that depends upon the Path which you are following. If we use the term prayer very liberally, then I would suggest praying as the finest way to turn your Mind towards good thoughts. And how to pray? Well, well, now—if we haven't just touched upon a hot topic for debate. Or have we? That's what you can often hear: "Never argue about religion, because there is no end to the argument," say some critics. Keeping good thoughts in Mind, I'll disagree with that. Here is what I say:

Do YOU think your religion is right? Does it make YOU happy? Does it keep YOU from trespassing against others? Yes? Then, brother or sister, you have found the right religion for YOU!

What difference is it to me how Your religion balances out on the scale of mine? If it doesn't belong on there, then I won't put it on there—then it won't affect the balance of mine, eh? Now, if You will accept all that, then there won't even be a beginning for an argument about our methods of prayer—we'll just say to each other: "Yours is good. . . . Yours is good."

And what if you don't accept my suggestion of "what's good for you and doesn't hurt me is good"? Well, I'll show you my garden; give you a sample of the harvest; hope I've inspired you; and let you go back to survey the extent of your own weed patch. If you still like it, then that's good, too. Just give me a little respect. . . .

Now, back to planting that garden of desires to have only good thoughts—planting through praying. From various things that I've said—today and at other times— You've probably gathered that my Mind is very much inspired by the Spiritual Powers that have long inspired Native People who spent their whole lives with the Nature of this North American Land. I'm inspired by the sight of Birds and Animals—the climbing of Mountains—the smell of Flowers and Trees— the feeling of Wind and Rain—the falling of Snow—I'm inspired by living with these things; I'm inspired by mentioning them in my prayers—they remind me of the many things in the Universe that flow so beautifully together in Harmony with Nature. I'm inspired to know—to make myself aware that I am just like All those things—a part of Nature—able to flow beautifully if I make an effort to live in Harmony with Nature—my brothers and sisters.

Since thinking of All these good things during my prayers is so inspirational to having, always, good thoughts, it follows that the more I pray the more I will be inspiring myself to have good thoughts—the more good thoughts I will have. If You can't comprehend what I'm saying, then I beg You to try it—try praying in such a way as to mention those things that exist (anywhere in the Universe) and that inspire you to have good thoughts. Do it through whatever form of prayer you think is right for you— loudly or meditatively. Better yet, try several forms—try loudly and meditatively. Remember: it's not the method of praying that counts—it's the thoughts that You have while praying.

And don't think that I'm suggesting You will find happiness in life by giving lip service to some "prayers." A bunch of words falling from your mouth won't make the weeds in your garden disappear. Do your praying with your Mind! Let your mouth help, if you want, by saying words and singing songs that inspire good thoughts to enter your Mind. But don't let Your prayers come only from your mouth. For we all know where *that's* at, eh?

If you make a regular effort at praying—by thinking good thoughts—and you live in an environment that makes you happy, then You will soon find that many of the things you do in your daily life give you good thoughts and can, thus, add strength to your prayers. Your prayers can involve more and more of daily life—by spending more and more of your time doing those things that are good enough to pray about—until You (and I, says my Mind) find yourself doing only those things good enough to pray about—and then all the goodness will make Your Life a Prayer.

A TRIBAL CAMP OF THE 1970's

Most of You probably have Dreams about the sort of place You would someday like to live in. A number of You have shared your dreams with me, and have asked for my comments. Perhaps, by sharing my own Ideal with you, I can inspire some of You while you are planning an Ideal of Your own.

In the earlier Companion Issue, some of You will remember hearing the old-time philosophy about tribal life. The following paragraph states the idea:

"If dreams of a life of culture accompany Your Desire for a home in Nature, then look for Companions. Seek others whose Dreams are like Yours. Get Together—give each other motivation. Get Together—Your ideas and resources. The results of respectful coalitions will be seen in the strength of Your success."

Now, assuming you have found some others who share

273

your ideas and ideals—how can you turn your Dreams into a way of Life? Of the countless blueprints which have been made for such a life style I can add but another one.

First, you must obtain a piece of land. For permanence and stability—forget about squatting, homesteading, or the like. The herds of Buffalo are gone, and so is the free land. Like it or not, You'll save yourself much sorrow if You'll just accept that. You *might* try to find a sympathetic landowner for whom a bunch of you could do some really heavy work, in exchange for a small parcel. Better yet, though, try to locate some other groups whose aims are even remotely similar to yours. Between all of you buy a quarter section (160 acres) and let natural boundaries (or original investment) divide up what's there. Quantity of land is *much* less important than physical and spiritual Nature. Many, many People who own quarter sections really make little use of more than a tenth of that amount. A tiny place that adjoins a national park or a large mountain has a thousand times the spiritual value of a huge place surrounded by thriving farms and homesteads. Mountains and animals generally make much better neighbors than thriving farmers, believe me.

So—now that you and your brothers have scraped up the money and found yourself 20 acres, what to do next? Camp on the place for a while, I suggest. Besides checking around for best soil, availability of water, and protection from weather, it will take you a while to find *the* spot that Your Spirits will like best. Perhaps, more important—if you and your companions have only been dreaming—is that, while camping, you will find out each other's abilities and desires—and the strength of your motivations. If you can put these all together and come up with an honestly pretty picture, then you may be able to settle minor differences of opinion through group discussions. Those who don't agree with that are probably not really ready to share themselves in a tribal life.

For your tribal activities you will probably want a central gathering place. Perhaps it would be best to build such a place first. This would give all of you a chance to

274

demonstrate group effort for group benefit. And it would give you all a sturdy shelter. My choice for such a building is a basically round, many-sided log building with many windows, large cook stove, workbenches, and convertible cots. Here you will be able to make group meals, have group discussions, dances, room for guests, a group library and toolbox, and a place to gather without imposing on anyone's home.

Adjoining the "community hall" might be your outdoor meeting place—a round clearing—perhaps surrounded by benches—for outdoor praying, dancing, singing, discussing, or just sitting in the Sun. If the thought of an annual Sun Dance—outdoor gathering and celebration excites your Spirit, then the round clearing can be the place to have it. A tall pole in the center can be your masthead, your holy center, your spiritual path up to Sun.

The community hall and the adjoining round clearing can be surrounded by a park-like field of grass—also a large circle. Surrounding it might be a rustic log fence.

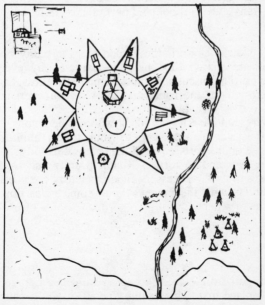

Then we come to the individual houses which, naturally, surround the tribal circle and gathering place. To give the feeling of privacy that I think every individual needs, rustic log fences could enclose each person's home and personal garden. I like the triangular shape for these individual plots—mainly because of the spiritual pattern that is the end result. Subdivision with spiritual flavor, if you will. Each individual designs his own home, and provides the materials that can not be naturally obtained. With group effort, all the houses could be built this way in one Summer. An open screen door, or a little cloth banner, can be used to display desire for company. That way, visiting in private homes is never an annoyance, and full privacy can be enjoyed without worry of interruption—and keeping in Mind that one's home is, for many, also one's chapel.

The central park would be great for playing children—within sight of all the houses, yet not too close. Teach them respect—teach them to share their love and understanding; teach them devotion through inspiration day and night. Let each adult teach all the children what he knows best—make their schooling a part of everything they do in life.

Next to the camp is the garden and the barnyard—the chores are shared, just like the harvests, by everyone. Again, group discussion must remain the boss and the master—all for the tribe, and the tribe for everyone.

There you have it—an ideal, without the details. Those you must fill in according to your tribe's abilities and wants. Tribal efforts at hand-made furniture, instruments, dishes, toys and so forth will add to unity and can, with desire, supply the necessary funds to satisfy the occasional encounters with the money world, some miles down the road, somewhere.

A NIGHT-TIME CEREMONY ON THE PRAIRIE

All day the People have rested—tonight is the Ceremony of Holy Smoking—tonight the People will stay up all night to sing and talk and eat and to say prayers of strength with the smoking of their pipes. Tonight will be a holy night.

Late afternoon is here now: see the coming of darkness —see it as it covers up the last shades of orange over the mountains in the Western sky. Darkness comes soon up on these Northern Plains, during these cold days of early Winter.

In their houses the People who are going to the ceremony tonight are now getting themselves ready—inside their houses that dot the Prairie here and there; some are surrounded by a sheltering growth of trees and bushes; some are nestled under a bluff by the side of a river; but most of them sit out on the open Plains—like tiny landmarks announcing the presence of People amid the vastness of the Universe—on top of endless Earth and underneath all-covering Sky.

Now lights come on inside the houses—yellow glowing through framed glass windows: some diffused by sheets of plastic protecting windows from the Winter storms soon to come. Horses and cattle graze near by different ones. A large Owl sits somewhere in a tree, hooting softly, in the now-almost-darkness in the yard of one of the houses. A bunch of dogs bark and play, by another. A voice is heard singing, from a third one—the tune can be heard across the Plain:

. . . Man, he says, my tipi is powerful.
Woman, she says, my tipi is powerful.
Rain is my Medicine.
My children, they hear me.
The Earth, it is powerful.

The chant goes on—the words are only a small part of it—the chanter can be seen inside his little house, moving around in a room lit by one bare light bulb. He is picking up things here and there: the wood stem and stone bowl for a large smoking pipe, which he puts in a paper bag; a small buckskin pouch of tobacco, and the old woolen cap, which goes on his head. Nearby him, his old wife sits in a chair, re-braiding her hair—she wears one of her long, print-cloth dresses. She sings the song too, for she knows it as well. It belonged to their long-ago Medicine tipi. At the ceremony they will sing it again—remembering when —and hearing the others sing like songs. Out on the Prairie, around them, in the chilled air of evening goes the song:

278

        . . . Man, he says, the water is our home.
        Woman, she says, the water is our home.
        Water, is my Medicine.
        My tipi, it is powerful.
        My tipi, it is powerful.
        Woman, my tipi, it is powerful.
        I mean it, my tipi, it is powerful.

Some while after full-dark comes, the People begin to arrive for the ceremony—not many will come, for not many have TIME now! Few, today, see the vastness of the Spirit that is with Us all the time. But those few—well, tonight they will gather: to help each other make themselves remain aware. Some of them come to see more than others—but they must see, at all, to even be there.

Few come in cars—few here have them: young relatives and others drop them off. The drivers halt momentarily to leave the old ones, before they hurry away from they-know-not-where. In the house by the coulee the old ones gather, to be with All the Spirits who will be there.

A few young ones have come to the ceremony—a few young ones who know some Spirit they will find There. They come, and the old ones are happy, thinking: "Sad, so few, but at least some will be here."

A hush of respect greets the Old One—though on canes and nearly blind, he's like a Bear: Sacred Earth on his face—sacred bearing—Sacred Earth adding red streaks to long, white-grey hair. Coming inside, towards the back he moves—slowly but surely: taking the place of honor, for the leader must sit there. His couch: and old, folded robe of Buffalo bull; his shoulders draped and covered by a blanket; and on his moccasins: a flower, beaded there.

Before the Old One: an altar—a box of dirt to represent our Earth Mother—a small pipe inside it, lying there. To each side of the Old One sit the others—on cushions, for the room is cleared bare.

With a prayer, the Old One starts the ceremony: "Hiyo

Spirits, we're gathered with You here. Hiyo Old Ones, Hiyo Medicines, Hiyo All of You Powers, hear our prayers, hear our songs that we sing for You. Be with Us, give Us guidance everywhere."

With prayers and songs, the Old One fixes the sacraments—some Sage leaves and Sacred Earth to remind Us of the Spirit of Prairie Life. As each one takes the sacrament, he says words of goodness and asks for blessings from the Spirits that only He knows are There.

Around goes the sacrament: to young and old—each one says a prayer, short or long. A helper brings a hot coal from the fire, with a forked stick he carries it to the altar. The Old One sings a song, brings forth his incense, puts some Sweetgrass on the coal that's lying there.

The night is long—soon some food is brought to help the physical discomfort that All must bear. Wooden bowls filled with meat and rolls—cups of tea—many apples; the talk is good—the food fills up bodies—Minds think of prayers.

Into paper bags goes the surplus food—carefully saved to be eaten at later times—when the ceremony will only be a strength-giving memory during the cold Winter days and nights. Outside goes one old man with his apples, putting on a fur cap before opening the door. In comes a cold draft—causing some to pull tighter their coats and blankets. Outside: to his team of Horses walks the old man with his apples—over to where they are standing beside each other; an old, green-painted wooden wagon hitched on behind. A few words of comfort he mutters to his Horses, that old man, and from his hand he gives them each an apple. Then he comes back inside and sits down—the others, too, are again settling in their places.

The attendant brings another coal from the fire—more Sweetgrass is placed on the coal—again, the air becomes pungent; again, the songs and prayers begin.

Now, a man goes outside: out into the dark, cold air to bring in a large object from its quiet, sacred place of resting. The object represents the Spirits who are with the gathering this night—things fastened to it are symbols that help everyone present to think of the powers of the Universe: Eagle Plumes to tell Us of the Birds and the Sky; fur to tell Us of the Animals and the Ground; Sage to tell Us of the Earth and the power of growth; crossed sticks to tell Us of the four directions and the powers which come from them; other symbols, too, with holy meanings to those present. More prayers are said—prayers inspired by the symbols of the powers known to be present.

The Old One sings a song:

"Sacred Paint, I am looking for it."

He reaches into a sack of things and brings out some old buckskin bags, while he's singing the words,

"Sacred paint, I have found it. It is holy."

He lays the buckskin bags of sacred paint before him. He brings out a piece of cloth in which is wrapped a small chunk of fat. Like a bar of soap, he rubs the chunk of fat between his palms until his hands are coated with a greasy layer. Carefully, he feels of the buckskin bags—his sight is too dim to let him see them well—he feels of them until he is content that he has found the right one. He unties its buckskin thong, opens up the bag, and dips two of his fingers inside: into the powdered mass of Sacred red Earth. Chanting all the while, he mixes the red Earth into the grease on his hands until his hands are thickly coated with shiny red. Then begins the ceremony of the painting.

Those who desire to be anointed with the Sacred Earth—those who feel that the anointing, done by the Old One, will later bring them memories to inspire strength when needed—they take turns going up before him, kneeling down, looking into the Old One's already red-painted face, hearing up close his songs and prayers of good wishes, and feeling his greasy, gnarled, old hands rubbing the Sacred Earth across their foreheads, over cheeks and chins, around the wrists, and over their hair.

Thus painted, each one turns his back, still kneeling, and receives the Old One's blessing as he passes the Holy Symbol of the Universe over their heads and bodies.

When it is finished—the ceremony of painting—a pause is taken to allow everyone time to prepare for the next part of the ceremony.

Outside, the night is clear and cold—Stars twinkle brightly—and a fine ring of orange surrounds Night Light's bright, full body like a thick circle of Sacred Paint. Nostrils tingle with each breath as the still, cold air freezes the moisture inside them. Each one hurries quickly back, and through the doorway—back to the cozy warmth, by the old wood stove, that waits in there. Only one comes back slowly—feeling no more the need to hurry—his body worn —his Mind strong, for the speed of his presence: no care.

Again seated on the floor around the room is the gathering—sacred things, and the altar, in their midst. Some light talk, making pleasant the gatherers: some laughter, some good memories in the air. Cups of tea, held by hands slowly rewarming. Says the Old One: "What foolishness, this; drinking warmth to fight cold caused by drinking so much warmness—like wiping dust from the wiper of dust!" Still, he drinks, like the others, the warm liquid; he drinks the tea among the gathering, there.

Half the night is over, when begins that part of the ceremony in which All participate, and each devotes. For now comes songs, and smoking pipes, and holy prayers; and words of courage passed on from ancestors, for Us to hear.

Next to the altar are stacked the smoking pipes of the partakers—each has his own, among the pile that's resting there. One of the helpers dumps out the herb, from sacks used while smoking; he dumps it out, in a pile, on the cutting board. With a knife, he cuts the herb—mixes it up to prepare it for smoking; fills the pipes—one by one— that are lying there. One of the Old Men takes each pipe and says a prayer, holds it over—in sacred way—the smudge of incense. In sacred way each helper then takes them—to have some Old Ones light them up and say more prayers.

Around go the pipes—each one smoking—each one blowing sacred wisps out in the air. Before long, it is finished, all this smoking. Before long, begin the songs of those gathered there.

First, the Old One gets out four sacred rattles, from the bag of things he has brought along. Buffalo rawhide, sacred painted, are these rattles, in time with singing, they will be shaken by those who hold them, by those who tap them on scarves laid down before them. But not until the Old One has held them over the smudge of incense—in sacred way —has prayed in time to sacred shakings of them. Not until then are the rattles placed in the hands of those who will first use them.

Tsht-tsht-tsht-tsht . . . goes the rhythmic sound of the four rattles as the holy singing begins. The men take turns singing four songs each—the women in background accompany them. Each one tells the meaning of his singing— from where the song came—what sacrifice was made to obtain the song, and the spiritual article it came with. All those present are aware of the powers of what's described there—of the songs and ceremonies that are represented there. Many have owned the same items, in the past once, as have their forefathers who are mentioned—strong as their presence that we all feel, gathered there.

Tsht-tsht-tsht-tsht . . . on goes the rattling and singing, the pipe smoking, the incense burning. On goes the night. Many are the songs sung—many are the Spirits thereby represented. As each one knows the sacrifice and devotions that the different songs are representing, none would consider singing any songs but those to which he is entitled— though all might help with the singing of the different songs of the devoted. Only one young man in the group joins the singing—at this time he is the only one who is devoted enough to the Spirits present to make sacrifices for their help—to learn their songs and ceremonies. From his sacred bundle he sings the words:

283

"It is powerful, this sweetness, take some of it.
I use it for a sacred purpose. . . .
. . . There he comes, Old Man.
He is walking this way.
He is coming in.
Come in with safety.
'Let us have a sweat,' he says . . .

. . . Old Man he says:
'My old smoke, I do not feel it.'
Old Man, he says: ·
'My new smoke, I feel it.'
It is powerful. . . .

. . . Now then, that which is above:

He knows me.
It is powerful.
This here, that which is below:
He knows me.
It is powerful.

As the night goes on, more food is served. Afterwards,
the singing continues as does the praying, the talking, the
smoking, the spiritual thinking . . . on and on and on and
on . . . till finally comes the first sign of dawn—a thin, light
line separating dark, starlit Sky from horizon. The singing
is finished, the pipes are smoked out, done are the prayers,
happy is the crowd. A last meal is provided: sacred blood
soup cooked with sacred tongue. Like our ancestors have
always done before Us, so we take a piece of tongue and
hold it up—let our Minds dwell on the Spirits represented
—say our prayers of good wishes for everyone. After eating, at last, goes out the Old One—soon we won't see his
presence any longer—but his Spirit will be with Us everywhere.

The Breath of one who prays to his spirits while crossing
a frozen lake with his Dog-team in the far North joins the
Breaths of others like him up there—joins their Breaths
and those of the Walrus and Polar Bear—the Seal and the
Reindeer—all those Breaths joining and coming South—
coming in a Sacred Way to bring those who are South
some of the Spirit of the Life of their Northern Brothers.

And so it is with the People far to the South—sitting in dugout canoes while floating on tropical waters, searching for the day's meal—their Breaths of prayer joining those of the Ocelot and Iguana—the Parrot and Llama—bringing to those of the cooler North some of the Spirit of the Life of their Southern Brothers. From East and West, also, come the Breaths of Brothers elsewhere. From the Earth—our Mother—come the powers of growth and strength—comes the Spirit of the Life of our long-gone Brothers, whose Earthly beings and belongings have become, again, a part of our Mother. And from Above come the powers of light and guidance—the Spirit of the Life of the Above Ones—Sun, Moon, Stars, and Sky; all the unseen others who live up on High.

See Them, Brothers—join Them. Let their Breaths give your thoughts cause to cry. Cry from happiness—knowing All who go where you go—send your prayers with Your Breaths to join the Sky.

Along the Columbia River, in what is now the state of Washington, there once lived a religious leader whom you will be interested to read about. His name was Smohalla, which means "The Preacher." Many of his people, however, called him by another name—Yu'yunipi'tquana—The Shouting Mountain, for a mountain spoke to him during some of his religious dreams, which he had while sleeping on that mountain.

Smohalla was a warrior and religious leader as early as the 1850's among his Wanapum People, and for a few members of the neighboring and related Yakima Tribe. Around 1860, however, he was involved in a fight with another leader, from a nearby camp, who left Smohalla lying on the ground for dead. Smohalla disappeared, and for several years the 200 or so People of his tribe saw nothing of him, assumed he was dead, and mourned for him.

Somehow, Smohalla had managed to drag himself down to the river and into a canoe, in which he floated off with the current and towards the Pacafic Coast. In those years, during his absence from his People, he traveled all over the West, physically. Spiritually, he also went a long way.

When he came back to his own People he brought with him the spiritual beliefs and ceremonies that had most inspired his thoughts among the different People with whom he had visited. To his People he was like Jesus—one that had been resurrected. They expressed their happiness for his return by their dedication and enthusiasm for the new Spirits he had brought along.

This is the way Smohalla described, for his followers, the meaning of Life:

"Once the World was all Water, and God lived alone. He was lonesome, he had no place to put his foot, so he scratched the sand up from the bottom and made the land, and he made the rocks, and he made the trees, and he made a man; and the man had wings and could go anywhere. The man was lonesome, and God made a woman. They ate fish from the water, and God made the Deer and other Animals, and He sent the man to hunt and told the woman to cook the meat and to dress the skins. Many more men and women grew up, and they lived on the banks of the great River whose banks were full of Salmon. The mountains contained much game and there were Buffalo on the Plains. There were so many People that the stronger ones sometimes oppressed the weak and drove them from the best fisheries, which they claimed as their own. They fought and nearly all were killed, and their bones are to be seen in the hills yet. God was very angry at this, and He took away their wings and commanded that the lands and fisheries should be common to All who lived upon them; that they were never to be marked off or divided, but that the People should enjoy the fruits that God planted in the land, and the animals that lived upon it, and the fishes in the water. God said He was the Father and the Earth was the Mother of Mankind; that Nature was The Law; that the animals, and fish, and plants obeyed Nature, and that man only was sinful. This is the old law."

"After a while, when God is ready, He will drive away all the people except those who have obeyed his laws," predicted Smohalla.

Regarding the new arrivals in his country, he said:

"They ask me to dig for stone! Shall I take a knife and tear my mother's bosom? Then when I die she will not take me to her bosom to rest.

"They ask me to dig for stone! Shall I dig under her skin for her bones? Then when I die I will not enter her body to be born again.

"They ask me to cut grass and make hay and sell it, and be rich like white men! But how dare I cut off my mother's hair?

"I want my people to stay with me here. All the dead men will come to life again. Their Spirits will come to their bodies again. We must wait here in the homes of our fathers and be ready to meet them in the bosom of our mother."

Upon his return, Smohalla urged his People to avoid most of the newly-arrived "civilization." Instead, he promoted a strict tribal life of fishing, hunting, gathering, and praying—a simple and natural life that he felt would bring for All the most in spiritual happiness.

In keeping with the spiritual feelings brought to the People by others, Smohalla proclaimed Sunday as a day for only holy matters. On that day he gathered with his People for morning, afternoon, and evening services. Any day, however, services were likely to be held, and anytime at all was right for the saying of prayers.

Smohalla's popularity, of course, was not happily accepted by those who were coming to "establish" laws which were not necessarily in Harmony with Nature. One of their representatives—a Captain E. L. Huggins, of the second Cavalry, reported the following conversations with Smohalla. The righteous captain conversed with his mouth open and his mind closed.

"Smohalla: 'My young men shall never work. Men who work cannot dream, and wisdom comes to us in dreams.'

"Captain: When it was argued that the whites worked and yet knew more than the Indians [quantity vs. quality, eh, Captain!], he replied that the white man's wisdom was poor and weak and of no value to Indians, who must learn the highest wisdom from dreams and from participating in the Dreamer ceremonies. Being pressed to explain the nature of his higher knowledge, he replied:

"Smohalla: 'Each one must learn for himself the highest wisdom. It cannot be taught. You have the wisdom of your race. Be content.'

"Captain: I contended that even the Indians had to work hard during the fishing season to get food for Winter.

"Smohalla: 'This work lasts only for a few weeks. Besides, it is natural work and does them no harm. But the work of the white man hardens soul and body. Nor is it right to tear up and mutilate the Earth as white men do.'

"Captain: I asserted that the Indians also dug roots and were even then digging camas in the mountains.

"Smohalla: 'We simply take the gifts that are freely offered. We no more harm the Earth than would an infant's fingers harm its mother's breast. But the white man tears up large tracts of land, runs deep ditches, cuts down forests, and changes the whole face of the Earth. You know very well this is not right. Every honest man [said Smohalla, while looking at the captain searchingly] knows in his heart that this is all wrong. But the white men are so greedy they do not consider these things.'"

Smohalla's beliefs and efforts inspired numerous Native groups along the Columbia River to follow his example. Religious ceremonies that combined Native with Biblical teachings gave much spiritual uplift to many People whose lives towards "civilization" had been filled with despair. One of Smohalla's disciples was a Yakima by the name of Kotai'aqan (Scattering Ducklings). A Major MacMurray visited with this disciple, pointing out that he was "pacific and gentle." Said MacMurray:

"He said all men were as brothers to him and he hoped all would dwell together. He had been told that white and black and all other kinds of men originally dwelt in tents . . .and that God in former times came to commune with white men. He thought there could be only one Saghalee Tyee, in which case white and red men would live on a common plane. We came from one source of life and in time would Grow from one stem again. It would be like a stick that the white held by one end and the Indians by the other until it was broken, and it would be made again into one stick."

Major MacMurray spent some time visiting at the camp of Smohalla, at Priest Rapids on the Columbia. Parts of his report from there help to give us a picture of Smohalla's People and their spiritual lives. He says:

"We reached the plain and were met by a procession, headed by Smohalla in person, all attired in gorgeous array and mounted on their best chargers. We wended our way through sagebrush and sand dunes to the village street, not a soul being visible, but from the mat-roofed Salmon houses there came forth the most indescribable chorus of bell ringing, drum beating, and screeching [?]. I noticed that the street was neatly swept and well sprinkled. . . . Our procession passed on beyond the village to a new canvas tent, which had a brush shade to keep off the Sun and was lined and carpeted with new and very pretty matting. Smohalla said this had been prepared especially for me . . . he had constructed a bench for me, having sent more than 90 miles for the nails. Fresh Salmon . . . were regularly furnished my party. . . . The River was within two yards of our tent door and was an ample lavatory [Indeed! I hope they caught your fish downstream from there, Major!]

"When I awoke the next morning, the sound of drums was again heard, and for days it continued. I do not remember that there was any intermission except for a few minutes at a time. . . .

"There was a small open space to the North of the larger house, which was Smohalla's residence and the village assembly room as well. This space was enclosed by a whitewashed fence made of boards which had drifted down the river. In the middle was a flagstaff with a rectangular flag. . . . Smohalla explained: 'This is my flag, and it represents the world. God told me to look after my people—All are my people. There are four ways in the world—North and South and East and West. I have been all those ways. This is the center. I live here. The red spot is my heart—everybody can see it. The yellow grass grows everywhere around this place. The green mountains are far away and all around the world. There is only water beyond, salt water. The blue is the sky, and the star is the North Star. . . .

"There are frequent services, a sort of processional around the outside of the fence, the prophet and a small boy with a bell entering the enclosure, where, after hoisting the flag, he delivers a sort of sermon. . . .

"This house was built with a framework of stout logs placed upright in the ground and roofed over with brush, or with canvas in rainy weather. The sides consisted of bark and rush matting. It was about 75 feet long by 25 feet wide. Singing and drumming had been going on for some time when I arrived. The air resounded with the voices of hundreds of Indians, male and female, and the banging of drums. Within, the room was dimly lighted. Smoke curled from a fire on the floor at the farther end and pervaded the atmosphere. The ceiling was hung with hundreds of Salmon, split and drying in the smoke.

"The scene was a strange one. On either side of the room was a row of twelve women standing erect with arms crossed and hands extended, with fingertips at the shoulders. They kept time to the drums and their voices by balancing on the balls of their feet and tapping with their heels on the floor, repetition wore them out, and I heard that others than Smohalla had seen visions in their trances, but I saw none who would admit it or explain anything of it [to a cavalry major, I probably wouldn't either].

"Those on the right hand were dressed in garments of a red color with an attempt at uniformity. Those on the left wore costumes of white buckskin, said to be very ancient ceremonial costumes, with red and blue trimmings. All wore large round silver plates or such other glittering ornaments as they possessed. A canvas covered the floor and on it knelt the men and boys in lines of seven. Each seven, as a rule, had shirts of the same color. The tallest were in front, the size diminishing regularly to the rear. Children and ancient hags [forgive me, grandmothers—I'm only repeating the Major's words!] filled in any spare space. In front on a mattress knelt Smohalla, his left hand covering his heart. On his right was the boy bell ringer in similar posture. Smohalla wore a white garment which he was pleased to call a priest's gown, but it was simply a white cloth shirt with a colored stripe down the back [the major wore a blue outfit, which he was pleased to call a soldier's uniform, but it was simply a blue cloth coat and trousers with colored stripes on the arms and legs].

"Smohalla's son was said to be in training as his successor. He was a young man, apparently about 23 years old, tall, slender, and active in movement, and commonly kept himself apart from the body of the People. He ordinarily wore a short gown of surplice, sometimes yellow and other times sky blue, with ornate decorations of stars or moon applique cut from bright-colored cloths. The sleeves were extravagantly trimmed with beads and silver ornaments."

While busy noting technical details, the Major may have missed a few basic points. The ceremony performed by Smohalla and his People was a group effort at Spiritual unity and awareness. The combinations of songs, prayers, bells, and drums, with the physical involvement and personal beauty that the participants strived for brought about an immense Spirit that was only their version of the religious experience that has been sought and found by many. The group goal is spiritual unity—the individual goal is of ecstasy during which individual members often experienced their Minds passing out of their bodies. Upon their return, and during various breaks in the ceremonies, these individuals would recite their visions and experiences to their brothers and sisters. Every factor was another color in the picture of spiritual happiness sought by ALL.

I am happy to tell you that a number of descendants of Smohalla's followers still fill their lives with his methods of prayer and devotion. Here and there, in the Columbia

River country, People still dress in their finery and gather to the sound of bells and prayers and chants—gather for the inspiration that they receive from the spiritual sessions and the holy feasts of water, salmon, and berries which always follow. It is well.

A STORY OF LIFE
FROM THE SIOUX PEOPLE

Wazi was chief of the People who dwell under the world, and his woman, Kanka, was a seer. Their daughter, Ite, the wife of Tate, was the most beautiful of women. She gave birth to four sons at one time, which proved these children to be gods. Yet Wazi was not content, for he wished to have powers like a god. Iktomi knew this and he schemed to have Wazi play his pranks. He told Wazi that he should have the powers he wished for if he would help make others ridiculous. Wazi was afraid, but he told Kanka what Iktomi had said. She said that if they had the power of the gods no one could take it from them and then they could laugh at Iktomi. Iktomi, lurking near, heard her say this, and smiled.

He went and sat in the tipi of Kanka. He told her that she was a wise woman and a seer and that for a long time he had thought she ought to have power to do as she liked. He said he would be pleased if he could help her get such power so she could do much good for the People. He then talked of the beauty of her daughter, Ite. He said that because of her beauty she was the wife of a god and the mother of gods and therefore ought to have a seat with the gods. He talked much like this. Kanka asked him how he could help her get power to do as she wished to do. He said he would think about this and then tell her.

When Iktomi had gone, Wazi told Kanka that if she was not careful Iktomi would make the People laugh at her. Again, Iktomi came and told Kanka that if she would help him play his pranks he would give her power to do as the gods do. Kanka said that if he would first give her and Wazi such powers and they could prove that they had them, then they would help him to do what he wished.

Iktomi agreed to this and gave them the powers they wished for. Then he talked of the beauty of their daughter until the night was almost gone.

Early the next morning he came and told Wazi and Kanka that they could prove their powers by making anyone more beautiful. He showed them how to make a charm that would make more beautiful anyone who would carry it on the body. He then went to the tipi of Ite and sat and talked with her. He told her that she was very industrious and modest, that she was as beautiful as Hanwi, and that if she were more beautiful she would be the most beautiful of all human beings.

Ite told her mother what Iktomi had said and Kanka told her that she would sit with the gods. Again, Iktomi sat and talked with Ite. He told her that Wi, the chief of the gods, had noticed her beauty and had spoken of it. Again, Ite told her mother what Iktomi had said, and Kanka said that Ite would sit with the chief of the gods. She gave her daughter the charm and bade her carry it on her body. Ite carried the charm and grew more beautiful each night. Iktomi told Wi that the wife of Tate was the most beautiful of all beings, that she was the wife of a god and the mother of gods, and that she ought to have a seat with the gods. He then sat and talked with Kanka and told her that it would please Wi to see Ite.

Wazi told Kanka to be careful or Iktomi would cause the People to laugh at her. She said that they could laugh at Iktomi, for he could not take from them the power he had given them; that when the People that now lived were forgotten, People would speak of Wazi and Kanka because their daughter sat with the chiefs of the gods. Iktomi lurked near and heard her say this and he smiled.

Ite adorned herself, but there was no fire in her tipi, neither was there food nor drink, and her little sons cried because they were hungry. She walked with her father and mother, and they passed before the face of Wi. Wi saw that Ite was very beautiful and then he remembered what Iktomi had said to him. So he talked with her and invited her to sit at the feast of the gods.

295

Iktomi sat in the tipi of Ite and talked with her. He told her that Wi was tired of his companion, Hanwi, and wished for a younger and a more beautiful companion. Then Ite told him that Wi had invited her to sit at the feast of the gods. He told her that when all were seated at the feast, she must take the vacant seat. Kanka helped her daughter to adorn herself and foretold that Ite would live forever like the gods.

When the feast was ready, Iktomi was talking with Hanwi. He told her that Wi thought that a woman, Ite, was the most beautiful of all beings and had invited her to sit at the feast of the gods. So Hanwi stayed to adorn herself and came late to the feast. Ite came early and when all were seated, she saw a vacant seat beside Wi, and she took it. Wi did not frown. He smiled and talked with Ite. Hanwi came and saw a woman sitting in her seat. She covered her head with her robe and stood behind Ite. The People saw this, and they laughed at her. Iktomi laughed loudest and longest. Kanka sang a song of joy, but Wazi was afraid. Tate left the feast and went to the tipi of Ite. He painted his face and the faces of his little sons black.

After the feast, Hanwi stood before Skan hiding her face with her robe. Skan asked her why she hid her face. She replied because she was shamed by Wi who had permitted a woman to sit in her place so the People laughed at her and Iktomi laughed loudest and longest.

Then Skan asked Wi why he had permitted a woman to sit on the seat of Hanwi. Wi replied that because of the beauty of the woman he had forgotten his companion Hanwi.

Skan asked Ite why she sat on the seat of Hanwi. She replied that her mother foretold that she would sit beside the chief of the gods and had made her more beautiful, that Iktomi had told her that she was the most beautiful of all beings, that Wi was tired of Hanwi and wished for a younger and more beautiful companion, and that Wi invited her to sit at the feast of the gods, that she had seen the vacant seat beside him and sat on it.

Skan asked Kanka why she had schemed to have her daughter sit on the seat of Hanwi. She replied that as a seer she foresaw that Ite would sit beside the chief of the gods, and that she and Wazi had gotten from Iktomi the powers to do as the gods do. By these powers they had made their daughter more beautiful, so that Wi would not be ashamed of her when she sat beside him, and that Iktomi had told her that Wi was pleased to see Ite.

Skan asked Wazi why he had gotten the power from Iktomi. He replied that he wished for the power so that he could do more good.

Then Skan told Wi that the gods must not forget; that because he had permitted the beauty of a woman to cause him to forget his companion, she would be his companion no more, that she could go her own way and travel as she pleased; that he and she had ruled the two periods of time, day and night, but that forever after she would rule the third period, the interval between the time she went from him until she returned to him; that because he had caused her to hide her face for shame she would forever hide her face when near him, and only uncover it when she was far from him.

Skan told Ite that because she had forgotten her husband and little sons she would be with them no more; that her unborn child would come before its time and it would forever be a little child and abide with Tate; that because she was so vain of her beauty that she dared try to usurp the place of Hanwi, she would go to the world and there live forever without friends; that she should keep her beautiful face forever, but she would have another face so horrid that those who looked upon it would fly from her or go mad; and that she would be known as Anog Ite, the Double-Woman, or the Two-faced.

Skan told Kanka that because she had obtained the power of a god by fraud she should go to the world and there live alone forever, until she could use her powers to help little children and young people, and that she would forever be known as Wakanka, the Old Woman, the Witch.

Skan told Wazi that because he had not used his powers to do good, but to cause shame for his kindred and the gods, he should live forever alone in the world until he could use his powers to help his grandsons and that he should forever be known as Wazi, the Old Man, the Wizard.

Then Iktomi laughed loud and long and taunted Wakanka and said that she would have cheated him to get the powers of a god and then would have laughed at him, but that he had made her and her kindred ashamed.

Skan then asked Iktomi why he had schemed to make Wakanka and her kindred ashamed and to cause shame for Hanwi. Iktomi said that he was a god and the son of a god, that his father, the rock, was the oldest of the gods, that he had named all things that are named and made all languages that are spoken, that he had done much good and should be treated as a god; but because his other parent, the flying god, had no shape, his form was queer and all laughed at him; that when he did good all laughed at him as if he were making sport, that because everyone laughed at him he would laugh at everyone; that he had made the chief of the gods and the most beautiful of the gods ashamed; that he had made the chief of the People and the most beautiful of women ashamed; and that he would make all the gods and all the People ashamed.

Then Skan told him that because he laughed when others were ashamed or suffered and because he threatened the gods, he must go to the world and remain there forever without friends; that all of mankind would hate him, and all the gods despise him, and that the sound of the rattles would be torture to him.

Then Iktomi laughed loud and long. Skan asked him why he laughed. He replied that Skan had forgotten the birds and the beasts; that he would dwell with them and talk with each in its own language, and that he would have pleasure and would make fools of mankind.

Then Tate blackened his face and with his four sons

sat before Skan. Skan called him his comrade and asked him what he wished. Tate told Skan to look upon his face and the faces of his little children that were blackened because their mother was taken from them forever. He said Ite was but a woman and that others stronger than she had caused her to forget the woman's place; that though his sons were gods, they were little children and wept for their mother's care. He begged Skan to let him bear his punishment of Ite and let her remain with her children.

Skan told Tate that because of his love for Anog Ite, he would dwell near her until the fourth period of time and then he could do with the woman as he wished, that he could send a token to Tate and then Tate would send four sons to establish the directions on the world and they would make the fourth period of time.

Hanwi blackened her face and mourned with Tate, and the People laughed at her no more.

Before the directions were given to the world, Tate with his four sons and his little son dwelt in his round lodge beyond the region of the pines. At midday the Sun looked through the door of the lodge toward the place of honor to see that all was well with Tate. The seat of Tate was the place of honor and that of his oldest son, Yata, was beside him. The seat of the second-born, Eya, was at the right side of the lodge, and that of the third-born son, Yampa, was at the left side, while that of the youngest son, Okaga, was beside the door. His little son, Yum, had no birth; therefore, he had no seat in the lodge, but sat where he chose.

Tate did the woman's work in the lodge. Each morning his four sons set out to travel over the world. Sometimes Yum traveled with Okaga. One time when all the sons were away, something shining fell near the lodge, and Tate went to look at it. It was a woman wearing a soft white dress. She carried a queer pouch that was marked with strange symbols. He asked her whence she came, and she said she came from the stars. He asked her whither she would go. She replied her father had sent her to find friends on the earth. He asked who was her father; she replied that the Sky was her father. Then Tate told her to come with him to live in his lodge. He bade her tell his sons nothing of who she was or whence she came. He gave her the woman's seat in the lodge. When he began to made a robe of tanned skin, she said she would do the woman's work in the lodge and so he gave her the skin.

She took from her pouch a sharp stone and cut the skin into queer patterns. Then she took from her pouch an awl and sinew thread and quickly sewed the pieces together and made a garment which she gave to Tate and showed him how to wear it.

In the evening, Yata came striding to the door and jerked the flap aside and looked inside the lodge. He saw the woman and then he gazed at his father. He went away from the lodge and sat and stared at the ground. Soon Eya came, singing and hallowing, and threw the flap up and looked inside the lodge. He saw the woman and his father; he looked from one to the other and sat beside Yata and gazed at the ground. Then Yanpa strolled up to the lodge and raised the flap and started to go in, when he saw the woman. He looked at her and then at his father, and then at the lodge inside and out. Then he went and sat with Yata and Eya and he, too, gazed at the ground.

Soon Okaga and Yum came back together. Okaga asked his brothers why they sat and gazed at the ground. Yata said that the witch was in the lodge; Eya said that their father was wearing a strange garment; and Yanpa said there was nothing to eat. Yum ran to the door and lifted the flap and saw the woman. She looked at him and smiled, and he went inside the lodge. She bade him to sit beside her. He sat down and continued to gaze at her eyes. She put her arm around him and he smiled at her. Okaga came to the door and saw Yum sitting beside the woman and smiling at her, so he went inside. He saw that the woman was young and beautiful and that her braided hair was long and smooth, and her dress was white and clean and that even her feet were clothed. He sat at his seat. Then Tate remarked that he had forgotten his work, and it would be late before he could prepare the food for the evening. The woman offered to prepare the food. Immediately there was a fire in the fireplace and there were hot stones in it. She put the stones in the cooking bag and the food boiled. Then she told Tate that the food was ready to be served. Okaga gazed at her, astonished, but Tate only smiled as if he were well pleased.

He called his sons who were outside to come and eat. Yanpa said that there was no food prepared when he looked in the lodge. Eya said that no one had brought wood or water and the food could not be ready. Yata was sure it was the witch who had bewitched their father and the food. Again, Tate called. Yanpa consented to go in. He sat at his place and stared at the woman. Yata said, "She will bewitch him also." Eya said, "The witch was old, but this woman is young." Again Tate called. This time Eya said that this was but a young woman and he would go inside. He went in and sat at his place and stared at her. Then Tate called again, saying that the food was prepared and they were waiting for Yata so that they might eat. Yata said, "She is the witch, but I will drive her from the lodge." He strode to the door and stepped into the lodge, scowling. The woman looked at him and smiled. He gazed at her and then meekly went to his place and sat down. He looked around the lodge, at his father and at little Yum who sat beside the woman. When the four brothers were seated, all silently gazed at the ground though Yum continued to gaze at the woman's eyes. Tate gazed at the fire and smiled as if something pleased him.

Then the woman asked Tate what he most wished to eat. He replied he would like tripe and wild turnips and soup. She took from her pouch a new wooden bowl and platter and from the cooking bag tripe and boiled turnips, and she dipped the bowl full of soup from it. She gave these to Tate and called him her father. The brothers all looked at her and then at their father, but he only gazed at the fire and smiled. Then she called Yata her brother, and asked him what he most wished to eat. He said he wished boiled flesh and fat and pemmican and soup. She took from her pouch a new bowl and platter of wood, and from the cooking bag, boiled flesh and fat, and she dipped from it the bowl full of soup, and she placed pemmican on the platter and gave it all to Yata. Then she called Eya her brother, and asked him what he wished to eat. He told her he wanted a boiled Duck and wild rice and soup. Again, she took a platter and bowl from her pouch, and from the bag a Duck and rice and placed them on a platter, and dipped the bowl full of soup and gave them to Eya. Then she called Yanpa her brother, and asked him what he wished. He said he wanted tripe, flesh, fat, a Duck, turnips, rice and soup. She put all these things on a platter and in the bowl that she took from her pouch and gave them to Yanpa. Then she took from her pouch a little platter and a little bowl. On the platter she put strange food and in the bowl strange drink that had an odor of sweetgrass. She handed these to Yum and told him to give them to his brother who sat by the door. He did so. Then Yata said that as he was the oldest of the brothers, she should give him the best food instead of to the youngest, Okaga looked at the food—there was little of it—he looked at the drink and there was little of that. Then he looked at the woman, but she and Yum were eating together. He put all the food in his mouth and it made only one mouthful. He ate it and it was good. He looked at the little platter and there was more food on it. This he ate and still there was more food on the platter. He drank all there was in the bowl and immediately it was full again. So he ate and drank until he was satisfied.

When it was time to lie down to sleep, the four brothers went out of the lodge and found a new tipi nearby. They lifted the door flap, and inside they saw four beds, one at the place of honor, one on the right, one on the left side and one near the door. Yata said it must be the witch. Eya said the witch had treated them well. Yanpa said he wished the witch would always prepare their food. Then the three brothers went inside the tipi. Each lay on his bed to sleep, but Okaga sat beside the water, and played on his flute. The music was as soft as a whisper, but the woman heard it, and she smiled. Yum asked her why she smiled, and she said because he was always to be her little brother. Far into the night, Okaga sat by the water and gazed at the stars.

In the morning Okaga rose early as was his wont, to bring wood and water for his father; but when he came to the door of the lodge he found much wood and the water bag was full. The fire burned with hot stones in it and the cooking bag had food in it. The woman was astir but she did not look at Okaga. The father called his sons and all came and each sat in his place. The woman served them with food, and it was good. When all had eaten, the father told his sons that the time appointed by the Great Spirit was completed, and now there would be a fourth period of time. First, he told them, they must fix the directions of the world, but when they returned to his lodge, it would be the fourth period; that since they were four brothers, they should fix a direction for each of them, and thus there would be four directions; that they should go to the trail around the edge of the World and travel together until they came to the place for each direction, and there they should pile a great heap of stones to mark the direction forever. He said Yata was the oldest son and entitled to the first direction, which must be where the Sun goes over the Mountains and down under the World when his day's journey is done. The direction for Yanpa must be where the Sun comes up by the edge of the World to begin his daily journey. The direction for Okaga must be under the Sun at midday. He told them that the journey must be long, that it would be some Moons before they returned to his lodge, and that there would be as many Moons in the fourth time as had passed from the time they left the lodge until their return. He told them to prepare for four days and start on their journey on the fifth day.

For four days they prepared; on the morning of the fifth day they went from their father's lodge. When they had gone, Tate mourned for them as for the dead, for he knew they would abide in his lodge no more.

The wizard was not permitted on the world, so he traveled around on the edge until he made a trail there. He spoke to the Stars as they passed near him and asked each for permission to go to the World, but they never granted his request. He saw that some Stars never came down to the edge of the World, so he set up a lodge under them and dwelt in it so that he might be near if they should come down, for he thought one of them might give him permission to go on the world. In this lodge a vision came to him in which he was told to go on the trail again where a message would come to him. He followed the trail around the edge of the world and a bright star spoke to him. It appeared in the form of a beautiful young woman, who told him she was the daughter of the Sky and that her father had sent her with a message to him. She told him to return to his lodge and abide in it until the Moon was again round and then go upon the World, where he would find the sons of Tate. When he found them he must with his power as a wizard aid them in the work they were doing. When this work was done, she told him to go to the lodge of Tate, and then he could forever afterwards go upon the World as he wished.

He did as he was bidden. He found the sons of Tate camped for the night, for they were making their journey. He said, "Ho, my grandchildren," and asked permission to camp with them that night. Because Yata was the firstborn, he was the leader of the party. He answered in a surly manner and turned his back towards the old man. But, Okaga, the fourth-born, spoke kindly and bade the wizard sit on his side of the campfire. When the brothers ate, the old man said he was hungry. Yata replied that he should not travel without food, for he had none to give away; but Okaga gave him some of his food which he kept in a little bag. The old man ate much of it, but when he returned the bag to Okaga it was full of food. Ever afterwards, it remained full of good food, though Okaga often ate from it until he was satisfied.

When they had eaten, the three older brothers wrapped their robes about them and lay down to sleep. Okaga gave his robe to the old man and it spread until it was so large that both Okaga and the old man could lie upon it and cover with it. So they slept together that night.

In the morning, the robe was small and light, but ever afterward it remained like new, and would stretch so that Okaga could lie upon it and cover with it at the same time. He asked the brothers where they wished to go. They told him that their father had sent them to make the four directions and put them on the edge of the World. He told them that he lived on the edge of the World, and could guide them to it, and that if they would do as he bade them, he could bring them there quickly.

They agreed to do as he would tell them. Then he gave each of them a pair of moccasins, for before this their feet had always been bare. He showed them how to put them on and bade them stand side by side with him. Then Yata said his direction should be first because it was his birthright to be first in everything and that his father had told him that his direction must be on the edge of the World where the shadows are longest at midday. He ordered the old man to guide them to that place. Then the old man told them that with the aid of the moccasins they could step from hilltop to hilltop far away. He bade Yata step first; but he was afraid and would not move. Then the old man bade Eya, the second-born, to step, and he did so and was soon on a hilltop far away. Then Yata stepped forward and was beside Eya. Yanpa, the third-born, then stepped, and he too stood beside his brothers. When the three brothers had gone, the old man asked Okaga to come with him; they stepped together and went far beyond the three brothers. He called them. When they came he told them that they could travel best under Clouds and immediately it became so Cloudy that neither the sun nor the Sky could be seen. They traveled under the Clouds more swiftly than the Birds could fly and in the evening they came to a high Mountain where the old man told them to camp that night. In the morning he told them to go over the Mountain and there they would find the edge of the World and could set up a great heap of stones. This was the first direction.

When the first direction was made, they saw the Sun. They saw that the Mountain stood where the Sun went down at the close of the day's journey. When they saw

305

this, Yata raged, for this was Eya's direction and it was first. The old man stood before the brothers and told Yata that because he was cruel and surly, and a coward afraid to step first in the work his father had sent him to do, his birthright had been taken from him and given to Eya and that Eya would forever be considered first in all things. Then Yata hid his face and wept.

Wohpe dwelt in the tipi of old Tate and served him and his sons. The skins she dressed were soft and white; the moccasins she made were good and comfortable; the food she prepared was always abundant. She kept the fire burning and the talk pleasant so that all were happy in her presence.

Yata said to his brothers, "I want Wohpe for my woman." Yanpa replied, "You are too cold and cruel for Wohpe. Were she alone with you, she would soon perish. Remember your touch upon her dress. Wohpe should have a man who is happy and has no cares. I want her for my woman." Then Eya said, "Wohpe delights to serve others. This is her happiness. My pleasure is to be served. I would have her for my woman."

Thus they disputed, while Okaga said nothing and Yum fled to his father's tipi. They strove day by day each to still the others and make his claims good, till Okaga said, "Brothers, ask Wohpe. Whom she chooses she should serve," and they were quiet.

Yata said to Wohpe, "I want you for my woman. I am strong and my will is right. I am dreaded, for I am mighty. I will give you a part in my powers. Will you be my woman?"

Said Eya, "Wohpe, if my rest is undisturbed I do no harm. My evening's walk is my only want. Only when I am called early in the day do I fume and plague others that I may be left at my ease. Will you be my woman?"

Wohpe heard them and looked into the eyes of Okaga. That was all. Then she said, "He who will do that which pleases me most, in his robe will I stand, and him will I serve."

With this decision they must abide: the brothers were again at wordy war over who should first make an offering for the pleasure of Wohpe.

When Wohpe came to stay with Tate, he gave a feast to Taku Wakan. He consulted with his sons as to whom he should invite. They first chose the Wakan Tanka. Wi was the first chosen because he was Wakan Tanka. Hanwi, his wife, was the second chosen because she was Wakan Tanka. Inyan was the fourth because they were Wakan Tanka.

These four, with Tate, were the chiefs of Taku Wakan and formed the council. They made the rules by which all things should be governed. Then others were invited: the Unktehi who are the Wakan of the waters, the Unk-heegila who are the Wakan of the lands, the Wakinyan who are the Wakan of the air; the Tunkan who is the Wakan of the rocks, the Tatanka who is the Wakan of the Buffalo; the Can Oti who are the Wakan of the forests; the Hohngica who are the Wakans of the tipis; the Nagi because they are the Wakan of the shadows. These Tate told his sons to invite.

Okaga made the invitation wands. They were twice as long as his foot, meaning to travel with both feet; decorated with bright colors, meaning a joyous festival; and tipped with a red plume, meaning that Wakan business was to be discussed. The West Wind was to deliver them.

Old Tate gave a feast because Wakan Wohpe came to live with him. Wohpe made invitation sticks and ornamented them beautifully. Tate sent them out by his sons. They took the sticks to Iktomi, Ikcegeli, Inyan, Wasicun, Wakinyan, Takuskanskan, Tunkan, Hoya and many others.

On the day they met, both the Sun and the Moon shone. The brothers each brought his own kind of food, which Wohpe prepared. They feasted. Then they held a council in which Tate held the place of honor and told stories. Iktomi asked each for his story. Tate told of his origin. He told of the birth of his sons, of their characteristics, of the coming of the Wohpe, and of his hopes for grandchildren.

Ikchegila told of his origin and his powers. Inyan told of his origin. Wasicunpi told of their origin, their pleasure, and powers. Wakinyan told of their origin, their kinds, powers, hates and likes. Taku Skan-Skan told of his origin and power. Tunkan and Hoya related their origin and powers. Iktomi tricked them and lied.

Then the guests said to Tate, "You have given presents to each of us as we desired. What can we give to you?" He said, "It is because of my daughter, Wohpe, that you have feasted. Give your presents to her." So they asked her what she would have. She sang her reply:—

"The Sun is my father.
The Moon is my mother.
Let no one have power over them.
The Sun is all wise.
The Sun is all powerful.
No one has power over them."

They all agreed that no one would have power over the Sun and the Moon. But Iktomi played a trick on the Wankinyan and often hid the face of the Sun and the Moon, while Hoya was so greedy that he would bite away a portion of the Moon. They then asked Wohpe if she did not want something for herself. She arose and stood by Okaga, who folded his robe about her. She said, "I want a tipi for Okaga and myself. A place for him and his brothers."

They made the World and all there is in it for them. Iktomi made the unpleasant things. Old Tate came and dwelt with them, but he left his powers at the old tipi. Then they all found that it was good and came to dwell on the Earth. Iktomi stirred up strife between the brothers, so they agreed to dwell in different places, but each would visit the other.

Yata dwells in the regions of the pines. Eya dwells in the mountains where the Sun retires to rest. Yanpa dwells where the great waters are, where the Sun begins his daily journey to view the whole World. Okaga and Wohpe have their tipi in the center of the World where the Sun is highest, and little Yum lives with them. Each year they come and bring life and warmth, but as soon as they turn their backs, Yata brings cold and death. Then the birds fly to Okaga and beg him to come to their help. When they come to his tipi, they find him and Wohpe so contented and happy, that they return rejoicing, and mate and raise their young.

Tate gives presents to all the guests.

Then they all dance. Yum dances better than all and is the favorite, but Yata hates him for this. Then the Wasicun dance and Wohpe dances with them and her hair shines and flashes. Since then, when the Wasicun dance there are flashes of light (the Aurora Borealis).

Waziya joins with Yata. Waziya is the Man from the North (the region of the pines). They do many things that are strange in order to amuse the company. Iktomi gives the choice of color. They choose white. Then Yanpa does things to amuse his company. Iktomi gives him a choice of colors. He chooses blue. Then Okaga does things so wonderful that the company never tires of watching him. Iktomi gives him a choice of colors, and he chooses red. Then Wohpe asks Okaga to do some favor for each one of the guests, and he promises to do so. Okaga asked Ikcegila what he most desired, and he said he wanted to have power over everything. Okaga asked where he wanted his power. He answered that he wanted his power in his horns and his tail. So he received power. But Iktomi made his horn very soft and his tail very brittle. His women lived on the earth and his home was in the water.

Then Okaga asked Inyan what he most desired, and he said he wished to be able to resist anything. Okaga made him very hard and very large so that nothing could give him pain; but Iktomi made him very brittle so that he would break in pieces but remain undestroyed. Then the Wasicun were asked what they most desired, and they said they wished to be invisible. They were made invisible, but Iktomi deprived them of form or shape so that when they wished to communicate with others they had to steal the form of something else. Then the Wakinyan were asked what they most desired. They said they wished loud voices and bright eyes.. Their wishes were granted, but Iktomi made their voices terrible and the glance of their eyes destructive.

Then Takuskanskan was asked what he most desired, and he asked to have powers over everything moving in order to protect it and do it good. He was given the power, but Iktomi made him a very sleepy one. Then Tunkan was asked what he most desired, and he said he wanted many children, so that he would be revered and cared for. They were promised him, but Iktomi promised that his children should strive among themselves, and forget him save when in trouble. Then Eya was asked what he most desired. He said he wanted to have plenty to eat at all times, so he was promised this, but Iktomi declared that he would always be hungry and his food would give him pain. Other gifts were given to the other guests.

"In those days came John the Baptist, preaching in the wilderness of Judea, And saying, Repent ye: for the kingdom of heaven is at hand." St. Matthew 3:1-2

TIPI LIFE

This is not a handbook for Tipi-making, nor for daily tipi usage, for that is not what I am qualified to pass on to You. I wish, instead, to inspire within You some spiritual feelings—for real Tipi Life must begin that way.

To get the technical matter of Tipis out of the way, here is some pertinent information:

Ready-made tipis may be purchased through the following suppliers:

CANADIAN WHOLE EARTH TRUCK STORE
250 Robert Street
Toronto, Ontario

MOTHER'S TRUCK STORE
Box 75
Unionville, Ohio

Practical knowledge relating to Tipis can be found in a number of books that have been written about old-time culture. One book that was specifically compiled for the tipi-maker is: THE INDIAN TIPI, by R. & G. Laubin; Published in 1957 by the University of Oklahoma Press.

First Snowfall of the Season—the bottom layer of white—
    a few more feet to come, yet—to make the Outdoors bright.
By middle of the Winter—You'll stand above the door—
    climb down to get inside, then—lay your shovel on the floor.
Inside you'll feel quite sheltered—as though beneath the ground—
    Hang your food-pots over the fire—as it's spreading its warmth
    around.
While Snowflakes strike the tipi—and Wind flies through the Air—
    You'll feel as One with Nature—for Nature's with You in there.

To experience the thrill and satisfaction of Tipi Life
you need not have a manicured cover of heavy canvas and
a dozen or two perfectly-straight, peeled, and dried poles
of 20 or 25 foot length. You may well *want* to have these
things in order to experience Tipi Life in the most comfort
and luxury, after trying something more simple.

—To know the joy of eating does not require a four-
    course meal eaten with silver forks and porcelain
    dishes—

Two canvas painter's drop cloths, some hours of cutting
and sewing, and a dozen reasonably-straight, cleaned poles
of 10 or 12 foot length will give you a serviceable lodge
to set up by your house or cabin (for a spiritual retreat),
or to take into the mountains (for a few nights of inspirational camping).

312

What I'm saying is, as usual, that happiness from doing something is in your Mind—so, I think You can experience happiness by trying a lot of things in a simpler fashion than "experts" of those things think is "proper." Many Native People in the old days—some whole Bands and Tribes of them—were happy to have the shelter of lodges that many people today would claim not be tipis. Yet, that is what they are, in the liberal interpretation of the word (being the way that Your own Mind wishes to interpret it). With that out of the way, let us get On with a few details of making a simple tipi.

If you follow these directions (physically or spiritually), then you will end up with about a ten-foot lodge (physically or spiritually) that will entertain four to six People comfortably, and provide living shelter for two. It will make a reasonably small bundle to pack around, and can be set up wherever you can locate enough twelve foot poles to drape it over, and enough sticks to lace up the front and stake down the bottom.

First, you need enough canvas to make a solid piece measuring ten feet by twenty. You might just buy a ten by twenty piece of duck or canvas; or, you might buy two ten by ten drop cloths—sew them together in a sturdy way (with a regular sewing machine, if your material is light); or you might buy or find several smaller pieces of canvas (if You're in a peasant mood) and have to sew them together and trim them—just so you end up with a piece that's ten by twenty, all right?

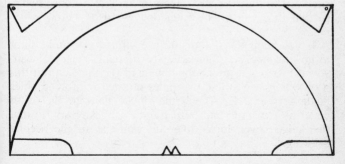

The kind of material you buy is up to You and your budget. You will have to decide what use you will make of the lodge—the more you use it, the heavier should be your material. Same goes for waterproofing (which flying dust and dirt really like to cling to). If I'm buying material for a new lodge, I go and feel of it and then decide which one I want—I never can remember the technical details. Sorry! That's how the Old People always did it.

So, now take your piece of ten by twenty and lay it out somewhere on a flat surface. With a pencil and measuring string mark up the canvas according to the first drawing, herewith. If you can't do it right the first time, throw everything away and start all over (buy Laubins' book next time, and make a really neat one).

With a good pair of scissors (or a really sharp knife) trim the material along all the lines until you end up with the basic semi-circle of the lodge cover and the two pieces that will be the smoke flaps. If you brought along your pipe, now is the time to get it out and smoke it while you dwell on the thought of Tipi Life and marvel at the effort you are making toward it. Then go on with the tipi-making experience.

Some sewing is now in order, as you are making your new lodge. Again, a sewing machine can be used if 1) your material is thin enough; 2) you know how to use a sewing machine, and 3) you have one. If not, get a spool of nylon thread, some beeswax, a thimble, and a large needle. Overlap the two pieces, wherever you're sewing, so that they will direct water downwards.

If you want the tips of the poles for your smoke flaps to go into pockets, then attach a triangular piece of canvas at E on each smoke flap. Some of the People do it this way; others stick these two poles through reinforced holes made at points E. Attach the smoke flaps to the lodge cover by sewing G and H to I and J—or, anyway, so that the lodge cover looks like the example in the second drawing.

314

If you want your lodge cover to wear well and look neat, then fold all the exposed edges back a quarter or half inch and sew this down for your hem. Even big stitches can be used here—so long as you get that double edge to avoid frazzling and tearing the lodge cover during use.

A double row of holes needs to be cut above and below the door on each side. The holes will be for the lacing pins, so they should be reinforced by sewing, like button-holes.

A piece of rope or leather thong should be sewn to the triangular piece that exists between the smoke flaps. With this you will tie the lodge cover to the raising pole.

All around the circular part of the cover should be sewn canvas or rope loops for the pins which will hold the cover down.

Now You will have to do some woodwork. Most important are the poles for the frame. In keeping with the funkiness of this particular tipi, any kind of poles will do, as long as they are reasonably straight, free of major cracks or breaks, and anything over 10 feet long. Try to find some with a butt diameter of two or three inches, and tapering toward the top. Clean the poles of bark and branches. Look for sharp branch joints along the poles and remove them—they will tear your cover. Next in importance are a handful of lacing pins (for as many double pairs of holes as you made above and below the door). These should be about ten inches long and the thickness of your little finger (or the next finger, if you gave up your little finger as an offering, already). Peel the bark off these, clean them, and sharpen the ends. Finally, cut a set of stakes for holding down the lodge cover. These should be a foot or two long and an inch or more in thickness, with one end sharpened. When you have all these things that I've so far mentioned, then You will be ready to set up your own tipi and build yourself a camp around it (but don't tell anybody where you learned all this if it doesn't turn out good).

A fellow named Gilbert Wilson spent some time with the Old People in their tipis many years ago. He was so inspired that he wrote an article about tipis for young boys back in 1916. In those days only young boys were given the privilege by Society to make efforts at fulfilling their Dreams and Fantasies. Poor Gilbert Wilson had to return to his city life, from the Prairies, and fulfill his own desires indirectly by telling young boys about them. Let Us give a prayer of Good Thoughts for Gilbert Wilson, brothers and sisters. (Gilbert's brother, Frederick, incidentally, Satisfied similar desires by making some fantastic sketches of his Dreams and Fantasies. They have been used to illustrate THE SPIRIT AT HIDDEN VALLEY—a book of the Good Medicine series.)

As for setting up the lodge: Reading Gilbert Wilson's description of this process makes me realize that he says it as well as it can be said, so I'll just quote him. Says Gilbert:

"There are two ways of setting up the tepee frame, called the three-pole and the four-pole ties. The three-pole tie, used by the Mandans [with whom Gilbert spent most of his time], is perhaps the simpler [more on the four-pole later].

"Lay three poles on the ground as in Fig. 6, and bind firmly, two feet from the top.

"The poles are set up in a tripod, Fig. 7, for the skeleton frame. Poles A and B, in front and spread apart, will inclose the door.

"Positions of the other seven poles of the frame are shown in the ground diagram, Fig. 8. A, B, and C are the three poles of the skeleton frame. Poles D, E, and F, on the left, and G, H, and I, on the right, are raised in the order named. The rope or lariat L, Figs. 7 and 8, used for tying the skeleton frame, has been left hanging. This lariat is now drawn out through the door, between poles A and B, is carried quite around the frame, and is drawn tight about the tie.

"The pole J in the rear of the tent is the last to be placed. On this pole the canvas cover is raised.

"Lay the cover on the ground, weather side up, and

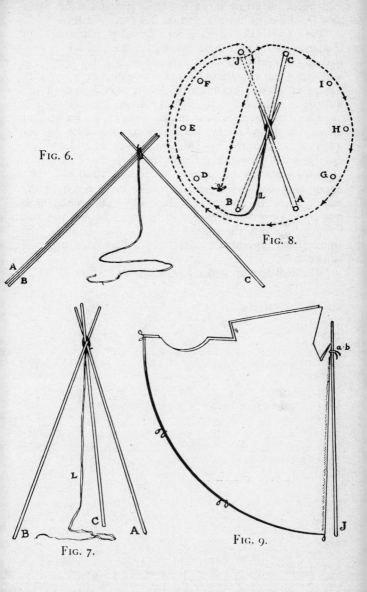

FIG. 6.

FIG. 8.

FIG. 7.

FIG. 9.

fold once over. Lay down the pole J, and tie the cover to it by the cord ab, Fig. 9, two feet from the top.

"Pole J with the cover is then raised in place between C and F. Before the cover is drawn, the lariat L is carried to the rear of the tent, around pole J, back into the tent again between J and C, and anchored firmly to a pin. Figure 10 shows the anchored frame. (Pole J is raised, but the tent cover is omitted in the figure.)

"The tent cover is now drawn around the frame and laced. The loops at the lower edge of the cover are secured to the ground by tent pins, driven in a slant. The door is hung over one of the lacing pins.

"Two poles are yet unused. They are raised and their upper ends are thrust into the pockets (or hole) of the smoke flaps. By means of these poles, the smoke flaps may be propped downwind, so that the smoke may not be driven down the smoke hole. In wet weather, the smoke flaps may by the same means be folded over the smoke hole.

"The tent, set up and ready, is shown in Fig. 11."

A Sarsi home in the foothills of the Canadian Rockies. The Old Lady is mashing berries to make Pemmican, while her lodge stands part-way open to let in fresh air. The family was forced to salvage scrap canvas to make their home with—yet the cover was sewn with some artistic display.

The lariat that is left hanging down from the crossing of the poles is usually tied securely to one or two pins that are driven firmly into the ground on the windward side of the fireplace. The reason is obvious. The pins around the outside bottom of the tipi also help to hold the cover down. However, during a busy period we once left a Good Medicine lodge set up all Summer, Fall, and Winter—through Wind, Rain, Sleet, and Hail—without pinning down the bottom or anchoring the lariat, and the darned thing never budged. During one of the Windstorms some of the boards even flew off our barn roof!

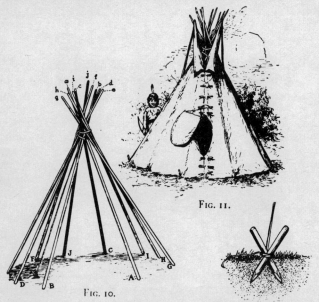

Fig. 11.

Fig. 10.

Now that you've made this Good Medicine lodge and it is set up on your homestead, listen to a few more comments about it. First of all, don't pack up your little lodge, your pipe, and your bead necklace and head for the nearest pow-wow, expecting to be welcomed as the mythical long-lost brother of the Natives. Others who have tried that were disappointed to find themselves laughed at or, worse, to have their camps turned upside down during the nighttime. Pow-wows and gatherings that occur nowadays help to serve as occasions for the People to keep alive some of their old traditions and customs—unless you understand these quite well, you may well unintentionally insult them.

Part of the People's efforts nowadays is to demonstrate to their friends and relatives what they've accomplished—a large, clean lodge, a new dance outfit, fancy Western clothes, or a brand-new camper. Very few People would appreciate your efforts to capture the Spirit of the Old Life by your primitive methods, especially if representatives of your ancestors killed theirs for doing the same things.

INSIDE THE LODGE

Your small lodge will be fairly cramped for space—especially when guests come and you are entertaining. In any case, though, your fire must be in the center. Dig out a pit, remove grass and material from around it, and line it on the outside with some stones. The fireplace can be quite small for a small lodge. Once you have a fire going, use a few sticks stuck into the center of the fire like spokes into the hub of a wheel. As the sticks burn, push them further into the fire, and occasionally add new ones. In this way you will have a fire of hot coals and small flames. A modern camper's fire will burn your food, your guests, and maybe your whole lodge. When retiring for the night, pull the remaining sticks out of the fire and bury their ends in the ashes—when done right you will still have hot coals for starting your fire in the morning. Blowing through a pipestem works well for turning the coals into fire. A bird's wing or tail can be used that way, too. Firewood is usually kept to the left of the door, just after you enter. In good weather it can be kept outside on the ground, or in a box made for that purpose.

Seating arrangements used to vary among tribes and different families. With your small lodge you can't be very choosy. In all cases, however, the place of most honor was to the rear, opposite the door. Among some People this was reserved for the head of the household and no other. Among others it was given to distinguished guests.

Still others used it only for keeping their Medicines. People usually slept end to end—one side for the women and the other for the men. This, of course, varied. When entertaining, however, the men always sat on one side and the women on the other. The man of the house sat just to the right of the rear, center, as one entered the doorway; the woman sat to his right. The first guests to arrive sat next in order, men to the right and women to the left, as they entered. If an honored person showed up—an old one, a bundle owner, or a leader, room was made for him and his wife to sit next to the lodge's owners. Unless unavoidable, others never passed between those who were seated and the fireplace, and under no circumstances between the fireplace and the owner (and his bundles). Passing through such a spiritual path with one's body was worse than interrupting a speaker. Children were taught this from the very start—their behavior towards guests was to be strictly with respect.

If you sew up a nice inside lining, the interior of your lodge will look quite neat, and you will be happy. Some bedspreads or sheets, however, tied securely to the lodge poles, will provide you with the same benefits, practically. This inner lining, of course, is for insulation from the hot Summer Sun and the cold Winter Winds, in addition to directing upwards the drafts of air which come in under the main lodge cover. Some People who lived in less Windy areas (like the Flatheads of the Valleys and Mountains) only put their tipi linings next to the cover, behind the poles.

If you have sacred articles, place them at the rear of the tipi—perhaps tied to one of the lodge poles there. In front of them, but in back of the fireplace, is the altar place where incense is often burned. The altar was usually a circle or square of Earth with the top layer removed. If particular bundles within the tipi required it, the Earth within the altar had certain decorations traced over it, and sometimes filled in with Sacred Paint. On this altar was placed a glowing coal from the fire, and the owner's customary incense was shredded or sprinkled on it. Common plants for incense include Sweet Grass, Cedar leaves, and Sage. Perhaps You will be directed to Your own, when You stay in Your tipi.

In the Summer home of Louison, a Flathead chief in 1908. His Buffalo-robe-covered backrest sits in the background, while carpet and furs line the floor. A trunk and other belongings fill the space down in the bottom corners, and fancy dress clothes hang from a rope tied to the lodge poles.

Some old rugs or quilts can be placed on the floor, for much of your time will be spent there. Pine boughs, ferns, or reeds from the Water can also be used in this way. If you have extra flooring material, it would be well to stuff it in the bottom corner of your tipi, all around; or, at least, where your beds are. Rolls of extra clothing and other belongings can be kept there too, if you wrap them with waterproof material or place them in rawhide containers. This stuffing will help your lodge to be more Air-tight. Trunks became very popular among tipi dwellers after they gave up much of their roaming and obtained wagons for their moving. You may find a trunk very handy for keeping your belongings safe, in order, and out of your everyday way. Food, especially, is well-kept inside a trunk in your tipi.

For cooking you may want to try the old way of hanging a pot from a chain or rawhide rope suspended from a sturdy tripod, the legs of which are planted firmly around the fireplace. Sometimes two forked sticks were used instead, one each side of the fire, with a third one lying crosswise and resting in the forks. From this the pot can be suspended, or meat and vegetables can be pierced onto a green Willow stick and cooked with the stick resting in the forks. In the Summertime, when the heat from a cooking fire is no longer bearable, two things can be done. Commonly, the pins were removed from the bottom of the lodge cover and it was rolled up a few feet on one or all sides. Often the women put up separate cooking tipis—made simply by tying together a few poles to form a frame, and draping part of an old tipi, or a tipi lining over it so as to protect the occupants from Sun's heat and expose them to cool breezes. Some People built more elaborate Sun and Cooking shelters. One that is often still seen among People of the Central and Southern Plains is a patio-like framework of poles covered over with many pine boughs.

A Sun-shelter in a Cheyenne camp around 1900.

Water, in the old days, was kept in a cleaned paunch and hung inside from one of the lodge poles, or from a tripod. Canteens were used when obtainable. Large metal milk cans are most commonly used today.

If Your Spirit directs You to express Your Dreams and devotions for others to see when they visit your household, a common place for such expression has long been the rear panel of the inside lining. Pictographic stories of Horse raids, battles, hunts, and visions were often drawn there by the owners. Bright blankets and colorful cloth material were often used for the rest of the lining, after the Buffalo were gone and if canvas seemed too plain or too expensive.

And always be prepared for guests! Keep extra blankets, if they need a place to sleep for the night. Keep some extra dried meat and beans for their Supper. Always have your pipe and smoking mixtures by your bedside—a quiet smoke should be your welcome to All who visit your lodge.

This camp of a wandering Cheyenne family was photographed in Montana around the turn of the Century. Behind their practical tipi is parked the family "camper." A pole sticking out from underneath its canvas cover supports some drying meat and sausages. Way beyond the wagon are the family's grazing Horses —the lead one was probably staked out or hobbled. At night the Horses were usually tied close to the tipi, to prevent them from wandering off and to give alarm in case of approaching danger.

While Mom prepares breakfast the rest of the family still sleeps under their blankets and covers—their feet pointed towards the fire. Mom is making fried bread during one of the recent encampments of her Stony People, by the Canadian Rockies. Long after midnight visitors were still coming to the door looking for a place to sleep. Over twenty persons ended up unrolling their sleeping gear (or borrowed blankets) on the floor.

The scene below shows a part of the Stony Encampment in the foothills of the Canadian Rockies. The Stonies have long been noted for their Mountain climbing and hunting. Several of their tipis have designs on them that were inspired by their Mountain life—such as this Mountain Sheep Tipi.

Year-round Tipi Life is an adventure reserved nowadays for the very hardy, to say the least. Though I have, myself, thought of attempting permanent tipi living—and may, yet, do it someday—I do not feel that I am anywhere near learned enough in the skills and Spirits of total Outdoor Life to risk Spiritual Happiness with possible physical danger. The People who did this in the Old Days were born into that kind of Life, and had countless generations' worth of knowledge and training to grow up with. In addition, Life in a Tipi was, for them, a necessity!

When the idea of cabin building spread across the country with the new settlers, long ago, some families and bands among different tribes became attracted to it. The Flathead People under Chief Charlo, for instance, built cabins at their home base in the beautiful Bitter Root Valley, in Western Montana. Though Grandma was born in a tipi during the Summertime there, she well remembers her family's cabin and those of their neighbors. Through unusually pleasant relations with the missionary-minded Priests who set up a Mission by the river in the valley, Charlo's People were inspired to adopt some forms of Old Country farm life. Though no one person "owned" any of the tribal land, each family had an area that others respected as being under someone's control. On that area the family (or families—brothers and parents and friends and relations often joined together on these ventures) built a log cabin, kept their Horses, and, perhaps, a milk Cow (bought or traded from settlers nearby). They raised feed and grains, and tended a vegetable garden. A mill at the Mission ground their grains into flour. All this during the old days, when the men packed up now and then and headed out to the Prairies for a Buffalo hunt or up North for some Horse raiding among enemy camps.

Charlo's Flathead People found that some of the ways of the new settlers improved their own way of living without taking away from its spiritual happiness. In the Wintertime they found that it was easier to heat a log cabin than a tipi. This promoted the good health of the

327

People—especially the Old Ones and the little Babies.
Things could be stored better in the cabins, year around.
And Children found the forced indoor life of much of the
Winter more enjoyable without the crampedness of a
tipi filled with People and centered around a burning fire
and hot cooking vessels.

Now, during the warmer times of the Year—especially
during Summer—when the People spent much of their
time out of doors anyway—they usually made their homes
in tipis. That is, they kept their bedding there, cooked and
ate there, and entertained guests there. The cabins were
used mainly for storage of food and extra belongings.
Some days the family members packed up their living
necessities, rolled them up in the cover of their tipi, packed
their Horses, and rode over to some relatives a few miles
up or down the valley, there to set up the household for
a relaxed time of visiting. Again, they might pack up their
home and, in company with a few others, make a short
or long excursion to some favorite hunting or root and
berry-picking ground, setting up their homes there until
the purpose for their coming was completed. Until just a
few years ago, Grandma still took her tipi and furnishings,
packed them on a Horse, and rode along with others like
her—often back down to their beloved Bitter Root Valley—to camp and hunt and gather in peace and harmony.

People of some other tribes combined Tipi Life with
solid-home living long, long before any settlers ever
showed up in their country. Most of these People lived

on the Eastern Plains—the region known today as the MidWest. They included the Mandan, Omaha, Ponca, and Pawnee tribes, to name a few. Other tribes often referred to these folks as Earth People, because their solid homes were large Earth lodges.

Rather than building solid homes for Winter use, as the Flathead did with their cabins, the Earth People generally built theirs for Summer use. One reason for this was that they raised vegetables in gardens (principally maize), and thus needed permanent sites for planting their crops and storing their harvests. They used tipis in Winter because their hunting required them to be constantly on the move out on the Prairies. The Earth Lodges were built in places of open exposure to Summer Sun, as well as fresh air for ventilation; thus they were not well protected from the storms of Winter. The tipis, however, could be set up in dense brush or tree groves down in some protected river bottom.

A good narrative of the tipi and solid home type of life among the Omaha People around 1820 was recorded by John Dougherty, the deputy agent for them and some of their neighbors. Parts of this narrative read:

"The inhabitants occupy their villages not longer than five months in the year [the permanent village, then located on the banks of Omaha Creek, near the Missouri River, in present-day Dakota County, Nebraska]. In April they arrive from their hunting excursions, and in the month of May they attend to their horticultural interests, and plant Maize, Beans, Pumpkins, and Watermelons, . . . dress the Bison skins, which have been procured during the Winter hunt, for the traders, who generally appear for the purpose of obtaining them [another advantage of permanent villages—permanent addresses, if you will]." About June, "after having closed the entrances to their several habitations by placing a considerable quantity of brushwood before them, the whole nation departs from the village." At that time they went on their Summer Buffalo hunt, bringing along their tipis which "are often fancifully ornamented on the exterior, with figures, in blue and red

Many tipi-using People on the West side of the Rockies covered their lodge frames with mats of woven tule reeds instead of hides. This mat tipi was used by a Kutenai family in Southern British Columbia.

paint, rudely executed, though sometimes depicted with no small degree of taste. . . . On the return of the nation, which is generally early in September, . . . property buried in the Earth is . . . taken up and arranged in the lodges, which are cleaned out and put in order. The weeds which during their absence had grown up, in every direction through the village, are cut down and removed. A sufficient quantity of Sweet Corn is next to be prepared, for present and future usage." By the end of October the People were again ready to go on a hunting excursion with their tipis, taking along their newly-tanned robes in order to do some trading on the way. "This hunt continues until towards the close of December, and during the rigours of the season they experience an alternation of abundance and scarcity of food." After the trading and meat-hunting expedition was finished, they returned to the village to "procure a supply of Maize from their places of concealment, after which they continue their journey, in pursuit of the Bisons. . . ." This Bison hunt, from which they brought back quantities of hides and dried meat, was completed in April—time again for planting.

For your interest, a technical description of one of these old-time Earth Lodges follows. The narrative is from the Long Expedition during their visit with the Kansa People of the Prairie in the late Summer of 1819.

"The village is situated . . . within about ¼ of a mile of the river. It consists of about 120 lodges, placed as closely together as convenient. . . . The ground area of each lodge is circular, and is excavated to the depth of from one to three feet. . . .

"The lodge, in which we reside, is larger than any other in the town, and being that of the grand chief, it serves as a council house for the nation. The roof is supported by two series of pillars, or rough vertical posts, forked at the top for reception of the transverse connecting pieces of each series; twelve of these pillars form the outer series, placed in a circle; and eight longer ones, the inner series, also describing a circle; the outer wall, of rude frame work, placed at a proper distance from the exterior series of pillars, is five or six feet high. Poles, as thick as the leg at base, rest with their butts upon the wall, extending on the cross pieces, which are upheld by the pillars of the two series, and are of sufficient length to reach nearly to the summit. These poles are very numerous, and agreeable to the position which we have indicated, they are placed all around in a radiating manner, and support the roof like rafters. Across these are laid long and slender sticks or twigs, attached parallel to each other by means of bark cord; these are covered by mats made of long grass, or reeds, or with the bark of trees; the whole is then covered completely over with Earth, which, near the ground, is banked up to the eaves. A hole is permitted to remain in the middle of the roof to give exit to the smoke.

Around the walls of the interior, a continuous series of mats are suspended; these are of neat workmanship, composed of a soft reed, united by bark cord. . . . The bedsteads are elevated to the height of a common seat from the ground, and are about six feet wide; they extend in an uninterrupted line around three-fourths of the . . . apartment, and are formed . . . of numerous sticks, or slender pieces of wood resting at their ends on cross pieces, which are supported by short notched or forked posts, driven into the ground; Bison skins supply them with a comfortable bedding [think of the spiritual atmosphere of such a bed, for a while!]. Several Medicine or mystic bags are carefully attached to the mats of the wall. . . . Of their contents we know nothing. The fireplace is a simple shallow cavity, in the center of the apartment, with an upright and a projecting arm for the support of the culinary apparatus."

"THE INTERIOR OF THE HUT OF A MANDAN CHIEF"
Karl Bodmer, 1833

GRANDMA'S
LITTLE TIPI

Until a few years ago, Grandma took this lodge with her whenever she went berry picking and root gathering up in the Mountains. Its small size and short poles made it convenient for packing around on short journeys; yet there was still always room for everyone who came along.

It took Grandma just about twenty minutes to set up the whole tipi—not bad for an 86-year old lady! Said she, when it was set up: "I'm just too old—not even good to put up tipi. When I was young I could just put it up in a hurry!"

". . . My Old People always used four poles to set up tipi on—I heard about some other Tribes using three poles. . . . I guess our tipis don't fall down any more than theirs do. . . ."

"This door pole always has to face that way (East)....
in the morning when You first go out You always remember to give thanks to Him (Sun)...."

"... Pretty easy way to fix up a house—just some
poles and then You pull that thing [the tipi cover] around
them and close it up with a bunch of sticks—like this..."

"There . . . now You can cook in it and live in it just like the Old Days . . . just like when I was born in Tipi. . . ."

Small rustic lodges in a camp of Northern Déné People, on the Alberta Prairie. The tipi covers were made of Elk, Moose, and Caribou skins, with canvas used for patching.

The home of a Sarsi family on the Alberta Prairie. The travois used for moving camp were often tied together, as in the right of this scene, to be covered with canvas for shelter, or to support items hung from their middle. Behind the girl on the Horse hang the owner's Medicine bags from a tripod, where they were usually kept in the daytime.

SUMMER CAMP

Every Summer I look forward to camping with "Grandma and Grandpa" in their tipi out on the Plains of Montana. Heading for 90 are the "Old Folks," as that "young fellow" who lives with them (Makes Summer—he's a couple of decades younger than they) calls them. Still, every Summer they pack up their blankets and pots for a few days of memories—enjoying, again, the Tipi Life of the annual encampment of the Tribe.

Without prior announcement I arrive on the first day that camp is being set up. Only a dozen tipis are in their places, but I know the Old Folks will be there—it is one of the year's highlights for them. Over in the NorthWest corner of the camp circle I see their tipi—in its usual spot by the lodges and empty places of others whose fathers and grandfathers lived and hunted together in the same band. Other bands have their own places within the circle.

An old striped blanket is sewn to the front of the tipi and serves as the door. It is tied at each side to a stick that hangs across the doorway and keeps the blanket stretched out. I lift the stick up on one side, put my left leg inside the tipi, bend low and put my head through the doorway, and step in with my right foot, being careful to keep my balance, and let the stick and curtain fall back across the door properly. . . .

. . . Ahhhhhh . . . . and other exclamations of surprise and pleasure come from the two occupants of the lodge, seated on blankets towards the back of the tipi. Smiles and handshakes, while I hold my bedroll in my left hand. "Hello Grandfather [Bear Child] . . . Hello Father [Makes Summer] . . . Where is Grandma?" "She went around looking for a boyfriend," the Old Man says, slyly. "The Old Lady went over visiting," says Makes Summer, wanting to oblige my question. He lives with the old folks and helps them keep house and run errands—though none of the three suffer from any particular handicaps.

"Well, you might just as well camp with us," says old Bear Child (who is also known as Many Treaties—the first was his father's name, the last was given to him by his father, who served as a guide and scout during the last century and made Many Treaties with People whose country he took parties through). He points out a place just to the right of the rear of the tipi for me to spread my bedroll on. Makes Summer has his spread out on the North side of the tipi (the door faces East, of course), and a bunch of blankets and bedding on the South side marks the sleeping area of the old folks. So I unroll my bag and sit down.

"We was just talking about you this morning," says Bear Child, "we figured you'd show up pretty soon." Makes Summer nods agreeably—his teeth illuminating an overpowering grin that only disappears during times of shyness or contemplation. He is wearing his usual dark glasses, to protect his aging eyes from the light. He is short and slight, and wears a cowboy hat over his gray hair. Bear Child is taller, but also lightly built. He has on a pair of beaded moccasins, slacks, and a plaid shirt. The ends of his braids are wrapped with red cloth, and his eyes are protected by a pair of airline pilot's glasses. A large button pinned to his shirt reads "OLD AGE POWER." He grins when he sees that I've noticed it.

For a while we sit in silence—only the distant sounds of People and Dogs reminding us that we are still in camp. All we can see of the outside is a bright blue Summer Sky, through the congestion of tipi poles as they reach out of the tipi top and point the way up High. The smoke flaps are slowly moving back and forth in the breeze, but the air is quite still and warm down where we sit.

Quietly, the door curtain lifts up and a small, moccasin-covered foot enters the tipi, followed, of course, by the Old Lady. Gracefully she walks to her place, at Bear Child's right, and is almost ready to sit down before she notices me. She puts her hand before her mouth (a modest exclamation of surprise) and utters a barely-audible "Ohhh!" as I step over to give her a hug. She is so small and so cheerful that I want to just pick her up and carry her off with me—her snow-white hair and twinkling eyes, surrounded by many pleasant wrinkles, would melt the heart of the strongest man.

Black Woman (her inherited name) sits down to the right of her husband and takes off her scarf and heavy wool shirt (which she wears outside, in spite of the warm weather). She reaches in her purse and brings out a little pipe with an ornate clay bowl and a willow stem. As she rummages in her purse for the tobacco, I reach into my bedroll and bring out my own—grown back home in Canada. She puts some of it in her pipe, and I ask her to say a prayer. She holds up the pipe—offering it to the Spirits of the Universe—and says a prayer of thanks that we have been reunited and are all in good health, and asks that we have a good time during the encampment and can meet again at another time. Then she lights the pipe and puffs on it for a while, before passing it around to the rest of us in the tipi.

For a while there is again silence in the tipi. Each one of us is absorbed in some experience within our Minds. The roundness of our dwelling gives me a very strong feeling—like being inside of a geometric molecule and tumbling through the vastness of the Universe—physical old age next to me, Spiritual everlasting age all around: just People, Earth, poles, and tipi covering, with a natural Skylight up above our heads and light diffused by the canvas walls all around. A very serene feeling in the warmth of the Summer, there.

339

Makes Summer breaks the silence to tell about one of his spiritual fathers from a few years ago—a long-gone old-timer by the name of Lazy Boy. It seems that Lazy Boy was once directed in a Dream to build a sweathouse inside of his cabin, which he had built at his place on the reservation. He cut a round circle into the floorboards in one corner of the cabin. These he reassembled on the floor nearby and attached to each other with crosspieces, so that he could fit the whole thing back into the hole in the floor. With the circle lifted out, he could step down into the Earth floor beneath the cabin.

Now, his Dream directed that he should take ten sweats inside of his house, that way, and that he would know from his Dreams when to take each one of them. After his final sweat inside the house, he was told to be prepared to go without the physical presence of his wife. Lazy Boy and his wife were pretty old People by that time.

So, Lazy Boy took his indoor sweats whenever he felt moved to do so. Before each sweat he would go out and cut fresh willows for the frame, while his wife heated the rocks inside their wood stove. By the time he had the frame built and covered with blankets, the rocks were ready and hot. He would sit inside the lodge, smoke a pipe and say his prayers, and sing a certain song that he learned in his Dream. His wife would pass the rocks in on a small ash-shovel. When he got through and lifted the cover, the whole house filled up with steam.

Lazy Boy was, at last, directed to take his tenth and final sweat, after which he permanently replaced the cut-out floorboards. Shortly after, his wife passed away during her sleep at night. In a few more years Lazy Boy, himself joined her.

The Old Folks had already had supper by the time of my arrival in camp, so I took my bowl along with me as I went to do some visiting. I knew that I would be invited to eat at the first place where food was being prepared. I headed over to the other side of the camp circle to see my friends George and Molly Kicking Woman.

The Kicking Woman's big, yellow-painted Medicine tipi is easy to find with its large drawings of Deer around its sides. The right to use this drawing, and the Spirit that goes with it, was transferred to them during a sacred ceremony some years ago. It originated in the Dream of some long-gone Person from the Old Days.

George had just hauled some bedding to camp for a neighbor, so I found him standing by his truck, next to the tipi. Attached to the rear of the truck was George's home-made tipi pole trailer, which is a modern version of the old two-Horse wagon that many loggers used to haul their logs with.

I followed George's invitation and we went inside the tipi. A bunch of hollow hooves, hanging from a thong by the door curtain, rattled softly as we brushed against the lodge cover while entering. George went to the rear of the lodge to sit down, offering me a place to his left. After a smile and a greeting, Molly continued her cooking—pausing only to chase out some kids who were looking for play-space. George and Molly take great pride in their tipi. A nice Oriental rug covers much of the inside floor space. Willow backrests hang from sturdy wooden tripods, and several Buffalo robes cover the floor and beds. The lining, tied to the poles on the inside of the tipi, is painted with traditional geometric designs in several colors. Some bags for sacred articles are kept at the rear. From one of them George took a large sack of Sweet Pine needles, which he and Molly burn daily for incense, as is required of their duties as the owners of a Medicine Pipe Bundle. Knowing that I also use Sweet Pine as incense, George gave me a quantity to take home. George is forced to leave at home some of his ceremonial items and obligations because many of the camp's younger People (both children and adults) were never taught the respect required to be in the presence of Medicine Powers from the past. George's lodge is always filled with visitors, and he feels that the worry of disrespect would bring more unhappiness in the presence of his Medicines than the happiness that their Spirit can bring for those who seek them.

Some of the proper tipi etiquette for those who believe in the old ways is as follows:

Visitors should always be acquainted with their host's Medicines, so as to show the proper respect for them and for their owners.

When entering someone's tipi, a vistor waits inside the door until the host points out a place to sit—women to the left and men to the right. Medicine Pipe Owners are always given a place by or near the host, others making room for such a person. The general seating is according to the importance of the guests—the most respected are always invited to sit near the host, at the rear of the tipi.

When going to and from a seat in the tipi a visitor should avoid passing in front of someone—those seated usually lean forward to let others pass behind. In no case must someone pass between the fireplace and the owner or his Medicines at the rear of the tipi—such disrespect would greatly trouble the Spirits of the Owner.

Children are usually not brought along to a gathering of visitors—but left, instead, to play with their own fellows. If older children are brought along, they are expected to remain still and quiet. Under no circumstances may children be allowed to roam freely or play in someone else's tipi, unless asked by the owner to do so. Small tipis were often made to give the children a place in which to practice their own housekeeping—for play only, of course.

Molly asked me for my bowl, and before long we were eating our Supper—boiled meat, beans, bread, and coffee. The sponsoring tribe or groups at most encampments provides daily rations for all those who are part of the camp. To encourage the use of tipis, a small money reward is usually paid to each tipi owner. In addition, dancers receive a few dollars for each night of dancing, and the drummers and singers receive payments as well. Members of the tribe who originated the encampment often give away presents to visitors who have travelled some ways to take part. Blankets and gas money are common gifts, while feather bonnets, buckskin dresses, and dance outfits are among the finer things given to honor a visitor. Thus, a family who makes the Summertime "pow-wow circuit," traveling from one encampment to another, usually is provided with enough, at each stop, to keep going. The dry rations usually last for a week or two. Meat is provided for all the meals, with enough left over to fill a rope stretched across the tipi, for drying. With mom and the kids dancing, and the old man doing some singing, money is earned to pay for gas and oil to get to the next place, while the extra presents of money and blankets can be used directly, or exchanged for whatever else the family is in need of. In case of any unexpected troubles, visitors are always taken care of to the best of the hosting Peoples' abilities. Later, when the hosts at one place become the visitors of their guests, they will be treated in like fashion.

By the time we finished eating and visiting, Sun was covering the camp with the mellow lighting that foretells the upcoming dusk and then darkness. A breeze that served to remind us of the Prairie Wind was lightly flapping lodge covers around the encampment, and the smell of cooking foods was everywhere mingled with the fresh outdoor air. Kids were still playing—but closer to their parents' dwellings, and enough camps were set up now to give the place a definite village air. Though for most who were present the encampment was purely a social occasion—feelings of the Old Ways long gone from their lives (or never entered)—yet the Spirit of the Old Days and the Old Nature People could be easily felt. The tipis were set up on an old, favorite campground—many of their covers were decorated as they were way back when. Looking beyond the immediate physical changes, the Universal Power of Earth, Sky, and Mountains seemed as vast on this day as they must have seemed then.

As I walked back, from a distance I could hear singing inside of our tipi; as I entered I found several guests were visiting. I shook hands, then sat down, feeling much like the junior—by four, five decades I was the youngest one there. The Old People went on with their conversation; I listened quietly to see what I could hear. After a while my good father, Makes Summer, suggested that the time was right to make our transfer—said that he was now prepared. Already I had approached him in a ceremonial manner, to obtain one of his two rattles which signified membership in the old-time warrior group called the Crazy Dog Society. The Spirit of the old warriors is almost gone, as are most members—yet the Power of belonging can still be had. From within the Mind can come most any Power—just seek the Spirits and when you find them, be very glad!

Makes Summer made a smudge, with Sweet Pine for incense, then three men who were members sang some songs. I was painted, given my rattle, shown how to shake it, then Makes Summer and I danced in the tipi to a rattling song. The brief ceremony soon was over, amid congratulations, after which we all had cups of tea. Old Morning Owl, who had also come down to visit the camp from Canada, wanted to give me some of the Power from his Medicines, so he sang for me a song from his own painted tipi. This song would, from now on, be for my use whenever I wanted to have Power by thinking of his old tipi. While giving him and Makes Summer ceremonial "payments" of blankets and money for their help, the Old People got to talking about painted tipis and the Tipi Life of the old days.

In the Old Days one could have found decorated tipis among most People who used this kind of a dwelling. Among many of these People a tipi with paintings on the outside signified the home of a particularly prominent man —the head chief or the keeper of a sacred bundle. No matter what significance lay between the owner and his painted tipi, however, the originals for such tipis were nearly always seen first in some Person's holy dream.

345

The painted tipis that existed in the past among many People of the greater Siouan family (which includes the Dakota, Assiniboin, Omaha, Ponca, Kansa, Missouri, Winnebago, Crow, Mandan, and Biloxi) were usually very individualistic—any number of combinations of symbolic designs were used to represent the tipi owner's vision. Thus, when social pressures discouraged the traditional practice of individuality among the Old People, most of these Vision Tipis were used until they wore out and then not repainted. The designs and stories of a number of these tipis were recorded, fortunately, so I will pass on to you the Spirit of them.

Among the Omaha People lived a holy man, long ago, named Nikucibcan. He was one of the two leaders of the Thunder Medicine Men, who were all very holy. The story of the origin of his tipi was told this way by his widow (just before 1900):

"I myself did not see him, but I have heard what was told. They say that he had a vision of the Thunder-being, so he made that rainbow which appears on his tipi. The old woman, his wife, has told this. They say that he said that the Thunder-being had carried him up on high, and that the place there resembled this world. The man was regarded as very mysterious; therefore, he decorated his tent according to the pattern that he wished to make. The painted spots represent hail."

A chief of the Omaha People, named Fire Chief, had a tipi with Cornstalks painted on it. Fire Chief did not tell anyone about his Dream (as was common in the Old Days—no one considering it proper to ask). His People, however (as well as others around them), considered Corn as their Mother and Buffalo as their Grandfather. It was good that a chief should have a vision of so Powerful a Spirit, thought his People.

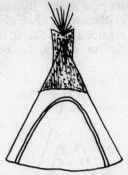

TIPI OF NIKUCIBCAN'S THUNDER VISION

FIRE CHIEF'S CORNSTALK TIPI

Waqaga was a member of an Omaha clan known as the Keepers of the Pipes. According to another Omaha man, only the members of this clan painted pipe decorations upon their tipis. Among other tribes, such as the Arapaho, the keeper of a Sacred Pipe also had a pipe stem decoration on his tipi. This Omaha man made the following comments about this tipi, and the pipes of his People:

"When, in my childhood, I saw the tents in which the People dwelt, they were of this sort. I saw the tent decorated with the pipes having feathers attached to each pipe at right angles. I saw a tent of this sort when it was occupied by Waqaga of the Pipe sub-gens. Though these pipes closely resemble peace pipes, they are made with the feathers attached to the stems at right angles. These are

347

the pipes used in the pipe dance. By means of the pipes the People made for themselves that which led to chieftainship. So they regarded the Sacred Pipes as of the greatest importance. Even when the People were very

SACRED PIPE-STEM TIPI OF WAQAGA

bad, even when different tribes continued to struggle with one another; even when they shot often at one another, when some persons came forth with the peace pipes, and bore them to a place between the opposing forces, carrying them all along the lines, they stopped shooting at one another. The Indians regarded the pipes as precious." Though basically-similar Sacred Pipes did and do have Power among many different tribes, not all followed the "peace pipe" observance.

Among the Blackfoot People of Alberta and Montana there are a number of painted tipis whose designs are basically similar. They too come about through individual dreams, but the dreams were represented in a more tribally conventional manner. Thus, most of these tipis have a dark band around the bottom, which represents the Earth, or at times, Water. In the band of dark are usually large, light-colored circles that represent the fallen Stars. Pointing up from the dark band are often a series of triangles, which represent Mountains. At the top of the tipi is another dark area which represents the night Sky, at the time of dreaming. In that Sky, at the back, is a large cross

348

which represents the Morning Star and, to some, a Moth. Moths have the Power to bring People Dreams, if they are meant to have them. On the smoke flaps are always found circles which represent the two constellations of the Great Bear and the Pleiades. In between the Earth and the Night Sky are drawn representations of the Power which came to the original owner in his dream. These Powers were most often Animals. With each painted tipi goes the story of its origin dream, some songs and ceremonies, and a Sacred Bundle of a few items put together by the original owner.

Back in the days when all the Blackfoot People lived in tipis, the owners of painted tipis were usually band leaders and other prominent men who could afford the transfer ceremony—or else men who were holy enough to believe in the power of their Dreams if they were directed to make up such a lodge. The People were so close to the Spirit of Truth that no one dared to make up any sacred object—such as a painted tipi—without being certain first of the Power of his Dream. And certainly no one ever dared to copy another man's spiritual decorations for his own selfish reasons. Good Spirits do not dwell among imitations of anything. Among the Omaha and Ponca People it was not generally considered proper for a man to decorate his tipi unless he had shown enough prior spiritual power to have become a member of one of the orders of Medicine Men.

Among the Blackfoot, painted tipis whose designs and stories of Power are still in existence include several Otter, Mink, Fisher, and Weasel tipis, with drawings of the Dream Animals around their sides. Most of these were given while the dreaming originators were taken Underwater and invited to visit in similar tipis lived in by the Dream Animals, there. Several tipis were first given by the Buffalo, and have on them drawings of those Animals, or particular parts of their bodies. Several Thunder tipis are still in existence—their usual decorations being colored spots painted over the whole lodge cover. These represent hailstones, and the original Dreamers were generally spiritually acquainted with the many aspects of weather.

To obtain the spiritual Power of such a lodge, one must feel drawn by the Spirit and the knowledge about a particular one. He then takes a filled pipe to the lodge's owner and asks him to smoke it. If the owner smokes the pipe, he is then prepared to agree to whatever one has come to ask him. A ceremonial transfer then takes place, including praying, singing, and feasting, and the owner is paid by the buyer (in Horses, guns, and blankets). The painted lodge cover, itself, is considered useless without the spiritual transfer of its songs and Powers. During the time of the encampment I felt particularly drawn to an aging lodge painted all over with Sacred Red Earth—a yellow circle on its back side to represent its original Dream Power—our Sun. The owner was old Maggie's son Sits Behind, and he agreed to transfer its Power when I ceremonially approached him. The memories of that encampment, as well as the songs and stories that are its Powers, will long be with me through the use of that tipi.

Facing East—"an aging lodge . . . a yellow circle on its back side to represent . . . our Sun."

Part of a camp of Ute People near the Colorado Rockies in 1874. These People spent a lot of time travelling in the Mountains, so they made their lodges small and light, and their poles short and few. The lack of smoke flaps must attest to the Peoples' liking of the feeling of Rain and Snow, as well as the taste of smoke whenever a direct gust of Wind drove the smoke back inside. (Bureau of American Ethnology.)

WINTER IN CANADA

THE SPIRIT AT
HIDDEN VALLEY

A GOOD MEDICINE STORY
TOLD BY
ADOLF HUNGRY WOLF

Illustrated by — F. N. WILSON

Hidden Valley was created to inspire the Dreams of my family—my Children and their Mothers. . . . to inspire Good Thoughts in my Brothers and Sisters—All of You who dream of a Life In Harmony With Nature. We All belong to One Family and All our Spirits are as one with the Great Spirit of Universal Life. . . .

Makwi Unoche

The inspirational drawings which illustrate this story, were done by Frederick N. Wilson back in 1912, when he accompanied his brother Gilbert to the camps of the Hidatsa People to learn their ways. Though Frederick is no longer living, his Spirit remains with his art work and causes me to think of him as a Brother.

HIDDEN VALLEY

The place that You are about to visit in this story is somewhere High Up in the Rocky Mountains. It is truly a Hidden Valley, for no one else knows its actual location. If You become inspired to look for this Holy Valley, after reading my story, I only wish You Happiness along Your trail. If Your reasons for finding the Valley are Holy enough I assure you that You will have success. You might find the Hidden Valley of this story, or you might find another Hidden Valley—in some other place. I'm sure that many more exist. Then, perhaps, you can write down a story like this, for You, too, will have The Spirit Of Hidden Valley.

Let me tell You a bit about the People who live in the Hidden Valley of this story. You may know some of them already—in person or in your Dreams. Others will come along and meet You on Your Path, if You look for them and are aware of their presence. Knowing them will give You strength and happiness—together You will be able to increase the Powers that will allow You to find the goodness there is in All of Life, and to overcome any evil that may try to block your Path. Your Dreams will become Your Life—Your Life will become as a Dream. Maybe this story is Your Dream, too?

SONGBIRD is a most powerful member of the tribal family that lives in Hidden Valley. He is the camp's oldest Person—his years on this Earth are numbered close to 100. He is the leading orator and story-teller among the People of the camp. He is the *camp crier* at all gatherings—the announcer, you might say. His sturdy body is still in fine physical shape, and his Holy Mind is filled with all the spiritual Dreams and Wisdoms which have come his way. His long hair is gray, and his hands are gnarled like the roots of an ancient tree.

SINGING IN THE NIGHT is the camp's Holy Woman —she has spent all her young life being instructed and prepared to lead and inspire the other women and girls to put spiritual meaning into all that they do—whether it be cooking, hiking, sewing, or dancing. She was orphaned shortly after her birth, and an old Holy Woman from the Past adopted her and fed her warm broth, allowing her to suckle at her wrinkled breasts after she had eaten enough. Amazingly, the Old Woman's breasts began giving milk after the fourth day of this suckling, so that the little orphan was nursed properly until she was quite grown. Singing In the Night takes care of the ancient Holy Woman's Headdress Bundle which the Old Woman brought up into the mountains from the Plains many decades ago. At the end of every Summer the Holy Headdress is taken out and worn by the Holy Woman to recall the Powers of all the Autumn Harvests of the Past. She then leads the People of the camp to the gardens where thanks is given by All before the first fruits of the Season are harvested. The People of the Camp have never suffered for want of food.

STONE PIPE is the camp's Mystery Person. Though he is but a boy, he has the ceremonial knowledge and abilities of an Old Man and, indeed, admits to have the Spirit of the Holy Leader of the People's ancestors, come back to guide them All and to give them the Spiritual Powers of the Past. With the help of his many Supernatural acquaintances he is assembling a Bundle of Holy Things which will represent All the Powers of the Universe. In his Bundle is the ancient Sacred Pipe Stem which belonged to his forefathers long, long ago, and was last kept by his father. To prove to the People his power from the Past, Stone Pipe went far into the Mountains and recovered the Sacred Pipe Stem from the cave where his father had put it when the New People started coming to this land and taking the Old Things and Ways from the People.

THE OLD LADY is a kindly, wrinkled old woman who shares her lodge with Stone Pipe. She looks like his grandmother, but she was Stone Pipe's child bride when his Spirit was in an Old Man during his last life. That is how long he has been gone. Now they are reunited and ask no more than respect from the others—who are spiritually awed by the union.

TWO CROWS is a young man who has not long been married to his childhood sweetheart, Yellow-Painted Sky. The two live in a tiny log cabin most of the year, except when they go off hunting and fishing, or during gatherings of the whole camp, when most everyone lives in a tipi. Two Crows is the great-grandson of the chief factor who originally owned and operated the trading post at Hidden Valley. The factor had been well-educated in Universities of the East, where his wealthy parents raised him. Upon graduation, however, he took the money his parents gave him to set up a business and moved West to live with the Native People, whom he very much admired. He brought with him several trunkloads of books, which were laboriously packed up to Hidden Valley by Mules. Two Crows very carefully protects these old volumes—teaching others to read them and gladly lending them out. Included are books about Wildlife and Natural History; arts and artists —works by Audubon and Paul Kane; books about Native People around the World by writers like Grinnell and Maximillian; books about medicinal doctoring and philosophy; and a black-leather-covered Bible that is well worn from use. Two Crows feels that every good book is worth reading and contemplating when one is learning True Life in the Universe. Two Crows expresses his spiritual feelings about Life through the many drawings and paintings that he is constantly creating. The walls of his cabin are filled with scenes of Birds, Animals, Mountains, and events around the camp. His work can be seen throughout the Valley, on the sides of cabins and lodges, in the colored-Earth designs of the Holy Altars, and on the sides of cliffs and boulders.

LITTLE BEAR is the father of a household of grown sons, whose coordinated efforts often make an unbeatable work force. They maintain the many trails in the Valley, and they do a large part of the People's hunting and fishing. Little Bear has a great passion for music of all sorts, and his family can always be called upon to provide the entertainment at any gathering. A huge drum made of rawhide and covered with painted designs is always hanging from its decorated stand in the middle of the family's household. Often the father gathers his sons around it to beat a lively rhythm with their drumsticks while singing some of their many dancing and festival songs. Little Bear is also the camp's Horse Leader—supervising the breaking of young Horses and the harnessing of older ones that are used for plowing, packing, and dragging in everyday camp life. He long ago began studying the characters of Horses and learning how to care for them when they are healthy and how to doctor them when they are ill. He has a large rawhide bag filled with little sacks of herbs and Medicine objects, and it is said that he seldom fails to restore a sick Horse to good health.

SUMA is the camp's minstrel—often wandering from lodge to lodge with some of his instruments, performing in exchange for a meal or some mending. His father was an old trapper from Scotland, and it is not remembered who his mother was. Suma has never had a family of his own other than his instruments, which he cares for as though they were little children. He often goes into the mountains alone, for days, usually returning to tell fascinating stories and sing wonderful songs, often accompanied by some new instrument which he designs and makes while he is away.

MY FATHER here, at the camp, is looked upon by others as a wise spokesman, though he is quick to point out that everyone in the camp has an equal voice in all that is done. He has taken me as his son since my mysterious arrival in the camp, and he has made me feel like I have always been a member of his family. This includes my Mother—a cheerful, plump little lady who is ready to take lightly any subject, and is sometimes reprimanded by Father for her joking and her carefree, ribald humour.

Her mother, old Grandma, is part of the household. She delights in correcting everyone's mistakes, in telling of the difficulties that were sometimes encountered during the camp's earlier years, and she is great for taking care of my smaller brothers while Mother and Father and my two older sisters go out to work in the garden or attend some tribal affair.

THE SPIRIT AT HIDDEN VALLEY

. . . . I am trying to open my eyes. I am wondering: Am I really waking up, or is this my Dream, continuing—I seemed so safe on that trail up the mountain, so safe and sure that I would reach the top. Then I fell! I fell and fell and thought so much that it was The End. Was it The End? Or was it The Beginning? How can there be The End? Does not The End mean at once a New Beginning? . . . .

. . . . But here I am, so it is no end. Here I am, hearing voices and seeing colors. A bright light I see most, and I feel as though the voices and colors are coming at me through a huge funnel—a funnel that sits upside down and fully covers me.

. . . . A hospital room. . . . I must be in a hospital room! Ohh—how badly did I get hurt. . . . I wonder? Waking from an operation. . . . that's it—the anesthetic must be wearing off after the operation. But I don't feel hurt. . . . drowsy, but not hurt. And this hospital room? Nurse. . . . Nurse. . . . there's a fire here! . . . .

The room is round—round and tall and pointed at the top. It has a framework of poles and I can see the Sky through an opening at the top. And there is smoke going up, up and out through the opening at the top. There is a fragrance to the smoke—a sweet and pungent fragrance— a distinct fragrance, though I notice there are others in the air: of foods and strange things. . . . I close my eyes. . . .

Another look: still the same. And the presence of People. I turn my head and look beside me: a strange scene of things I am not familiar with—things that look bright and colorful and alive. And there are People—amidst all the unusual things. And these People look different, somehow, than the People I am accustomed to. They are good to look at—so good to look at that I get a funny feeling by looking at them. Though they must be total Strangers, I feel that I know them—can trust them—can love them —should be here among them. . . . for whatever the reason. I Am Here: is the proof of this! I close my eyes. . . .

I look again, though the good feeling remains even with my eyes closed. A sound like sails flapping in a breeze draws my attention overhead, the sound slides downwards, making the walls of our dwelling ripple against the tall poles, and it brings with it a faint gust of cool, fresh air, followed by the sound of rustling leaves on unseen trees and bushes whose presence I suddenly feel all around. Some Birds voice their approval, and I close my eyes. . . .

For the fourth time I open my eyes, and the scene, as from a Dream, is still there. . . . I am still Here. And who are these People who are here with me? I lift myself up on an elbow—raise myself up with my hand. No one pays any attention to me—perhaps it is still a Dream. I look around:

Across from me there are some women, sewing—four women, there are. One of them is much older than the others—while two of them are about my age. One must be the Mother. Her body rocks gently with each stitch she takes with her sewing—her thoughts seem to flow with the stitches, too. . . . she looks as though pictures are there, where each stitch goes. Many small wrinkles radiate outward from the outside corner of each eye. . . . and her small, dark eyes seem to twinkle. Her hair is darkish, not too heavy, and she wears it in two braids. She is covered by a Buckskin dress which hangs almost to her ankles and is decorated from the waist up by beautiful patterns of attached beads.

The Old Lady just watches, sometimes she closes her eyes. The girls, too, are sewing something—their hands barely moving and their thoughts buried deep within their work. They are dressed in light-colored, cloth dresses, with large sleeves that hang down in loose folds. Their faces are partly hidden by their long hair, which falls down way past their shoulders. They are seated on some furs—like those beneath me. All around this neat dwelling are spread other furs. Some fine, old trunks are standing here and there. I am here, in this home—I am here, in this tipi —I am here, but I don't know where.

While I wonder whether or not to interrupt the pleasant silence which surrounds me sounds from outside draw my attention towards the door. Quiet laughing, like children playing somewhere, the bark of Dogs, the sound of water, running along. Then sounds of footsteps falling softly on the ground. A shadow approaches outside now—the doorway opens to let in light—and someone's leg. A man enters—smoothly and gently—gives me a glance and a smile comes to his face. The man has on a shirt and pants of Buckskin, long, braided hair with strips of cloth tied on the ends. He walks over—saying nothing, but still smiling—and sits beside me on the furs that are lying there. For a moment he looks into my eyes—a feeling of happiness is conveyed. Then he looks towards the door and holds his right hand out, as though inviting someone else to come inside.

Through that door you were brought into this household, he says, pronouncing clearly every letter in each word. *Why You were sent here you will find out in time. But this much I will tell you at this moment: We are your family for as long as you stay here—that is your bed, this is your lodge, ours is your food. What You were Seeking in Your life's dreaming is yours to live now—your dreams were strong, for THEY guided You here. After you've been here for a while you'll know this better—perhaps the Power of your dreams will then be clear.*

He ceases talking and sits silent for some moments, then he turns and reaches for something behind. I hadn't noticed the rear of this tipi—there are bags and pouches hanging up. Underneath the wooden tripod from which they are hanging is a mound of clean dirt, piled like an Anthill. In the center is a circle of bright orange, made from some kind of powder sprinkled there. From that

361

circle are many lines of red going outwards—like the spokes of a wheel—all done with care. At the base of the mound lies a small pipe with a black bowl and a short, wooden stem. This is what he is reaching back for. He takes it and brings it to him from back there. He reaches back again for a small sack, which he opens, filling from it the bowl of the small pipe. He takes a stick—holds it briefly in the fire—while he raises the small pipe into the Air.

For my new son—let our first smoke bind our Spirits. Hear me, Powers who are around us Everywhere. Give my new son strength and guidance—make him happy. Let his dreams become as one with our prayers.

He looks into my eyes once again, smiling, and causes a smile to cover my face, as well. He takes the stick from the fire and holds it in the pipe bowl, puffing, at the same time, on the other end. The gray smoke curls upward— the fine smell goes all around us. He blows a wisp of the smoke up, four wisps to the directions, and another wisp to the ground. He turns the pipe in a Sun-wise direction and hands it to me, stem first, without a sound. I do likewise, as I just saw him do in his smoking, but he corrects me as I hand the pipe back to him.

When passing a pipe to another, he says to me, in a kindly way, *you must turn the pipe in the direction Sun travels, and thus wish your brother a good day.*

After we finished smoking the pipe my new Father asks me to empty the ashes from its bowl into the fireplace.

As I turn to do this the Old Lady looks over at me with a smile and a wink, and says:

You'd better be careful, Sonny, that boy of mine, there, is a pretty mean father and will soon have you doing all his work so that he can stay around this lodge to bother us ladies!

My new Father smiles embarrassingly and nods his head towards the Old Lady, saying:

This is my mother. She likes to tease everyone a lot. Luckily, she is not as mean as she looks. You'll be calling her Grandma in no time, like we all do. I guess I should tell you, too, about the others in your new family, he goes on. *You may already have guessed that the older of the others, here, is your new Mother—you just call her Mom. The other two will be your sisters from now on.* Then, while they continue their work and act as though they are not aware that our attention is on them, Father adds:

You may call either of them sister, or you may prefer to call them by their names. 'Long Way' is what we call her with the lighter hair, while her sister with the braided hair we call 'Good Faith'. You may even find that their names take on meaning, as you watch them in daily life. But, no matter how we may differ in some of our ways, we always seem to end each experience with that Powerful feeling of One-ness that has helped to bring You here.

After some moments of silence Father begins to rise, saying:

I think we should go outside now—the men from the camp are gathered down by the lakeshore and are expecting our company.

So I follow him out of the tipi—stepping into the Outside for my first time. Outside: standing in the warm, fresh air—a sight takes away all my senses—a sight that is more fantastic than any I have ever dreamed of—a simple and fantastic sight. Like a massive painting from a child's fairy tale book lies the scene that is before my eyes. Green and blue dominate the scene—green meadow and green forests, with a vast blue Sky above. The rocks and snow on the massive mountains, which rise up all around us, reflect the green from below and the blue from above—reflect them and combine them to take on a tone of their own which blends harmoniously that which is Above and that which is Below.

It is difficult to attempt even a walk into a painting which is so beautiful as this one—a scene so majestic—but it is almost impossible to believe that I am actually A PART of that scene! Yet, Father and I, ARE a part of it, just like the tree to our left, the tipi behind us, the Horses straight ahead, and the countless other living Spirits who surround us to add color and strength to this fantastic experience of Universal Life.

It is a short walk down the shore of the lake. Grasses and flowers grow almost to the water line, which is barely moving—like the slow breathing of a silent giant. The water is clear—or course—and for some distance out, away from shore I can see the yellow sand that rests below it, broken here and there by some stones or small growths of green plants. A stone's throw ahead of us is the gathering of men—most of them seated. Several of the younger men are off to one side, playing a lively game amongst themselves. One of them is rolling a rustic sort of wheel—about the size of a man's head—towards the others, who wait for it with arrows in their hands. As the wheel passes by, each one throws his arrow at it. A shout goes up from the participants and some of the spectators as the wheel topples over and comes to rest on the ground, one of the arrows stuck in its center. The wheel itself is made from twisted grasses which are than wrapped with a wet strip of rawhide which hardens when it dries. The wheel has numerous spokes of rawhide lacing in which the successful thrower's arrow becomes entangled. Father tells me all this, adding that the game sometimes goes on all day—often to the tune of such wagered items as tobacco and craft work.

We sit down on the ground and join the gathering,

364

which has no air of formality about it whatever. Since Father's first mention of this, back in the tipi, I have been dreading the thought of formal introductions in front of a scrutinizing collection of wise men and minds. At the moment I do not feel that type of a situation at hand.

Father has begun a conversation with a man seated near him, who appears to be about his same age. The man has two dark braids, as do most of the men, and he is shirtless—only a necklace of not-too-large Bear claws covers his chest. He wears loose trousers of some sort of beige-colored cloth, and Buckskin moccasins. Though each man in the group looks distinct from the others, this man's description could be called typical—if I could call anything here at this place, typical.

The young men on the side are still playing their wheel game. Some of the men gathered here are quietly conversing with each other, while others of them are sitting quietly and gazing in various far-off directions. Their features vary widely, as do the tones of their bodies. They do not appear to be related much amongst each other, physically. Yet, there is a definite air of close relations there, among everyone. It makes me wonder if I, too, may be related, somehow, to them all.

As I contemplate these various thoughts and try to absorb the Power which I know is around me my eyes notice an Old Man sitting alone, quite nearby. Somehow I have missed seeing him until now—but, suddenly, I cannot stop looking at him—something about him is like a whirlpool pulling towards it the current of my Mind. An old, wrinkled, gray-haired man with a worn shirt of leather covering the top of his body. From beneath his massive brow peer small, dark eyes at the cliffs along the opposite shore. A fur robe covers the lower half of his body—his arms resting on it, a pipe in one hand. As I look—in total rapture—he begins, softly, chanting. One by one the others stop talking to hear. The young players sit down, their game finally ended. All attention is given to the chanting of the Old One—though still scattered about at the edge of this lakeshore—All of Us who are here seem suddenly more near.

After chanting for some time, praying words with his singing, the Old One stands up and smiles kindly towards me. He says, with the tone of a kind old Grandfather:

I am glad We are All happy with this life we have here. Tomorrow I will tell our new Brother about Us, for I know he has Good Thoughts, and that his Mind will hear me clear.

SONGBIRD'S STORY OF THE VALLEY

. . . . Tomorrow:

. . . . So, I wait. . . . and, finally, he comes. He wears only moccasins, with high tops covering his ankles, and a large yellow-and-brown fur, wrapped around his waist so that the legs and tail dangle down at his sides and back. He comes. . . . and he motions for me to follow. I do—I follow and say nothing.

Soon we are away from the camp circle—away from the sounds and sensations that hover there—and out into the domain of the sounds of Wind—the vast stillness that isn't—the rustling of leaves in the tree tops—Birds gliding from one to the other in the breezes up there. I follow his footsteps along a narrow path that takes us through thick bushes, where our view is limited to a few steps ahead. Now the bushes give way to a small clearing, and the path leads us through the middle of knee-deep grasses and purple flowers—Songbird halts momentarily, thrusts both arms deep into the growth, then brings his fists up to touch his left breast, at the same time he has his eyes closed, his lips are moving in silent conversation —silent prayer—then a gentle smile engulfs his face and he glances at me—glances through me, into the unseen Spirit world that is around us. All this has taken but a few moments, and already we are on our way again, following the path back into the dense bush growth and past tall tree trunks. He says nothing, and I dare not ask.

We come to a brook, half hidden by the flowers and grasses that grow along its banks and hang out over its waters—many trailing their tops in the brook's gentle current. The path turns right, here, and ascends by short, steep layers. The green growth is very low for several steps to each side of the brook, and the path is visible some ways ahead at all times. Where the path and the trees come close together the ground is covered by a carpet of brown pine needles, and a sweet and pungent odour fills the air. I pick up a handful of the needles—the odour is definitely from them—and I'm tempted to take a bite of them—they attract me so much.

Up, behind the trees of this forest, rises the massive stone face of Stone Face Mountain—a steep incline broken only by barely-visible narrow trails which run like wrinkles across the Stone Face, and a few shrub-covered knolls that stick out like small hair-covered moles from the looming Face. Father has already pointed this out to me from our camp.

Up Stone Face Mountain we climb, after leaving behind us the growth of the forest. A well-worn trail—a steep, rocky path—takes us rapidly higher, and our breath grows noticeably shorter. Up . . . up . . . up . . . up . . . the Old One keeps right on climbing and leading us like tiny explorers across the great Stone Face

I think my body is about to give up its efforts, as the Old One finally motions towards a small knoll just up ahead—he is planning for us to halt there. We come up from below the out-cropping—it looks like a vestibule in an opera house from down here (only much larger), but, as we go around and above it, the impact of its size shrinks away with the view down the mountain, until we are standing directly above and behind it, and it suddenly seems like a small place to stand upon in the vastness of the Universe, here, up high.

From our place behind the knoll the worn trail divides into several branches—one of them leading out to the point of the out-cropping itself. From up here, now, I can see that the shrub which I saw growing from down below is actually a tiny forest of stunted and twisted pines, some of which stand twice as high as I. Everywhere I look there are droppings and track marks—the knoll must be a favorite look-out and gathering place for many of the animals hereabouts. Here and there are flat places in the grass growth—indicating some visitors have, recently made here their beds.

On the ground, before a large boulder, the Old One sits down on his fur robe—he sits so that his back leans against the boulder and his eyes can take in the breathtaking scene all around. Likewise, I sit down by him—for some time not a word can be said. Down below are the camps of the People—in the valley, by the lake, they look so small. The lake—I can see from one end to the other—like a long sheet of blue glass spread out below. The forest—like the hair upon a fur robe—a solid mass, with some additional patches growing here and there. In the distance, all around, a wall of mountains. Up above, the solid Sky—the endless Air.

His voice sounds strangely near after my eyes and Mind have wandered so far. *I come often up to this place—to see our Valley,* he says, while gazing away, out there. How many places, that he sees now, does he know close-up? How many adventures can he see in this one view?

For most of my 92 years of Life I have known this place, he now continues, *hardly anything seen from up here has changed at all. The Great Spirit of the Universe wants us to know THAT—for, compared to the Universal Power, the lives of men, like ourselves, are very small.*

It was meant that this Valley be populated by a People whose lives remain at Nature's call. For this valley enjoys complete isolation, from the wounds that other People in the World befall.

Now, since your strange arrival, you have wondered about this Valley, and how it is that all these People are living here. My name is Songbird, as was my father's before me; as tribe historian—I tell the story for one and all.

Now he has raised his left hand to his forehead, shading

his eyes from the bright rays of Sun. The hand is wrinkled and scarred from old age, and only a stump remains where his small finger once was. He squints his dark eyes with a grimace that draws attention to his full lips and the remainder of his teeth—some on top, some on bottom, that are stained yellowish-brown and worn flat. Gray braids hang down behind his ears. He remains absorbed in the view he is watching—some time passes before he says anything at all. Finally, he breaks the vast silence that isn't—and again, his closeness strikes me so strongly —just two human bodies among the All.

Over there, as he points Westward, *are what we call our Sunset Wall of mountains. There, at one time was the Hidden Valley Pass. A narrow, rocky trail led from this Valley to the outside—through canyon and gorge, and sometimes along treacherous rock faces, where a misstep meant a thousand-foot fall. Through that Pass came both trappers and hunters—some to camp here and some to live here. Strong was the Valley's Spirit, through its call. Later on came some new men from far-away lands. They came to meet, to trade, explore, and just to see—what the land of our Old People had to offer—what the call of Hidden Valley could be.* He breathes deeply, several times. His hand drops from his forehead, his gaze turns to the ground. His eyes close—he is apparently reminiscing:

So it was, when I was a young boy. The new men came to Hidden Valley, and many stayed. They built a mine, a trading post, and little houses. They brought supplies, they brought their women, they brought great changes, to the silence that Hidden Valley once had.

Now, these new men got along fairly well with the Old People. They prayed (though not like we), and sang strange songs. They worked hard daily—they traded things to the Old People for meat and hides. Peace existed, by that time, among the tribes who knew this country, so little groups moved to the Valley now and then. They'd often visit, and entertain, and pray together, and the new men, when they had time, would join right in. He hums a short tune—smiles, as he explains that the new men

369

taught some of the Old People their strange songs. All together they would sing—some old, some new songs, all loudly singing, moving bodies, feeling strong.

Came a time, late one Spring—it was almost Summer—came an old man, to this place, from somewhere West. Said a dream had brought him up—that night he'd tell us, let us decide to do whatever we feel is best. The old man was almost naked—just breechclout and blanket—but painted black from head to foot, except for a large white circle over his left breast.

That afternoon, in the camps, there was much talking, as each one wondered what the old man had to say. My father's brothers were seated and smoking—they came to talk of the old man, and to pray.

Our camp, that time, numbered twenty-four lodges—mixed bands of Blackfoot, Bloods, and Piegans, from the Plains. Camped near us were a half dozen families of Sarsi's, and next to them were some Stony's from Kutenai Plains. At the trading post were a dozen employees—their wives and families were also living there. In its courtyard were camped trappers and miners—perhaps two hundred People were gathered there.

My father and some friends set up a large lodge—one with two covers fastened together to make an oblong. Thus they made room for most of the adults who wished to hear the old man speak. Much food was cooked, and all were served, who felt like eating; then pipes were filled and all sat down in proper order—just whispered words while all were smoking and saying prayers. Came in the old man—his blanket draped over his shoulders and tied in front with two sewed-on thongs. His weight was supported by a large stick—some Eagle feathers and some other small bird skins tied to its top. His face was still black-smeared from painting. Down to his shoulders hung the loose locks of his gray hair. On his cheek a large scar made a shadow, and his right eyelid was closed—no eye was there. He walked slowly to the front of the gathering

—and though all were silent and waiting, for some time he just stood there and stared.

'My children,' he began, in a strong voice for an old man, *'my Medicine has guided me to you here. I must tell you of an event about to happen—an event which for some of you will bring fear. For many years have my Dreams foretold me, that the mountains would be the place of my end—ever after should continue my Spirit, among a People who will live where my thoughts shall dwell.'* For a moment the old man paused—his face seemed to twitch and quiver—then he cried—an old man crying—it was moving, it made everyone feel strong. He sang a song—and from the mourning sounds in it, we all knew that it was his death song. Right there he was singing THAT song that once his Spirits taught him—told him to keep alone, to carry along. We all knew what would be caused by its singing—we knew his Life here on Earth would soon be gone.

'My children,' he addressed us all again. *'My children, it is here that I must leave my body—and it is RIGHT here, where some of you will always belong. My dream has told me that the need for the Pass into this Valley is about to pass—there is to be NO way in here, before too long. Already, my Spirits told me, too many are coming—but soon: no more, no matter how brave or strong. I am to go through the Pass, said my vision, go through singing my sacred death song. Somewhere up there the mountains are to answer—the boulders falling will take my body along. In four more days, I tell you, all of these things will happen—just four more days, and those who stay will become strong. Ask yourselves, now, my children, if it's for you—this life that will follow, here, in this valley; if it's for you—to live a Life that can't go wrong. For, with my Power, I will give All my guidance to those who stay here—I'll be with you, whenever You sing my song.'* And, again, the old man sang his song.

So, look now, again, over to Sunset Wall mountains, says Songbird slowly, stretching his long arm towards the

371

West. With his thumb in advance he points carefully. *What the old man said came to pass—for gone, from over there, is the old Pass. Only four more days he lived, after that night, and then he left us, never to return.*

Songbird continues his story, after a brief pause:

There was much confusion in the camps and at the trading post, after the gathering broke up and everyone returned to their homes. There were those who thought the old man was crazy—there were those who believed him and begged him to call it off. "It is not our place to guide the destiny of the Universe—we are but humans— good for companions—but just so strong," he would answer each one.

By the second day some camps were packing—were leaving. Many new men took their packs and went along. By the fourth day the trading post was half deserted, many lodges from the Old People's camps were gone. Only lodge poles and blackened fire-pits bore solemn witness of the families no longer there—forever gone. Of those who stayed, most were sure that's what they wanted —that the old man's dream was very strong. In his final hours we gathered to hear his words of wisdom, his songs and his prayers, to keep US strong.

'Everywhere are coming new people,' he told us. *'Many of these are good people. Many of ours are good People. But the few remaining ones on both sides will cause much*

trouble—they will see things with only their eyes—not with their Spirits. They will forsake the Old Spirits and let the desires of daily lives design their gods. For many years will these people live that way, before their children will seek, once again, the Spirit of our life. You, who remain here, will keep alive all that Spirit so that, someday, it may grow again in the hearts and minds of a People who will be loving our Mother—Earth—with prayers and songs.'

The next morning the old man went: down, past the lakeshore, out of the valley past the waterfall, above the treeline up to the canyons and far out of sight, he went, while the People remained in camp—waiting silently. Still was the air—very quiet—till, from afar, came a rumbling sound. Everyone's eyes went up the mountains, where a dust cloud formed quickly and hid the view. Many voices joined together in prayer, while the rumbling on the mountains continued. We knew for sure, then, our fate was sealed—all together. The dream of the old man, indeed, had been strong. When the dust cleared only physical was our reaction—for all those present knew it would happen all along. The familiar sight of our old Pass was gone—so was the South side of yonder mountain. For several days, words were seldom spoken, but the bonds of brotherhood quickly grew strong.

Few of us are left today from the original People in this Valley, but the same Spirit exists today as did back then. For all these years we knew someday our Dreams would be answered—someday a new old-time-spirit People would come along.

That is why You are here with Us, now! You were guided here by the Spirits of the Universe because You looked to those Spirits of the Universe for guidance—because You believe they exist and have met them in Your Dreams and visions. All together We can make great things happen with All the Spirits who are here for Us to find.

Physically, we here in this Valley have been very fortunate. Many things to help us were stored for trapping, trading post, and for the mine. We have been careful to use just what we really needed, and to use each thing as long as it continues to have some use left. How many knives we've made anew, when they were broken; how many handles, for all our axes, were made with knives. How many clothes were worn to shreds, then sewed together, to make a new thing with a new purpose, in our simple lives. With pencils we all learned the art of writing, with needles every man and woman sews. With nails and saws we build Winter-time housing; with pots and pans we cook all our Natural foods.

But, most of all, is the strength of our isolation—it's brought together all our People to one belief: that we're all here on this Earth for a purpose, to harm no one—to give to All—to have Belief. We believe that following Dreams is what makes one happy—when one shares happiness with others, they become happy, too. Thus, all the time, someone is happy; thus, all the time, we're happy too. . . .

. . . . Nighttime—back in the lodge of my family:

My son, did Songbird tell you, today, the story of our People here, asks Father.

Yes, I reply, *a most moving story it is—a most Powerful story. It strengthens my belief in the Power of my Dreams, which have brought me here.*

You must have had a very strong belief in your dreams to begin with, continues Father, *to have gotten here at all. We knew all along that someday someone like you would come. For You will now help us to go on to the next stage of our lives here. Nothing can go on forever without change—not even the Spirit at Hidden Valley!*

I nod my head silently—Songbird, too, made some mention of expected changes here, in the Valley, due to my presence. I wish that were not so, for I would like to spend the rest of my life here, living just as I see these good People living.

Do not worry yourself, my son, says Father when he notices my silent stare, *the goodness of this Valley will continue to be, and its Spirit will be yours as long as you wish it. But there are others in this World who should know about the Spirit—for there is enough to share with All the People of this Earth.*

I would rather not even think about the rest of the World, at this time. I can not imagine what might happen if that World found out about Hidden Valley—for some it would bring great happiness, for others only envy. But the many who control the destinies of Nature—those spiritually-insignificant but physically strong and demanding ones—I fear for the plans and schemes they would develop that would quickly destroy the Spirit at Hidden Valley.

We are not expecting to re-open a pass in order to intercourse freely with the World outside, explains Father to my concerned look. *We would wish for some additional People to come here with us—to bring us their skills and knowledge of positive things in exchange for the life we can give them. We would wish for more families to add new blood to our children of the future—to keep us from becoming lame without the introduction of new thoughts and new ideas. You must wait for the Summer's End Ceremony to hear more about this,* Father concludes. *We will seek advice, then, from our long-ago Old Ones as to what we should do, now that you have come, as they predicted.*

THE YOUNG BOY AND THE OLD LADY

I go today to pay a call on the Old Lady who lives with a young boy in a small, bark-covered lodge down by the lakeshore—there, just past the edge of the forest. I met the old lady the other day, when I came up behind her on the forest trail, where she was struggling with a large load of dried wood for her fire. I offered to carry the wood, and she shyly accepted, covering her mouth with her right hand—in modesty—as she spoke to me. She led the way to her lodge in such a fashion that no one saw us enter. Not till later did I learn that she would have felt disgraced if some other woman had seen me doing her work. Inside the lodge I felt strange, though I could not understand why. A young boy sat in there, naked except for a small apron hanging from his thin belt. His hair was tousled— cropped above his shoulders and in bangs across his forehead. His face was painted strangely and he was singing. Before him lay a small animal skin, turned so that its tanned side was facing upward and only a few wisps of dark brown fur showed along its sides. The boy was in the midst of drawing figures and designs on this skin, using small bones for brushes and beautiful sea- shells to hold his powdered paints, which he mixed with grease from a small bag. The figures and designs were made with many shades of reds, yellows, greens, and blues, blended so as to attract my eyes beyond my control for several moments. Meanwhile the fire crackled and blazed with the new wood, which the old lady was adding and the unusual odours of the place became even stronger as they got warmed.

This is my man, Stone Pipe, the Old Lady said, know- ingly interrupting my prolonged gaze at his artwork.

He lives in a Dream World, though he seems to be here, she added, perhaps not meaning to confuse my thoughts so. Her explanations, right then, of the young boy were simply beyond my understanding.

In reply to my nervous statement of necessity for departure, she thanked me for the assistance and asked for my company at supper in the evening, two days hence.

So, that is why I am going back today to call on the Old Lady and the young boy. Not knowing what to make of her statements, the other day, I have carefully avoided making any mention of her at the lodge of my Father, and no one yet knows that she and I have made any acquaintance.

. . . . The signs of evening are in the air as I make my way along the forest trail to get around to the far side of the Old Lady's tipi: Sun's light filters through openings in the dense growths of bushes, and Birds sing their Sunset serenades. Through the trees, now, I see their tipi, smoke rising from its center, curling up, and away, into the Air. Not far from the tipi—in front of the nearest tree—I see a fire, by a canoe turned over and propped up to serve as a shelter. The Old Lady sits smiling, before that fire; the young boy stands silently there. As they see me, the boy begins singing—in the distance there's an echo, somewhere.

Come, my boy, have a seat by this fire, the Old Lady says, as she beckons me near. *My man's Spirit tells him to be fasting, but two Fish for us he has caught. . . . I am now cooking;* and there, on sticks by the fire, I can see the pair.

The singing is from a boy's voice—high and gentle; but the song seems to convey wisdom seen with gray hair. Can a boy do such singing? I wonder—for the Spirit of his songs shows great care.

I sit down by the fire—smell the roasting Fish, and the burning wood—see the firelight reflect from the grease and paint covered faces of the Old Lady and the young boy, see it throwing eerie shadows on the large Pine that looms behind us—practically over us. A sense of one-ness pervades the whole scene—a one-ness that I feel I am a part of—I want to join the boy's song; to stroke the Old Lady's hair; to melt myself like wax and pour myself among them.

Quietly, the Old Lady brings before her two wooden

bowls. In each bowl she places a Fish and, from a small sack, a handful of dried berries. Without a word she gives me one bowl, takes the other and bows her head down in prayer:

HiYo you Spirits who are with Us: we thank you for this food—thanks for the Air; we thank you for our lives, and for the water; may we continue to be together, forever; and so, you Spirits, I end this prayer.

She lifts her head with a smile—a look of satisfaction. She sees me—as I am looking right at her—she gives a wink, with her left hand she smoothes her hair. Soon, busy eating, while the boy goes on singing, my thoughts are of everything there: of the People, of the camp, of my presence—of the Spirits that have guided me there.

We finish our meal fairly quickly, and clean the places where we sit. *Let us go into the lodge,* says the young boy, *let us go, for I feel another prayer.*

So we go into the tipi—the young boy leading. Behind me, the Old Lady brings the bowls and the foodstuffs; inside, she puts away what she carries and starts a fire in the center of the home. The boy, meanwhile, sits down on a pile of furs behind the center—across from where we entered through the door. He motions me to a place on the right side—to his left—where other furs are piled to sit on—a seat prepared.

My Mind often puts my words into prayer, begins the young boy, *and though my body has the appearance of youth—my Mind has before been in bodies—will again be in others, someday, somewhere.* I am not able to make any response to these words from this young man—I only wait—I know that something has brought me there.

The boy goes on: *Age, you know, is a physical thing confined to bodies—for the Mind is a Spirit and knows no time. If your Mind can be left free from your body— your life on Earth will seem like nothing compared to the Spirit of Minds that exist everywhere. Keep your Mind always searching—your Spirit happy. . . .*

A song comes from his lips then, as though it were still a part of the sentence *your Spirit happy*. . . . The young boy's eyes close—his mouth quivers, his face looks smooth and shiny—the song—the chant—goes on and on. I close my eyes—I release all of my muscles—I become detached except for feeling the songs flowing with my Mind. I float along, feeling musical colors—seeing sights of softness and beauty and an endless garden of colorful darkness. I hear his voice say—I hear an echo repeating: *My friend, I can see you with me there;* and sure enough —as though in real life—I see a vision: I see the young boy as an old man sitting somewhere.

I see you there, said again the young boy, this time with more emotion, *I see you there—yes, my friend—I'm with you there.*

The boy stops his singing and looks at me quite brightly —as though he'd found what he wanted in song and prayers. *Yes, you and I are truly brothers—the story's long, that's why you're here. . . . that's why you're here. Yes, once before you were beside me—another life time— another place—but you were there. Let my Old Woman, here, tell you how it is between Us, all.*

The Old Lady speaks: *Well, as I told you the other day, this boy is my man Stone Pipe—once with me while I was still quite young. I was his child bride—he was married to my two older sisters—when my parents were killed, one day while hunting—he took me in, made me as one of his wives. Before he left, he often said I should wait for him, he said that someday he would be back for his young wife.*

Well, continues the Old Lady, *he is here now, his body and his Mind, to help us All in our search for the highest Spirit in Life on this Earth. In the night, when we make love, we both find the Power with us—we feel the Spirit of those who are around Us, and those who were before Us. We hear the songs—see the colorful ceremonies, we learn to know them—for they can later help us to recall the Powers of Life that brought them to us in our Visions.*

379

So it is, says the boy named Stone Pipe, *that I am gathering together the powerful Bundle of Life. My strongest memories of those before me, and those around me come to me nightly—to direct and guide me—to give me Dreams which show me all the good Thoughts of Life.*

From long ago come the memories of my grandfather—how the People came to him in times of need. He would pray and sing his songs, and they left, smiling—for he had words that were of wisdom, come from devotion: to constant thoughts of happiness in All that he knew.

Sometimes my grandfather made use of certain things to help the People who came to him—to remember the Powers of the past, the present, and of All time. He used incense—many kinds—that All remembered, for many times they had smelled the sacred scents before. Way back in the days of our early ancestors the same kinds of incense curled their smokes from altar floors.

My grandfather always filled a pipe and gave his guests a smoke. It pleased him to see that pipe smoked all around. So I fill now this bowl with wild plants—we'll smoke with Nature. To our awareness of Nature's presence I will now pray:

HiYo Above Ones—You here on Earth, we seek to know you; you Underground, we ask that you shall remain strong. See that our Minds, like curls of smoke, can be united, with the vastness of the Spirit that's All around. Smoke with us here, Spirits, and let our thoughts be good.

With a stick from the fire he lights the pipe. He blows the smoke out, then he draws another breath in. Inside the bowl: the faint glow keeps getting brighter—a wisp of smoke comes up from it with every puff. Then on to me—to smoke the pipe—then the Old Lady—round and round, we pass that pipe, till All's smoked out.

My grandfather's proudest duty was the keeping of the People's Sacred Pipe Stem—all wrapped and bundled and kept from view by furs and skins of Animals. The Pipe

Bundle—with its stem the length of a young child—hung above the Old Man, tied to a lodge pole. Every morning and every night he prayed before it—a prayer of humbleness to the Spirits which he knew were always present there. For, as far back as anyone could remember that Sacred Pipe Stem had been among the People—as a physical reminder of the Powers that have grown for Us, here, through the thoughts and prayers by All who Were, before. My grandfather often said that those whose faith was in the Powers represented by the Pipe Stem could do or have anything they really wanted simply by drawing on that Pipe Stem and thinking strongly about their wish!

Ah—is that not a powerful, wonderful thing—so much Spirit represented by one object. Ah—to capture some of that Spirit in one's Mind. . . .

. . . . Know you now, my friend—no, my Brother— know you now, that I am, here, the keeper of that Pipe.

Every night I pray before it, and see the People, the Ones, like I, who prayed to Spirits not in their sight. For now those People who were, before me, once with that Bundle, now they are present when All of the faithful pray every night.

Each night in my visions I see some Old One, doing something that is Holy, I try to remember, each night, that Holy sight. And so I'm learning the sacred ceremonies for my final: Bundle of Life. Shall I tell You about some of my Holy visions, my Brother? Well then, hear them:

In my First Dream—some while ago—came the call to gather: Bring together, come together, think of One-ness, said a voice from out of the depths of the Universe where was floating my Mind. Soon I saw them—a few old men— I watched them gather. They sang a song to give respect to Mother Earth:

> This, where we sit, it is Powerful.
> This, Holy Earth, it is Powerful.

I remember that song very clearly. One of the men then looked at me and spoke: Young man, You are chosen to help bring People together. We have not chosen you—no, You have chosen yourself, by coming here and believing Us. That is good—it will give you much happiness, this belief in our spiritual existence. We hope you will always believe in your Dreams, for they are guided by the Spirits with which your Mind dwells. You have chosen Us—our way is happy—it leads to goodness. Hear what we tell you, see what we do, remember it well!

The man who was speaking to me then unrolled a blanket and brought out the Old Sacred Pipe Stem— wrapped up in a bundle. He held it aloft, up towards Sun, and sang some songs, while he took the coverings off:

> *Man, you must say it, this Pipe it is powerful,*
> *Man, you must say it, this Pipe it is powerful.*

and

> *You stand up, you take me, you untie me,*
> *I am powerful.*
> *You stand up, you take me, you untie me,*
> *I am powerful.*

This last song sounded as though it was coming from the bundle itself, IT seemed to be singing, while the man untied the thongs and wrappings. Finally he brought out the Sacred Pipe Stem, which I immediately recognized as the same one my grandfather had, and that I now have. The man held the Pipe Stem before him, while its decorations of Eagle plumes—countless numbers of them— vibrated gently in the soft breeze. He prayed that Sun should yet become aware of the Power of the Universe and the Spirits of the Sacred Pipe Stem. And then he sang a fourth song—a chant, it was, without words—a tune so moving that each note seemed to beckon my Mind to join it on its journey into Space. While singing this fourth song, the man held the Pipe Stem close to him and danced in a slow circle, going first to the East and bowing, then to the South, the West, and finally the North. When he was finished singing and dancing he handed the Pipe Stem to the man on his left, who prayed with it and then involved himself in a similar dance. So it was with each of the men there, gathered in a circle in my Dream—each one prayed, danced in a circle, and bowed to each direction. The same song, meanwhile, filled the air.

Then the man looked at me again, and said:

Young man, we have now shown you the dance of the Sacred Pipe Stem—as it has been performed by countless generations of the past. You must remember and continue this ceremony, for someday a new generation will again be seeking the Old People's power—and this ceremony will inspire some of them on their way. You need not become a leader, or strive for power—for those who need you will come and find you anyway. Give what they ask for—tell them about Us, our ceremonies. If they should follow, and find new meaning for their lives by seeking Spirits, then you'll be happy, for their new strength will be in Your Life, as well as theirs.

Then the man reached inside of his buckskin shirt and pulled out a thin cloth bundle. He said, to me:

Sometimes it helps, while praying, to look for signs of the Universal Powers. While you pray in the morning, for instance, you see Sun's light—you feel warmth coming down to the Earth. After dark shines the face of Night Light—and of countless Stars that make the Heavens bright. In a storm you see the Clouds—you see the Lightning, you feel the Rain as it drops to the Ground. When you walk, you feel Earth—our good mother; when you swim you feel Water all around. When you pray you should think of All these Powers, let your thoughts make You, with them, feel as One. For All that IS makes the All into One-ness, and your prayers should bring that One-ness within you.

Now, young man, you have the Spirit of your Old People with that Pipe Stem, to be with you whenever You wish them there. But some of our relatives from the Bird and Animal kingdom, wish to be represented, too, when you make those prayers. In this cloth bundle is a whistle, for you to have—to help you with all your prayers. For when you blow upon its mouthpiece You will remember what you are seeing before Us All, gathered right here.

The man had pulled out the whistle and began to blow into one end, causing a high-pitched tone to come out of the other end. He blew softly, he blew hard, he made it vibrate, and soon some sounds in the forest we could hear. As he continued, the sounds continued to grow louder— soon many Animals and Birds joined our gathering there. In a circle, they stood around us—it was like magic—my Dream seemed real, like breathing in and out fresh air.

Here, young man, now take this whistle; take with you All the Spirits whom you've met right here, he told me. Play your OWN tune, and always trust yourself to Nature, and All of Us will be with You, no matter where. We men, here, will come to you again in future Dreaming, so will our brothers, here, these Birds and Animals. Learn what we teach you—let your Dreams give you guidance. Now go—for Life is short, while with your body. Your new companions will be, from now on, with you on your Paths. Keep them in Mind with your songs and ceremonies, They'll give you strength to put in food for daily eating, they'll give you strength to feed your Mind during your fasts.

And so, my brother, I obtained the whistle that I now keep with the Pipe Stem. I left that Dream down a new Path, with my new friends. Since I awoke they have been with me in my new Life—by day in thoughts, by night in dreams as strong as Life.

At later times I will tell you about all this dreaming

and later on You, too, will have dreams about which you can tell. Each of Us, here, at Hidden Valley, has dreams to guide us. We let that guidance decide the paths of our daily lives. We live by day what we dream in the nighttime, we let good thoughts and happiness be the dream of Our Life.

THE TALE OF SUMA, THE MUSICIAN

It is quiet this evening inside the community lodge—the families are all at home cutting up the meat from the day's hunt—shadows of meat strips hanging from strings reflected from all the lodge covers as I passed by them, on my way over here. Father was just tying more strings

between the lodge poles as I left—three strings were already hanging across the tipi with drying meat.

Only Suma, the Musician, is in the big log lodge with me now. He smiled pleasantly when I came in, and has been immersed in a slow song ever since.

Rrrrratt—rrrratt rrrratt—rrrratt is the sound that is filling every corner of the otherwise-silent lodge. Suma has his big Music Stick before him—his favorite source of accompaniment whenever he sings alone. It is a branch from a Poplar tree, longer than a man's leg. Suma has carved the branch into an object resembling a knife, with large notches on the back of the *blade*. At the end of the handle is the carved head of his Medicine Animal, with beads and small bells wrapped around its neck. Suma has the point of the Music Stick on a piece of tanned buckskin which is spread on the floor. He is rubbing a stick made from a Service Berry branch across the notches.

Rrrratt—rrrratt—rrrratt—rrrratt comes the sound from the notches as the stick bounces smoothly over them. . . . rrrratt—rrrratt—rrrratt—rrrratt. Suma is wearing his Buckskin suit with the red and white beadwork and the fringes of sewn-on Gopher tails. His hair is loose down his back, as it usually is in the evening, when he is singing. He is sitting, right now, on one of the low benches over against the log wall, away from the fire in the center of the lodge. I am sitting in one of the large chairs with the tree-limb armrests. It has a back and seat made from Willow branches. The lodge is comfortably warm from the fire inside the stone-edged pit. Water is boiling quietly in a kettle that hangs some distance above the fire—suspended from a steel rod that is also used for cooking.

Rrrratt—rrrratt—rrrratt—rrrratt, Suma's song goes on. He is singing some words, now and then, but I can't understand them. Mostly he just chants—the mood of his chanting is very strong and far-away.

O-WO-O-HO O-WO-O-HO O-WO-O-HO O-WO-O-HO-
HE-JA-HE-JE-HE-JA

I close my eyes to listen to the song more carefully. Just as I begin to let my Mind wander up some grassy slope towards a forest, Suma stops his singing. He rubs his Music Stick a while longer, then he sets it aside also. He looks over here, at me, and continues with his pleasant smile.

You bring a smoke along? he asks me in a self-inviting way.

No, it's in my bag—over my bed. I can go and get it, though, if You want.

You no need to go, he replies, *is some smoke here, in the trunk with the Sesame Seeds. You smoke with me?*

Sure, I said, happily. What else could I say to a pleasant man like that? It is a real experience to be able to sit close by and watch Suma's pleasant face. I get up and sit on one end of his little bench.

Better you sit on the big bench by the fire—we have some tea when done with smoking, he advises. I oblige—the big bench has more room, and is further from the coolness of the floor.

Shortly he comes back with a little Buckskin bag—like the ones most of the People keep their *smoking* in. From inside his Buckskin shirt, somewhere, he brings out another bag—a little larger than the first—from which he takes a little stone-bowled pipe. The short stem has a carved snake twisted around it. The whole stem is smooth and shiny from being greased with fat, and reddish-colored from occasional applications of Sacred Earth Paint. Father's pipe looks similar to this one of Suma's. He fills the pipe, lights it, offers it, and we smoke—the firelight flickers and throws huge shadows of ourselves against the sloping log ceiling and the sturdy log walls.

. . . . Finished smoking—now drinking tea from gray, colored-with-age, tin cups. Tea made from Rose buds which the People gather in the Fall, just about the time of the first Snowfall. Father says the tea provides much nutrition during the Winter, when only meat can be gotten fresh. Songbird once told me that Rose buds are good for cold or fever if they are ground up and mixed with a meal, or taken as a drink. Suma has also brought over a dish with some Sesame seeds piled on it. They are good to grind up with the teeth, between sips of hot tea.

That was a Thought Song, says Suma, as though his singing had just ended. *Always gives me good Thoughts about near and far friends, and companions that I might somehow meet, yet,* he adds, as explanation.

One time I sing that song, sittin' in the afternoon Sun

387

by myself, he says, as much to himself as to me, *I sure got myself some good thoughts, then—visiting with some folks I never knew before—never seen since.* I wait—quietly and patiently—while Suma stares into the fire. His pleasant face is still smiling—his eyes seem to be watching scenes in the flames that I can't see. He has introduced a story, and is now getting it together right. I say nothing— I try not to move. He may decide not to tell his story if he thinks I am impatient.

Was three of Us—three young fellows—walking along like partners, he begins in a reminiscing tone. *Walking along in the Summer Sunshine—having nothing to do but just to look around and see the living Spirits with Us. Exerything was making Summer sounds of pleasure in Sun's warmth: Bugs, Insects, Birds, Squirrels, Bushes, Frogs, all our relatives whom we can hear and see.*

As we went along through the woods we came out into an opening and found ourselves along the top of a ridge. We looked down below us and saw a thin column of smoke rising from out of the trees on a point of land that went out into a bay of water. We wondered who might be camping there, so we proceeded to climb down and see.

Was a lot of Brush on the way down—somehow I got separated from my two Dream companions and was soon making my way through the Brush and tangles alone. Up ahead of me I could see nothing but green growth, with the column of smoke rising up from it towards the blue Sky above. For a bit I entered some growth so thick that I could barely even see Sky above me, then I came out upon the bay's sandy shore. I looked all around, but there was no sign of a camp or a fire, and I couldn't see the smoke column any longer before Sky. Suddenly I felt very empty and alone, so I decided to sit down and wait for the arrival of my two lost companions. I sat down in the sand—too soft, I think—soon I was asleep, there on the shore of the bay. . . . Dreaming. . . . dreaming. . . . happiness. . . .

. . . . Water was splashing somewhere near me—laugh-

ing and giggling sounds, I heard. Thought there must be some People playing in Water. My eyes opened and I looked out at the water of the bay: a young girl was out there—standing out in the water: bathing, laughing, giggling, splashing Water, she was. I felt like part of the sandy shore—just eyes watching pretty girl bathing. Another girl came to shore near the first one—laid down her robe on the Sand and waded slowly out into the Water. Long, dark hair hanging way down behind on girl wading out—now blowing to this side, then to the other . . . My eyes just looking, my body all numb, like part of the shore. The girls splashed each other with water, rubbed themselves with their hands—my Mind flowed out across that Water to join them like a Cloud, it flowed away from my body in the Sand.

As I watched, one of the girls dove beneath the Water. Then I heard some splashing quite near by—I looked to my right, by some Bushes, and saw the Sand open up before my eyes. Suddenly, by those Bushes, there was a pool of Water, and a beautiful head came up from below—it was the girl whom I last saw diving, smiling to me, she said, "You are wanting to go?" So I quickly got out of my Buckskins, and got into that Water from the Sand. She motioned for me to come and follow, so I dove under with a tug from her hand. . . .

. . . . I found myself in a long water tunnel—the Sun light seemed to come up from below. With little effort I found myself drifting behind the girl who was swimming very slow. The silence of that Water was more than loudness, while the lighting gave everything a golden shine—like a dream was that beautiful, swimming body, going on as though flowing with All Time.

After a while the other girl swam down to join us—she came up close, I saw directly into her dark eyes; then she turned and the two swam ahead together—I felt their water trail still vibrating, from the movement of their arms and legs and thighs. When our heads finally surfaced above that water, I knew we must be at about the place, where I first saw the girls join each other, from where they first caused my Mind to become dazed.

389

So we all three splashed water and laughed, and they still giggled, though the sound was more from pleasure than youth. It seemed so real—being in that water—part of Heaven. . . . just they and I, the Land and Water, and the Sky.

Slowly we seemed to play towards the shoreline, and soon we were standing by the robe. One of the girls picked it up with a laugh and began running, then we behind her, stepping softly in the sand. The warm air dried the water on my body, while locks of wet hair trailed behind from my head. Into a white lodge the girls kept on running, and when I entered they seemed to be asleep on a Buffalo robe bed. . . . . I went over and lay down between them, feeling warmth flowing all around—in that tipi with a blanket of Heaven, and a pillow of soft, warm Ground. I just let my whole self go, kept my thoughts on Sun, above—the girls were chanting, soft and low, while Everything on Earth made Love. . . .

JOURNEY TO THE LAKE OF MANY ISLANDS

The other day I was out on the lake Fishing—in my canoe—all by myself. I caught a few fish in the morning, which I tied to a braided Horse-hair rope and threw overboard. As Sun got near lunchtime I grew tired of Fishing —for some time I had caught no more Fish. So I got out my pipe and had a smoke, then rolled out my robe on the canoe floor and lay myself down. I looked up at the blue Sky above, and listened to the tiny splashings of water on the sides of the canoe, as it gently rocked to and fro. . . .

. . . . and I dreamed. . . .

. . . . The Fish on the braided Horse-hair rope were pulling my canoe along—we were headed across the lake. I felt like I was tied into the bottom of the canoe, and I could not get up. I just lay still and looked up at the Sky and listened to the water splashing off the sides of the canoe. Finally I was able to sit up—just as I heard a nearby sound of rushing water. I looked ahead and saw that my canoe was caught in a swift current that was heading for a huge rock-faced wall. I grabbed for my paddle and tried to control the canoe, but it was of no use. Just before we reached the rock wall I noticed—looking over and through the waves which were rising and falling all around me—that all the water was rushing into the opening of a cave that barely showed above the water level. Quickly I laid myself back down and called on my Guide to protect me. . . .

Whoosh—sh—sh—sh Tush—sh—sh—sh. . . . the sounds were like many waves breaking on shore during a heavy storm on the lake—I dared not look—several times the canoe jarred against boulders and other solid objects, and each time fear made my muscles tighten and my heart call a halt to its beating. Yet, in no time. . . .

. . . . silence. . . .

the sound of the rushing water quickly faded into the background; I raised myself up to look around: I was on a large, green lake that stretched as far as I could see, and was dotted by many islands—one of these was nearby. I noticed that I was sitting in water, and a hole in my canoe's bottom caught my eye. I had nothing with which to bail water, so I took my paddle and worked furiously to reach the nearby island's shore. The beach of the island was level and smooth, and the water before it was calm. I was almost up to it when my canoe gave a final start and dropped out of sight below the line of the water. I was able to stand up on the lake bottom, and the water felt very warm. I took hold of the Horse-hair rope and dragged the canoe along as I waded into shore. Once on dry land I dropped the rope and continued my walking. The smooth sandy beach went inland for half of a mile; before it ended where some low cliffs rose abruptly, hiding from my view whatever was beyond. I reached the cliffs and climbed up through one of the rain-washed gullies that looked like a tiny canyon in the mountain of sand. If I had hopes of finding food or shelter, on the other side, I was soon disappointed. The cliffs were like a solid sand wall that only enclosed another body of water—a lake within a lake. I hiked back to my canoe and sat down to ponder my fate. . . .

. . . . stranded on a strange island with only a sandy beach and nothing to repair my broken canoe with. . . . when I heard again the sound of rushing water—this time only briefly before the sound was replaced by that of a water spray—and it, in turn, by the sound of countless drops hitting the lake top. I looked up to see a most gigantic fish floating at the top of the water— its eyes and back and part of its tail sticking up in the air. At this sight I became very much afraid. . . .

. . . . but the giant fish spoke to me, in a deep, gurgling sound that was more comical than fearsome. . . *My friend, have you a light to make a fire?*

I have my flint and steel, sir, I answered hesitantly, *but it won't work in water.*

That is all right, said the large fish, *for you may light my pipe for me on the shore.*

At that I saw an object floating towards me across the water—shaped like a pipe, it was, and it was headed ashore. I drug the thing out of the water—it had a stem as long as my leg, and a bowl as large as a kettle. Inside the bowl was a tangle of leaves and vines that looked like an uncut salad. I was surprised to note that all was quite dry. The large fish spoke again:

You must light my pipe and offer smoke to the Spirits. After that float it out here to me. When I've smoked I will be able to help you—now, go ahead, strike your light and make my smoke.

So I reached into my own little tobacco sack—its contents all wet from my adventure—and brought forth my little waterproof bag made from a Rabbit's intestine. I unrolled it and brought out flintstone and steel. To the top of the pipestuff I put a pinch of moss-fuzz. With the flintstone I struck the steel in my hand. The spark flew, right away I started blowing, and the pipestuff began to crackle and burn. To the mouthpiece I ran, in a hurry, but to draw on such a pipe I had to learn.

The mouthpiece was huge—at least by what I was used to. I was not able to suck air through a stem of such length, but I found that I could blow down the stem to the pipe bowl, and the weight of its contents was not disturbed at all by my breath. However, the pipe stuff was soon heavily smoking—like a campfire just doused with water from a large cup. While the bowl rested securely in the soft sand I moved the long pipe-stem all around—I pointed it, first, to the Four Directions, then held it upward, and finally down, towards the ground. Once more I blew some of my breath down through the pipe-stem, to make sure that the stuff was well lit, but a breeze came and forced the smoke down the stem and back out at me —and right down my lungs it did hit. . . .

. . . . I tried to lift myself back up from the ground— I could see nothing, for the smoke still hung around. The sandy Earth felt like smoke—into which I kept sinking— I relaxed and something lifted me Up to my feet.

Be careful, my boy, that stuff will get You, said the big Fish, *that's from a good crop—I picked it from the deep-*

est part of the lake. I dried it there, on that shore—an old
Crow helped me, all seven days he slept and dreamed,
while wide awake. But where I keep it that's my own
secret—I can not tell You, but I can help You find finer
places, here on this lake.

The large fish instructed me to push the pipe back into
the water. I gave it a light shove and let it float to where
he was. I quickly did as he asked me, while I wondered:
Where would he take me? What would I see? How would
this end?

For awhile he smoked his pipe occasionally blowing
streams of water up into the air—while he looked off
across the big water to I knew not where. Then, all at
once, the pipe was gone, his eyes were gleaming, he half
sang out: *Are you ready?* Then he swam close up—I
swam to meet him—I got aboard him. His big, tough
wrinkles gave my feet a real good grip. I stood above him
while he propelled us through the water. Like a fast
canoe, we went along, but without the strain of paddling.
A warm breeze made my braids float behind me—into the
Air as though to join the Birds that flew around. A flock
of large ones was nearby circling—what kind they were,
or where they came from, I never found.

I used my bow to keep my balance while a fine
spray of water tingled my body—bathed in Sun's light—

that light came like a River from behind soft clouds—
sometime to go yet, before would come again the night.

As we went along we passed by close to some islands—

one, two, three; and at the fourth one we stopped. With a jump I was back in the water, a few strokes, a little wading, and I was back on solid ground.

If You should need me, after I'm gone, said the big Fish, *just stand in this water; take four big mouthfuls and spit each one as far as you can. I will come to meet you, smoke my pipe, and try to help you; but next time I do that, is the only other time I can.* With that he swam away, and I was sad to see my new friend go. Yet, I knew that his life was quite unlike mine. While I live upon the Earth and not the water, his home—the lake—gives him the stuff to make HIS life just fine.

When the big Fish was gone from my sight I looked around the shore of the island. There were footprints in the wet soil everywhere. I looked forward to being, again, with other People, and hoped that they could help me on my way.

I followed a path which led through the willows, that grew in a moist hollow close to the shore. A cutbank surrounded all but the water-side of the hollow. The path went up and over the lowest part of the cutbank and into a light forest of bushes and tall shrubs. The path led along, through several small clearings, till it finally came out to a meadow of good size.

In the middle of the meadow was a strange lodge like I had never before seen. It was long and low—quite different from the lodges we use here. A Person, stooped over, was just going inside. The back of the Person's robe was brightly decorated, and the colorful art made me feel much at ease.

I approached the strange lodge, wishing someone were outside—I grew nervous at the thought of having to go inside announced and seeing all the occupants staring at me. From the sounds of voices and other noises which I could hear, I knew that a number of People would be within. I walked up to the door while two Dogs watched me closely, I looked in the door and my heart skipped a beat. I couldn't decide on my first reaction as I saw the strange gathering there, ahead of my feet. A number of Persons were seated in that lodge, some with most hideous faces. Someone said, *Come inside,* and as I went in they all rose and offered me their places. At the rear was a man who was surrounded by smoke, and he motioned for me to sit beside him. I was brought up to respect the meaning of the place beside the host's seat that is offered to an honored guest, so I went to the rear and sat down. I forced myself to look at some of the other People in the lodge, out of courtesy, but I was careful not to focus my eyes upon them. I was afraid of myself, what my expression might be, if I dwelled on the thought and the meaning of this group—if I rested my eyes on their physical appearances.

I am Smoke Head, said the man beside me in a thin, strained voice that sounded far away. *Did Huka, the Fish bring You to our island just recently, or have You been lost?* he asked.

I have just arrived, said I, quietly so as not to attract too much attention to our conversation. The others in the lodge seemed to have forgotten about my presence very quickly, and were again involved in their own visits and chores. *I came here hoping that you would be able to give me some assistance to get back to my People,* I said, very hopefully.

Of course we will assist You, said Smoke Head, *that is what We are All Here For, don't You know?* He seemed to imply something that I could not figure out. He continued to smoke constantly, his head being barely visible, at times, inside the cloud. Strangely, the cloud of smoke stayed only around him, and seemed to rush immediately upward and out through the roof opening, without affecting anyone else in the lodge.

May I spend the night here, with you People, before setting out on my journey home in the morning, I asked, confidently. Everyone's hospitable manner had made me feel very much among helpful friends.

Certainly You will spend the night Here, replied Smoke Head. *We will know when You are ready to go home.* For a moment I thought that in his efforts to make me feel welcome he was inviting me to stay with them for a visit. His following conversation, however, added quite a different light to this idea than I had expected. He said:

All of Us are Here to learn some Lessons—to understand different things we never understood before. Some People on Earth think others' Lives should be in their power—they think that Power means having control of others' lives. When they do this they get sent here, to our Island of Purgo, to live with their own power, feel its evil, and cast it out. If they do this then they go back to rearrange their Earthly ways, after their deaths their Minds will live on in Universal Happy Days. But if they cheat, and try again to control another's destiny, their Minds will forever dwell in misery!

My own fault is that I am immensely fond of smoking, so much so that my Mind always seems clouded up, and I am never quite sure about what I am doing. I harshly criticise others without knowing the pain I may be causing them, because the smoke reddens my eyes so I can hardly see. But here, the others pay no attention to me— all my bad thoughts stay in the smoke around my own head. When I go back to my Earth home I look forward to looking around myself—to speak to others, to find out their desires. My days I'll spend with others, sharing happiness, to make my smoke filled with good thoughts during the night.

Smoke Head ended his conversation with a moment of silence, followed by a mighty siege of coughing. After awhile he tapped my knee and said: *See those two ladies with the funny heads?* as he pointed out two women down the way. Both had spooky faces that nearly frightened me, and one had a strange growth on her head.

Back at home they are known for their gossiping— everyone always says they have big mouths. The one talks a lot about just everything, the right one pries a lot into

397

*other People's lives. All day long, now, they just sit there
gossiping, while no one here pays them any Mind. Pretty
soon they will see the ugliness in each other, if they're
left alone, then they may try just to be, again, good wives.*

*Come outside and I'll show you the Frog Chief, he's
the one who gave everyone commands. All day long his
loud voice disturbed the peacefulness, as he shouted his
orders through the camp.* We walked out of the lodge and
I was greatly relieved—the place was just too strange for
me. I still wondered for the reason of my presence there—
I wasn't like them—that was easy to see.

*There is that Frog Chief—in his water hole, when he
shouts only croaking can be heard. He is finding that life
goes on around him anyhow, even if he doesn't say a
single word.* And there, in a small water hole near the
lodge sat the strangest frog I have ever seen: a feather in
his long hair, a pair of earrings, a Chief's arrow that his
odd fingers held between. His croaking sounded funny,
the way his face appeared, as though he were shouting in
vain. I could see how obnoxious he could try to be, but
as a Frog his Spirit gave me no pain. I hoped, for his
sake, that he could learn to keep quiet, now, and that,
with silence, he would still have the same strength. Where
words can add little to others' Spiritual needs, actions can
often raise them to great lengths.

*Let me show you the three brothers who are unhappy
now,* said Smoke Head, as he led me through the field.
*One had more success than the other two, so the two tried
to have the third one killed. Their brother is still at home,*

but his Spirit's here, to show them what might happen if they proceed—with their selfish plans to take his happiness—like robbing a good hunter of his meat. And there, down below, I could see them now—two sorrowful runners being chased, by a laughing, huge skull that kept behind them right along, now and then tapping their backs with its bony face.

Next thing I knew I was walking away from them— leaving those weird People and their strange lodge. They were waving, making strange sounds, till I lost sight of them—as I hurried back to the water and, I hoped, home. I waded out and took four mouthfuls of water; I spit each one out, just like the Fish said I should do. . . . then I woke up and found myself in my canoe!

Get up, says my father, splashing water in, *you're lucky the Wind blew you this way. Some others, in the past, went fishing like you, today, and they got lost in some faraway place. They've returned, telling stories of strange People there; a hidden and magical race. They came back, very frightened, from whatever they had seen. It must be powerful, whatever it was that they had seen, for they came home and changed their Paths to better ways.*

So speaks my father, here at the shore, as I wake up. I'm not sure just what to tell him so I'll just think: Make others pleasant, before seeking my own pleasures; avoid ugly gossip—tell things about others right to their face; don't shout orders or use words for what You can do better—let actions take the place of spoken words; don't think evil of others who have what You want— be happy for them and they may show You their ways; and, finally, think carefully about all your dreaming—let it be the mirror of Your Mind throughout your days.

DREAM OF THE GIANT

The brother of Father is visiting with us this evening. *Uncle Big Snake* we call him. A handsome man in his 70's. Uncle Big Snake is good to look at while he accents his story telling with hand signs. His shiny, brown forehead goes some ways up where his hair has receded, while his silver-gray locks fall to his shoulder behind. He is telling us now:

Once I dreamed I was in a very strange place: all the natural things seemed to be the same as here, in the Valley—the trees and mountains and streams—but all the signs of human life that I saw were very large—several times larger than they usually were. I came upon a place where some tall trees had been chopped down—apparently to make firewood, or else, perhaps, a shelter. The trunks were all gone—only the stumps were left standing. Yet, all the remaining stumps were two or three times as tall as I—there was enough useable wood left just in these trunks to supply most of our camp with a Winter supply. In addition, more than a Winter supply of firewood, for our camp, was scattered about in broken branches, left by whoever had taken the trunks.

I looked around me on the ground and noticed some very large depressions—large enough for me to lay down in. Walking around them I discovered that they were in the shape of footprints—huge footprints, they were! Following the direction the footprints were leading—first with my eyes—I saw a path clearly ahead—a wide swath of crumpled bushes and broken small trees, as though a landslide had here finished its downhill run. Yet, there were no piles of Earth or large boulders—just those huge footprints sunk down into the ground.

I was amazed and curious—not yet afraid or angry—so I followed this trail of destruction to see where it would go. I had not picked my way along the tangled trail very far when I came upon the carcass of a Deer. It appeared to have been butchered, but only one hind quarter was actually gone—other parts were just lying about, while most of the animal seemed to have been torn and shredded as though someone had hacked around on it with a hatchet. As I looked more closely I noticed several pieces of sharp flint protruding here and there from the body— each one as large as the blade of a knife, but somehow driven into the body without any handles. Other pieces of flint were scattered about, some of them were stuck in a large pine tree behind me. The tree's life-juice of sap was already oozing out.

I continued to follow the tracks to a stream bed, where whatever it was must have stopped for a drink, for at the water's edge I found the remains of the hind quarter, and in the warm air it sure did stink. One footprint was left right in the water, and the creek, at that place, flowed out upon the ground—in a hundred small branches it divided, and everything was muddy, all around.

I went on, and up ahead I heard loud noises—from some bushes were coming loud sounds. I approached with my bow and arrow ready—I expected a huge Bear, ready to pounce. But—oh! how I shrank back with horror when I saw what was making all the noise: it was a man of gigantic proportions—a huge man with a bellowing voice:

"What brings you here—you weakling—you servant. . . ." as his huge hands reached out and grabbed hold of me. . . . "Come with me—I'll find use for your presence. Can you cook well? Can you chop down a tree?" Though he asked questions he must have thought of his own answers, for he never gave me a chance to speak. He just roughly threw me into his big basket, which from filth and contamination did reek.

Outside, I could hear him laughing loudly, and at times he seemed to be grumbling some song—he was rising, and planning to take me along.

"Another warrior, perhaps, I have captured—another weakling to fight my enemy's men; seven hundred he has killed, of those I've sent against him; there'll be no peace until for every one I've killed ten!" So I heard him talking, then loudly grunting—but all the odours made me feel pretty weak. He swore loudly about stepping into something; he kicked the basket, and I fell on my cheek.

A sudden updraft brought fresh air into my basket, as he took my conveyance upon his back; His steps and

*bouncing sent the basket swinging madly, and, oh! how the
forest did crack.*

*I found a loose piece of the basket to hold on to, and,
for the first time, had a chance to look around. The basket,
to me, was quite a big one; and through the space between
the basket weavings, I could see, way below me, the
ground. A nearby sound suddenly caught my attention,
and I noticed another person by me; he was covered by
loose leaves and branches—it looked as though he were
sleeping, to me. He sat up and looked at me sadly, then
he asked, "Have you been here very long?" I shook my
head and said, "Just a few minutes," and he told me, "You
should have never come along."*

*It turned out that he, too, had been captured, and he
knew what our fate was to be. He said, "Two giants are
at war with each other, and for fighters they use captives
like you and me."*

*I asked him where the two giants were living, and he
told me on opposite sides of a lake. "They lived at one
time together, like two brothers, but then each wanted
more than he could take. So they fought, and threw words
at each other, and each one claims that the other is bad.
They're too busy making war on each other to notice that
All around them is sad."*

*My companion-in-plight told me how the country has
suffered, since the giants have lost all common sense—
wrecking forests, killing game, and cursing Nature; using
innocent little People for their defense. I asked him of the*

*Deer that I saw earlier, and he told me how the giant kills
with flints—"Instead of using one accurate arrow, he
throws a handful, quite blindly, at what he wants. He
often hunts when his stomach is filled up, so he takes only
what he sees fit. At his rate there will soon be no Nature—
his desires fall into a bottomless pit."*

*I asked my friend if there was any way, now, that we
could save each other's life. "Not a chance," said he, with*

a look of dejection, "Not unless we can find us a knife."

Well, then, it did just so happen, that my knife was still tied to my side. We took it and started quietly cutting that basket till we fit through it, and dropped quietly outside. The giant just kept right on walking, his noises covered any that we made. My friend said that without his two captives, the giant would find his war hard to be made.

So, in my dream, we gathered my friends' People, we had them move near my own People's campsite. The giant was quite upset at the desertion, for, without them, his existence soon died.

THE THREE FAMILIES

There once lived three families whose members were all close friends—they lived as neighbors, and were happy together. The men hunted and smoked with each other, the women cooked meals and sewed clothes together, and the children went hiking and swimming together. They shared each others' joys and sorrows, and they helped each other with whatever they had.

So they lived, until one day one of the women, looking up, saw an Eagle of exceptional size and beauty flying overhead. Though she had no particular need or use for the feathers, she said—aloud—"I would certainly like to have the skin of that Eagle."

After some little while one of the other women, looking up at the cliffs nearby, saw a herd of Mountain Goats. Though she had plenty of skins and furs in her lodge, she said—aloud—"I would certainly like to have the skin of such a Goat."

The third woman, after thinking over what the other two had said, saw a beautiful golden Snake sunning itself on a boulder nearby. Though she could think of no use for any part of such a creature, she said—aloud—"I would certainly like to have something from that beautiful Snake."

Now, the three men of the families were sitting nearby, smoking. They had heard what each of the women had said and, though knowing that the statements were made from idleness and had no meaning, they each said—aloud —"I am able to fill my woman's request."

So, the men went off to climb the nearby mountain— one looking for the large Eagle, one for the herd of Goats, and one for a golden Snake. They found the Eagle, first of all, quietly nesting. As they approached, the Eagle asked what it was they wanted and, when it learned the intent of their mission, it asked them to come near. From its tail the Eagle gave each of them a few feathers and said: "Your People shall always wear these to remember the power of the Eagles—you may return home, for that one woman will now always have Eagles dropping feathers in her hair."

So, the men went on to find a Goat skin. As they neared a herd of Goats, one old nanny came forward and asked them what they wanted and, when she learned the intent of their mission, she asked them to come near. She gave them each a fine suit made of Goat skin and said: "Your People shall always wear such clothes to remember the power of the Goats—you may return home, for that one woman will now always have Goats rubbing their fine fur on her body."

So, the men went on to look for a golden Snake. As they came to some boulders they were startled by a loud hissing, and shortly they saw some gigantic Snakes coming near. The Snakes hissed and shouted at them: "You came for us, but yet you stand there with cold fear. Your People shall always fear Snakes, when they see them, and all they will get is a good run for their lives, because of our power—you may return home, for that one woman shall have plenty of Snakes curling around her feet, now!"

So the men ran home, now rather frightened. From a distance they saw their three tipis, but none of their families seemed to be about. As they came closer they found only some piles of their clothing and their foot-

404

prints that showed where they had gone: in the back-
ground, where in the past only flowers had been standing,
stood three pine trees, tall and dark. From the one flew
an Eagle, losing feathers, on another a Goat had rubbed
its hair, and the third one had Snakes that were coiling
in the Sunshine by its roots, upon the ground, everywhere.

SAVARO—THE MAKER OF THINGS

For several days I have been hearing the distant tap-
tapping of Savaro's tools while he has been making a new
canoe from the trunk of a large tree. I have seen him,
from a distance, sometimes working alone, sometimes
working with the help of one of the other men in the
camp, or even with the help of his woman, Raspberry.
Savaro and Raspberry live in a large log house covered
with Earth, which they built on a knoll by the shore of
the lake. Savaro did not want to build too close to any-

one else's home because, as he once told me, *only I can enjoy the musical sounds of my tools as they help me to create all the things that I think of.*

Whenever I see Savaro around the camp he always asks when I am going to come by to see some of his creations. Today I will take advantage of his invitation, so that I can also see how it is that a tree trunk can be turned into a balanced canoe.

Hello, do you have a few minutes to visit. Savaro shouts eagerly from a distance as I walk down to the edge of the lake where he is working on his canoe. It is a warm day, and he is taking advantage of the weather by letting his skin feel the air and soak up Sun's rays. He has a strip of buckskin tied around his head to keep his hair back, and a black beard covers most of his face.

Our house is a little out of the way, so we don't get visitors too often, he explains with a large smile on his face. *Hey Raspberry,* he shouts in the direction of the house, *make some tea—we have company.* My visit seems to have aroused much enthusiasm within him.

Little Bear and his sons helped me to haul this huge tree here, he says, pointing to the canoe-shaped hulk before him, *after I felled it with the use of various tools. I've been hollowing it out with my chisels for a couple of weeks, now, and I'm just about ready to try it out.*

I build small fires in the parts that are hard to chisel, though I have to watch carefully that the fires don't burn too far into the side. Today I've been using my planer to smooth the surfaces and make them even. I use a fire for this job, too, if a large area needs to be leveled. I just run a torch back and forth along the high spot, and then I scrape it off after it has been scorched well enough.

I guess I can leave this go for awhile—I'd like to show you our house, he says questioningly. I tell him that I'd love to see it, and he eagerly guides the way along a winding, stone-laid trail that takes us up the knoll and into a clearing in the growth of trees, where sits the large Earth house.

It doesn't look very high, but mighty big, I comment as we approach a small vestibule with a door, which is a part of the house.

Oh well, wait until you see how it is built inside, he explains to me, as he opens the plank door to the ringing of many strands of shells that are tied to a bouncing willow stick which is fastened to the inside of the door. A strong accumulation of odd and mysterious odours rushes for the door as we step into the vestibule. Coats, shoes, and caps are hung on the vestibule wall, while various wood and Birch-bark containers stand in rows on the floor. Another doorway—without a door—leads into the main room of the house, which is several feet lower down than the vestibule.

You see, the house looks low from the outside because it is actually partly underground, Savaro explains triumphantly. *This knoll is exposed to rough weather from across the lake,* he goes on, *so we stay pretty snug and protected way down here. Besides, Raspberry and I feel real secure living down here in our Earth Mother's womb!*

We spent a long time digging out this pit and making it level. Then we lined it with logs, which we continued above the ground for four more feet, before laying the logs across to support the roof. I fitted the upper parts of the walls so that there were plenty of openings for windows, which is why it looks so bright down here. Don't you think it's bright down here? he asks hopefully. Indeed, it is a very cheery home that actually gives no indication of being partly underground unless you look out through one of the open windows and see that the bottoms of the nearby trees are about eye level. The floor space inside here must be four times that of a large lodge in the camp— at least thirty feet in each direction. A large, colorfully woven blanket hangs across a far corner of the building, making a triangular room behind there. I have been hearing noises from that area since we came in, and now I find that it is the sleeping section, and Raspberry is just arising from a nap. She looks startled to find us in the house, but immediately joins the conversation.

How are you—how is everything in the camp, she asks. Before I answer she continues, *have you seen Savaro's canoe? He's been working on it for quite awhile now, and expects to finish it very soon.* She seems to be fully informed about his activities and eager to tell someone else about them.

Why don't you make us some tea from those roots you dug yesterday, Savaro suggests to Raspberry. *I want to show our guest some of the things we have around.*

Some of the People in the camp scoff at me because I'm always working with tools and building things. They think I should spend more time just wandering around and daydreaming. But this is my life, right here—that's what I do the best and what I enjoy doing the most, he says, while making a sweeping motion with his arm to take in all the contents of his home. *Some of the People called me Tool Man, sometime ago. I told them I didn't care much for that name, so then some of them started calling me Not-Want-To-Be-Called Tool Man,* he said, with sort of a puzzled look on his face. *I'd rather be called Savaro— or else just plain Neighbor. I mean, we're All neighbors, aren't we?*

Where did you get all these odds and ends, I finally had to ask. The ceiling beams are just covered with hanging things like pieces of chain, metal rings, big skeleton keys, parts of old guns, and numerous things that I don't think I've ever seen before.

Ohh—just scavenging around, he replies, acting somewhat as though I'm prying. *It's really amazing what stuff you can find around the old trading post—stuff that got lost and broken. I don't figure anything should be left to waste if there's a chance something can be made out of it; everything's got some use to it, if it's handy when you need it.*

Here and there I see baskets with Food, bowls with dried plants and herbs and mysterious little bags. They must sample many of Nature's things. In the center of the house is an open firepit with a waist-high wall made of rocks. Raspberry is pulling on a rawhide rope that is attached to some sort of a pulley at the edge of the fireplace. Soon a clay vessel comes up from the fire and, as she pulls another rope, swings out to the edge of the firepit. *I rigged this thing up so that we can control exactly how fast our food cooks over the fire.* Savaro explains. *This other rope lets us swing whatever is cooking out here, to the side, so that we don't get burnt leaning over the fire. I made these bellows,* he goes on, pointing to an affair on the floor that has a wooden foot-pedal, attached to another rawhide rope which hangs from the ceiling beam above. A folded leather bag is fastened beneath the pedal. *I made these bellows from a tanned Elk hide that I soaked in Bear grease, to make it air-tight. The rawhide rope has just enough give to let me push this pedal down—as soon as I take my foot off it comes right back up to place. When we get up in the morning all I have to do is toss a few sticks of kindling into the ashes, here, and pump on the bellows for a few moments, and the fire starts up. The nozzle from the bellows fits into a hole that I left when I made the stone wall, around this fireplace. I can pull the nozzle out and use the bellows for other things—such as providing the air to play this harmonica that I found the pieces of,* he goes on, pointing to a strange object that is roughly the size of a harmonica, but is made mostly of smoothed and polished pieces of wood. One side has a leather cover constructed so that a round piece protrudes, big enough to stick my thumb into. *I just put the nozzle of the bellows in here,* he points to the protruding round piece, *and pump the bellows. To play a tune I just cover different holes up here, in the front. I'll show you.* He fits the nozzle of the bellows into the hole on the harmonica cover and pumps the bellows with the instrument's other side. Horrible squeaking sounds can barely be heard above the puffs of air from the bellows. *I told Suma he could have this when I get it perfected,* he says, *but Suma doesn't want to carry too many things around with him when he wanders, I guess. He said it would be*

409

better if I learned to play it—then I could maybe accompany him. I've tried talking Raspberry into learning to play it, but she says she doesn't have enough time.

Savaro lays down the bellows and harmonica as I walk over to a massive workbench along one wall of his house. *By the way, I use the bellows and firepit to do a little blacksmith and jewelry work, too,* he adds as an afterthought. *Every once in awhile somebody brings me a piece of rock with some workable metal in it—some Copper or Silver—and I make them bracelets or a ring or some earrings out of it, in exchange for what's left over. With the bellows and a good fire I can work with a lot of metal —though I really prefer wood.*

Here is your tea, says Raspberry, as she brings over two wooden cups of steaming liquid. *I hope you like it; Savaro and I like this kind real well,* she explains. We sit down on a bench made from half of a log, with wooden stems for legs. The tea is dark reddish-brown in color, and smells like something in a pharmacists collection. It has an odd taste that I can't describe, but it is pleasant to swallow. Savaro takes out a little Buckskin pouch from his back pocket and a small, clay-bowled pipe. *Would you care for a smoke,* he asks, as he fills the bowl with tobacco from the pouch. *I call this smoking mixture my Tops and Stars, because I made it from the smallest and softest parts of my smoking plants—the parts closest to the warmth of the Heavens above,* he says in a reminiscent tone. *The Summer's End Ceremony will begin pretty soon,* he continues, *and with it we'll have our harvest. Here's to a good crop of everything,* he calls up, as he points the mouthpiece of his small pipe towards the Sky. He puffs on the pipe for some time before passing it to me. Raspberry shakes her head when I try to pass it to her. Taking the pipe from me Savaro explains, *naw, her head's up in the Clouds most of the time, anyway, she doesn't like to have smoke floating around her, too.* He chuckles quietly, while Raspberry assumes a look of having her head up in the Clouds.

We sit quietly for awhile, feeling the warmth of the

410

afternoon through the windows nearby. *Would you like to go back outside,* ask Savaro, apparently feeling also the beckoning of Sun's rays. I nod and get up, handing my empty cup to Raspberry with a smile of thanks. She smiles, in return, and continues to scrape at some wrinkled, brown roots with her knife, up on her cooking counter.

Outside there is a warm vibration—an almost-silent sound of brightness, warm air, Birds in the Trees, and countless insects busily at work in unseen places. Savaro walks to the edge of the knoll and sits down on a huge stump that he has evidently moved there himself, as it just sits on top of the ground like some giant's footstool. I sit down on the stump, by Savaro, and there is yet room for a couple more People to sit. The view out on to the lake is most overpowering from this point. Like a huge, blue mirror, it reflects its frame of green forest and high, rocky pinnacles. To think of the World which exists at the bottom of that lake, alone. Fish, Plants, and Insects living together in an environment so much different than the one up here, yet so much in Harmony with it.

Do You see that little island out in the middle of the bay, over there, asks Savaro. *That's going to be the next goal of my Dream Life. I want to build a small version of my Earth Lodge over there. And I'm not going to use any tools or metal things there—just for the Experience*

411

of doing it that way, he says. I am trying to picture a small Earth-covered lodge on top of the island.

The trail down to the water, in that bay, is a real steep one, Savaro goes on. *You see, the whole bay is surrounded by rocky walls that drop off straight for a hundred feet or more to the water. I figure that even if People from that World Outside ever find their way to our Valley, they're not going to be very anxious to disturb me out on my island home!* He gives me a sly wink at that.

I'm going to try to pack whatever supplies I'll need over there in along the frozen lake-top this Winter, he continues, still looking over at the Island with a dreamy film over his eyes. *Then I can hike in and out during the Summer at my leisure—depending on whether Raspberry and I like this place better than that one,* motioning to his present and future homes with his chin.

Are you planning to use your new canoe to reach the island, I ask.

Yeah, he says, in a far-away voice, *and to explore other parts of the lake from there. That reminds me,* he says, in a sudden tone, looking towards his canoe. *I would like to finish smoothing down the inside and outside of that thing today. Would you care to give me a hand?*

There are still several hours left to the afternoon, so I'll go ahead and help Savaro with his canoe. I'll just leave my clothes up here, on the rock. They would only get in my way while trying to work in this warm air.

My grandpa used to do a lot of travelling in a canoe, Savaro informs me. *He came over here from France and traded with different groups of People for furs. He'd load up a big freight canoe with trade goods like knives, axes and beads, and paddle several hundred miles upstream, trading on the way. When he had his canoe filled with what he wanted he just drifted back down to where he started out. When he got older he went to work for the factor at this trading post, and married his daughter. So,*

412

you can see that I am related to Two Crows, whose great-grandfather was that factor. Quite most of us are related here, by now, and the subject has caused some concern among the People in the camp, I know. They're worried about the future. Let me tell you a story about the First Canoe, as my grandfather used to tell it to me:

STORY OF THE FIRST CANOE

A tribe of People made their homes on the West side of a wide river, far from these mountains, here. Every Winter they would migrate to the Plains to hunt Buffalo and bring back their hides to tan during the Summer. They crossed the River toward the East, and came back West, to their land, before break-up in the Spring. At the end of one such Season of hunting a young man, his wife, and his baby son fell behind the rest of the tribe as they were moving back to their country. The young family had brought more Buffalo hides than they could conveniently carry, so they were forced to travel very slowly. Now, by the time this family reached the banks of the wide river, break-up had already started, and they were no longer able to cross. They sat on the bank and mourned over the situation that they were left in.

While the man and his wife were so mourning, and their child was crying along with them, a Coyote came along, floating down the river in a carved tree trunk. This was back in the days when the bodies of animals still looked pretty much like those of the humans. This Coyote saw the mourning People so he floated his craft over to them and asked them why they were so upset. The People told him how they had gotten stranded on this side of the river because their heavy Buffalo hides had not let them travel as fast as the rest of their People.

Now, Coyote had an idea. He said to the People: *This body that I have does not quite suit me. I float along this river with my carved tree trunk, but I am not wise enough to make any good of this travelling. No Animals will have me in their camps because I am too much like a human. Yet, no humans will let me come near because my face*

413

*is that of an animal's. Since my face looks that way, it
would be best for me to just be an animal. So, if you will
give me one of those fine robes that you are packing, man,
then I can cover the rest of my body with fur. And if I
may have one of the braids of your hair, woman, then I
can unbraid it and wear it behind as a tail. And if I may
learn your mournful wail, young child, then I will have a
sound that will make all others pity me. In exchange for
all this, I give you People my carved tree trunk, for it shall
be of no use to me, anymore. You can fill it with your
things, and float it over to the other side, and join the
camps of your People.*

And so came the first canoe to the People, says Savaro
with a knowing look. And we let our Minds wander to
those long-ago days of Animals and Humans, when they
were learning how to get along with each other. . . .

THE HUNT

From a deep sleep I awaken to hear someone talking
quietly into my ear. Startled momentarily, I look up to see
my Father smiling—looking anxiously at me.

It is time for the hunt! he says, when he sees that I am awakened.

Ah yes! Now I remember—the hunt—this morning we are to go for a hunt. Fresh meat to add to our meals of fine vegetables and berries—fresh meat to give our bodies strength—hides for the women to tan and sew into things —sinew for sewing—hooves to carve children's toys from—scraps for the dogs—and. . . . the Spiritual Adventure of the hunt itself!

I pull myself up to my elbows—my fur-robe-covering slides down and exposes my chest to the damp morning air. I feel good—looking forward to the warmth of my clothing. My hair is tangled and my mouth feels as though still asleep—but, shortly, I am up and have my clothes on, my hair brushed, my mouth rinsed, and my face and arms washed with cold water—my skin feels alive with a stinging warmth underneath the security of my clothing.

By the fireplace sits a bowl of grain-meal, which Father is now and again dipping his fingers into, as he leans his head back and opens his mouth. I do likewise, throwing the meal into my mouth with gusto, fiercely chewing up the grains and dried berries, and then swallowing each mouthful down to feel the new activity in other sleeping parts of my body—which are now waking up and making me feel even warmer—and stronger.

I sit down at the edge of the blankets and furs that make up my bed and I put on my moccasins—folding the tall flaps firmly around my ankles and wrapping the long

thongs several times around them. I tie my knife sheath to my belt—the blade was just sharpened last evening while we all sat around the fire, talking—and I tie a rolled-up scarf around my head to keep my hair from falling into the way of my eyes. From the rope that holds up the tipi's inside lining I untie the thong by which hangs my bow case and quiver and their contents. Proudly, though just for a moment, I look at them: my own bow and arrows—made by the hands of Savaro, that bearded, magical craftsman who lives with his woman and his work in an Earth-covered lodge, over on the other side of the bay. A strange man whom everyone likes, but no one really knows. I look forward to visiting with him.

While I was admiring my fine hunting gear, Father has stepped outside and, from the sounds that I hear, he is preparing his Horse for the ride. Quietly, I stand up, pick up my bow and attachments, and lift aside the Elk skin door covering—looking back, momentarily, at the still-sleeping occupants of the lodge, all looking so comfortable, so warm—giving me a warm feeling inside.

Outside: the air is much more damp and chilly than I expected—the moisture on the blades of grass looks cool and gray. I hang the bow and arrows over my back—the strap across my shoulder. I learned some time ago to wait for this part of dressing until outside—after getting outside the lodge once or twice and finding my bow and arrows stuck crosswise inside, between the lodge poles on each side of the door.

Father is mounted now, and ready to go. I hurriedly slip the main piece of my hackamore over Matsoaki's nose, pull her ears through the neck strap, untie the rope around her foot (she makes a couple of meek efforts to have me leave that rope by lifting her foot up), throw the reins back over her head, and leap smoothly up on her back. She is restless from her night of standing and doesn't want to hold still while I get a proper hold on the reins and make better my sitting position. I give her just the faintest nudge with my heels and she immediately tenses her hind end and makes an effort to leap forward and take off at a gallop. I check her with the reins, and we move quietly away from the big, red-painted lodge. No one else in camp seems to be awake yet, which makes it hard for me to decide whether this is the very end of yesterday or the very start of today. I dwell on that. . . .

The mist in the air gets thicker as our trail takes us into the forest—it looks more like fog, hanging there among the trees. At times Father is far enough ahead of me, on the trail, that the details of his figure begin to fade into the mist that he appears to be continually riding into. The Horses' hooves make squishy, thudding sounds as they pound down upon the dark, damp Earth. We ride in silence while the morning light slowly dawns on us and, bit by bit, makes more of the details of our surroundings become visible to my eyes. We cross a tiny, rushing stream, and pause to let the Horses suck up some of the water. Suddenly: in the woods—there's a CRACK!. . . . Matsoaki halts her drinking immediately and lifts her head several inches—her ears turning one way, then the other, water draining from the sides of her mouth back into the creek. I hold my breath to listen, but I don't hear any more sounds. The Horses finish drinking, and we continue along the trail—all of us giving expectant glances into the trees in the direction of the sound. . . . CRACK! There goes the same sound again—followed by silence, as we come to a dead stop in our trail. Father looks carefully, then gives me the signal to get down from my Horse. Silently I dismount—lifting one leg over Matsoaki's back and sliding my body down her side, opposite from where the noise came from. Father is tying his buckskin gelding by the front legs with a long thong, which we both carry for that reason. I do the same.

I believe there is an Animal in that brush just off to our right, he whispers in calm words. My breath, by this time, is coming in short gasps, since the excitement has mixed with the cold. *I will go around to the other side of the sound and give you the Owl call when I am ready. Then you may enter straight into those bushes, as quietly as you can, and one of us, at least, will see what is making that noise. . . .* and he is away, silently.

I do not need to wait very long to hear the faint *Ooh-Hoo, Ooh-Hoo,* of Father's voice. I have gotten my bow out and slipped the loose loop over the notched end. Now I get out two arrows from my quiver, mount one, and hold the other one with my bow hand, parallel to the bow. Picking each step carefully, between small brush and occasional branches, I advance into the bushes where we last heard the noise. . . . on and on, the distance passing slowly with such careful steps. Suddenly: like an explosion of brush and animal, a large shape bounds out just a few feet in front of me and away in a straight line. . . . the main thing I can see is a large white tail, waving in the air like a flag in the hands of a nervous flagman. Two or three long bounds the beast takes, covering distance so fast that I don't even get my bow into shooting position, much less aimed for a most difficult rear-shot—when up jumps Father, about one bound ahead of the Animal, with his bow drawn and ready. Only the top half of his body is visible in the tall grass where he has been hiding—he must have known just about where the Animal

was and suspected its route of travel. The twang of the bowstring is almost immediately followed by a light, thudding sound. A twitch in the Animal's body signifies that the arrow has found its mark. Yet the Deer—a large white-tail, it turns out—continues with its long bounds and is shortly out of view inside the next bunch of bushes. Father holds up his hand, motioning for me to stand still, so I listen: a loud crashing sound has followed the last sound of a jump, and now the crashing sounds become general, as though the Animal is rooting and thrashing around in just one bush. . . . then there is silence. Father remains still for a few more moments—I do likewise—then he heads in the direction of the last sounds, drawing his knife from its sheath as he walks. By the time I catch up to him he is pumping the Deer's hind legs, forcing the blood to run out of the opening in its throat which he has made.

My brother, it hurts me to do this, he says, towards the Animal's body, *but my family is in need of the food which you will provide for us. I pray that your Spirit continues to dwell here and that it may be good for those whom you will serve.*

Having said that, Father begins to open the animal up with his knife so that he can clean and prepare it. He looks to me and says, *You may as well go on ahead without me. I will prepare this Deer, and then pack it back to camp. If you have not arrived back in camp by mid-afternoon I will come and find you. Continue down the trail we were following, and turn to the left at the first fork that you find. In a short distance your trail will drop down into a small clearing—stay at the edge of it and you may be able to observe some feeding Deer or Moose. Sometimes they bed down in the thick of the brush, there.*

I nod my understanding—at the same time sweeping my right arm away from my stomach, as Father often does when he means, *It is well.* I walk back out to the trail and untie Matsoaki's feet, and jump back on top of her.

I head Matsoaki down the trail as Father suggested, and soon we come to the fork, where I head left towards the mountains that form a high, solid wall on that side of our World. Looking over the tops of the trees ahead, where they appear to be downhill, I can see a light area that must be where the clearing is that Father mentioned. I dismount and tie Matsoaki's rope to a solid, old stump, just off the trail, that sits by itself and has no brush or other trees near it. There she can find a bit of grazing without being able to tangle her rope up in any growth.

As I continue on foot the trail makes a sharp right turn and then drops downhill, as the trees thin out, away from it. At the bottom of the small hill I can see part of the clearing—covered with low, green bushes, green grass, and numerous white and purple flowers. What a breath-taking view:

The width of the clearing is equal to the length of a tall Pine Tree. The ends of the clearing are hidden from view by the forest at my right and left. On the other side of the clearing, straight ahead on this path that I am standing in, begins the thick, dark forest again. It lays like a continuous carpet, in all directions. It ends more than half-way up the mountains which loom over this clearing with immenseness. Above the line of the forest can be seen the bare slopes of the mountains—large boulders strewn here and there along the paths of old slides. A few of the high-up ridges have green tree growths on top of them—like hairy moles in the faces of the mountains. The mountain which is somewhat off to my right has a sheer cliff of red and yellow Earth facing my way. The lower reaches of the cliff's face are lost somewhere in the green forest below it. Patches of white, here and there, represent the remnants of the one-time glacial covering of these mountains. And above all this the Sky forms a bright blue backdrop to an everchanging pattern of clouds that seem to rise up from the top of the mountains and flow this way—as though they were being brought to life by some magical power just behind the high peaks above us. If I let my eyes dwell on the clouds for a few moments I get a strong desire to reach up and touch them. . . .

After looking over the clearing and inspecting the paths and tracks, some of which are quite recent, I've picked a spot from which I can remain best hidden while still able to cover the most likely parts of the clearing. I'm seated on my blanket at the edge of the trail that I came in on—just a short distance above the main part of the clearing. I brought over some broken Pine branches and built a simple wall that will hide my movements and presence from the eyes of any game which might be inspecting the surroundings before venturing out to graze in the little meadow. I've made a few trial sightings, and should be able to reach most of the meadow with my bow from right here.

Sun is well up in the Sky by this time, and the air is warming up—so much that I might as well unbutton my shirt. A contemplative smoke would go well right now, so I might as well bring out my pipe and fill it. My small travelling pipe and its bag are fastened to my quiver. I untie the knot in the tie string and unwrap the mouth of the bag. I pull the little bag open at one end and pull out the short wooden stem with its wrapping of sinew. I reach into the bottom of the bag and bring out the little, black stone bowl, shaped like a small elbow and polished till shiny with grease. I fit the tapered end of the wooden stem into the smaller of the two holes in the bowl and draw

on it, to see if the passage is clear. It is. Again from the bottom of the little pipe bag I bring up a pinch of my smoking mixture. I put this into the larger hole in the pipe bowl—the one with the black crust around it that gives off a sweet smell from many smokings. I tamp the mixture down with a twig lying nearby me. . . .

. . . . I awaken with Sun shining hotly upon my face from its middle-of-the-afternoon position in the still-blue Sky. For some time I have slept—dreamt of the Earth and all the things upon it: the Pebbles and Twigs, the Insects and Flowers, the Birds and Animals, the Sky up above. I have been as one with them in my dream—I am as one with them, lying here, waking up, on this warm afternoon. I take my shirt off to feel the faint breeze uniting with the moisture on my body. My face feels hot and tingling from lying motionless in the path of the hot rays for so long.

The afternoon breeze brings with it an overpowering sound, out here in this mountain forest—a sound that is the voice of everything which is around here—a HUSHhhhh —a visible sound in the tops of the nearby trees as well as an invisible droning that seems to be coming down the canyons and mountains and through the forest from the vastness above. Leaves rustle; twigs snap; an occasional tree trunk groans as if passively greeting the rush of the unseen air or commenting upon the burden that it must continuously bear.

I will have another smoke from my pipe, while deciding whether to remain here or to get up and wander around, in order to locate the object of this hunt. I knock out the cold ashes left in the bowl from my earlier smoke. I fill the bowl with another pinch from the bottom of the pipe bag, and tamp it down again with the same twig, which still lies where I last tossed it. I wonder what will become of this twig after I leave this place—for I will probably never see it again.

I must cover the match well to keep the breeze from blowing it out. I must marvel at the ingenuity of that Savaro—making these matches from twigs, Pine sap, ancient gunpowder, and sulphur from the cave of an abandoned earlyday mine. Though all the People in the Valley take with them their flint and steel, when travelling away from home, these matches are a great convenience when one only needs a quick fire like this. . . .

. . . Big, gray wisps of smoke drift away from the top of the pipe bowl and out from the corners of my mouth. The heat from the burning mixture stings my tongue and warms my mouth. Slowly I puff—blowing the smoke out and watching it rush off with the breeze—mingling with it to disappear into the Universe.

Suddenly! I am consciously aware of some sounds that my subconscious Mind has been making contact with for some little time—occasional sounds somewhere out in the forest—sounds like twigs breaking and brush rustling. . . . I listen silently—Silence! Just the Wind in the mountains and down here in the trees. Silence! Then! There are the sounds again—sounds such as would be made by a child quietly playing with sticks inside of some dense bushes. Couldn't be a Person—though the sounds seem much too strong to be any small Animal. A large Animal, then— what kind? I wonder. . . . as my heart begins to beat faster and my hands begin to feel moist and tense. Again, I hear the sounds—as though they seem to be a bit closer each time. The sounds are coming from the brush on the other side of the clearing and some ways off to the right. But I can not see a thing moving.

Quietly! I remove my bow from its case and gently place one end against the instep of my foot—bending the other end so that the center of the bow bulges outward. I pull the loose end of the bowstring up towards the top notch of the bow. I almost have the loop over the notch when the whole affair breaks loose of my nervous hands— the bow almost propels itself into the air as it straightens out. Luckily my hands have enough of a grip to keep this bungling silent. Again I bend the bow—this time more quickly so that the loop is over the notch before my hands can lose their grip again. I take four arrows from my quiver and place three of them in front of the bow, where I can hold them with the same hand as the bow itself. The fourth arrow I lay in place, carefully fitting the bowstring between the notch. I hold the arrow in place with the index finger of the same hand which holds the bow and the other arrows. Using my right hand for support I raise myself up very slowly and quietly. . . .

. . . . I almost lose my balance getting up—I am dizzy from being on the ground so long. The sounds now seem to be fairly close—yet I can still see no movement in the brush, nor any other sign of the noisemaker. I wonder if it could yet be some very noisy small animal?

I am carefully making my way down the trail toward the clearing—each step is a studied and measured one, so that my presence will not be announced. During my smoking I noticed that the gray wisps went hurriedly in a direction away from the clearing, so my scent should not make its way over to whatever is making the sounds. Ahead lies the upturned trunk of a dead Cottonwood tree—an ideal shelter for me to make my stand behind. I lean myself against the trunk to rest my body from the strenuous few steps it has taken.

There! The tops of some tall bushes are swaying unnaturally—that must be the location of my quarry. Like a chain-reaction in slow motion, the movement in the tops of the bushes comes slowly towards the edge of the clearing, over on the other side. If the maker of the movements continues in that direction he or she will step out into the clearing almost directly across from me, a stone's throw away. A chill rushes through my body, and I wish I had kept on my shirt—to help silence the loud beating of my heart, if nothing else.

The bushes at the very edge of the clearing are swaying now—and I can barely make out some dark object through the many leaves. Suddenly! The quarry steps out into the open—so defiantly that it must not have any awareness of my presence. It is a Moose—a large, dark cow Moose with an appearance which makes it look almost awkward: a large head at the end of a massive neck, which ends in a large hump above the Animal's shoulders. A monstrous nose hangs almost comically at the end of the cow's face, and a little, dangling beard hangs under her chin. She is huge—about the size of my Horse Matsoaki, though some of the huge appearance is due to unusually long legs. The cow's hind parts seem small and incomplete when compared with the massive front. She stands still, as though waiting for something to happen, and I begin to raise my bow into position to shoot. . . .

. . . . Crack! More of the sounds which I was hearing for some time, though the maker of the sounds seems to be standing silently out in the clearing. Crack! Crack! And out from the bushes comes another Moose—a powerful-looking Bull with his weapons of horn adding a great deal to the massiveness of his head and shoulders. His shiny coat of hair is almost black, except down around his feet, where he seems to have on golden-yellow socks. His tiny eyes seem inadequate for such a large body and, indeed, I have been told that he relies on them much less than his nose and ears. He does not seem to be concerned about any possible challengers—he appears to be very relaxed. Few beings in Nature would dare challenge such a monstrous combination of legs, horns, and muscle.

The cow begins to wander along the edge of the meadow in a direction away from me. I was hoping that they would come this way, to give me a closer and more powerful shot. I will have to aim carefully and shoot quickly if I am to have any success with this challenge. . . .

. . . . Thummmmm—goes my first arrow, the bowstring snapping sharply against my wrist. The cow stops and the bull doesn't move—not a muscle. Quickly I fit another arrow to the bowstring and pull it back—I must hit him this time, though I felt sure that the first arrow hit the mark, also.

Thummmmp—goes my second arrow, making a definite sound of striking its mark. The bull twitches his body once, but otherwise stands still. I fit yet a third arrow to the bowstring and start to pull it back when the bull turns—and begins to trot towards me. I aim carefully below the swaying hump on his back—long, black hairs bristling noticeably on its top.

Thummmmp—goes the third arrow, its feathered shaft protruding over the bull's big ears. He makes a momentary lurch, then halts in his tracks. I fit my last arrow to my bowstring—the others are deep in my quiver which hangs on my back. As I fit the arrow the bull begins to trot towards me again—though much more unsteady than at first. He is now close enough to be on fairly intimate terms with me. I can clearly hear his labored breathing, which only adds to his apparent ferocity. I aim again below the swaying hump—hoping to strike some vital area underneath. It is the only clear shot that I have from this head-on position.

Thummp—goes the fourth arrow, striking harder and more quickly than the others. The big bull crashes to his knees as my heart skips a beat. The feathered shaft is barely left sticking out from his back. His shiny eyes have a look of disbelief as well as a look of conviction to do harm to this unexpected challenger who looks so weak, standing there before this ruler of the forest. With loud, labored breaths he again begins to rise. I quickly pull the quiver from my back and reach in for more arrows—dropping the quiver from my hand as I fit one of the arrows to the string. The battle will shortly be over—but the big bull is not yet ready to accept defeat. He still has left enough power to take me with him on this last physical journey. With a few more steps he will be upon me. . . .

I begin a song—a loud song of courage for myself—an announcement of victory—a demand for his acceptance of defeat, and I let fly another arrow.

Thumpppp—the arrow goes deep into his side, which he has left barely exposed to me. Crash—the bull goes down on his side. His legs make an effort to lift the big body up once more, but the damage which has been done is too heavy to lift back up. He raises his head in defiance, looking about for me in his last attempt. I let go of another arrow—this one deep into his heart from very close range —and he drops his head with a last sigh. My song continues as loudly as I can sing it, while the tears run from my eyes and fall to the Earth below. I feel badly for ending the life of this powerful being; I feel badly, and in my song I tell him so. . . .

HiYo my Brother—forgive me for doing this to you. Let Your Spirit always be with me in exchange for this physical ending which I have caused. Give spiritual strength to all those who will strengthen their bodies with you. HiYo-HiYo, HiYo-HiYo!

Go now, woman, I find myself shouting-singing to the cow, *go now, for he is mine. You would not have stayed with him long anyway—another will find you and take you soon, in this forest.* The cow will not listen to me—

she challenges my right to her slain man's body as she stands as close to him on the other side as I am standing from him here. She snorts loudly, and paws the Earth with her large hooves. *Go,* I shout again, waving my arms at her, *go, or I shall have to take you with me as well.* I have one arrow left, which I fit to my bow, fearing that she may attack me. I do not wish to shoot the cow, if possible, for she may give the forests many young bulls, yet. Again I shout at her, *Go, go from here—your man is mine now,* and as I wave my arms and my bow she begins to retreat, stopping now and then to snort loudly—a snort which echoes menacingly from the trees around the meadow. All of Nature is watching this powerful Drama of Life.

With my knife I take care of the first part of the operation which will end up providing many meals for the People at home. It is a tedious operation, which must be done carefully so that nothing useful is damaged or ruined. I leave my bow case and quiver lying by the big bull, to keep away any hungry Bear or other marauders, while I go back to Matsoaki to ride her down to the camp. I will need the help of some others to bring this massive food supply back home. . . .

Night is half-way over by the time I take a plunge into the cold waters of the creek, where they flow out into the lake. We have finally completed the job of hauling my success of the day back to camp and hanging it from the branch of a tree out of reach of the camp's Dogs—hanging it so that it can cool and mellow naturally. As I am cleaning off the labours of the day, it is hard to believe that all this has happened in just one day—how dramatic can be the events of some days!

SUMMER'S END CEREMONY

Early in the morning it is, again—finally the start of the day on which is to begin the Summer's End Ceremony, which we have All been anxiously awaiting. Songbird is walking around the camp with some bells in his hand, which he keeps regularly ringing. His deep, penetrating voice can be heard all over the campground loudly proclaiming the spiritual event that is to take place on this day. Now and then he calls out someone's name and reminds them of the duty that he or she is to fulfill for the ceremony.

Arise, my friends and neighbors. . . . arise, all my relatives, here, he is now saying. *This is the first day of our Holy Season—this is the day on which we start our Summer's End Ceremony.*

Hey there, my young friend Two Crows! It is for you to take along some boys and gather the material for the sweat lodge, which you must have built by this afternoon. Send a boy out to gather some fine rocks that will heat well. It is for you to decorate the insides of our Holy Lodges—to make the Earth altars and decorate them with Earth paints and feathers, so that they will be ready for the incensing during our ceremonies.

Hoka hey, my friends, hoka hey! Let Us be moving along now—let us make ready for the busy day. This evening will be the first ceremony inside the West lodge. When Sun sets our food will be roasting over the firepit inside that lodge, and we will all gather in there, at that time, to partake of the food.

Okeh, my friend Little Bear! Are your boys getting up and making ready for the work of today? You will be bringing the firewood to the West Lodge, and covering its framework with those grass mats and lodge covers that are

428

*in the storeroom. Tonight you will be singing for the Owl
Dance, which will be bringing this day to a close many
busy hours from now. Let's go! Let's go!*

*Good morning, all you women! Help to get your men
started so that everything will be ready this evening. We're
going to have a good time together—happy days, Holy
days. Hoka hey! Bring your berries and meat to the Camp
Hall for cooking—let us have a good feast tonight. Hurry
up! Hurry up!*

Someone pulls aside the door curtain and calls to me,
interrupting my involvement in the wake-up song that
Songbird is loudly in the midst of. It is Two Crows, looking in.

Can you help me with my work, he asks. *I have sent
someone out to gather the rocks for the sweat lodge, and
I will send out another young boy to cut the willows. I
would like you to help me in putting the sweat lodge up
and in preparing the altars and Holy lodges. Will you
come?*

*Yes: yes! I'd love to—perhaps you can teach me some
things about the ceremonies,* I eagerly reply. Since Two
Crows is a man younger than I, I will be able to ask him
about things that are not proper to ask the older man
with whom I visit.

Two Crows is waiting outside, sitting on the ground in
the early morning Sunlight, whistling quietly to himself.
Other People in the camp can be heard talking, coughing,
and singing, as the households prepare for the day. The
new baby in Low Horn's lodge is having its wake-up
exercise of crying while its parents are probably trying
to get themselves ready, as well, for the day. As soon as
I finish braiding my hair I will be ready to go with Two
Crows to see what is to be done. None of us will be eating
anything until the feast this evening. We are getting ourselves prepared for the four days of fasting, which will
begin after these first four days of the opening ceremony.

Two Crows is still whistling as I step out through the

doorway. The camp has a feeling about it—a vibration— of many Spirits coming together for some major event. The lodges look particularly bright and cheerful—not an unhappy note anywhere. Songbird has mounted a Horse and is now riding around the inside circle of the camp, still singing his songs. He is dressed in all manner of elegant plumage—looking like a proud creature of the Forest and Mountains, parading before his peers. A head-dress of black-tipped Eagle feathers covers his head, tufts of Horsehair floating away from each feathers' tip. White

Weasel skins hang from the sides of the strip of quillwork which seems to join the feathers together over his fore-head. More Weasel skins hang from the arms and legs of his Buckskin leggings and shirt. The smooth looking Buckskins gleam shiny yellow in the bright light—partly because they have been rubbed with a light-yellow colored Earth that is found under a cutbank by the far side of the lake. Some use the yellow Earth to paint their faces, others color their moccasins and even their tipis with it. Songbird has painted his Buckskin suit with it, simply by rubbing it gently into the grain of the hides. He has a bead-embroi-dered martingale hanging over his shoulders of his favorite Buckskin-colored gelding—small bells jingle from the ends of the tassels at each side. A number of People around the camp circle have paused to admire the Old Man as he gaily makes his rounds on the Horse—a colorful and glistening sight that gives Us strength and inspiration.

Let us go over to Little Bear's and see if one of his boys can go out and cut the willows for us. We can, mean-

while, gather some firewood and prepare the ground around the lodge, says Two Crows, *while we walk towards the lodge of Little Bear.* Inside the lodge several voices can be heard singing a slow song, while others inside are making various sounds and noises getting themselves ready. The songs are being practiced for the Owl Dance, tonight.

Hello, Father, says Two Crows respectfully to Little Bear. *Can one of your boys help us for a short while to obtain the willows for the sweat lodge,* he asks. Little Bear smiles and looks around at his boys, of whom there are several. His wife cheerfully volunteers the services of Horse Rider, their youngest son, who is braiding a long Buckskin rope that is tied to one of the lodge poles. She says to him, *You go and give some help to these People, what they are going to be doing is very important. Us older ones have to get that West Lodge all ready for tonight, and you would probably just be in our way there. Here, you take along this big knife of mine—and be careful that you don't cut yourself! You'll be needing that if you're going to go and cut all those willows.*

Work well, says his father while giving him a pat on the shoulder. In a moment Horse Rider is out of the lodge and walking along side of us, acting like a pony that has just been let out of a corral. Two Crows tells him what he is to do, and he listens very carefully: *We need one hundred good willow sticks for this sweat lodge,* he explains, *for a Holy sweat lodge must be strong, and it must be large enough to have room for many People. Get straight sticks about the thickness of your fingers, and twice as tall as you are. Trim the leaves and branches off where you find them, so there won't be a mess here in the camp. We will help you to cut the last four—the big, long ones. Now go—we will be in the middle of the camp circle preparing the ground. Bring the sticks there.*

Horse Rider heads for the trail which will take him over to the point of the small bay, where there is a dense growth of willows on the shore and some ways out into the shallow water. Two Crows, meanwhile, is leading us over to the storeroom to pick up some things we will be needing for our work. Two women are just leaving the storeroom with some of the camp's cooking gear—including a large brass kettle and a metal tea pot that is as large as a bucket.

Inside the storeroom everything is cool and quiet. The storeroom is actually a large building made from massive Cedar logs. A heavy door made from rough-hewn planks is the common way of entering the building, but there is also a double set of doors—one set on the inside and one on the outside—that are suspended from sturdy runners. These open wide enough for eight People to walk through side by side. The lighting inside is dim, but covers every part of the building. It comes in through numerous small window openings that have been placed around the log walls. A thin-scraped sheet of rawhide covers each window opening and is well tacked down all around, to keep out air, moisture, and smaller visitors who might wish to take up living among the stores, there, and eat up some of what is being carefully preserved.

The building is a maze of framework, inside, on which rests a great variety of material stacked in many separate layers to allow air circulation, Two Crows tells me. Some wooden canoes rest upside down near the ground. A dozen, or so, wooden spoked wheels are stacked nearby. Numerous boxes and crates line the floor space, while countless tools and implements hang from thongs fastened along the walls. Two Crows walks over to a section of farming tools and takes down a heavy metal rod—one end sharpened like the point of a spear. From a suspended pole covered with thongs and laces he takes a handful of thin leather strips.

Now we can start, he says as he heads for the doorway, *we will come back here later to get some other supplies*. I close the latch of the heavy door and hurry to catch up to Two Crows as he walks to the center of the camp. From one side of the camp is coming Horse Rider—already carrying a bundle of cut willow stems.

Every year we build a new sweat lodge, says Two

432

Crows, as he locates the place that we will work. *We take down the old one when the ceremony is over,* he continues, *and make a new one to be strong enough to hold all in camp. We make our family sweat lodges from the willows when this lodge is taken down.*

First I will dig the hole for the rocks—you can just watch me for a few moments, he tells me, as he begins lifting out pieces of sod with the pointed shovel. He is taking each shovelful to a place that is directly East of where he is digging. *This will form the Sacred Mountain of Earth,* he explains about the place where the sods are being piled. *This Holy lodge is so large that I must dig four holes—each of them will be filled with red-hot stones, in order to thoroughly heat the lodge up.*

In just a short while Two Crows has finished digging the four holes— all of them equal in size and round in shape —*to represent the roundness of the Earth and the Universe,* he explains. The Sacred Mountain is quite large now, and Two Crows tells me, *we will prepare the Mountain later on, before the ceremony.*

With a long stick Two Crows carefully traces a line in the dirt—a large oval that goes way around the four holes which he just dug. Handing me the metal rod with the sharp point he says: *You make the holes in the ground, along that line, while I sharpen the willow stems and cut them in the right length.* He tells me to make the holes about the width of my foot apart from each other. There will be very many stems making up the framework of this sweat lodge!

As I proceed around the oval with the metal rod, driving it down as hard as I can, pulling it out, and driving it down again, Two Crows follows me. He inserts the sharpened end of a willow stem in each hole that I dig, and soon we have a small corral of upright willow stems, the ends of some are waving in the breeze as they point their way up towards the Sky.

Now he brings forth the small bundle of leather thongs

433

and asks me to bend one of the willow stems from my side into the center. He bends one the same way, from the other side, and we tie them together with a thong where they meet. This we must do to all the parallel willow stems, until we have a long, arch-like framework over the marked out area. . . .

Two Crows has gone out and cut the eight main willow stems—big, long ones that are used to tie the lodge frame down length-wise. Four of the big stems are put into the ground at each end, then bent toward the center and tied together. Next, we tie the long stems cross-wise to the many short ovals, to make the willow framework very solid.

The rocks have all been brought beside the lodge by the boy who was sent out by Two Crows earlier. Some distance directly out from the doorway of the lodge Two Crows now digs another hole—quite a large one. Together we start a fire in it, which Two Crows tells me to tend while he goes to the West Lodge and scatters Pine branches on the floor and arranges the altar in back for tonight's gathering. I have to begin putting the rocks into the fire when it gets hot enough. . . .

Sometime later in the afternoon the People begin gathering at the sweat lodge, bringing with them their robes and some other hide or mat to contribute as a temporary covering—for the length of the Ceremonial Days. Two Crows has sent some boys out to gather armloads of Sage, which he is spreading over the sweat lodge floor. The rocks are all glowing red inside of the big, hot firepit. As soon as Two Crows finishes with the flooring, the People begin crawling through the doorway and finding their seats inside the lodge—men to the right and women to the left, and children with their mothers or fathers. Two Crows and I stay behind to pass in the many rocks—four sets of four fist-sized rocks are placed in each of the four pits inside the lodge.

Hot air comes drifting out of the lodge—hot, burning Air. The People pass out their robes, which we lay in two piles by the sides of the door, before we enter the lodge ourselves. After the door coverings are tightly pulled in place we find room for ourselves and sit down. The Earth beneath our bare skin feels cool and damp compared to the heat and dryness of the air around us.

Songbird sits at the rear of the lodge, two large Eagle wing fans in his hands. The four rock pits look like underground lanterns—red eyes of the Earth. Everything in the lodge is illuminated by a deep, red glow. The tanned bodies of the People fade into the dark lodge coverings behind them, but the whiteness of their teeth and their eyes gleams brightly all around. Songbird begins singing: *He-Ja, He-Ja-Ha. He-Ja-Ha. Hey-Ja-Ha; He-Ja. He-Ja-Ha, He-Ja-Hi-Yo. . . .* His Grandson, Dreaming-of-Elk, is sitting near him in front of one of the rockpits, takes up the tune in time to the dipping of four cups of water, which he splashes on the rocks before him. *Tushhhhhhh. . . . Tushhhhhhh. . . . Tushhhhhhh. . . . Tushhhhhhh,* is the sound of the meeting of those Powerful Elements— Water and Fire. Clouds of steam rise up from the rocks with each splashing—up to look for an escape into the Air above. Finding only the lodge's thick coverings, the steam clouds billow out and begin to engulf the lodge's occupants, who are still bathing in a red glow. Sways-with-the-Wind sits at the next pit after Elk. He is a shy young boy, so his singing can barely be heard above the voices of the other two, and the splashing of water on the rocks that are before him. More steam rises into the Air, and hangs over us like a nighttime fog. Good Man is next in line, and he joins in the song and splashes water. His rocks sizzle and pop, and he smiles with satisfaction, as the steam spurts upward.

The song ends after four cups of water have been splashed on the rocks in each of the pits. For some time we all sit quietly, barely being able to breathe the thick, wet air, and feeling the sweat running along the skins of our bodies as though we were in a shower. Songbird signals for the curtain to be opened, and a number of People crawl outside to sit in the warm, fresh air for a spell. The steam pours out through the doorway and soon the inside of the lodge is cool again. The others come back in, and we start the singing and steaming again. . . Four times we do this. By the fourth time I can't tell anymore whether I am inside or out, or how many others are still present in the lodge. Some of the People have remained outside after the first or second round—especially some of the women with children. Now the rest of us go outside and rush over to the mouth of the creek, where it flows into the lake. Amid sighs and loud *Ahhh's* all the People jump into the knee-deep water and lay down, to feel the coolness of the creek passing over their bodies. I close my eyes and put my head under water, facing upstream, I feel like I am falling through endless Space after I let go of my hold on the weeds growing at the bottom. My knees scrape the bottom and I regain my Earth-consciousness, as the current has flowed me to the edge of the lake. I get back up on my hands and knees and gasp for breath, my head just above the water's surface. I have to stand up to breathe as full as my lungs demand—though I almost pass out again while getting up. Hardly a word is spoken by anyone, as the People continue to bathe, or sit at the water's edge and gaze out across the lake, or wander back up to their robes by the sweat lodge. . . .

Not long after the sweat is finished the People all gather again—wrapped in their robes and seated in their places inside the West Lodge. The lodge looks like a tipi that was cut in half and had two parallel walls placed between the two tipi halves. It is built on a framework of tipi poles, and covered with several old lodge covers and numerous mats made of Tule reeds woven together. Along the top runs an open space that lets us see the Sky and allows the smoke from the fire within to escape. The fire is built in a narrow pit the length of a man. The women are preparing the meat which has been roasting over hot coals for part of the afternoon—choice pieces of Deer, Elk, and Moose. Two large kettles, also hanging over the coals from cross-sticks, contain the thick, bubbly substance that we call Berry Soup. Mom once explained to me that the People consider their Berry Soup as a Holy Meal, because their forefathers in the long ago, once, survived a whole Winter on soups made from their dried Berries and Roots, while all the game had left their country for some mysterious reason. She said that the Soup is usually made by boiling water and adding many Service Berries and some cleaned Bitterroots. Pieces of Wild Turnip are put in to thicken the Soup. The roasted meat, the cut-up pieces of vegetables, and the Berry Soup represent all the Holy Food of the People, and makes an especially relishing menu after a Powerful sweat. After our bowls are filled we all take out one berry and hold it aloft, saying our prayers of thanks, for the Good Food, the Good Lodges, the Good Gathering, and the Good Life. Then we put the berries down at the edge of the firepit as a spiritual offering to our Mother Earth. Those who are sitting further back pass their berries up to those near the firepit.

.... After eating we all pick up our bowls and any scraps left over, and clean up around ourselves. We will all go home to our lodges to get dressed and comb our hair—to rejoin here later for the singing and dancing. We leave the Lodge looking as it did before we came in....

I join my own family in walking back to the tipi. We are all elated, filled with food, and excited about the upcoming dance. Father says he is going to take a short nap and I think I will join him. That will give the women a chance to get dressed without us in their way....

.... Father awakens me to tell me that the women are already gone to the West Lodge and that the singing there has begun. We both feel a bit foolish for napping so long and must now dress in a hurry so as not to get there too late to be inconspicuous. I get out the rawhide that is folded into a large envelope and contains my fancy dress outfit that the women of the household have been making for me during the past weeks. I take out my new Buckskin leggings, shirt, and aprons and put them on. I've tried the outfit on several times while it was being made, so I know how it goes on and how it fits. It would take me too long to comb and braid my hair, so I'll just brush it well and wear it loose. Father hands me a white Eagle tail feather with a black tip and a tuft of hair.

You should wear this in your hair, he says. *It will represent your great experience of coming to us, here, in this Valley. All of Us, here, know that a single feather in a man's hair means that one event in his Life has been particularly strong for him.* That seems like a most spiritual reason for wearing such a feather, so I gladly tie it to a bunch of hair at the crown of my head. It will sway gently as I move, and its tuft of hair will float in the Air. After I put some garters around my leggings at my ankles, and tie my moccasins, I am ready to go. I'll carry along the beaded sash which was given to me by Two Crows— his great-grandfather had it given to him by the chief of some Eastern tribe as a token of friendship long, long ago. Father is adjusting his Eagle feather headdress. When he sees that I am ready to go he motions me out.

An evening breeze is blowing outside, making the Eagle feather on my head tug at the bunch of hair that it is tied to. The fringes on my shirt and leggings ripple up and down and back and forth as I take each step, while the softness of the Buckskin hides gives me comfortable security and protection from the breeze. The feathers on Father's headdress shimmer in the breeze and rustle quietly—much like the sound made by a gliding Eagle's wings when he sails by with the Wind on a noiseless day. Father is wearing his Buckskin suit, also, and the fringes make his whole body appear to be flowing along. He carries a stick with a single Eagle feather, to remind him of some dramatic experience during his life.

As we approach the West Lodge we can see that the dance has not yet formally begun—since a number of People are still standing around outside. They all have their robes wrapped about their bodies to keep back the chilling evening air. The long fire inside lights up the lodge brightly, and much talking and warmup singing can be heard. I will stay outside for a few more moments and let Father go in by himself, at first. . . .

Some while later the dance is about to be started. Everyone sits down in the same places as they did for the earlier eating—men on one side, women on the other.

438

Little Bear is handed a filled pipe with which he says a prayer. He then lights the pipe and passes it down the row of men, each one smoking four turns, then passing it on to the next one. The last man passes the pipe back up towards the first man, no one smoking while it goes that way except for young Stone Pipe. As the Keeper of the Sacred Pipe Stem he has inherited the ancient custom of honor by being allowed to smoke from pipes no matter from which direction they are passed to him, as he is spiritually also smoking for the Sacred Stem. The others will only smoke pipes passed to them from their right, in the direction that Sun travels around the circle of the Universe.

While one pipe has been travelling down the row of men, another one has been going down the line of women. Little Bear's woman Fine Sewing lit the pipe for that side and said a prayer with it. The pipe was then passed down to the last woman in the line, who smoked first, so that it could be passed to each smoker in the proper direction.

With the smoking completed Little Bear walks over to the center of the lodge and sits down in front of his large drum, where three of his boys have already seated themselves. A large cup of water is handed to Little Bear, who takes a drink and passes it on to the other boys. The tall one, called Black Eyes drinks a swallow, then takes another mouthful and spurts some of it over his left shoulder, then his right shoulder, then on to the ground between his legs, and the rest into the palms of his hands, which he briskly rubs together. With an almost-coughing tone he makes the sound, *Huh, huh, huh, huh!* Then he rubs his palms over his glossy hair, giving a final and triumphant *Huh!* as he tosses his dangling locks behind his shoulders, shows his white teeth in a big grin, and winks real conspicuously to one of the younger girls seated by her mother in the line of women. Some of the women giggle, and most of the men chuckle from amusement. Meanwhile, Low Horn begins the singing with a drawn-out opening note that is several scales higher than the screaming of most women. Then the drumming begins—rapidly, at first, as the four singers take quick, short strokes with their springy drumsticks. A moments pause in the shrill note and the rapid drumming. . . . then all four begin chanting in a medium-high tone to the loud and steady thumping of the drum sticks.

Father gets up, nodding to two of his friends, Suma and Pemmican and the three slowly begin dancing. Little Bear lays down his drumsticks, picks up an Eagle's wing fan, and wraps his Bear robe around him. He joins the other three men, and the four together now circle around the inside of the Lodge in front of the People—they are the honorary dancers who usually lead off in the dancing. All four men dance in a stately fashion—not hopping about like the younger ones will do. They hold their bodies erect and turn their heads from side to side with each step. And their footsteps—their feet move with barely more than a shuffle. Yet, it is a very smooth shuffle that causes each leg to give a slight upward jerk with every drumbeat. Sometimes the men shuffle a bit towards the right, then a bit towards the left, all the while making a smooth and casual circle around the dance ring.

After the honorary dancers have made four circles around the Lodge others begin to get up and start dancing. The dance is just warming up, so no one moves very quickly. Some People stand up and just dance in place, by bouncing their bodies lightly to the beat of the drum, and swaying from side to side. I stand up and join them, and soon the desire for dancing begins to circulate along with my blood. . . .

Little Bear has rejoined his sons in the singing and drumming, and the song is a more lively one. A number of People still remain standing in one place—or dancing within a small area close to their seats. Others are beginning to loosen their bodies a bit—soon they will be involving themselves fully in the ever-increasing tempo and enthusiasm of the drumming and singing. . . .

What a colorful scene is made by the People in their beautiful costumes. Buckskins, furs, feathers, beads, and bells are everywhere. Each one is wearing these things which he or she feels expresses their life with Nature. And each one dances to his own thoughts of the Natural experiences which he has had.

There is old Big Snake, wearing his ancient Buffalo horn headdress. It was given to him long ago by his father Eagle Plume, who made it from the skin and horns of the first Buffalo Bull he ever brought down—years ago, when Buffalo Bulls were still common in the country below. He is blowing on a bone whistle to which are attached the feathers of various Birds that he has dreamed of. His dance imitates the slow, boasting movements of the leading bull in a Buffalo herd. At intervals he blows on his whistle, bends his head low, and prepares a mock charge at one of the other People dancing nearby. Big Snake is a good-natured old man, and everyone is cheered by his antics.

Young Horse Rider is involved in a more lively dance —lifting his knees up high as his feet tap the ground in time to the drumbeats. He turns constantly to the right or

left, moving in and out of the dancing group with ease. On his head is a roach made from the hair of a Porcupine, which ripples in the Air from the constant movement. Compared to the measured steps of old Big Snake the rapid movements of Horse Rider make him look like a lively calf running around a serious bull. Yet, both bull and calf seem to be flowing with the same rhythm—dancing to the same tune.

Behind the circle of drummers stands Low Horn's woman, quietly watching the People's involvement with her husband's singing and drumming. The drumsticks bounce far into the air between each beat. As one the sticks come back down to strike the surface of the skin drum another blow, another loud *thump* which joins the ones before and the ones after to make a rapid steady *Thum, thum, thum, thum,* in rhythm with everyone's heart beat. Low Horn's woman is holding the sturdy

442

carrier into which their small child is safely strapped. Elaborate beadwork covers its Buckskin bag as well as the Buckskin which is stretched over the long, oval backboard. She often carries the backboard over her shoulders by a strap which is fastened to its backside. The white background of the beadwork contrasts brightly with the yellow-brown color of the smoked Buckskin from which her dress is made. The top of the dress is covered with numerous teeth from Elk which Low Horn has brought home for their meals—each tooth represents a hunting experience and a lot of good meals.

Whenever the drummers and singers take a break someone gets up before the group to tell some brief, old-time story, or to explain about some new article of dress that is being worn for the first time tonight, or to sing some song for the entertainment of the People. The others take seats around the floor, or step outside for some cool air or a short walk.

At intervals between the fast and energetic dance numbers come the slower Owl Dance tunes. They are recognizable by their hard-soft, beats and by the reaction among the People. These are the dances where men and women join together in couples—arms around each others' waists—as they dance sideways in a circle around the lodge. As each Owl Dance progresses, the various couples join others, until a long, Snake-like line forms and coils its way back and forth around the lodge. The dancers move to the left, picking up their left feet first and stomping them down in time to the loud beat. With the soft beat they drag their right feet behind, thus taking short steps while their bodies rise and fall with each beat. When all the People have joined in one line those at the front weave around so that they are dancing past those at the rear. Often the Snake is so coiled around the dance floor that all one can see is many smiling faces, bouncing bodies, and tapping footsteps, going to and fro.

Songbird's voice has awakened us early, again. Father and I have just returned from a plunge into the lake to help awaken our bodies. I am rubbing myself dry with the help of my robe. Outside, I can hear the distant splashing of water at the lake, as others awaken themselves likewise. Sun is just about to show His Power over the mountain tops—already His streams of light are making bright the early-morning blue Sky.

Today and tomorrow—the second and third days of the Summer's End Ceremony—we will all be going to the gardens to bring in the Season's harvests. During the afternoons and evenings we will have more drumming and singing—and we will continue to dance. First, we will all be meeting at the Sacred Tobacco Garden. . . .

. . . . The Tobacco plants have been growing all Summer in a small plot of land which juts out into a quiet, tiny bay of the lake near the camp. The soil there is continually damp from the surrounding waters, while Sun's rays are able to reach the plants all day long. Yet, the spot is so protected by low, surrounding bluffs that the strong breezes which regularly blow across the lake pass right over the top of the plants without causing them any harm.

The garden is divided up into numerous small plots—each one belonging to one of the camp's families. Each plot has a spiritual guardian—represented physically by one or more tiny dolls made from Buckskin and hair. The little dolls are attached to long, carved sticks which are planted in the ground at the head of each plot. Bells and chimes made of shells and beads are attached to other sticks planted around the plots, and little colored pieces of cloth and ribbon wave gaily in the air. At first glance the scene looks like a carnival for little People held in a forest of towering, green plants, with banners waving and musical notes coming from the different things hanging on sticks.

Only the upper parts of the People are visible as they wander among the Sacred Plants in the garden—each family coming together at the head of their own plot. Everyone present plucks a leaf from one of the Plants

444

and holds it aloft, towards the warm-shining Sun. Someone begins to pray and then we all join in—each one giving thanks for the goodness of the past Summer and for the wealth of the Sacred Tobacco crop. When we finish praying we put our leaves into the soil around the carved sticks with the guardians attached—a symbolic sharing of the crop with its spiritual guardians. Then everyone begins to pull up the plants to the tune of a song that is started by Songbird. The words say: *Sun, Above is Holy. Earth, Below is Holy. These Sacred Plants are Holy. Our smoking will be Holy. Our lives will be Powerful.*

The plants are pulled up firmly and carefully, so that the roots will remain attached. The soil is then carefully shaken from the roots and the plant is placed in a pile. It is saddening to watch the disappearance of that beautiful garden of swaying, living green. But it is pleasant to think of the many spiritual gatherings and ceremonies which will be started by the sacred smoking of these plants.

Mother has explained to me what we will do with the plants when we get them back home. The roots will be cut off and washed. They keep well and will be used to season our Winter's cooking. The seeds will then be carefully picked and placed in special Buckskin pouches— to be saved for later plantings. Father told me that some years the plants grow too slowly to give mature seeds, so that the People must always be very careful with their seed gathering and try to keep enough to last for several years. The rest of the plant is then hung upside down from the ceiling of the lodge until it becomes dry and brittle. The leaves are then carefully removed and ground up inside of large pouches, where they will be kept until needed for smoking. The stems are cut up into small pieces and mixed with the leaves of the Bearberry plant to be used for just everyday smoking. Sometimes the stems are put in with fried foods to be used for seasoning, though they are too tough and bitter to be eaten.

After all the plants have been pulled up—even the little ones that have spent most of the Summer hidden in the shade of the tall plants—the head of each household brings out the family's Eagle plume offering to the Spirits who are at the Sacred Garden all year. One of Little Bear's sons is selected to take all the plumes down to the shore of the lake and place them in the ground in a row. Before the Winter snows come the men will return to the Garden with loads of manure, which they will give to the Earth in exchange for what they have taken today. Then they

will each take up their Eagle plume offering and plant it in the center of their family plot. Every year the People have taken their Sacred Tobacco harvest this way—and every year they have had a successful crop.

With a Powerful feeling of one-ness we return to our lodges, everyone's arms filled with huge bunches of plants, their wispy roots dangling down towards their Mother Earth for the last time—their bright green leaves swaying in the breeze once more, before they will be turning into smoke and joining the breezes forever, at later times.

. . . . Tonight we dance, again. The dance is to start outside of the big Earth Lodge before the coming of evening. Little Bear will lead the singing—the drumming will be done on the Turtle drums that were made by Suma during one of his visits to the mountains. They are made of the thick part of a Moose hide—taken from behind the neck. They were cut out in the shape of the Turtles that Suma saw in his dream, and then sewn up while still wet. Sand was stuffed inside of them so that they would keep their shape until dry. Little Bear's sons will be taking

turns standing before the entryway of the Earth lodge and giving prayers of thanks while holding the smoking pipe. While praying, Little Bear told me, they will be thinking of the many good songs and dances that the People have enjoyed during the past year, and they will be asking for another year of such goodness. Later on, as darkness comes, the singers will move inside the Earth lodge, where we will all gather for our evening meal and for more Owl dancing. . . .

. . . . Tomorrow we are to harvest the fruit from the trees and the vegetable from the garden—it has been a very successful Season and we will have a large harvest. Much of the crop will be dried for Winter use. Some of it will be stored in the underground cellar, where it will keep as it is. Some of it will have to be eaten within a short time after the ending of the days-long Ceremony. The harvest will be prepared during the four days of the Sun Dance, by those who are not taking a direct part in that ceremony. The preparing will be done around the sacred shelter lodge inside of which the Sun Dance itself will be going on. I have not yet been told much about the Sun Dance Ceremony, except that it will begin on the day after Stone Pipe opens his Bundle and brings out the Sacred Pipe.

This is the fourth day of the Summer's End Ceremony —the day that Stone Pipe is to open his Bundle and take out the Sacred Pipe Stem, so that we can all give prayers of thanks for the good Summer, and the plentiful harvest,

447

and that we can all encourage each other to look forward to a good Winter.

All night long Stone Pipe's voice has been drifting across the bay into the camp. He has been praying and singing while he is on top of the rock cliff that faces the camp from across the water. He will soon begin his walk back to camp to lead in the Holy Ceremony. Two Crows has been preparing the double lodge in which the ceremony will be held. The double lodge is made from two sets of lodge poles built up in such a way as to take two regular lodge covers—thus forming one oblong lodge that is large enough to seat everyone comfortably while still having enough room for the sacred dancing which will be a part of it. Mother is just giving me some of her robes to take over to the big lodge to use for making couches for the People. I will take them over and help Two Crows with his duties. . . .

. . . . Some time has already passed since Songbird went around the camp playing Stone Pipe's sacred flute and calling out to the People to assemble in the double lodge. Everyone has come in and taken a seat among one of the two rows of People. In the center, at the West end of the lodge, sits Stone Pipe. Songbird sits at his left and the Sacred Bundle rests on a pile of furs between them. Stone Pipe has been telling us the story of the Dreams which have been directing him in assembling the Sacred Bundle, and he is just now telling about the Sacred Pipe Stem that is kept within it:

. . . . *So my father followed the instructions of his Dream and went into the Mountains to hide the Sacred Pipe Stem in a cave. He hiked for four days before he reached the top of Chief Mountain, fasting the whole time. He carried the Pipe Stem tied across his back, and brought with him only a blanket, his knife, and a sack of Pemmican to eat on the way home. Several times he encountered Grizzly Bears on the trails along the high, barren slopes of the mountains. Each time he took the Pipe stem from his back and held the Bundle out to give the Bears a smoke, singing one of the Pipe's ancient Power Songs. Always the Bears let him pass without harm.*

Just below the flat top of Chief Mountain my father
found the cave—and just then the Winds, which had been
increasing, began carrying drops of rain which quickly
turned into a torrent. My father found safety inside the
cave and looked out at the Lightning ceremony which was
taking place in the gray and black Sky. He was exhausted
and quickly became overpowered—His Spirit left his body
there and travelled on a fabulous journey. He travelled
ahead in Life and saw scenes which were not to occur for
many years, yet.

The first thing he saw was the approach of countless
People coming Westward across the Plains. The People
were similar to the ones that had, by that time, already
been building cabins and towns here and there in our Old

Country. But they were thousands of times more numerous—swarming like flies over the Land so that the Land was barely visible any longer. In between these hordes of People my father was able to get glimpses of the Land, and it looked frightening—the many feet and hooves and wheels had broken down the bushes, scraped all the trees, smashed all the grasses, and left muddy ruts and tears in our Earth Mother's skin that he could hardly bear to see. He saw what happened to the camps of our People—they were knocked over and the pieces were scattered all over —only those People survived who joined the masses and moved along with them. Here and there a handful of others were saved—usually those who were off on some sidehill or up some mountain seeking visions or otherwise involved in Holy Thoughts.

My father was shown that the Spirit of the Old People would be lost unless some of it was taken up into the mountains—to some remote area where it would be safe. Our own valley, here, was the one he saw as the safe place for the Spirit to remain. He saw the closing of the mountain pass—our only gate—which he correctly predicted for the People before it happened. He saw our People living in Harmony with Nature, here. And he foresaw that someday the thoughtless mass of new People would begin to think again. He foresaw that the Spirit of the Old People would come back to Life someday in the Persons of the Young People, everywhere. He said that when that Spirit was to be reborn, and not until then, would we, as the Keepers of that Spirit's living Powers, again come in contact with People outside of our Hidden Valley in the Mountains. He said "a tiny hole will burst in the dam of this Sacred Reservoir of our Spirit—a tiny hole in the form of a Person. And that Person shall be carrying the Spirit of Me and shall have the Power to distribute All the Power which has guided our Old People through their lives. And when that Person comes," my father said, "he shall dance the Sun Dance with you and during those four days I will let him know who I am, what Power I have to give him, and how he will have to pass that Power on to the many who will come after him from his part of the World, seeking It." That is what my father said, my rela-

*tives, and that is the reason why this Summer's End Cere-
mony will be the most Holy and Powerful of All the ones
we have had, for the time has come for Our Power to go
forth and bring Happiness throughout the Land, wherever
it is needed. The tiny hole has burst and our reservoir is
now connected with the outside World!*

The howling of a Wolf somewhere across the lake brings
the startling reality of Natural Life back to everyone's
Minds—not a sound has been made since Stone Pipe
finished speaking. Now Stone Pipe looks up with a smile
and says:

*My father's sacred guardian was the Wolf—whenever
he was in need for the Wolf's power he gave the Wolf's
howl. His Spirit is with us now.*

I suddenly have an immense feeling of insignificance—
my own thoughts seem petty and small. At the same time
I feel as though the Earth is balanced on my head and
my arms could stretch out endlessly across the Universe.
What Power there is in existence to cause all of this to
happen. As nothing is the human body, with its limitations,
when compared with the limitless expanse that makes up
the realm of the Mind. Perhaps just a minor test to see
if our Universal Minds can escape the confinements of
our Earthly bodies.

From two large, skin sacks behind him Stone Pipe
brings out several handfuls of rawhide rattles of the kind
that I once saw him make. He sews together two pieces of
wet rawhide cut out with necks for handles. Through the
necks he pours sand and pounds it down with a short
stick until the main part of the rattle looks like a round
bulb. After the rawhide dries in that shape he pours the
sand back out, inserts a few pebbles, and puts the stick
inside the neck to make a stronger handle. Each of the
rattles is covered with Sacred Red paint. He passes the
rattles around until most everyone has one. He also brings
out some bunches of dried and cleaned Animal hooves,
fastened to long buckskin thongs which are tied together
at one end. They are used as rattles, also, and their jingling

sounds can be heard while they are being passed from hand to hand among the People.

. . . . And now we are all singing the Holy Songs in time to the beating of the rattles—Stone Pipe and Songbird are leading each song. Dozens of rattles at once: *chk, chk, chk,* in harmony. Dozens of voices chanting the tunes that we have often sung together in the past, while Stone Pipe and Songbird add the words about the holiness of our thoughts, our lives, and our Spirits. After the fourth song Stone Pipe lays down his rattle and turns towards the Sacred Bundle, though he continues to sing with the rest of us. This is the song that we always sing when sweat bathing, but Stone Pipe adds some words to it this time:

> *You stand up, you take me, you untie me. I am Powerful;*
> *You stand up, you take me, you untie me, I am Strong!*

He sings the words as though they were coming from the Bundle to him, while he reaches towards the knot at the end of the Bundle's buckskin thong. Once he reaches for it. . . . twice he reaches. . . . three times. . . . and the fourth time he takes a hold of it and gives it a quick jerk which brings the knot loose. He unwinds the long thongs and stands up with just the Sacred Pipe Stem Bundle in his hands—the skin of a Wolf wrapped about it so that it cannot be seen.

Songbird, meanwhile, has taken a glowing coal from the fireplace with his Sacred Tongs made from the forked branch of a berry bush. He sprinkles some of the Sweet Pine needles on the coal, while the song still goes on. For a moment the smoke from the needles wavers just above them, then it spirals hurriedly up into the air and passes throughout the lodge, the wonderful sweet scent brings happiness into our bodies and good thoughts into our minds. Everyone grasps a handful of the Holy Smell and brings it to his heart to signify the becoming of one with the goodness and the heart.

452

Stone Pipe passes the Sacred Pipe over the smoke four times, and is now getting back down on his knees to bring the Holy Stem out from its wrappings of skin and fine, ancient cloths. Meanwhile, he sings the words:

Man, you must say it, my Pipe it is Powerful;
Man, you must say it, my Pipe it is Strong!

He lifts the Sacred Stem from its last covering and holds it up in the Air for All to behold. Its covering of countless, white Eagle plumes ripples in the vibrations of the Air within the lodge, caused by the Power of our singing and rattling. As smiles of recognition and happiness cover the singing faces, hands reach into the air towards the Pipe and are brought back to rest on breasts. The People take the Power represented by the Pipe into their hearts. Stone Pipe begins a new song, which everyone quickly takes up. He sings the words:

> *There comes the Old Man, he is coming walk-*
>   *ing;*
> *He Ja Ha, He Ja Ha, He Ja He Ja Hey.*
> *He's coming in here, sitting down, that Old Man*
>   *is Powerful!*
> *He Ja Ha, He Ja Ha, He Ja He Ja Hey.*

During this song he dances slowly, with smooth, jerking steps, to the Four Directions, beginning with the East, where Sun rises. At each place he holds the Sacred Stem at arm's length, offering a smoke to the Spirit of that direction by aiming the mouthpiece that way. Next, he dances to the North, where the North Star shines brightly from one place, and where the Powers of Winters dwell. As he dances to the West the words of the song change and tell about the Old Woman, who is coming in to be with the Old Man Spirit, and Us. To the West is Sun's nighttime home, where the other half of the World begins. Finally, he dances toward the South, from where come the warm winds of Summer that help to make everything grow.

After Stone Pipe sits back down with the Sacred Pipe he begins another song, this one with the words:

> *Old Man he says, "let us smoke," It is Powerful!*

He turns the Pipe all the way around once, holding the mouthpiece towards each one of us as it goes around. Then he sings:

> *Old Man, he says, "my old smoke, I do not feel it."*

At this he shakes the Stem four times, so that the Eagle plumes dangling from it sway wildly in the air. The chant continues, and Stone Pipe now sings:

> *Old Man, he says, "my new smoke, I feel it." It is Powerful!*

As the rattling continues with a steady beat and a number of People go on chanting softly, Stone Pipe holds the Sacred Stem close to his head and begins to pray aloud:

HiYo Sacred Stem—All of You Powerful Spirits who are here with us! We thank You for letting us be here all together again, at the end of another good Summer. We are thankful for our good health—our good food—our good homes—our Sacred Valley Home. We ask you to show us always your Powers, Sacred Pipe. Show us your Powers so that we will be inspired to live Holy and that we will have the strength to live well. Give us strength by letting us know that you are always with us—All of you Powers of the Universe—All of you who are Holy. . . .

Stone Pipe asks for continued strength and happiness and talks about the times to come, before the next Summer's End Ceremony in Four Seasons. Then he passes the Pipe to his left, where my father is sitting. Father accepts the Pipe Stem with both hands and, beginning at the top of his head, rubs the Sacred Stem down along each side of his body twice while praying aloud and asking the Powers to be fully with him and help him to keep away from any evil. After he finishes his prayer he, too, passes the Pipe to his left, and so it continues around the lodge, each one saying a prayer loudly or silently and spending some intimate moments with the Ancient Holy Thing.

After the Sacred Pipe has gone all around, Stone Pipe takes it again and stands at the back of the lodge with it—holding it aloft again so that all may see it. My father removes his robe and his shirt and kneels down behind the ancient Buffalo skull in front of the altar. He takes the smoking pipe from the place where it is resting on a frame of willow sticks—mouthpiece toward the Sky so that All the Spirits may feel invited to smoke. He holds the pipe up and calls out:

Great Power of everything! Smoke with us now, as we take the first taste of our Holy Smoking Crop of this Season. Be with us through the coming Seasons and give us good thoughts even when times are hard. Let the glowing warmth of this smoking mixture represent the warmth we will have this Winter. Let the greenness of the unburnt leaves represent the good food we will then be eating. Let this stone bowl represent the strength of our bodies. Let this pipe stem represent the straightness of our lives.

So, now the smoking pipe makes its way around the lodge, passing from Person to Person—each one taking four slow wisps of the Holy Smoke. When the pipe returns to the rear of the lodge father refills it and puts it back in its place against the willow support. Stone Pipe walks forward and places the Holy Pipe Stem against the willow support, next to the smoking pipe. He goes back to his place by the rest of the Bundle and sits down. From behind the Bundle he brings forth his long flute, licks his lips, and puts his mouth against the mouthpiece—exhaling softly to cause the flute to exclaim a quiet and pretty note. The musical sound flows through the lodge like an unseen cloud of smoke, joining us all together in its tonal sea of beauty. We all close our eyes, as Stone Pipe asked us to do earlier, and bring to Mind the dreams which he told us about. The Thoughts evoke visual scenes of his serenades for the many Birds and Animals with which he

visits in his dreams. We All know well the ways of those Birds and Animals, so it is easy to see them now, walking alongside of young Stone Pipe who is playing his Sacred Flute. . . . For some time he plays his Sacred Flute, while I sway my body to the rhythms of his tunes. Some are humming along with the tunes—causing a vibration which makes the music become more than sound, as it goes into my ears and throughout my body and Mind.

The sound of Stone Pipe's Sacred Flute begins to grow dim, but the humming, swaying, and vibrations continue. Stone Pipe makes gentle grunting and growling noises, and I barely open my eyes to watch him lifting up the skin of a Black Bear and swaying back and forth with it, while squatting on his haunches. He sings a song, in rhythm to our humming, and calls out the words:

In Summer I eat Berries; in Winter I stay warm and sleep. My life is good. My Life is Powerful.

He hands the Bear skin to father, on his left, who immediately covers his head with it and quietly begins chanting a song-prayer. Stone Pipe, meanwhile, brings out a Bird skin from his Bundle—the skin of a Loon. He holds the body of the Bird in his left arm—cradled like a baby—and with his right hand he holds the head up in such a way that the Loon seems to be swimming. He moves his arms back and forth and sways with his body and sings these words:

I live where there is water. Water is my Medicine. My water life is good. My water life is Powerful.

With my eyes still barely open I can hardly see Stone Pipe. But I can see the firelight reflecting brightly from the Loon's shiny feathers, while the flickering shadows on the lodge walls begin to look like the continual movement of the water at the edge of a river. I see the Loon swimming back and forth in that water—I begin to feel as though I, too, were swimming along with that Loon in the water.

Father has, meanwhile, passed the Bear skin down the line, to his left. Stone Pipe now gives him the Loon skin, which he also cradles in his arms and sways with in time to his chanting.

Stone Pipe reaches into the Bundle and brings out the shiny, brown skin of a Beaver—the paddle-like tail hanging from the almost-round body. He hangs the skin over his right arm and grasps the tail with his left hand. He slaps the tail on his back and sings the words:

457

*My food is on the Land, but my home is safely
in the Water. My Earth Life is good. My water
life is Powerful.*

Like the Loon, the Beaver seems to come alive as
Stone Pipe moves it back and forth as if it were swimming—now dipping its head down into the Bundle and
bringing back a short stick whose ends have been noticeably Beaver chewed. The Beaver makes the motions of
building himself a home, and I begin to feel as though I,
too, were carrying sticks with me to help him with the
building of his home. . . .

. . . . Stone Pipe continues to bring out the skins of
other Birds and Animals—for each one he makes the
gestures which seem to bring it to life. For each one he
sings the song of its Life Power. The Duck's song says:

*I fly in the Air. I fly where my food is. Air is my Medi-
cine.
My life in Air is Powerful.*

The song of the Grouse says:

*I make my home in the bushes of the forest. That is
where I drum and dance. The forest is my Medicine. My
forest life is Powerful.*

By this time everyone in the lodge has some Bird or
Animal skin and is either humming or praying while swaying with it. Some of the People are making the sounds
of the different Animals, and it feels as though All of
Nature were taking part in this ceremony of Life. Many
Spirits are flowing about and being interchanged from
one to another. The feeling is very Powerful. . . .

.... There will be four of us dancing during the four holy days and nights of the Sun Dance Ceremony. Songbird will be guiding us and Singing in the Night will sit in her sacred booth and fast along with us. After Stone Pipe completed the ceremony with his Sacred Bundle, last night, Songbird asked me if I understood, now, that I was to take part in the Powerful Sun Dance Experience. He told me to eat lightly of the tasty Berry Soup that was served after the ceremony, and to prepare my self spiritually for eating nothing at all during the next four days. I had been planning to eat nothing but light portions of Berry Soup during that time, as everyone else in camp is doing, but I had not planned on going without food altogether. Yet, I know that everyone in the camp will be praying for me and anxiously awaiting my meeting with my Guardian Spirit—Stone Pipe's long-gone father. I could only hope to accomplish that meeting by going without food, as was required by the Ancients in the long ago. So, I knew that I could endure the fast.

It is not yet light outside, but already the camp is astir. Old Songbird will be taking us four holy dancers up on the cliff to await the coming of Sun. The Sky is clear outside and it promises to give us a fine day.

I am to wear only my breechclout and a pair of moccasins and a large fur robe to keep warm my body. As I step outside I see Songbird waiting at the place of the Holy Lodge. It is still fairly dark, but I can see that he, too, is wearing a large fur robe around his body. On his feet are a pair of beautifully-beaded moccasins, and in one hand he carries a large fan made from the wing of an Eagle. His hair is hanging down in loose folds. And perched on top of his head—tied to his hair—is the body of his Guardian Power—a powerful Eagle. Songbird stands silently. The air about him seems more sacred than ever.

I walk over and stand near Songbird, neither of us saying a word in the cool darkness. Stone Pipe joins us a moment later, dressed in robe and moccasins like myself. In a few more moments the other two holy dancers join us from out of the dark—Savaro and Little Bear's son Low Horn. Songbird turns and quietly walks towards the shore of the lake—the four of us following noiselessly.

. . . . After walking all the way around the edge of the bay and then passing through the forest trail, we are now climbing up the last slope to reach the top of the cliff which overhangs the lakeshore. Countless persons have come here to seek visions or just meditate and sing Power Songs in private.

. . . . Three times Songbird calls for the boys outside to lift the door flap—but we don't go outside. The fourth time he pours the remaining water on the stones and tells us to rush into the cold lake water to rinse off. A scramble follows, after which the only sound is the breaking of water as four bodies dive into the deep pool which lies just beyond the sweat lodge. . . . I feel much like a hot ember just taken from a fire and dropped into a vessel of water. . . . the coldness only tingles my skin, but does not enter my body. Quickly I return to the surface and swim to shore. Songbird is standing in the shallow water, rubbing handfuls of it over his body. He is afraid that a sudden plunge into the cold water might be too strong an experience for his aging body, so he rinses off more casually. In just a few moments we all have our moccasins and breechclouts on again as we follow Songbird over and into the Holy Lodge.

Songbird has us sit down in front of the Center Pole, which seems to be supporting the whole lodge as the hub of a spoked wheel. Its top points toward the endless heights of the Sky, while its base is wrapped with seed necklaces and strings of dried berries which the People tied there as symbolic offerings to the Universal Spirits, with good thoughts of having much more of these good things. A dozen steps beyond the Center Pole, in the direction which we are facing, is the Pine bough arbor in which sits Singing In the Night—the spiritual representative for the women. She sits with her head bowed, her unbraided hair hanging loosely over her robe.

Your sacrifice of dancing before this Center Pole for the People, while not eating for the whole time, will give inspiration to All and life-long Powerful thoughts to yourselves, says Songbird, while looking at each of us with his pleasant eyes. *This Pole before you is Your Center of the Universe—Everything radiates from here in equally never—ending paths. All those paths converge right here, and You may choose to walk down any of them that You wish. You must only WISH. During your days and nights here, if anything inspires You along these paths that you will visit, share your inspirations with Us. We will be All Together, here, to give strength to each other.*

Songbird walks over to the arbor and helps Singing In the Night to get up. He lays his robe inside the arbor and picks up his Buckskin pipe bag, which is laying in there. Then the two come and sit before us.

Let your thoughts dwell often on the Power of our being here, says Songbird, *so that your sacrifice will express your gratitude for that Power. Life here, on Earth, would be of no use if it gave us nothing to be grateful for. Be happy that you are here, All of You, and You will have more than enough to be grateful for!*

461

Songbird has filled his pipe and he now rests the stem against the Center Pole, sitting the bowl carefully on the ground beneath it. He rises up and, again, assists Singing In the Night to do so.

Dawn has already made its appearance by the time we finally reach the little clearing at the top of the cliff. Songbird still says nothing—he only turns toward the East and stands in silence. We stand behind him and wait for the golden glow with him.

. . . . Not long—and the Eastern horizon begins its daily, spectacular color show. First orange, then red, then pink, and then orange again, as that ever-present Spirit of Sun comes into view over the mountains.

HiYo Sun—you bringer of warmth and brightness, calls out Songbird in a loud, clear voice. *HiYo Sun— You are the center of our Universe, so vast that we cannot begin to imagine All the Power. Pity Us—we here, on this Earth. We, who are so small and insignificant compared to All that there is. Guide Us to live in harmony with All of the Spirits of the Universe. Make our Paths bright so that we may see the way to goodness. Make our hearts warm so that we will give each time that we take. Shine down on Us, Holy Sun, during each one of these next four days, and be with Us completely while we give up our thoughts to the Power of You. And let that Power remain with us during the coming Seasons.*

With his prayer finished Songbird turns and begins walking down the path towards camp. Silently, the rest of us follow him—down from that high cliff to the shore of the water that can be seen far below. The rocky trail zig-zags back and forth before entering the forest, where it becomes a dirt trail with a more gradual grade. Sun's light filters through the trees and gives the forest and clearings a contrasting appearance of dark and bright. The coolness of the morning forest is already broken in those places where Sun has had a chance to enter. It will be a very warm end-of-Summer day.

Back at the camp the People have already finished covering the framework of the Holy Lodge. Pine boughs have been laid over the roof poles, which radiate outward from the tall center pole—the pole which stands in the middle of the lodge. At their outer points the roof poles are fastened to upright posts, which are attached to other cross-poles, the whole forming a round structure similar to the main camp hall, but without any siding, roofing, or floor, other than the numerous Pine boughs.

Songbird leads the way to the sweat lodge at the edge of camp, down by the lakeshore. Several young boys are there tending the fire which is heating the rocks. The coverings are aready on the lodge, so we crawl through the doorway and sit down around the inside—Songbird sitting at the rear. Unlike the spacious camp sweat lodge this one has barely enough room for the four of us and our leader. We pass our robes outside—and the boys begin pushing red-hot stones in through the doorway with forked sticks. Eight stones is all that Songbird wants them to pass in—eight stones, each the size of a fist. Songbird sings the Sweat Bath Song as he begins to sprinkle water on the hot rocks. . . .

We will have a Holy Smoke after Singing In the Night purifies her body in the sweat lodge, says Songbird, *then we will begin with our dancing.*

The four of us sit quietly while Songbird and Singing In the Night walk down to the lakeshore. There is silence in the camp—all the People are in their lodges awaiting the start of the dancing. Voices can barely be heard, talking in low tones. Only Birds continue to talk about daily life, while flying through the Air and hopping about, unseen, in the many trees around the camp.

After some time comes the distant sound of breaking water—telling us that Singing In the Night has completed her sweat bath. . . . In a while she comes back into the Holy Lodge enclosure with Songbird. She is wearing her robe about her body, her loose hair hanging over it in dark, wet locks.

After we are all seated together again, here in front of the Center Pole, Songbird picks up his pipe and holds it aloft, asking the Spirits everywhere to smoke with us and give us good thoughts. He lights it and puffs briefly, then passes the pipe to Singing In the Night, who does the same. The pipe makes several rounds before it is smoked out—all of us remaining still and silent during the smoking.

To give our Minds and bodies further Power, during these holy times, Songbird tells us, *we will paint ourselves with the Sacred Earth Paint.* He reaches into his pipe bag and brings out a rolled up little sack. The sack contains a quantity of the powder-like red Earth which is found up on the side of one of the mountains, and which the People use at times for painting their faces or covering their holy things.

Songbird reaches into the powdered Earth and brings out a piece of fat, which he begins rubbing between his palms as he gets up on his knees and starts the painting song. The words are:

Sacred Paint—I am looking for it.

He puts the piece of fat back in with the paint and presses one of his greasy, red palms upon his forehead—leaving a bright red imprint which looks like the rising of Sun in the morning. He sings the second song, which says:

Sacred Paint—I have found it. It is Powerful.

At that he wipes his hands all over his face, his hair, his neck, and his arms. Then he turns to Singing In the Night and does the same, singing the second song as he begins painting. He does the same to each of us, in turn, each time singing the second song. After all our faces are covered with the shiny coat of Sacred Paint Songbird removes his robe and motions for us to do the same. He passes the paint-coated piece of fat around so that each of us can rub it well between the palms of our hands, then he motions for us to follow him in rubbing the paint all

464

over our bodies. All the while he continues to chant the second song, without singing the words. When we finish, Singing In the Night puts her robe back on—the rest of us stand up and get ready to begin the dancing. Singing In the Night returns to the arbor and sits back down, hanging her head in prayer. From a rawhide case next to her she takes out an object of upright feathers and hanging skins and beads. She places it on her head. It is the Sacred Headdress which she inherited from the Old Lady who adopted her while still a baby. The headdress has been worn by countless Holy Women in the past, during their People's Summer Ceremonies. Its presence is a constant reminder to Singing In the Night of the example she should make of her Holy Life.

Songbird goes to the arbor and brings out his hand drum—its hide covering stretched tightly across its round, wooden frame from the heat of Sun. On the cover is painted a large red circle, to represent the Power of Sun, and many small, white circles, to represent the Powers of Hail and Thunder. He turns and faces the Center Pole—and Us—and holds the drum up towards the Sky with his left hand. In his right hand he has a slender stick with Buckskin wrapped around its end. Very slowly he lifts his right arm up to bring the drumstick close to the drum—raising his wrinkled face upwards at the same time. His eyes are closed and both of his arms are trembling from excitement and old age.

WHUMM! is the sound that echoes from inside the handdrum out to our eardrums—and all around the camp, as Songbird gives the face of the drum a swift tap with the stick. I look Skyward to peer into the depths of the brilliant blue which surrounds all the Earth.

WHUMM! goes the drum again, with a sharp, penetrating sound that makes my body start as though it had been hit by the drumstick.

WHUMM! goes the drum for a third time and *WHUMM!* again for a fourth time. At the last beat comes a high, shrill scream from within the arbor that can only

465

be the voice of a woman. It is a musical scream—a song from deep within the lungs of Singing In the Night. It tapers off in a tremolo caused by a rapid flicking of the tongue against the upper roof of the mouth—the moving, crying song of a Holy Woman in rhapsody. For a moment there is silence in the camp—even the Birds in the Air and trees have paused to listen to the echoes in the mountains of Singing In the Night's voice which has been carried far and wide by that one deep breath of Universal Power. . . .

. . . . The cry seems to echo and re-echo countless times from canyons and mountain walls around Us and above Us. At last it echoes no more, and Songbird brings his arm down, though leaving his face up towards the Sky, and begins a steady *Whumm, Whumm, Whumm, Whumm* beat on his drum, while Singing In the Night begins singing a most haunting tune of long, drawn-out vocables.

Haaaaaaiiiiiiiii-Jaaaaaaaaaaah. . . . Waaaaaaaaayyyyyy-yyyy-Yooooooooooooooooaahh. . . . her voice floats away with the drum beats. The voices of other women around the camp now join her voice to make a chorus, singing a vibrant mountain song.

After a brief pause in the singing—while only the steady drum beats go on—Singing In the Night begins the song again, joined by the women and then the men, some singing with deep voices and some with the high shrill ones of younger age. The other voices are growing louder and coming closer together as the People of the camp come out from their lodges and walk slowly to the Holy Lodge. . . .

Around the inside of the Holy Lodge the People march, slowly, while the singing and drumming continues—the procession of the Gathering in the Holy Lodge. Only after All the People have come inside and circled the Center Pole several times does the singing stop. The People spread their robes on the ground and sit down upon them. There is silence, again.

Songbird breaks the silence by calling aloud for All to Hear:

We are thinkful, Spirits of the Universe, for Being! We are thankful for Being during these past Seasons, and ask All of you Powers to continue to Let It Be! Continue to give Us the strength to endure, to find Happiness in All and Everything, to lead a Holy Life, and to be who

*we are. . . . These next four days that we will spend fully
with You, Powers of the Universe; let them be Holy Days.
Show Us that You are with us—give Us Your continued
inspiration and guidance. Let It Be. . . . Let It Be good!*

Everyone, here, repeats, *Let It Be Good, Let It Be
Good,* then everyone begins praying loudly—putting into
words the Good Thoughts which are theirs right now for
being here together, in good health.

After the last Person has finished praying, Songbird
speaks again:

*My People, let Us All be happy and strong together, as
we have been in the Past. Let this celebration give Us All
the Power to go on living this Holy Life during the coming Seasons—the Power to accept those things directed
by Nature and to see Everything as being a part of the
goodness which Is the Great Power of the Universe.*

And so begins the drumming again. Others have
brought hand drums, like Songbird's, and are now joining
with him to keep the spiritual rhythm going. The songs,
too, are sung by many voices, while my eyes are still
deep in the blue which colors the vastness Above. . . .

. . . . Much later—I lie down upon my robe which is
spread behind me on the ground. I still keep my eyes on
the vastness Above, where many more Spirits are beginning to make their appearance in the forms of Stars. The
drumming and singing has been going on continually all
afternoon. . . . Going on continually all night. . . . going on
continually all the next morning. . . . the next afternoon.
. . . the next night. . . .

. . . . Dancing—dancing—dancing—looking upward,
forever upward. To where? Endlessly—endlessly, as the
Universe goes on to a Forever that will take Us forever
to experience. . . . giving me a feeling of great insignificance—a grain of sand in the ocean. . . . giving me a feeling of great Power—to be continually surrounded by so
much, that there is no way to come to an end, even if this
insignificant, Earthly body of mine ceased right now to

function. . . . I lie on my robe—feeling as though my body actually IS ceasing to function—only a numbness left, physically, while my Mind traverses the Universe with great, leaping bounds—looking back down at the tiny ball that is Earth—unable to even see this Hidden Valley, much less my body. . . . Now back to Earth and my body again—hearing the call of the drumming and singing—feeling the need of the others in the Holy Lodge for my presence to be there. . . .

. . . . I sit up and look around in the Star-lit darkness—feeling that others are there, but seeing nothing. The drumming and singing seems very distant—like the echoes in the mountains. A faint orange glow shows at the top of the mountains—I think it is in the direction where Sun sets each evening— it is a faint orange glow that looks like liquid, softly undulating as if being stirred by some distant breeze. . . . undulating at the top of the mountains, as if balanced there and making an effort not to flow over. . . . now it seems so far away—again it seems to come so close that I can reach out and dive my hands into it. . . . I reach both of my hands out for it—closer. . . . and closer. . . . and closer it comes, turning brighter orange as it comes near. . . . and a breeze comes with it— the breeze that is causing the undulating, for the breeze and the movement of the orange has a harmonious rhythm. . . . a warm breeze, it is—warm and whistling, it rustles through the Pine boughs that surround me—I can hear them swishing together and flapping against the poles to which they are fastened. . . . stronger it grows—the rushing of that breeze—stronger as the orange glow becomes brighter and continues to come nearer. . . . and still there is drumming and singing around me—somewhere, near or far; I can't tell just where it's coming from. . . . the breeze has now turned into a full Wind, which sounds like a mountain stream as it rushes through the trees of the forest nearby—sounds, like a hundred People whistling and brushing against each other as it passes through the Holy Lodge and causes the pole foundation to creak and sway. . . .

. . . . The singing and the drumming, the howling of the

Wind all around—they seem to be as one, the song is carried by the Wind as though it were coming from the orange glow that now seems to be balanced on top of the Center Pole—an orange glow with no real form and no dimensions. . . . I lean forward—my arms and hands still outstretched—and grasp the Center Pole to steady myself while looking, still, upward. The Pole is warm—very warm—and it is vibrating to the singing. . . . somewhere there is a voice—I can barely hear it—talking, or singing-talking—it is hard to tell which. . . . a voice unlike any I have ever heard before—and it seems to be coming down from Above, down from the top of the Center Pole where the orange glow is still resting and hovering. . . .

Do You feel this Dream of the Sunset? says the voice—suddenly very plainly above the sound of the singing Wind. *Young man, this is the Dream of Your Life—THIS is Your Dream of the Sunset. Hear me well, now, for I will be returning to visit you often, like this. Hear me well, for this is what I say:*

The Power of the Universe has brought You to where you are. All of Us who are no longer physical—it is Our desire to help our ancestors, who are yet on Earth, to enjoy their physical lives to the fullest. You who have bodies can do wonderful things, there on Earth, that we, who are Spirits, can no longer do ourselves. We can only enjoy those things through the bodies of others—and only those others who know our Spirits and accept them. Those of my ancestors who are there with you now, they already know us. But the People at the places where we brought you from, they are often not aware that anything exists beyond their bodies. We can not help them to find strength in their lives, because they do not recognize our guidance—though they are our ancestors as well as the People who are right there, with you. For, only the Great Power of the Universe is everlasting—and we are All a part of that Great Power. If those others destroy their bodies—or even this whole Earth—it will be of no consequence to the Great Power of the Universe—for everything will still be a part of that Great Power. Only the wonderful experience of physical life will be shortened

470

for All who are concerned—their Spirits will join the rest of us in the Universe that much sooner—and they will have that much less happiness to bring with them after they leave their bodies behind.

You, young man, will be going back to your other People, to tell them about the happiness that they can find if they live their lives in harmony with Nature—if they seek to meet and know the many other Spirits who dwell all around them, recognizing the spiritual one-ness of Us All. You will be learning about the Spirits who are guiding others—for All of Us out here in the Universe wish to give guidance to our ancestors back there, on Earth. You will learn about the many other Spirits, and you will tell those who wish to know about Us—the Spirits who will be guiding You.

You must live a simple life—you must live it in accordance to the way we direct you. You will see Us any evening that you sit by yourself, quietly, and watch the ending of the day—for We are the Spirits of the Dream of the Sunset.

The boy who was my son while I lived there, on Earth, is there, now, with You. He has brought back the Sacred Pipe Stem which I once left in the mountains for You— for All of You. Long I have known You would be coming —to give Us your body to use. By your words and your actions we can inspire others to join Us in keeping alive our Spirit on the Earth. For We are Your People—we have brought You to Us because we long ago knew that You felt our guidance. I, too, was once guided to this life by Spirits more Powerful than I could understand. I once lived far to the South of where we are now. But the Spirits of our ancestors, even then, felt need of someone on Earth to help keep their Spirit alive. I, too, had a vision and was given the Dream of the Sunset, which guided me and brought happiness to my life. I became the Brother of the Sun and travelled far and wide over this land while following the Dream of the Sunset. I learned much from the different People with whom I camped, ate, hunted, and prayed. They are all with me now—our Spirits are All

471

together. Often we return to the places where we dwelled while on Earth—and often we are saddened because no one knows that we are there—no one feels the presence of our Spirits. Only at Hidden Valley do our ancestors still live in harmony with the Spirits of Nature—only at Hidden Valley can we give bodies the strength we wish to give everywhere. Here is how You will help Us:

In the Winter to come I will tell you the story of the Dream of the Sunset. I will tell You about the Powers which I found during my travels here and there. I will tell you about the People and the places and their legends. You will tell my story to those back where You came from who care. You will have the Sacred Pipe Stem as a physical reminder of our Spirits—our Power will be with You that way. The stories I will tell you are all long ones—of ceremonies, of hunting parties, of many tribes. You must be patient—hear everything that I tell you—for when the time comes it will be Your turn to visit there. You will go back to all those old places—tell others about the Spirits you find there.

I cannot yet tell you when you will be returning to your other People—it may be next Summer, or the one after that. All I can say is that You must first hear the whole story of my Dream of the Sunset so that You will know where All those Good Spirits are at. Along with my stories I will show you many of the People whom I met on my travels—I will show you their ceremonies and camps. They will sing again the songs they once sang for me— they will tell again the traditions of their tribes.

I will leave You, for now, my Son and Brother, I will leave my Friends and Sisters behind. I am happy to have brought You to this place, where my Relatives will All treat you kindly. Look for The Dream of the Sunset—be patient, for the story takes long to tell. The Power that YOU have found at Hidden Valley is now ready to help Your Life to be well.

. . . . With a sudden surge of Power I stand up to dance to the song which All the Spirits at Hidden Valley are singing—All the Spirits who will make my Life Strong. In my arms rests the Sacred Pipe Stem—its vibrating plumes make not a sound—in my head is the Sacred Vibration—making tears from my eyes fall to the Ground. Each drumbeat flashes through my whole body—causing me to sway up and down—while the People hold hands in a circle—dancing slowly around and around. Their faces are beaming with laughter, with smiling, with glowing happiness—so strong is this Life in Heaven, so Strong is this Life in bliss.

. . . . Will YOU come with me to Hidden Valley again? Will YOU hear with me the story of Brother and his Dream of the Sunset? Will YOU let YOUR Mind go wherever this Power wishes to take YOU? Please come along! Please come along! We All want to share with YOU this Power. We are Birds, we are Trees; we are Stars, we are Mountains; we are part of every colorful Flower. Let Our Spirits hold hands, let our Friends become our Bands, Let Our Minds All join this Great Happy Power—

OF LIFE IN HARMONY WITH NATURE.

I Pray: Can You hear me, Brothers and Sisters, Can YOU hear Me?